STUDIES ON THE TESTAMENTS
OF THE
TWELVE PATRIARCHS

STUDIA
IN VETERIS TESTAMENTI
PSEUDEPIGRAPHA

EDIDERUNT

A. M. DENIS et M. DE JONGE

VOLUMEN TERTIUM

STUDIES ON THE TESTAMENTS
OF THE
TWELVE PATRIARCHS

LEIDEN
E. J. BRILL
1975

STUDIES ON THE TESTAMENTS
OF THE
TWELVE PATRIARCHS

Text and Interpretation

EDITED BY

M. DE JONGE

LEIDEN
E. J. BRILL
1975

ISBN 90 04 04379 9

TABLE OF CONTENTS

PART THREE

PREFACE

The studies contained in this volume were written by H. W. Hollander and Th. Korteweg of the New Testament Department of the University of Leiden, H. J. de Jonge of the New Testament Department of the University of Amsterdam (formerly assistant for the Testaments of the Twelve Patriarchs-project at Leiden) and the editor. H. E. Gaylord, Jr., executive editor of the Compendia Rerum Iudaicarum ad Novum Testamentum-project assisted in matters of the Slavic versions and cooperated in the writing of chapter IX.

The chapters II-XII deal with various aspects of the textual tradition. In chapter XII some important results reached in these chapters are summed up and evaluated with a view to the forthcoming *editio maior*, prepared by M. de Jonge in cooperation with H. W. Hollander, H. J. de Jonge and Th. Korteweg. This section of the book gives much necessary background information and detailed argumentation not to be included in this edition. This textcritical section also contains a number of short articles on the history of manuscripts by H. J. de Jonge (chapters V and VI, and see also IV). In chapter I the same author describes the history of the use and the study of the Testaments in Western Europe between Robert Grosseteste and the beginning of the XVIIIth century. It supplements the existing surveys of research on the Testaments which usually begin with J. E. Grabe's edition of 1698.

The second part of the volume gives a number of studies dealing with the so-called higher criticism of the Testaments. Chapter XIII gives an introduction to research on the Testaments in recent years. Chapter XVII reviews two recent translations, in German and in Danish, with their introductions and notes; the first part of this study, again, gives a convenient summing up of the position of the moment, as well as the author's position in these matters. One of the chapters, XIV, is of a somewhat earlier date (1960), but it has been incorporated because it deals extensively with the relationship between the Testaments and the Dead Sea Scrolls. It is obvious that the author's thoughts on a number of questions have developed since then, and that particularly the textual data mentioned in the article need supplementation.

Some of the papers included here were earlier published elsewhere. For practical reasons they were reprinted photomechanically (with very minor alterations) by permission of the original editors and publishers. They are :

II.   H. J. de Jonge, Die Textüberlieferung der Testamente der zwölf Patriarchen, originally in : *Zeitschrift für die neutestamentliche Wissenschaft* 63 (1972), pp. 27-44.

IV.   H. J. de Jonge, Les fragments marginaux dans le MS. *d* des Testaments des XII Patriarches, from : *Journal for the Study of Judaism* 2 (1971), pp. 19-28.

V.   H. J. de Jonge, La bibliothèque de Michel Choniatès et la tradition occidentale des Testaments des XII Patriarches, from : *Nederlands Archief voor Kerkgeschiedenis* 53 (1973), pp. 171-180).

XIV.   M. de Jonge, Christian influence in the Testaments of the Twelve Patriarchs from : *Novum Testamentum* 4 (1960), pp. 182-235.

XV.   M. de Jonge, Notes on Testament of Levi II-VII, originally in : *Travels in the World of the Old Testament* (Studies presented to Professor M. A. Beek), Assen 1974, pp. 132-145.

Finally, chapter X. M. de Jonge, Textual criticism and the analysis of the composition of the Testament of Zebulun, is a slightly adapted version of an article written in 1972 in honour of M. Richard. It is also appearing in J. Dümmer (ed.), *Texte und Textkritik*, to be published in the series *Texte und Untersuchungen*.

For obvious reasons the incorporation of this already printed material made it impossible to achieve complete uniformity. The fact that contributions were written in English, German and French was also the cause of some divergency. Nevertheless consistency within each contribution has been attempted.

The editor recalls with gratitude the many discussions among the authors as well as consultations with others, which helped to shape the insights and convictions laid down in the various chapters of this volume. Each author pursued, of course, his own particular interests and everyone remains responsible for his own contribution.

Many people, at one stage or another, helped to translate or to revise earlier drafts of these articles. The editor wants to record here especially the help received from his colleagues H. E. Gaylord, Dr. J. C. H. Lebram and Dr. J. S. Vos. It is also a pleasure to mention the help given by the publishers' competent staff.

Lastly it should be mentioned that the preparatory work on the new edition was made possible by the financial support of the Netherlands Organization for the Advancement of Pure Research (Z.W.O.).*

Leiden, March 1, 1975   M. DE JONGE

Theologisch Instituut
Rapenburg 59

* The editor's dissertation *The Testaments of the Twelve Patriarchs.* A Study of their Text, Composition and Origin (1953), often referred to in this volume, has now been reprinted by the original publishers, Koninklijke Van Gorcum Comp. B.V. of Assen.

PART ONE

DIE PATRIARCHENTESTAMENTE VON ROGER BACON BIS RICHARD SIMON

mit einem Namenregister

HENK JAN DE JONGE

Im 16. und 17. Jahrhundert, als noch kaum ein Gelehrter von den *Testamenten der zwölf Patriarchen* Notiz nahm, fanden ihre Belehrungen und Weissagungen bei den Frommen im Lande soviel Interesse, dass z.B. in den Niederlanden zwischen 1541 und 1679 durchschnittlich alle vier bis fünf Jahre eine Ausgabe davon in der Landessprache erscheinen konnte.* Heute kommt dagegen fast alljährlich irgendeine wissenschaftliche Studie über die Testamente auf den Markt, aber ausserhalb eines kleinen Kreises von Forschern sind sie in Vergessenheit geraten. Der Untergang der Testamente als Volksbuch und ihre wachsende Beliebtheit als Forschungsobjekt sind zwei Seiten einer Entwicklung, die man nicht ohne ein gewisses Gefühl der Wehmut betrachten kann.

Wir wollen im folgenden nicht die Bedeutung der Testamente für die europäische oder gar niederländische Volksliteratur behandeln,[1]

---

* *Quantum sit, quod pagellae hae benignitati debent Viri doctissimi J. C. H. Lebram (cuius literarum judaicarum studia facultatem theologiae adornant Lugduno-batavam) vix dici potest. Qui, qua liberalitate est, mihi silvam comparanti rerum hic enarrandarum, quaedam attulit, quibus neglectis commentariolum meum melius blattis et tineis commisissem quam tibi, lector, obtulissem. Quod quasi non sufficeret, coepta mea perlegit, liberreque adnotavit, si quid esset quod supplendum, quod recidendum, quod planius dicendum mereretur. Quibus nondum contentus, quae belgice conceperam, Teutonitate donavit. Quonam successu, ipse videbis. Hoc quoque scito, magno fructui fuisse, quae Th. Korteweg et J. Smit Sibinga, adumbratione mea recognita, sagacitate qua solent me monere voluerunt.*

[1] Besonders in England haben die Testamente noch lange eine Rolle gespielt. Bis 1731 wurde die englische Übersetzung „for the Company of the Stationers" immer wieder aufgelegt. In einem Exemplar des Druckes von 1581, das jetzt in der Bodleian Library in Oxford steht (Douce L. 518), ist in der Handschrift des 1834 verstorbenen Bibliothekars des British Museum, Francis Douce, die kuriose Notiz bewahrt, dass der berühmte Redner John Henley (1692-1756), der sich selbst die Erneuerung der geistlichen Eloquenz zuschrieb, „used to preach festivous on the Testaments of the 12 Patriarchs". (Briefliche Mitteilung von Th. Korteweg, Leiden, 26. 9. 1972).

sondern uns der anderen Seite des erwähnten Prozesses zuwenden : dem Lauf, den die wissenschaftliche Untersuchung der Patriarchentestamente im Abendland nahm. Das Debut der Schrift im England des 13. Jahrhunderts ist, wie im fünften Kapitel geschildert, mit den Namen Michael Choniates, John von Basingstoke und Robert Grosseteste verbunden.[2] Bald nach diesem Eintritt in die abendländische Entwicklung erhielten die Testamente aber auch einen wesentlichen Platz im Werk von Roger Bacon. Bacon, der zu den universalsten Geistern seiner Zeit zählt, ist der erste europäische Gelehrte, von dem uns eine deutliche Stellungnahme zu den Testamenten bekannt ist, und damit einer von den wenigen, für den sie eine besondere Bedeutung hatten.

In den Jahren 1266-1268 hat Bacon sein *Opus majus*, ein umfangreiches philosophisches und wissenschaftliches Werk, verfasst. Durch dieses wollte er Papst Clemens IV. veranlassen, eine Erneuerung der Wissenschaften in Gang zu bringen. An zwei Stellen des Werkes werden die Testamente behandelt. Einmal in pars II, cap. XVI.[3] Der Zusammenhang ist folgender : die eine vollkommene Weisheit ist nach Bacon in der heiligen Schrift enthalten und wird mit Hilfe des kanonischen Rechts und der Philosophie entfaltet. Die Philosophie umfasst dagegen die Wissenschaften der Heiden, steht aber der Weisheit Gottes nicht beziehungslos oder feindlich gegenüber. Sie ist ursprünglich den Erzvätern und Propheten gegeben. „Soli enim patriarchae et prophetae fuerunt veri philosophi qui omnia sciverunt, scilicet non solum legem Dei, sed omnes partes philosophiae ... Ab istis sequentes viri philosophi philosophiae principium et originem habuerunt : Indi, Latini, Persae, et Graeci" (II,9). Somit ist die Philosophie nichts anderes als eine Entwicklung oder Entfaltung („explicatio") der Weisheit Gottes. Darum haben die Christen diese Weisheit der Heiden nötig, um die ungeteilte Weisheit Gottes finden zu können. Denn in der Suche nach der göttlichen Weisheit sind die Heiden ihnen vorangegangen, und zwar mit Erfolg, denn sie kennen bereits die wichtigsten Artikel des Glaubens : die Existenz Gottes, seine Einheit, Allmacht, Weisheit und

---

[2] Grosseteste hat auch als erster die Testamente zitiert : aus T. Jud. XXI,2-4 bewies er König Henry III., dass die Salbung die englische Könige nicht über die *dignitas sacerdotalis* erhebt. S. seine *Epistolae* (ed. H. R. Luard), London 1857, S. 351.

[3] Diese Stelle nennt schon L. Diestel, *Geschichte des A.T. in der chr. Kirche*, Jena 1869, S. 181, worauf J. C. H. Lebram, Leiden, mich aufmerksam machte. Für den Text, siehe J. H. Bridges, *The „Opus Majus" of Roger Bacon*, Suppl. Vol. : revised text. London-Edinburgh-Oxford 1900, S. 71-72.

Güte; die Dreieinigkeit; die *creatio ex nihilo*; auch viel über Jesus
Christus, die heilige Jungfrau, den Antichrist, die Engel, die Aufer-
stehung der Toten, das jüngste Gericht, das ewige Leben, die Höllen-
strafen; sie wissen etwas von einem Mittler zwischen Gott und Mensch,
einem Stellvertreter („vicarius") Gottes, des Herren der Welt. „Und
man braucht sich darüber nicht zu wundern, dass die Philosophen
solche Dinge schreiben konnten, denn alle Philosophen haben nach
den Patriarchen und Propheten gelebt, und darum haben sie die
Bücher der Propheten und Patriarchen gelesen, die in der Heiligen
Schrift stehen".

Nun erklärt Bacon, gerade in der Passage, die uns interessiert,
noch eingehender, warum die Philosophen so auffallend viele und
genaue Erkenntnisse über die göttliche Wahrheit haben konnten :

> „Et similiter alios libros fecerunt [*sc.* patriarchae et prophetae], tangentes Christi
> mysteria, ut in libro Enoch et in libro de testamentis patriarcharum et in libris
> Esdrae tertio, quarto et quinto, et in multis aliis libris de quorum aliquibus fit
> mentio in sacro textu, ut de libris Nathan et Samuelis et Abdon prophetarum.
> In hujusmodi enim libris tanguntur expresse articuli fidei, et longe expressius quam
> in canone scripturae. Nam praeter caeteros libros liber de testamentis patriarcharum
> ostendit omnia quae de Christo adimpleta sunt. Quilibet enim patriarcha in morte
> praedicavit filiis suis et tribui suae, et praedixit eis ea quae de Christo tenenda
> sunt, sicut manifestum est ex libro illo. Et hi libri licet non sint in canone
> scripturae, tamen sancti et sapientes Graeci et Latini usi sunt eis a principio
> ecclesiae. Nam beatus Judas de libro Enoch accepit auctoritatem, et Augustinus
> quarto [*immo* : quinto decimo] de Civitate Dei multum fundatur super illum librum
> ut ostendat quod prius fuit sapientia apud sanctos quam apud philosophos,
> et ait quod magis propter nimiam antiquitatem ille liber non est in auctoritate,
> quam propter aliud. De libris autem aliis manifestum est quod in usu sanctorum
> et sapientum antiquorum sunt propter hoc quod planas veritates de Christo
> continere noscuntur. Philosophi igitur curiosi et diligentes in studio sapientiae
> peragrarunt regiones diversas, ut sapientiam inquirerent, et ideo libros sanctos
> perlegerunt, et didicerunt ab Hebraeis multa".

„Ebenso haben sie (*sc.* die Patriarchen und Propheten) andere (*sc.* nicht
in den Kanon aufgenommene) Bücher, die die Geheimnisse Christi
berühren, geschrieben, wie im Buch Henoch, dem Buch von den
Testamenten der Patriarchen, dem dritten, vierten und fünften Esra-
buch, und vielen anderen Büchern, von denen einige in der Heiligen
Schrift genannt werden, wie die Bücher der Propheten Nathan, Samuel
und Abdon. In derartigen Büchern werden die Glaubensartikel ausdrücklich berührt, selbst viel ausdrücklicher als im Kanon der Schrift.
Denn neben anderen Büchern offenbart etwa das Buch über die
Testamente der Patriarchen alles, was sich mit Christus erfüllt hat.

Jeder Patriarch hat nämlich bei seinem Sterben seinen Söhnen und seinem Stamm verkündigt und geweissagt, was man von Christus glauben muss, wie aus jenem Buch deutlich wird. Und obwohl diese Bücher nicht im Kanon stehen, haben heilige und weise griechische und lateinische Schriftsteller vom Entstehen der Kirche an davon Gebrauch gemacht. Denn der selige Judas hat sich auf das Buch Henoch berufen, und Augustinus gründet sich im vierten Buch (Bacon meint Buch XV, cap. 23) des Gottesstaats nachdrücklich auf jenes Buch (sc. Henoch), um zu beweisen, dass die Weisheit früher bei den Heiligen, als bei den Philosophen war, und er sagt, dass jenes Buch mehr wegen seines zu hohen Alters kein kanonisches Ansehen genoss, als aus irgendeinem andern Grunde. Auch bei andern Büchern ist es deutlich, dass sie von alten Heiligen und Weisen darum gebraucht werden, weil bekannt ist, dass sie klare Wahrheiten über Christus enthalten. Also haben die Philosophen wissbegierig und sorgfältig in der Erforschung der Weisheit die verschiedenen Gebiete durchgearbeitet, um die Weisheit aufzuspüren, und haben darum heilige Bücher durchgelesen, und viel von den Hebräern gelernt".

Wie sich aus dieser Passage ergibt, meint Bacon, dass die heidnischen Philosophen eingehendes Wissen über Gott und Christus solchen Apokryphen wie Henoch und den Testamenten der zwölf Patriarchen entlehnt haben. In diesen würde deutlicher über die christliche Wahrheit gesprochen als in den kanonischen Schriften des Alten Testaments. Damit ist nicht nur das Détailwissen der Heiden über die christlichen Lehrsätze erklärt, sondern die Tatsache, dass die Heiden die verborgenen Büchern der Erzväter gebraucht haben, beweist auch, dass die Weisheit der Philosophen dieselbe ist wie die Weisheit Gottes. So ist die Wissenschaft der Heiden nichts als eine Komponente der allumfassenden Weisheit des Herrn: die Christen dürfen also das Wissen der Heiden nicht nur unbesorgt auf ihrer Suche nach der göttlichen Wahrheit benutzen, ja sie haben sie dazu sogar nötig. Das veranlasst Bacon, in den anschliessenden Teilen seines *Opus majus* eine umfangreiche Beschreibung der gesamten zeitgenössischen Wissenschaft zu geben: Griechische und hebräische Sprachwissenschaft, Mathematik, Physik, Optik und Perspektivkunde, Astronomie, Geographie, Chronologie, Musik, experimentelle und moralische Wissenschaften usw. Diese Wissenschaften muss der Christ kennen lernen, um das Verständnis der Wahrheit Gottes zu erlangen.

Aus dem Gesagten zeigt sich, dass die Testamente der zwölf Patriarchen im Denksystem Bacons eine bedeutende Rolle spielen.

Eine derartige Anerkennung ist ihnen niemals zuvor zuteil geworden, und sie haben sie auch schnell wieder verloren, wahrscheinlich für immer.

Ganz am Ende des *Opus majus*, in einer Passage, auf die die Untersucher der Kanongeschichte oder der Testamente unseres Wissens noch nie aufmerksam geworden sind, bringt Bacon die Testamente der zwölf Patriarchen nochmals zur Sprache.[4] Er geht von einem umfassend entworfenen und ins Detail gehenden Vergleich der Religionen der Welt aus, bei dem sich die Überlegenheit des Christentums u.a. darin zeigt, dass die christlichen Glaubenslehren schon den Heiden bekannt waren, und dass Christus von den jüdischen Propheten geweissagt worden ist. Die Wahrheit des Christentums konnte nicht zuverlässiger bestätigt werden als durch diese nichtchristlichen Zeugen, wie z.B. Flavius Josephus. Auch das vierte Buch des Esra, der doch lange vor Christus lebte, enthält klare Hinweise auf Jesus Christus. Dann fährt Bacon fort:

> „Item in libro duodecim Patriarcharum docetur manifestissime de Christo. Nam quilibet Patriarcha docebat tribum suam certificationem de Christo, sicut adimpletum est. Et si dicatur quod hi libri sunt Apocryphi, id est de quorum auctoribus non est certum, hoc non tollit veritatem, quia libri hi recipiuntur a Graecis, Latinis, et Judaeis. ... Multi enim sunt libri in usu Latinorum, Hebraeorum, et Graecorum de quibus non est certum qui sunt auctores: immo de paucis nos Latini sumus certificati, et in multis erramus. Nam cum aestimamus quod Avicenna fecit librum Coeli et Mundi qui communiter habetur, falsum est. ... Et in theologia libri Ecclesiastici et Sapientiae non habent certos auctores, cum alii aestimant hos esse Solomonis, alii Philonis, alii alterius. Unde non obstat quod liber sit ignoti auctoris, dummodo a multitudine sapientum comprobetur".

Übersetzt: „Ebenso wird im Buch der zwölf Patriarchen unverhüllt über Christus gelehrt. Denn jeder Patriarch lehrte seinen Stamm sichere Kenntnis über Christus, wie es (später) erfüllt ist. Und wenn man sagen wollte, dass diese Bücher apokryph sind, d.h. dass über ihre Verfasser keine Sicherheit besteht, dann hebt das ihre Zuverlässigkeit nicht auf, weil diese Bücher anerkannt werden von Griechen, Lateinern und Juden. ... Denn viele Bücher sind bei Lateinern, Hebräern und Griechen in Gebrauch, von denen nicht feststeht, wer ihre Verfasser sind: selbst wir Lateiner haben über wenige Bücher Sicherheit, und irren uns in vielen Fällen. Denn wenn wir meinen, dass Avicenna das Buch über Himmel und Erde, das allgemein verbreitet ist, wirklich

---

[4] Pars VII, pars iv. J. H. Bridges, The „*Opus Majus*" of Roger Bacon, Vol. II, Oxford 1897, S. 391.

verfasst hat, dann ist das falsch. ... Auch in der Theologie ist nicht
sicher, wer die Bücher Ecclesiasticus [5] und Sapientia [6] geschrieben hat,
da die einen meinen, diese seien von Salomon, die anderen von Philo,
noch andere von irgendeinem andern. Daher bedeutet es keinen
Einwand, dass der Verfasser eines Buches unbekannt ist, wenn es
nur von dem Grossteil der Gelehrten anerkannt wird".

Diese Passage ist wichtig, weil sie zeigt, was Bacon unter ,,apokryph"
versteht. Eine apokryphe Schrift ist für ihn ein Buch, dessen Verfasser
nicht feststeht. Dies ist eine überlieferte Auffassung: so bezeichnet
Augustin u.a. Schriften als ,,apokryph", weil ihre ,,occulta origo non
claruit patribus". Aber im Gegensatz zu Augustin folgert Bacon nicht
ohne Weiteres, dass Schriften eines unbekannten Verfassers keinerlei
Autorität besitzen. Wenn genügend kirchliche, oder gelehrte Schriftsteller die Autorität eines apokryphen dadurch bestätigen, dass sie es
benutzen, dann kann eine apokryphe Schrift als vollkommen zuverlässig
gelten. Bacon unterscheidet darum zwischen ,,authentisch" und ,,zuver-
lässig": ein Buch kann, obgleich seine Authentität nicht feststeht,
zuverlässig sein und darum eine bestimmte Autorität haben, was er
am Beispiel von IV Esra nochmals an anderer Stelle genau ausführt
(Bridges I, S. 291). IV Esra, so Bacon, ist zwar apokryph, d.h. es
ist nicht sicher, ob es von Esra geschrieben ist, aber es wird in
der Liturgie häufig gebraucht, ,,und darum, ob Esra oder irgendjemand
anders es geschrieben hat" (,,sive Esdras sive alius hunc fecerit"),
es muss in jedem Falle als Autorität gelten (,,supponendus est pro
auctoritate"). Die Authentität ist nicht sicher, aber auch nicht ausgeschlossen, jedoch die Zuverlässigkeit und Autorität stehen durch
den kirchlichen Gebrauch zweifelsohne fest.

Die Tatsache, dass für Bacon die ,,auctoritas" einer Schrift nicht
von der Person des ,,auctor" abhängt, ist auffallend, da andere
Scholastiker zwischen Authentität und Kanonizität keinen Unterschied

---

[5] Bei Clemens Alexandrinus und in der lateinischen Übersetzung des Origenes
wird vielfach Salomon als Verfasser des Buches *Ecclesiasticus* genannt. Cyprian zitiert
es durchweg als Werk Salomos, ebenso auch andere Lateiner. Hieronymus, *Comment.
in Dan.* 9: ,,Jesus filius Sirach scripsit librum, qui... plerisque Salomonis falso dicitur".
E. Schürer, *Geschichte des Jüdischen Volkes im Zeitalter Jesu Christi* III, Leipzig 1909[4],
S. 220-221.

[6] Origenes ist nächst dem Verfasser des muratorischen Fragmentes der erste, welcher
Zweifel hinsichtlich der salomonischen Abfassung der *Sap. Sal.* andeutet. Canon
Muratori bezeichnet wahrscheinlich Philo als Verfasser der *Weisheit Salomos*. Dass
Philo der Verfasser sein sollte, erwähnt Hieronymus, *Praef. in vers. libr. Salom.*,
als Ansicht einiger ,,scriptores veteres". Schürer a.a.O., S. 508-509.

sehen (Diestel a.a.O., S. 181). Bacon aber kann nur mit Hilfe dieses Unterschieds das Ansehen der Testamente aufrecht erhalten und damit ihnen den wichtigen Platz einräumen, den sie in seinem Werke einnehmen.

Bacons Auffassungen über die Testamente lassen sich somit folgendermassen zusammenfassen :

1. Es ist nicht sicher, dass die Testamente die authentischen letzten Worte der Patriarchen enthalten.

2. Ungeachtet der Frage nach ihrer Authentizität ist die Zuverlässigkeit des Inhalts der Testamente durch die kirchliche Benutzung der Testamente verbürgt (offenbar hat Bacon gewusst, dass die Testamente bei den griechischen Christen in Gebrauch waren).

3. Die Testamente haben nicht weniger Autorität als IV Esra, Sirach und die Weisheit Salomos.

Darüber hinaus verdienen noch zwei Tatsachen unsere Aufmerksamkeit.

Bacon erwähnt am Ende seines *Opus majus* die Testamente im Zusammenhang mit der Anführung nichtchristlicher Zeugen für die Wahrheit des christlichen Glaubens. Dabei beruft er sich neben heidnischen auch auf jüdische Gewährsmänner : die Propheten, Josephus, IV Esra und die Patriarchen. Unter den Juden findet man nach Bacon einflussreiche Gestalten, die auf Jesus als den wahren Messias hingewiesen haben. Hieraus ergibt sich, dass die Juden im Stande sind, ihr Unrecht zu erkennen. Sie müssten dieses eigentlich zugeben, und sich zum Christentum bekehren. Derselbe Gedanke findet sich im Kolophon der auf Anregung von Robert Grosseteste um 1242, also 25 Jahre früher, hergestellten lateinischen Übersetzung der Testamente. Nach diesem ist die Übersetzung der Testamente angefertigt, ,,damit die deutlichen Prophezeiungen, die in dieser Schrift klarer als das Sonnenlicht strahlen, noch heller leuchten sollen zu grösserer Bestürzung der Juden, und aller Ketzer und Feinde der Kirche''.[7] Die lateinische Übersetzung der Testamente hatte also

---

[7] ,,Quo sic luculentae prophetiae, quae in hoc scripto, luce clarius, coruscant, in maiorem confusionem Iudaeorum & omnium haereticorum & inimicorum Ecclesiae gloriosius prorumpant''. Auch Matthaeus Paris, *Chronica majora* (ed. H. R. Luard, IV, London 1877, S. 233) berichtet in Formulierungen, die offenbar mit der eben wiedergegebenen verwandt sind, dass Grosseteste übersetzt hat ,,ad robur fidei Christianae et ad majorem Judaeorum confusionem''. Nach Thomas Ittig, *Historia ecclesiastica secundi seculi*, Lipsiae 1711, ist das Kolophon von Matthaeus Paris abhängig. Da aber das Kolophon schon in Handschriften aus der Mitte des 13. Jhdts. vorkommt, und Paris seine Anmerkungen erst 1242 niederschrieb, ist die Abhängigkeit vielleicht umgekehrt. Siehe auch S. 100.

apologetische und missionarische Ziele, und stand im Dienst einer
Campagne zur Bekehrung der Juden in England. Den Grund dafür
ersehen wir aus den Ausführungen von Robert Bacon. (Vgl. S. 100).

Ferner kann man sich fragen, was für Kenntnis von den Testamenten
Bacon hatte. Natürlich wird er mühelosen Zugang zu einem der
Manuskripte der lateinischen Übersetzung gehabt haben, die in der
Mitte des 13. Jahrhunderts schon ziemlich verbreitet waren. Daneben
aber besteht die Möglichkeit, dass Bacon die Testamente auf Griechisch
gekannt hat. Die einzige, damals im Westen bekannte griechische
Handschrift des Buches war die im Besitz von Grosseteste. Bacon
war ein Schüler von Grosseteste und kann, wenn nicht von John
von Basingstoke,[8] mit dem er vermutlich Verbindung gehabt hat, so
doch über seinen Lehrer von dieser Handschrift gehört haben. Nach
dem Tode von Grosseteste ging die Handschrift durch Erbschaft an das
Franziskanerkloster in Oxford über. Zum Franziskanerorden gehörte
seit 1247 auch Bacon. In den Jahren 1250-1257, also auch in der
Zeit, als Grosseteste starb, hielt sich Bacon in Oxford auf. Dort
kann er, der feurige Vorkämpfer für das Studium antiker Quellen,
wie Bibel und Aristoteles, in der Originalsprache, die Testamente in
der Bibliothek seines eigenen Klosters in griechischer Sprache gelesen
haben, und zwar in der Handschrift, die Grosseteste aus Athen hatte
kommen lassen.

Roger Bacon hat aus verschiedenen Gründen nur wenig Einfluss
gehabt. Sein *Opus majus* wurde erst 1773, gut fünfhundert Jahre nach
seinem Entstehen zum ersten Mal gedruckt. Seine Ausführungen über
die Testamente haben darum auch nicht viel zur Entwicklung des
wissenschaftlichen Interesses für diese Schrift beigetragen. Zwar wurde
die lateinische Übersetzung der Testamente vielmals abgeschrieben,
aber erst in der Mitte des 16. Jahrhunderts begegnen wir bescheidene
Zeichen einer wiederauflebenden Beschäftigung der Gelehrten mit
diesem Buch.[9] Um diese Zeit werden nämlich die Testamente mehrmals
kurz nacheinander in lateinischer Übersetzung im Rahmen von Sammlungen altchristlicher und jüdisch-hellenistischer Schriften herausgegeben. Das erste Mal erscheinen sie auf diese Weise in dem 1550

---

[8] Siehe über Basingstoke Kap. V in diesem Band.

[9] Beiläufig sei auch bemerkt, dass Hugo von St. Victor (1096-1141) in seiner
De eruditione didascalica IV, 15 (Migne, *PL* 176, Sp. 787-788) eine ganze Reihe von
Apokryphen aufzählt, darunter auch (wenigstens nach dem Text bei Migne) *Testament
von Hiob*.

bei H. Petri in Basel herausgekommenen *Micropresbyticon. Veterum quorundam brevium theologorum, sive episcoporum sive presbyterorum, aut sacri ordinis aliorum qui aut tempore Apostolorum, aut non multo post vixerunt, elenchus*, S. 589-615. Der Sammlung, die dieser und ähnlichen Zusammenstellungen zu Grunde liegt, kann eine gewisse wissenschaftliche Bedeutung nicht abgesprochen werden, weil die Testamente hier deutlich in eine literarische Umwelt gestellt werden, mit der sie vorher nicht in Verbindung gebracht worden sind. In der Mitte des 13. Jahrhunderts hatten in England Robert Grosseteste und Roger Bacon und in Frankreich Vincent de Beauvais, wenn auch nicht die Authentität, so doch die Zuverlässigkeit des Inhalts der Testamente und wahrscheinlich auch ihr Entstehen in der Patriarchenzeit noch nicht bezweifelt. Nun stehen sie auf einmal innerhalb einer Sammlung von Schriften aus dem frühesten Christentum, die mit Ignatius von Antiochien beginnt und u.a. eine spätjüdische Schrift, wie das *Liber antiquitatum* des Pseudo-Philo, enthält. In einer anderen Sammlung, den *Orthodoxographa theologiae sacrosanctae ac syncerioris fidei doctores numero LXXVI ...*, zusammengestellt durch den Basler Dominikaner Johannes Herold, bekannt als Verfasser von viel gebrauchten Predigten, folgen auf die Testamente (S. 1440-1467) unmittelbar die Sibyllinischen Orakel. Diese *Orthodoxographa* wurden 1555 ebenfalls von Petri in Basel herausgegeben. Zum dritten Mal in verhältnismässig kurzer Zeit sind die Testamente auf Lateinisch herausgegeben in den 85 altkirchliche Schriften enthaltenden *Monumenta S. Patrum orthodoxographa ...*, Basel 1569, des reformierten Theologen Joh. Jac. Grynaeus. Im Übrigen wird in diesen Sammlungen kein gelehrtes Interesse an den Testamenten sichtbar : Wenn z.B. bei Herold unser Pseudoepigraphon als ,,plenum mysteriis" beschrieben wird, dann verrät dies eher erbauliche als wissenschaftliche Absichten.[10]

Stillstand, wenn nicht gar einen Rückschritt bedeutet die Ausgabe von Auszügen aus den Testamenten, die der lutherische Pfarrer in Salzwedel, Stephan Praetorius, ein aktiver Schriftsteller aus dem Ende des 16. Jahrhunderts, in seinen *Pauli apostoli ad Laodicenses epistola, latine et germanice edita. Adjecta sunt fragmenta Apostolorum et Patriarcharum Testamenta*, Hamburg 1595, besorgte. Wissenschaftlich

---

[10] Ferner erschienen die Testamente noch in den einzelnen Ausgaben von De la Bignes *Magna Bibliotheca Veterum Patrum* : Paris 1575, III, S. 798; Paris 1589, V, S. 731; Paris 1610, V, S. 611; Köln 1618, I, S. 173; Paris 1624-1644, V, S. 531.

noch unbedeutender ist die viel später im 17. Jahrhundert erschienene
Ausgabe des lateinischen Textes in den *Elogia Patriarcharum et Christi
Jesu Dei Hominis* von Emanuel Thesaurus Patritius Taurinensis und
Aloysius Iuglar, „è societate Jesu", Mainz 1665, an anderen Orten
1669 und 1711 wieder aufgelegt.

Inzwischen waren die Testamente schon auf einem andern Wege
in den Bereich der Wissenschaft gelangt, und zwar durch den gelehrten
Theologen Sixtus Senensis (von Siena). Sixtus Senensis (1520-1569)
war ein getaufter Jude, der nach seiner Bekehrung zunächst in den
Franziskanerorden, später bei den Dominikanern eingetreten war.
Er veröffentlichte 1566 seine umfangreiche *Bibliotheca sancta*. Dies
Werk, wiederaufgelegt in Frankfurt 1575, Paris 1610 und Köln 1626, ist
u.a. deswegen berühmt, weil darin zum ersten Mal zwischen proto- und
deuterokanonischen Büchern unterschieden wird. Im zweiten Buch der
Bibliotheca sancta gibt Sixtus in alphabetischer Anordnung eine mit
Kommentierungen versehene Aufzählung aller nichtkanonischen Autoren, die in der Bibel genannt oder zitiert werden. Dabei werden
die Testamente zweimal besprochen. Das erste Mal behandelt Sixtus
das im Judasbrief benutzte Buch Henoch und führt dabei die Testamente der zwölf Patriarchen als Testimonium an. Anschliessend
bringt er eine treffende Inhaltsangabe und teilt mit, dass Origenes
und Prokop das Buch benutzt haben. Damit werden, wie es scheint,
zum ersten Mal in der neueren Zeit die Testamente, wenn auch
nur beiläufig, für die Auslegung des Neuen Testaments herangezogen
und in ihrer Bedeutung von wissenschaftlicher Seite anerkannt.[11]

Zum zweiten Mal bespricht Sixtus Senensis die Testamente unter
der ausdrücklichen Überschrift *Patriarcharum duodecim filiorum Iacob
testamentum*. Er wiederholt die kurze Inhaltsangabe ohne nennenswerte
Änderungen, enthält sich aber einer literarhistorischen Beurteilung.
Allerdings hat man den Eindruck, dass Sixtus in seinem kleinen
Abschnitt über Henoch die Möglichkeit offenhält, dass die Testamente
wirklich die Worte der Jakobssöhne wiedergeben. So führt er gegen
die Zweifel des Augustinus und Hieronymus an der Echtheit von
Henoch an, dass bereits in einem sehr alten Buch Entlehnungen

---

[11] Es ist weder möglich, noch nötig, alle Werke und Schriftsteller zu nennen,
die im Anschluss an diese Stelle bei Sixtus Senensis die Testamente einfach als
Testimonium für das Henoch-Buch anführen. Als Beispiel nenne ich : Joach. Joa. Maderus
(1626-1680; professor historiae zu Helmstädt), *De scriptis et bibliothecis antediluvianis*,
als Praefatio seinem Werk *De bibliothecis atque archivis*, Helmstädt 1702², S. 18,
vorangestellt (öfters wiedergedruckt).

aus Henoch vorkommen und dass auch Tertullian in seinem *De cultu feminarum* gute Argumente für die Echtheit von Henoch vorgebracht hat. Die Berufung auf die Testamente hätte in diesem Zusammenhang keinen Sinn gehabt, wenn Sixtus nicht der Meinung gewesen wäre, dass die Patriarchen wirklich Henoch zitiert haben. In diesem Punkt hielt Sixtus den Bericht der Testamente für zuverlässig. Wenn er unter der Überschrift *Patriarcharum...* nochmals über die Testamente spricht, nennt er sie „sehr alt und aus dem Hebräischen übersetzt". Er entnimmt diese Angaben kritiklos dem aus dem 13. Jahrhundert stammenden Kolophon der lateinischen Übersetzung von Grosseteste. Entsprechend der Tendenz dieses Kolophons hat Sixtus Senensis jedenfalls die inhaltliche Richtigkeit der Testamente nicht bezweifelt.

Wie Sixtus Senensis denkt auch noch Benedictus Pererius, oder Pereira (1535-1610). Dieser stammte aus Valencia und war 1552 Jesuit geworden. Er lehrte seit 1576 in Rom. Als Theologe und Bibelexeget hatte Pererius bei seinen Zeitgenossen den Ruf grosser Gelehrsamkeit, bei späteren auch den zu grosser Ausführlichkeit. Immerhin wurden die in den Jahren 1589 bis 1598 in Rom erschienenen umfangreichen *Commentariorum et disputationum in Genesim tomi IV* 1606 in Köln schon wieder abgedruckt. In diesen bemerkt Pererius zu Gen. 48, 1, dass die Patriarchen des Alten Testaments, wenn sie ihr Ende nahen fühlten, ihre Nachkommen und Freunde zu versammeln pflegten, um zum letzten Mal zu ihnen zu sprechen und bei dieser Gelegenheit ihnen sowohl die Zukunft vorauszusagen als auch Ermahnungen zu einem tugendhaften Leben zu geben. Als ältestes Beispiel führt Pererius den Segen Jakobs an. Er vermutet, dass Adam, Noah, Abraham und Isaak dasselbe getan, dass aber die letzten Worte dieser Erzväter wohl „nichts Besonderes oder Bemerkenswertes" enthalten hätten („nihil insigne et notabile"), und darum nicht überliefert sind. Jedoch seien die Worte, mit denen Isaak Jakob, und die, mit denen Jacob seine Söhne segnete, wert festgehalten zu werden. „Dem Beispiel ihres Vaters Jakob folgten seine Söhne, die zwölf Patriarchen des hebräischen Volkes; jedenfalls war früher ein sehr altes Buch mit dem Titel *Testamente der zwölf Patriarchen* in Umlauf". An diese Bemerkung schliesst sich eine kurze Skizze vom Inhalt des Buches und die Erwähnung der Testimonia bei Origenes und Prokop. Als spätere Beispiele von „Testamenten" nennt Pererius die letzten Worte der Mose, Josua, Samuel, David, Tobias, Mattathias, Jesus, die alle in der heiligen Schrift überliefert sind, und die von Antonius, Benediktus, Franziskus und Dominikus. Wichtig ist schliesslich auch der

kritische Hinweis des Pererius auf die Auffassung des klassischen
Heidentums, dass Sterbende die Zukunft voraussagen konnten. Pere-
rius' Erwähnung von Xenophon, *Cyropaedia* 8, c. 7, sollte noch von
Andreas Rivetus als Parallele zu Gen. 49 angeführt werden (*Exerc.*
CLXXVII).

Die Worte „Einstmals war ein sehr altes Buch in Umlauf" („fere-
batur olim pervetustus liber"), mit denen Pererius seine Bemerkungen
einleitet, erwecken den Eindruck, dass Pererius selbst den Inhalt der
Testamente nicht kannte. Man muss sich fragen, wie er dann zu
einer so treffenden Inhaltsangabe gekommen ist. Die Antwort ist,
dass er sie mit einer einzigen unbedeutenden Veränderung von Sixtus
Senensis abgeschrieben hat. Tatsächlich hat er die Testamente wohl
nicht selbst gelesen, so merkwürdig diese Annahme auch scheint,
wenn man die damalige Verbreitung der Testamente berücksichtigt.
Über ihr Alter und ihre Herkunft kann Pererius kaum ein selb-
ständiges Urteil gehabt haben; wenn er dennoch eine Meinung äusserte,
hielt er sich offensichtlich an die Annahme, dass die Testamente
wirklich gesprochene Reden der Patriarchen enthielten.

1595 äusserten jedoch wenigstens zwei Kritiker die Meinung, dass
die Testamente nicht als authentisch oder zuverlässig anzusehen seien.
Erwähnung verdient vor allem, was Johannes Drusius (1550-1616),
Professor für Hebräisch in Franeker, davor in Oxford und Leiden,
hierüber bemerkt hat. In *De quaesitis per epistulam*, 1595 in Franeker
erschienen,[12] widmet er den Brief 105 den Apokryphen und Pseudoepigraphen, die er in zwei Gruppen einteilt: erstens, die, die in
kirchlichem Gebrauch sind, zweitens die, die überhaupt nicht anerkannt
sind und zu seiner Zeit niemals zusammen mit dem Bibelkanon oder
Teilen davon herausgegeben wurden. Auf die zweite Gruppe, die
nichtkirchlichen Apokryphen (gegenwärtig als Pseudoepigraphen bezeichnet), wendet Drusius die Charakteristik von Augustinus (*Civ.
Dei* XV, 23, 4) an, dass sie zwar etwas Wahrheit, aber viel Unwahres
enthalten („aliqua veritas, tamen multa falsa"). Drusius gibt danach
eine Aufzählung solcher Schriften, die keine kanonische Autorität
besitzen, die u.a. Henoch, die Patriarchen oder das Testament der
12 Patriarchen, das Gebet des Joseph, das Testament Moses, die
Himmelfahrt Moses, Abraham usw. umfasst. Diese Liste gibt Drusius
an ˙aus der Synopsis des Epiphanius zu kennen, womit offenbar die
Synopsis scripturae sacrae gemeint ist, die unter dem Namen des

---

[12] In den *Critici sacri*, Tomus VIII, London 1660[1], Sp. 2045-2112.

Athanasius in Umlauf war (in Migne, *PG* 28, Spalte 281-438).[13]
Dabei fällt auf, dass Drusius den kurzen Titel „Patriarchen", den
wir in der Synopsis finden, mit „sive Testamentum 12 Patriarcharum"
näher bestimmt; dies ist ein Zusatz, der in der Liste des Ps-Athanasius
fehlt. Weiter erwähnt Drusius, dass die Testamente durch Origenes
zitiert werden.

Dass die Testamente für Drusius als nicht-kirchliches Apokryphon
gelten, bedeutet, dass sie nach seiner Meinung teilweise „Falsches"
enthalten. Dies Urteil beruht nicht auf ausdrücklicher Argumentation,
sondern auf patristischer Tradition. Doch hat Drusius ohne Zweifel
die Testamente gekannt. In Brief 102 zitiert er ausführlich einige
Passagen, die seiner Meinung nach Zeugnisse für die Existenz eines
Henochbuches enthalten, nämlich T. Sim. V,4; T. Levi X,5; T. Levi
XIV,1; T. Zeb. (Drusius schreibt versehentlich Issachar) III,4 und
T. Dan V,6-7. Auch in einem seiner letzten Werke, das den Titel
Henoch sive de Patriarcha Henoch ejusque raptu et libro trägt, erschienen
in Franeker 1615,[14] sagt Drusius in cap. 18 beiläufig, dass das Buch
Henoch in einigen Testimonien „Lex Henoch" heisst, womit er ohne
genaue Quellenangabe auf die Erwähnungen des Henochbuches in
den Testamenten anspielt.

Auffällig ist die Zurückhaltung, mit der sich Drusius über Pseudoepigraphen wie Henoch (und sichtlich macht er keine Ausnahme
für die Testamente!) in cap. 21 seiner Henocharbeit äussert: „die
eine Gruppe der Apokryphen hat die Kirche anerkannt, die andere
verworfen. Doch ist nicht alles falsch, was darin als falsch angesehen
wird. Wir werden dies, wenn Gott uns Leben und Gesundheit gibt,
zu gegebener Zeit und an geeigneter Stelle zeigen". Noch kein
halbes Jahr später ist Drusius 66 Jahre alt gestorben.

Neben Drusius hat 1595 auch der calvinistisch orientierte englische
Kontroverstheologe Andrew Willet (1562-1621), Fellow von Christ's
College in Cambridge, später auch „incorporated" zu Oxford, auf
die Unechtheit der Testamente hingewiesen. Willet muss einen gewal-
tigen Arbeitseifer an den Tag gelegt haben: einer seiner Biographen
teilt mit, dass „He made it his practice to produce some new
biblical commentary or theological work every half-year". Er war
bereits einige Jahre „prebendary" in Ely, als 1595 in London seine
Hexapla in Genesin erschien (1608²), „that is, a sixfold Commentary

---

[13] Besonders Sp. 432.
[14] In den *Critici sacri*, Tomus VIII, London 1660¹, Sp. 2029-2046.

upon Genesis", wie der Untertitel mitteilt.[15] Willets *Hexapla in Genesin* ist eine Kompilation aus einer Anzahl damals berühmter Kommentare, und zwar aus dem des Calvinisten Johannes Mercerus, den Beza publiziert hatte, dem des oben genannten Benedictus Pererius S.J. und dem des französischen Protestanten August Marlorat. Der Kommentar heisst *Hexapla*, weil nach der Mitteilung auf dem Titelblatt einmal sechs Übersetzungen benutzt werden und zum andern die Behandlung jedes Kapitels auf sechs Rubriken verteilt wird. Die Testamente werden im Zusammenhang mit der Auslegung von Gen. 49 behandelt, unter Rubrik 3, „the explanation of doubtfull questions".[16] An dieser Stelle wird dem Josephus vorgeworfen, dass sein Bericht über den Segen Jakobs in *Antt.* II zu knapp ausgefallen ist, während hingegen andere die Segensprüche Jakobs zum Anlass genommen hätten, „to forge other fables upon this occasion". Willet nennt in diesem Zusammenhang die durch Origenes erwähnte „narration of Joseph the sonne of Jacob", und berichtet darüber, dass „Athanasius, in Synops. holdeth this to bee a forged booke : so is that other, called The testament of the twelve Patriarkes". Abgesehen von zwei Details entlehnt Willet alle seine Nachrichten nachweislich dem als Gewährsmann genanten Pererius. Die wichtigen eigenen Zusätze bestehen in Willet's Hinweis auf die Synopsis von Ps-Athanasius und seine Bemerkung, dass die Testamente ein „forged booke" sind.

Jedoch spricht sich Willet so beiläufig, kurz und ohne Begründung aus, dass Th. Korteweg[17] wohl mit Recht vermutete, dass Willet die Testamente überhaupt nicht auf Grund eigener Kenntnis beurteilt habe. Der Kontext, in dem er über sie schreibt, stammt aus Pererius; die Berufung auf Ps-Athanasius für den Erweis der Unechtheit der Testamente setzt wohl keine eigene Untersuchung der Testamente durch Willet voraus : das konnte man 1595 auch bei Drusius lesen. Allerdings hat Willet wahrscheinlich noch nicht Drusius' *De quaesitis...* benutzen können. Dennoch ist denkbar, dass Willet und Drusius in diesem Fall nicht auf eine gemeinsame Grundlage zurückgehen, sondern dass Willet von Drusius abhängig ist. Drusius dozierte nämlich 1572-1576 mit grossem Erfolg als Orientalist in Oxford; Willet erwarb dort in den achtziger Jahren den Grad eines master of arts. Vielleicht

---

[15] Meine Ausführungen über dies Werk, das sich in keiner niederländischen Bibliothek befindet, beruhen auf freundlichen Mitteilungen von Th. Korteweg, Leiden, der bei Gelegenheit eines Studienaufenthaltes in Oxford das Buch einsehen konnte.

[16] In der benutzten Ausgabe (London 1608) S. 455.

[17] Mündlich mitgeteilt am 4.7.1973 in Oxford.

hat Willet Gedanken von Drusius benutzt, die dieser zunächst mündlich vorgetragen, aber erst später niedergeschrieben hat.

Es ist sicher ein Verlust, dass Drusius den von ihm in Aussicht gestellten Beweis, dass die Pseudoepigraphen nicht ausschliesslich Unwahres enthalten, nicht mehr hat führen können. Zweifelsohne hätte er die relative Wichtigkeit verschiedener Pseudoepigraphen darlegen können und damit eine etwas positivere, jedenfalls mehr nuancierte Beurteilung und genauere Untersuchung dieser Literatur anregen können, als ihr ohne seine Mitwirkung zu Teil geworden ist. Denn gerade die Testamente der zwölf Patriarchen sind kurz nach Drusius' Ableben zwar Gegenstand einer für jene Zeit lobenswerte Untersuchung gewesen, die der französische Jesuit Jacobus Salianus (1557-1640) verfasst hat, aber die Ergebnisse waren über ein umfangreiches Werk hin zerstreut und hatten kaum Aussicht, Beachtung zu finden, sicher nicht in akatholischen Ländern.

Salianus war zuerst Rektor eines Kollegiums in Besançon, später war er in Paris tätig. Er publizierte 1619-1624 in Paris zum ersten Male seine *Annales ecclesiastici veteris testamenti ab orbe condito usque ad Christi mortem* (1641⁴).[18] Dies sechs Foliobände umfassende Werk bildet einen grossangelegten Versuch, alle bekannten Traditionen über die biblische Geschichte in einem chronologischen System unterzubringen. Salianus beginnt mit dem „ersten Jahr der Welt und Adams, 4052 v. Chr." und beschreibt in jedem Jahr die darin geschehenen Ereignisse, die die Bibel oder andere Quellen, wie Josephus, Philo, die Apokryphen, die Kirchenväter oder spätere Gelehrte, berichten. Dabei harmonisiert Salianus nicht nur soviel er kann, sondern er muss auch wohl oder übel alle möglichen Traditionen kritisieren oder abweisen. Für die Periode von ca. 1770-1625 v. Chr. beruft Salianus sich sehr häufig auf das in den Testamenten bewahrte Material.[19]

Auffallend ist, dass Salianus die Testamente nicht *a priori* als Quelle

---

[18] Auch in Paris erschien 1618 I. Tarinus, *Origenis Philocalia*. Zum Zitat aus der *Oratio Josephi* in *Philocalia* 23, 19 bemerkt Tarinus (S. 703-4) : „his consimilia pleraque in libro verè testamentario de testamento XII Patriarcharum". Torinus enthält sich aber jeder Beurteilung der Testamente.

[19] Kritik an den in derartigen Annalen gebrauchten Quellen wurde damals besonders von protestantischer Seite ausgeübt. Nach seiner Übersiedlung nach England, „Casaubon was compelled to give most of his time to the refutation of the *Annals* of Baronius", J. E. Sandys, *A History of Classical Scholarship* II, repr. London 1967³, S. 207.

verwirft, sondern dass sie bei ihm die Möglichkeit erhalten, ihren Wert unter Beweis zu stellen, wenn Salianus auch manchmal ihrem Titel die Bemerkung zufügt „wenn man diesem Buch glauben muss" oder Ähnliches. Manchmal, wenn Salianus die Testamente anführt, schliesst er mit einem Vergleich mit anderen Quellen an, um festzustellen, ob die Angaben der Testamente zuverlässig sind. Naturgemäss hat er an den zahllosen chronologischen Angaben Interesse, die an verschiedensten Stellen in den Testamenten vorkommen. Gerade diese Angaben sind es freilich, die sich bei näherer Prüfung als unhaltbar erweisen.

Ferner unterlässt es Salianus nicht, grosse Partien des Erzählstoffes der Testamente mitzuteilen, vor allem in den Sterbejahren der Patriarchen. Diesen Stoff gibt er oft ohne viel Kritik wieder. Wer sich in die Geschichte der Patriarchen in den *Annales* des Salianus vertieft, hat am Ende einen ziemlich zutreffenden Eindruck vom Inhalt der Testamente.

Salianus hat die Testamente wahrscheinlich genauer untersucht als sonst jemand in der Zeit bis 1698. Natürlich interessiert auch ihn nur ihre historische Zuverlässigkeit. Gegenüber Drusius aber ist bei ihm als Fortschritt zu verzeichnen, dass die Zuverlässigkeit der Testamente nicht mit einem Hinweis auf die kanongeschichtliche Tradition bestritten wird, sondern auf Grund von zahlreichen Einzelbeobachtungen untersucht wird, wobei das Urteil oft, jedoch nicht immer, zum Nachteil der Testamente ausfällt. Man empfindet es positiv, dass Salianus sich immer wieder die Mühe macht, die Haltbarkeit oder Unhaltbarkeit der Angaben der Testamente seinen Lesern vor Augen zu führen. Obwohl Salianus von ihrem geringen historischen Wert überzeugt gewesen sein muss, hat er ihnen einen bedeutenden Platz in seiner grandiosen historischen Harmonisierung eingeräumt. Auch hat er sich nicht zu den Schimpfkanonaden erniedrigt, mit denen sich die Gelehrten noch mindestens ein halbes Jahrhundert lang der Forschungsarbeit an den Testamenten entledigen sollten.

Was nämlich der Entwicklung einer wissenschaftlichen Erforschung der Testamente ernsthaft im Wege gestanden hat, ist die rein „historische" Betrachtung der Schrift, das einseitige Interesse der Renaissance für das Problem der Echtheit und der historischen Zuverlässigkeit. Das führte zu erheblicher Verachtung des Buches durch die Kritiker des 16. (und 17.) Jahrhunderts. Sie sahen die pseudoepigraphische Literatur als durchsichtigen Betrug an wegen ihrer Pseudonymität und der daraus erwachsenden inhaltlichen Unzuverlässigkeit. In dieser

Hinsicht ist das Urteil von Joseph Scaliger repräsentativ,[20] das er in seinem 1606 erschienenen *Thesaurus temporum* über den griechischen Henoch ausspricht, dessen Fragmente aus Syncellus er als erster gesammelt und publiziert hat. „Ich frage mich", schreibt Scaliger, „wer eigentlich wen übertrifft : die Juden mich in freier Zeit, um dies alles auszudenken, oder ich sie in Geduld, um das abzuschreiben. Denn es steht soviel Ungereimtes, Abstossendes und Beschämendes darin („quorum piget, taedet pudetque"), dass, wenn ich nicht wüsste, dass es nun einmal die Art der Juden ist zu lügen und dass sie den Unsinn („nugas") auch jetzt noch nicht unterlassen können, ich es (*scil.* das aus Henoch Zitierte) nicht für wert halten würde, dass es gelesen wird".[21] Und in einem Brief vom 30. Oktober 1605 endet Scaliger eine Tirade über Pseudoepigraphen wie Aristeas und Pseudo-Hecataeus mit einem Urteil über die Sibyllinischen Bücher, das tatsächlich zu denken gibt :[22] „Was ist über die Sibyllinischen Orakel zu sagen, die Christen gegen Heiden angeführt haben, obwohl sie doch ein Machwerk der Christen sind und in den Bibliotheken der Heiden nicht vorhanden waren. Für so machtlos hat man Gottes Wort angesehen, dass man daran gezweifelt hat, dass das Reich Christi sich ohne Lügen ausbreiten konnte".

Über die Testamente der Patriarchen hat Scaliger sich unseres Wissens nicht geäussert. Er hat nur im allgemeinen über die im *Micropresbyticon* und in den *Orthodoxographa* von Grynaeus (siehe oben S. 11) gesammelten Schriften, unter denen sich auch die Testamente finden, in häuslicher Konversation gesagt : „Omnia illa sup-

---

[20] Über Scaliger's *philologia sacra*, siehe „The Study of the New Testament", im Festschrift zur vierten Jahrhundertfeier der Leidener Universität, *Leiden University in the Seventeenth Century. An Exchange of Learning*, Leiden (Brill) 1975, S. 64-109.

[21] In der von uns benutzten 2. Auflage, Amsterdam 1658, S. 405 der „Notae in Graeca Eusebii'. Solche Bemerkungen (vgl. z.B. auch „Animadversiones in Chronologica Eusebi", *Thesaurus temp.* 1658[2], S. 185, wo Scaliger von „inepti Judaei", „eorum nugas" und „Anilitates sycophantiarum Iudaicarum" spricht) vergleiche man als Korrektiv mit „de veel te weinig bekende uitspraken over de Joden in zijn Scaligerana", die W. den Boer als „een monument voor het Leiden en het Holland van de zeventiende eeuw, dat voor Rembrandt's schilderijen nauwelijks onderdoet" bezeichnet, *Scaliger en Perizonius, hun betekenis voor de wetenschap*, Den Haag 1964, S. 10. (Ein schönes Beispiel, wie auch gutwillige Geschichtschreibung von Idealbildern der Gegenwart bestimmt sein kann).

[22] *Illustriss. Viri Iosephi Scaligeri… Epistolae omnes quae repereri potuerunt, nunc primum collectae ac editae*, Lugd. Bat. 1627, S. 303-304.

posititia, ... nihil ibi boni".[23] Ausserdem hat Scaliger in der Erst-
publikation des griechischen Textes der Stichometrie von Nicephorus
in seinem *Thesaurus temporum* (1606) auch den Titel Πατριάρχαι,
mit der Zahl der Zeilen, στίχων ,ερ, ohne Kommentar aufgeführt.[24]

Der englische Rechtsgelehrte und Altertumskenner John Selden
(1584-1654) ist der erste, der die Testamente ausdrücklich für ein
griechisches Machwerk erklärt hat. In seinem *De successionibus in
bona defuncti ... ad leges Ebraeorum* (London 1631, S. 98-101) nennt
er das Buch ,,ab Ebraeorum genio satis alienum" und eine Erfindung
von *Graeculi*, ,,qui Regno sacerdotium antestare (neque is morbus
recens natus est) inprimis voluere". Selden begründet diese antiklerikale
Deutung der Testamente mit einem Zitat aus J. Jud. XXI,1-4 und
mit Hinweisen auf TT. Rub., Sim. und Napht. Ob er mit ,,*Graeculi*"
Christen oder hellenistische Juden meint, bleibt unklar.

Aubertus Miraeus (1573-1640), Domdekan und Generalvikar von
Antwerpen, publizierte 1639 dort seine *Bibliotheca ecclesiastica sive
nomenclatores VII veteres*. Dieses Buch enthält ausser sieben ältere
Literaturgeschichten das ,,auctarium de scriptoribus ecclesiasticis",
eine Aufzählung von ,,kirchlichen" Autoren, von den Septuaginta bis
in das 17. Jahrhundert. Beim Jahr 1242 behandelt Miraeus Grosseteste,
erwähnt aber von ihm nur seine Übersetzung der Testamente. Er
bemerkt, dass diese Schrift ursprünglich hebräisch abgefasst war und
durch Origenes und Prokop zitiert worden ist. Er verweist auf Sixtus
Senensis, von dem er offenbar ganz abhängig ist.[25]

Der unkritische Gedanke eines hebräischen Originals der Testamente
war aus dem Kolophon zu Grossetestes lateinischer Übersetzung
in die gelehrte Literatur durch Sixtus Senensis gelangt und von diesem
durch Miraeus übernommen. Diese Vorstellung erhielt in der Mitte

---

[23] *Scaligerana* ed. Des Maizeaux, Amsterdam 1740, S. 454, *sub voce* ,,Micro-
Presbyticon". ,,Ce qui est dans le livre ainsi intitulé a esté mis dans les orthodoxographes
de Basle par Grynaeus : omnia illa supposititia, praesertim Epistolae Christi & Apostolorum ; nihil ibi boni".

[24] In der Auflage Amsterdam 1658[2], am Ende der Chronographie von Nicephorus,
S. 312.

[25] Die Nachricht von Sixtus S. ist ihm wahrscheinlich über eine *Bibliotheca sacra*
eines gewissen Molanus, deren Handschrift Miraeus gekannt hat, zugeflossen. Höchstwahrscheinlich handelt es sich hier um das Werk, das in C. G. Jöcher, *Allgemeines
Gelehrten-Lexicon* unter Johannes Molanus (Kath. Theologe in Löwen 1533-1585)
aufgeführt wird mit dem Titel ,,Bibliotheca theologica MSt" und das offenbar niemals
gedruckt ist. Über Joh. Molanus S. Joseph Lecler, Marius-François Valkhoff, *Les
premiers défenseurs de la liberté religieuse*, Tome premier, Paris 1969, S. 191-193.

des 17. Jahrhunderts einen Schein von wissenschaftlicher Begründung, als der aus Neapel stammende Jesuit Scipio Sgambati (1595-1652) in seinen *Archivorum veteris testamenti, seu de scriptoribus hebraicis tomi sive libri tres*,[26] einer hebräischen Literaturgeschichte von Adam bis zur Zeit von Augustus, den hebräischen Ursprung der Testamente auf Grund ihrer Sprache zu beweisen suchte : „Stylus ostendit Hebraicè scripta fuisse". Sgambati hält die Testamente für ein Werk aus dem ersten Jahrhundert n. Chr. Wichtiger ist, dass Sgambati als erster das Entstehen der Testamente literarisch zu erklären gesucht hat. Er meint, dass sie nicht geschrieben seien, um den Leser zu täuschen, sondern als literarische oder oratorische Übung, „ex more, quo solemus veterum orationes, colloquia, testamenta ex verisimili fingere". Für diese Anschauung hat er folgende Begründung : „quòd singula (sc. testamenta) scripta sint adversus aliquod vitium, aut pro aliqua virtute; ut testamentum Simeonis adversus Invidiam : Levi adversus Superbiam : Iudae pro fortitudine adversus Avaritiam, ac Fornicationem, quae ostendunt librum ab aliquo scriptum oratoriè, et ex ficto argumento". — Einfluss haben die Bemèrkungen von Sgambati kaum gehabt : seine *Archivorum veteris testamenti libri tres* wurden erst ein halbes Jahrhundert später (1703) in Neapel durch seinen Ordensbruder Thomas Strozza ediert.[27]

Ebenfalls vom hebräischen Ursprung der Testamente, vor allem aber von ihrer Minderwertigkeit war der dänische Lutheraner Thomas Bangius (1600-1661) überzeugt, wie aus einer Passage von gut einer Seite in Quarto hervorgeht, die er den Testamenten geweiht hat. Bangius hatte schon seit 1630 in Kopenhagen Hebräisch doziert, als er dort 1652 Professor der Theologie wurde. 1657 publizierte er sein *Coelum orientis et prisci mundi*, das mit einem neuen Titelblatt als *Exercitationes philologicae-philosophicae* in Krakau 1691 wieder herausgegeben wurde. Laut Untertitel handeln diese *Exercitationes* „de ortu et progressu literarum". Nachdem er über den Ursprung der Literatur und die schriftstellerische Tätigkeit Adams gesprochen hat, gelangt Bangius zu den Schriften von Henoch (S. 20). Die Existenz eines alten Buches, das Henoch zugeschrieben wird, ergibt sich nach Bangius ausser aus patristischen Zitaten, auch aus Hinweisen in „dem bekannten Volksbuch, das unter uns Dänen in unserer Muttersprache im Jahr 1601 bei Waldkirck erschienen ist unter dem

---

[26] 1703 in Neapel ediert durch seinen Ordensbruder Thomas Strozza, S. 206-207.

[27] Das Buch ist ziemlich selten. Ein Exemplar befindet sich in der Bibliothèque Nationale in Paris (A 1407). Siehe auch Anm. 32.

Titel „Testament der zwölf Patriarchen, der Söhne Jakobs".[28] Obwohl
Origenes und Prokop es benutzt haben, fährt Bangius fort, ist es
nicht wirklich eine Schrift der Söhne Jakobs, sondern „das Erzeugnis
irgendeines Rabbinen" („Rabbini cujusdam foetus"), ursprünglich
auf Hebräisch geschrieben und von Grosseteste übersetzt. Der Scribent
dieses unechten Machwerkes zitiert Henoch wiederholt. Soweit der
inhaltliche Teil der Bemerkungen des Bangius, aus dem sich ergibt,
dass er die Testamente zwar nicht als authentisch, aber doch als
ursprünglich jüdisch ansah. Mit grossem Nachdruck fällt Bangius
danach das Urteil, dass die Testamente voll Unsinn und Lügen sind.
Als Beweis hierfür zitiert er zwei Passagen, die nach seiner Angabe
aus dem Testament Gad, in Wirklichkeit aus dem Naphtalis, stammen.
Er retrovertiert sie übrigens aus dem Dänischen in ein perfekt klas-
sisches Latein, das mit dem von Grosseteste nichts gemeinsam hat.
Er benutzt Test. Napht. V,1-7 und VI,1-6, zwei Visionen des Naphtali,
die eine von der Erhöhung Levis, Juda und Joseph, die sich je mit
Sonne, Mond und einem geflügelten Stier zu erheben wissen, die
andere die vom unbemannten Segelboot, mit dem Jakob und seine
Söhne in See stechen und womit sie in einem Sturm Schiffbruch
leiden, sodass sie bis an die Enden der Erde zerstreut werden.
An solchen Erzählungen zeigt sich, meint Bangius, die Bedeutungs-
losigkeit und Sinnlosigkeit des Buches zur Genüge. Seiner Meinung
nach kann es ungeachtet seiner wiederholten Bezugnahme auf Henoch
keinerlei Autorität haben. Untergeschobene Erzeugnisse, wie die Testamente, die Leiter des Jakob und das von Gelasius genannte Testament
von Jakob verdienen durch Motten und Bücherwürmer verschlungen
zu werden, oder sind höchstens als Packpapier für den auf dem
Markt gekauften Pfeffer gut, wie Bangius mit einer Anspielung auf
Horaz (*Ep.* II, 1, 270) bemerkt : „foetus... dignus quo piper amiciatur
aut qui blattis & tineis esca fiet".[29]

---

[28] Diese Ausgabe steht nicht bei Robert Sinker, *A Descriptive Catalogue of the
Editions of the Printed Text of the Versions of the Testamenta XII Patriarcharum*,
Cambridge-London 1910, S. 26, „Danish".

[29] Die *blattae et tineae* des Horaz werden im 17. Jhdt. öfter als das verdiente
oder gefürchtete Schicksal literarischer Werke genannt, z.B. von Jan. Gruterus, *Inscrip-
tiones antiquae totius orbis Romani*, Heidelberg 1603, S. CXLVI, von Jos. Scaliger,
Scaligerana ed. Des Maizeaux, S. 112 „libros... blattis et tineis erosos", und von
Is. Vossius, *Ignatii epistolae genuinae*, London 1680², Fol. A3v. „si libri... blattis
et tineis absumendi relinquerentur". Auch der Pfeffer (*piper*) des Horaz gehört zum
festen Idiom der literarischen Kritik des 17. Jhdt.; S. z.B. Th. Crenius, *Animadversiones Philologicae et Historicae* XII, S. 68 : „inveni exempla [von Frid. Spanheims

Nicht viel anders urteilte Baltasar Bebelius, lutherischer Professor für Theologie in Strassburg (1632-1686). Schon in seinen *Ecclesiae antediluvianae vera et falsa*, Strassburg 1665 (S. 9) betont er den geringen Nutzen von allerlei Adambüchern, dem Evangelium des Nikodemus, Henoch, den Testamenten der zwölf Patriarchen, Berossus, Jubiläen und Sibyllinen als Quellen für die Geschichte der vorsint-flutlichen Gemeinde. Die Testamente enthalten krauses Geschwätz, das mit dem von Henoch vergleichbar ist, von dem doch „fabulosa sunt pleraque". In seinem zehn Jahr später publizierten *Adversus prae-existentiam animarum humanarum...*[30] legt er dar, dass sich die Präexistenz der menschlichen Seele nicht aus Väterzitaten beweisen lässt; denn „si quid de consensu Patrum fuerit probandum, necesse est, ut illud fiat ex authenticis, vel probatis & indubiis documentis; jam vero non minima pars eorum, quae h.l. producuntur, dubia, suspecta, falsa, & adulterina est. ... Tale est *liber Henoch*, ... *precatio Jacobi* (von Bebelius identifiziert mit dem *Testamentum Jacobi* bei Gelasius), ... *Patriarcharum XII. Testamentum*". Bebelius nennt die Testamente zwar sehr alt, aber darum nicht weniger unecht, „weil die Schrift nichts von diesem Testament der zwölf Patriarchen weiss".[31]

Abweisend und herabsetzend, aber mit einem neuen und wichtigen Argument wurden die Testamente auch von Joh. Heinr. Heidegger (1633-1698), seit 1667 Theologieprofessor in Zürich, kritisiert. Hei-degger, der vor allem durch seine Mitwirkung bei der Entstehung der *formula consensus Helvetica* bekannt ist, aber dabei eine mässigende Rolle gespielt hat, liess 1667 in Amsterdam den ersten Teil seiner *Historia sacra patriarcharum* erscheinen, worin er den hebräischen Text des Alten Testaments gegen Versuche der Jesuiten, dessen Quellenwert herabzusetzen, verteidigte. 1671 erschien der zweite Teil ebenfalls in Amsterdam, einer Anzahl führender Staatsmänner in den Niederlanden, u.a. Cornelis de Witt gewidmet, und den Curatoren

---

Exercitationes de gratia universali] olim delata in domum vendentem thus et odores et piper et quidquid chartis amicitur ineptis" und G. Beveregius, „Judicium de Canonibus Apostolicis", § 24, bei Cotelier, *Patr. apost.* ed. Clericus, I, Amsterdam 1724, S. 440, Sp. a: „hos canones unà cum Ignatii Epistolis, piperi & scombris devoveret". Vgl. schon Erasmus, *Ep.* (ed. Allen) II, S. 216. Z. 172.

[30] *Adversus praeexistentiam animarum humanarum, Errorem Christophori Sandii et Anonymi cujusdam, novorum Origenistarum, Exercitatio Theologica*, Strassburg 1675, S. 123. Wir gebrauchten das Exemplar der Bibliothèque Nationale in Paris (D² 3541).

[31] „Scriptura de illo XII. Patriarcharum Testamento nihil novit, nec ex aliis fide dignis monumentis, & vetustioribus de eo quicquam constat, unde igitur recentiores gesta illa sciverint?" (S. 123).

der Leidener Universität, die ihn vergeblich angesucht hatten, den Lehrstuhl des 1669 verstorbenen Coccejus, damals wohl der bedeutendste theologische Lehrstuhl in der protestantischen Welt, einzunehmen. Auch im zweiten Teil seiner *Historia* führt Heidegger aus, dass nur die hebräische Bibel die Geschichte der Patriarchen zuverlässig wiedergibt. Trotzdem, sagt er in Exerc. XVIII, hat „ein ebenso apokrypher wie anonymer Verfasser" („apocryphus juxta atque anonymus") gewagt, ein Testament der Erzväter „ohne Rücksicht auf die Schriften willkürlich zu erdichten und den leichtgläubigen Nachkommen vorzusetzten" („ἄτερ γραφῶν fingere pro lubitu & credulae posteritati propinare"). Danach zitiert er den Paragraph des Sixtus Senensis vollständig, teilt, als ob er sie selbst gefunden hätte, die Zeugnisse des Origenes und Prokop mit und spricht dann sein Urteil aus: „Es ist ein geschmackloses („insulsus") Buch, das sich durch seine eigenen Angaben schon verrät, sodass es mich erstaunt, dass Salianus und andere hier und da Behauptungen ohne irgendwelchen Wert („frivolas") auf die Autorität dieses Werkes gründen". Dieser Angriff auf Salianus zeigt die Voringenommenheit der antirömischen Polemik. Denn Salianus hatte in seinen *Annales* die Testamente zwar gebraucht, aber doch nicht kritiklos (siehe oben, S. 17-8). Tatsächlich beweist Salianus in seiner Behandlung der Testamente als historische Quelle schärferes kritisches Gefühl als Heidegger gegenüber der Genesis.

Immerhin ist Heidegger, soweit wir wissen, der erste gewesen, der die Testamente explizit als christlich bezeichnet hat: „Frühe Christen, die dann und wann den christlichen Glauben mit frommen Betrug verbreitet haben, scheinen dies Buch fälschlich unter dem Namen der Erzväter herausgebracht zu haben, um die Juden, bei denen die zwölf Stammväter stets grosses Ansehen genossen, auf ihre Seite zu bringen, ebenso, wie sie auch die Sibyllinischen Orakel gefälscht haben, um die Heiden zu bekehren. Es steht nämlich fest, dass diese Pseudopatriarchen nicht zukünftige Geschehnisse verkünden, was die Art war, in der im Alten Testament gelehrt wurde, sondern Ereignisse wiedergeben, die schon geschehen sind". Mag Heidegger sich auch aus polemischem Enthusiasmus verächtlich über die Testamente ausgesprochen haben, seine zitierte Beobachtung über die *vaticinia ex eventu* ist eben so richtig, wie neu. Denn dass Sgambati dasselbe bemerkt hatte,[32] konnte Heidegger nicht wissen.

---

[32] Sgambati schrieb: „Non esse autem librum hunc ante Christi tempora scriptum,

Um 1675 aber begann sich doch ein Umschwung in der Beurteilung der Schrift abzuzeichnen. Ein Zeichen dafür war die Tatsache, dass 1672 Jean Baptist Cotelier zum ersten Mal einige Zitate aus dem griechischen Text der Testamente als Parallele in seinen *Sancti patres qui temporibus apostolicis floruerunt*, Paris 1672, anführte.[33] Deutlicher gewahrt man die eintretende Veränderung in den Ausführungen[34] des sonderbaren niederländischen Gelehrten Johannes de Mey (1617-1678), geboren und gestorben in Middelburg (Seeland).[35] Nach seinem Studium in Leiden (1634-1639), zuerst in der philosophischen, später in der theologischen Fakultät, und nach kurzem Pfarrdienst auf einer der seeländischen Inseln, einer in England abgebrochenen Reise nach Indien, Promotion in der Medizin in Valence und nach folgender Tätigkeit als Pfarrer auf St. Eustatius, wurde De Mey 1649 Prädikant zu Middelburg. Obwohl er sich öfter gegen den Verdacht der Heterodoxie verteidigen musste, wurde er 1662 für eine theologische Professur an der Utrechter Universität nominiert, aber zunächst Dozent für Philosophie und schliesslich 1676 professor primarius theologiae am Athenaeum Illustre in Middelburg. Dies Institut versorgte gebildete Bürger, vor allem aber die ungefähr zwölfjährigen Abiturienten der Lateinschule mit höherem Unterricht, sodass die letzteren erst in etwas höherem Alter die Verführungen der Universitätsstadt zu bestehen hatten.

Unter den von vielseitiger Gelehrsamkeit zeugenden Publikationen von Johannes de Mey befindet sich das 1675 erschienene *Derde*

---

satis indicant apertissima vaticinia earum rerum, quae Christo acciderunt. Nam ex certis, ac veris vaticinijs Prophetarum Isaiae, Hieremiae, ac caeterorum discimus hunc Prophetis esse morem, ut futura, non nisi obscurè praedicant. Huius autem libri Auctor omninò apertè, ac perspicuè plurima de Christo scribit". *Archivorum V.T. libri*, S. 207.

[33] Dies bemerkt J. E. Grabe in der Praefatio zu seiner Ausgabe der Testamente, auch aufgenommen in J. A. Fabricius, *Codex Pseudepigraphus Vet. Testamenti*, I, Hamburg 1722², S. 516. Grabe verweist aber nicht auf Belegstellen, und wir haben solche auch nicht gefunden.

[34] Auf die wichtige Passage bei De Mey hat J. A. Gruys, Den Haag, uns aufmerksam gemacht.

[35] Für einen ausführlichen Lebensbericht sei verwiesen nach Pieter de la Ruë, *Geletterd Zeeland*, Middelburg 1741, S. 99-116; B. Glasius, *Biographisch Woordenboek van Nederlandsche Godgeleerden*, II, 's-Hertogenbosch 1853, S. 502-504; F. Nachtglas, *Levensberichten van Zeeuwen*, Tweede Deel, Middelburg, S. 158-163; und *Biographisch Woordenboek der Nederlanden*, Nieuwe Uitgaaf, 12, S. 764. Für De Mey als Theologe, S. Chr. Sepp, *Het Godgeleerd Onderwijs in Nederland gedurende de 16ᵉ en 17ᵉ eeuw*, II, Leiden 1874, S. 106-110.

vervolg van Euzooïa.[36] In den vorhergehenden Teilen hatte De Mey
zunächst theoretisch die Bedeutung eines gut regierten bürgerlichen
Rechtsstaates verteidigt; danach setzt er nun auseinander, dass ein
solches wohlgeordnetes Staatswesen vorbildlich in der Gesellschaft der
Patriarchen von Adam bis zu den Söhnen Jakobs verwirklicht war.
Seine Anschauung will De Mey dem Leser in einer kommentierenden
Darlegung der Berichte der Genesis nahebringen. Unerwartet unter-
bricht er dabei seine Besprechung von Gen. 49 nach Vers 13 mit
der Mitteilung: „Doch om de meeninge [Bedeutung] van de uytsprake
Jacobs over de 12 stammen ... te verstaen, is niet ondienstig seker
Boecxken, dat my onlangs ter hand gekomen is", worin „worden
beschreven de 12 Testamenten, welcke de 12 Sonen Jacobs, yder voor
sijne dood gemaeckt en hare kinderen voorgedragen en aenbevolen
hebben".

Es fällt auf, dass De Mey, abweichend von dem bis dahin gebräuch-
lichen Verfahren, nicht nur einzelne Zeilen oder höchstens eine Seite
seines Werkes den Testamenten widmet, sondern ihnen nicht weniger
als beinahe 4 Seiten in Quarto einräumt (S. 78-81). Von Testament
zu Testament gibt er eine kürzere oder längere Inhaltsangabe — zweifelsohne auf Grund eigener Lektüre —, und bei diesem oder jenem
Testament gibt er sogar Erklärungen, seien es auch nur zoologische.
Bei Test. Zeb. VI berichtet er z.B. von einem erstaunlichen Muscheltier,
das er auf seiner Reise nach Westindien das Meer durchpflügen sah,
und das die Matrosen „bezaan" genannt haben.

Danach legt De Mey acht aus den Test. Ruben, Simeon und Levi
entnommene Prophetien über Christus vor, und zum Schluss folgt
eine literarhistorische Beurteilung der Testamente, wofür De Mey
die auch sonst in seiner *Euzooïa* benutzte Form des Dialoges zwischen
einem Christen und einem Heiden wählt. Mit dieser Form meinte
De Mey nämlich, wie er in seinem ersten Vorwort zur *Euzooïa*
mitteilt, zeigen zu können, dass der christliche Glaube auf rein
vernünftigem Wege einsichtig gemacht werden kann, und dass gutwillige
Heiden ohne Berufung auf die heilige Schrift von der Vernünftigkeit,
Richtigkeit und Wahrheit des christlichen Glaubens überzeugt werden

---

[36] Die erste Ausgabe erschien zu Middelburg bei Th. Berry. Diese ist mit neuem
Titel und wieder abgedrucktem Vorstück nochmals herausgekommen in Middelburg
bei Bartholomeus de Later, 1678 (ein Exemplar dieser Ausgabe befindet sich in
Den Haag, Kön. Bibl. 2105 A 165/3). Auch ist das genannte *Derde vervolg van
Euzooïa* aufgenommen in De Meys *Alle de Nederlandsche Werken*, Middelburg 1681,
wieder aufgelegt in Delft 1704 und 1741.

können. Darum ist nun die Reihe der Prophetien auch kaum bis Test. Levi XVIII gelangt, als sie schon vom Heiden mit der Bemerkung unterbrochen wird, dass der Sprecher es für wahrscheinlich hält, dass die Testamente auf griechisch von Christen geschrieben sind. Sie seien jedoch als alte hebräische Weissagungen ausgegeben, um als Beweis für die Wahrheit des Christentums zu dienen. Als Parallele führt der Heide die Sibyllinischen Bücher an, die seines Erachtens ebenfalls von Christen verfasst sind, wie sehr sie sich auch als Schriften heidnischer Prophetinnen geben.[37] Der Christ antwortet, dass er hierüber kein Urteil haben könne, dass aber auch Andrew Willet, ,,een geleert Engels-man", die Testamente für nicht-authentisch gehalten hat, wenn auch die Schrift, ebenso wie die *Narratio Josephi*, von Origenes benutzt worden sei.

De Mey ist in seiner Beurteilung der Testamente beinahe vollständig von der oben genannten damals 80 Jahre alten Kritik von Andrew Willet abhängig. Dieser war seinerseits, ausser in der Echtheitsfrage, Pererius gefolgt, während Pererius wieder, ohne dass bei ihm eigene Kenntnis der Testamente zu Tage tritt, sich schon auf Sixtus Senensis verlassen hatte....

Hatte Drusius die ausdrückliche Verwerfung der Echtheit der Testamente in die Kritik eingeführt, so kommt De Mey das Verdienst zu, abweichend von der Gewohnheit seiner Zeit, mit der Ablehnung der Echtheit nicht mehr ohne Weiteres ein herabsetzendes Urteil verbunden zu haben. Er unterlässt nicht nur jede verächtliche Äusserung über die Testamente;[38] er nennt sie auch für das Verständnis des in Genesis 49 vorliegenden ,,Testaments" nicht nutzlos (,,niet ondienstig"). Ausserdem nimmt De Mey, jedenfalls durch den Mund des Heiden, christlichen Ursprung der Testamente an, obschon er, wie aus der Einleitung zu seinem Exkurs hervorgeht, die Überlieferung von deren jüdischem Ursprung recht gut kennt. Schliesslich distanziert sich De Mey (ebenso wie Selden) von der traditionellen, inzwischen auch pseudowissenschaftlich annehmbar gemachten Meinung, dass die Testamente ursprünglich hebräisch geschrieben sind : für ihn sind sie griechisch verfasst.[39]

---

[37] Vielleicht verrät sich in dieser Anspielung auf die Sibyllinischen Bücher verschwiegene Abhängigkeit De Meys von Heidegger, S. oben S. 23-24.

[38] Scipio Sgambati schrieb noch : ,,fabulosis narrationibus scatent haec testamenta, quae minimè Prophetam decerent", a.a.O., S. 207.

[39] Bemerkung von J. C. H. Lebram : Vielleicht müsste De Mey noch stärker hervorgehoben werden : der Rationalist will das (hier : politische) Ideal eines aufgeklärten

Auffallend ist, dass die (niederländisch gegebenen) Zitate aus den
Testamenten von De Mey nicht aus der gängigen niederländischen
Übersetzung des Buches entnommen sind. De Mey muss die angeführten Passagen selbst übersetzt haben. Er legte aber dabei nicht
eine von den lateinischen Ausgaben zugrunde, sondern eine der
zahlreichen englischen. Dies geht daraus hervor, dass er in seinen
einleitenden Bemerkungen die Testamente als aus dem Griechischen
durch Grosseteste übersetzt beschreibt, „en uyt sijne Copye in 't Frans,
Duyts en Engels. Waer van de oude Copye in 't Griecks geschreven
op Parkement bewaert wort in de Academie tot Cambridge". Diese
Mitteilung bezieht De Mey offensichtlich vom Titelblatt einer der
englischen Ausgaben der Testamente, wo ebenfalls erst die Übersetzung aus dem Griechischen von Grosseteste genannt wird und
danach folgt: „... and out of his Copy into French, and Dutch,
by others, and now Englished. To the Credit whereof, an ancient
Greek Copy, written in Parchment, is kept in the University Library
of Cambridge". Als De Mey die Mitteilungen über das Manuskript
zu Cambridge (gegenwärtig Univ. Libr. Ff. 1. 24) abschrieb, lag
diese Handschrift gerade ein Jahrhundert in der genannten Bibliothek:
1575 war sie an diese aus dem Nachlass des Erzbischofs, Kirchen-
geschichtlers und Handschriftensammlers Matthew Parker über-
gegangen.[40] Die Handschrift war durch Gelehrte des 17. Jahrhunderts
schon gelegentlich als Zeuge für das *Hypomnesticon* des pseudonymen
unbekannten christlichen Kompilators Joseppus[41] erwähnt worden:
so durch John Selden und Patrick Young.[42] Als Zeuge für die

---

Staatswesens nicht nur auf christlich-antike Traditionen, sondern auf eine Urüber-
lieferung begründen, die allen Völkern gemeinsam ist (vgl. Martinus Martinis Hinweise
auf die Chinesen). Räumlich, historisch und literarisch sprengt man hierfür die Grenzen
der biblisch-klassischen Überlieferung. Auch das führt noch nicht zur literarischen,
aber wenigstens zu einer mehr inhaltlich orientierten Würdigung von Überlieferungen.
Die Vorstellung von dem „vernünftigen" Kern der Menschheitsüberlieferung ist Vorstufe
ihrer literarischen Würdigung.

[40] Zur Geschichte dieses Manuskripts im 16. Jhdt. s. M. R. James, „Greek Mss.
in England before the Renaissance", *The Library* 4th Ser., 7, 1927, S. 337ff., vor
allem 341, 343, 350. Nach James hat Parker die Handschrift aus Canterbury gerettet,
möglicherweise aus St. Augustine's. Für die Schicksale des Manuskripts im 13. Jhdt. s.
Kap. V in diesem Band.

[41] Migne *PG* 106, 16-176. Jacques Moreau, „Observations zur l'Ὑπομνηστικὸν
βιβλίον Ἰωσήππου", *Byzantion* 25-27, 1955-1957, S. 241-276.

[42] Joh. Selden, *Opera omnia*, Vol. I, Pars I, *De Anno Civili Veterum Judaeorum*
Cap. VIII, Sp. 28: „Etiam in commentario veteri quod ὑπομνηστικὸν appellatur

Testamente der Patriarchen aber ist, soweit wir wissen, die Handschrift in der wissenschaftlichen Literatur das erste Mal durch Johannes de Mey genannt worden.

In der Zwischenzeit war aber auch in England die genannte Handschrift als Quelle für die Testamente nicht ganz unbekannt geblieben : zuletzt verfügte Thomas Gale, damals High Master von St. Paul's, über eine Abschrift[43] der Testamente, auf Griechisch abgeschrieben nach der durch De Mey angeführten Handschrift in der Cambridge University Library. Aus dieser Handschrift führte Gale Parallelen in seinem *Iamblichi De Mysteriis*, Oxford 1678, an.[44] Seit dem Tode seines Sohnes Roger im Jahre 1744 liegt Gales Abschrift in der Bibliothek des Trinity College zu Cambridge (O. 4. 24).

Offenbar haben in der anglikanischen Kirche mit ihrem Interesse für die alten Überlieferungen der Christenheit die Patriarchentestamente wieder Beachtung gefunden. Unter ihrem Einfluss steht Johannes de Mey, dessen Behandlung der Testamente völlig unbeachtet geblieben ist. Das dort erwachte wissenschaftliche Interesse für die Testamente in der Zeit nach De Mey kennen wir dank J. A. Fabricius besser. Allerdings bleibt ihre Beurteilung zunächst noch in den alten Bahnen. Doch beschäftigte man sich mehr mit den Umständen der Entstehung der Patriarchentestamente.

1688 erschien in London der erste Teil der *Scriptorum ecclesiasticorum historia ecclesiastica* von William Cave (1637-1713), Pfarrer in London, Hofprediger Karls II. und Canonicus in Windsor. In dieses Werk, eine Übersicht über alle europäischen Schriftsteller von der Geburt Jesu an bis zur Reformation, nahm Cave auch einen Abschnitt über die Testamente von 13 Zeilen Länge auf (S. 52). Er datiert sie zuerst gegen 190 n. Chr., später in den Anfang des 2. Jahr-

---

Ἰωσίππου Josephi (codice nimirum a Theodoro Cantuariensi antistite ante annos amplius septingentos in Angliam cum Graecis aliis, ut existimatum est, allato...".
Patr. Junius, *Clementis ad Corinthios Epistula Prior*, Oxonii 1633, Fol. N2r. : „De quo loco Josephus scriptor Christianus (quem nos ex codice MS. Cantabrigiensi descriptum habemus) in Ὑπομνηστικῷ suo, quaestione 121. sic habet...".

[43] Für Gales Abschrift s. R. Sinker, *Testamenta XII Patriarcharum ...*, Cambridge-London 1869, S. viii-ix, *sub* (2). Nach M. R. James, *The Western Manuscripts in the Library of Trinity College, Cambridge. A Descriptive Catalogue* III, Cambridge 1902, S. 274, war Gales Abschrift durch Patrick Young geschrieben. Young and Gale scheinen also den selben codex besessen und gebraucht zu haben. Siehe unten S. 113 und 115, *Addendum 3*.

[44] *Iamblichi Chalcidensis De Mysteriis liber*, Oxonii 1678. Dies war die *editio princeps* dieser Schrift. In ihr wird z.B. S. 210 Test. Levi III,9 zitiert.

hunderts,[45] aber „ob der Verfasser ein Jude oder ein Christ war,
ist nicht deutlich. Wahrscheinlich ein judaisierender Christ, wie es
jener Zeit viele gab". Obwohl Cave die Testamente als „plurimis
Ethicis praeceptis, iisque melioris quidem notae, passim refertum"
empfiehlt, unterlässt er nicht, ihren Inhalt im Übrigen als „ineptia"
zu bezeichnen. Interessant ist, dass Cave eine Abschrift des griechischen
Textes der Testamente erwähnt, die bei Thomas Smith liegt, Fellow
des Magdalen College zu Oxford, und nach einem in der Bodleiana
befindlichen Codex (Barocci 133) angefertigt ist. Schon lange vor
1688 hatte Thomas Smith versprochen, so Cave, eine griechisch-
lateinische Ausgabe der Testamente zu publizieren. Aus dieser Ausgabe
ist nichts geworden.[46] Beim Tode von Smith (1710) ging seine Abschrift
an die Bibliothek von Dr. Hearne über, der sie der Bodleian Library
vererbte, wo sie noch jetzt aufbewahrt wird (Ms. Smith 117).[47]

Bei der Abfassung seiner *Historia literaria* hatte Cave, vor allem
für die Periode nach 1300, die kräftige Unterstützung des damals ungefähr vierundzwanzigjährigen Henry Wharton (1664-1695)[48] gehabt.
Ein Jahr nach dem Erscheinen von Caves *Historia* veröffentlichte
Wharton selbst sein *Auctarium historiae dogmaticae Jac. Usserii de
scripturis & sacris vernaculis*, London 1689. Auch hierbei handelt es
sich um eine chronologisch angeordnete Literaturübersicht. Hinter
Polykarp, der 140, und Theophilus von Antiochien, der 184 n. Chr.
datiert wird, werden unter der Jahreszahl 190 die Testamente vor
Clemens Alexandrinus eingeordnet und besprochen. Wharton bemerkt,
dass die Testamente, obwohl einige sie als ursprünglich jüdisch und
auf Hebräisch geschrieben ansehen, doch von Christen geschrieben
sind. Unschön ist die Verachtung, in der sich Wharton — zugegeben:
im Alter von kaum 25 Jahren — über den Verfasser ergeht: „Zwar gibt
der Betrüger vor, von jüdischer Denkart zu sein, um von da mit
frommem Betrug den Juden seine Fälschung aufzutischen und ihnen
seine Prophezeiungen unter dem Namen der Patriarchen zu verkaufen,
aber der Betrug schaut überall hervor und wird durch unverkennbare
Hinweise offenbar". („sectam quidem Judaicam prae se fert Impostor;
ut exinde Judaeis fucum piâ fraude faciat, & sub Patriarcharum

---

[45] J. A. Fabricius, *Codex pseudepigraphus V.T.*, I, Hamburg 1722², S. 501.

[46] Wir verdanken Smith jedoch eine Ausgabe des Ignatius von Antiochien.

[47] Vgl. Sinker a.a.O. (Anm. 43), S. x-xi, *sub* (1). Das Smith die Absicht gehabt
hat, die Testamente herauszugeben, scheint Sinker nicht gewusst zu haben.

[48] Über Wharton, s. David C. Douglas, *English Scholars, 1660-1730*, London 1951²,
S. 139-155.

nominibus venditet profetias. Verum ubique pellucet fraus, manifestis prodita indiciis"). Als solche *indicia* sieht Wharton Weissagungen auf Christus wie z.B. Test. Aser VII,3 und Test. Joseph XIX,11 an; Stellen, die später nicht ohne Grund von R. H. Charles in Klammern gesetzt wurden.[49]

Zugleich aber erreicht die Wertschätzung der Testamente einen Tiefpunkt in einem Kapitel des Nicolas le Nourry, Benediktiner von St. Maur (1647-1724), das nichtsdestoweniger wegen seiner Analysen wichtig ist. Le Nourry, der an verschiedenen wissenschaftlichen Projekten seines Ordens teilgenommen hat, liess 1694 in Paris den ersten Teil seines wichtigsten Werkes erscheinen, des *Apparatus ad bibliothecam maximam patrum* (1703[2]). Dies war als literarhistorisches Hilfsmittel gedacht für die in Lyon erscheinende *Bibliotheca patrum maxima*. In einem besonderen Kapitel über die Testamente gibt Le Nourry zuerst eine ziemlich ausführliche Inhaltsangabe, wo er vor allem nicht versäumt, die Verweisungen auf Henoch anzuführen. Dann bemerkt Le Nourry, dass die Schrift nach allgemeiner Auffassung voll Phantasien, Fabeln, Fehler und Lügen steht, was er auf zwei Arten durchführt. Erstens nennt er sechs Widersprüche zwischen den Testamenten und der heiligen Schrift, zweitens weist er darauf hin, dass in den Testamenten wiederholt Gebrauch vom gefälschten Henochbuch gemacht wird, woraus sich die Minderwertigkeit der Testamente zur Genüge erweist. Anschliessend setzt Le Nourry auseinander, dass das hohe Alter des von Origenes bereits benutzten Werkes nicht gegen seine Unechtheit ins Feld geführt werden kann, da schon in ältesten Zeiten Bücher gefälscht worden sind. Der Verfasser muss angesichts der Weissagungen auf das Kommen und Leiden Christi ein Christ gewesen sein, der mit seinem Buch Christus verherrlichen („ut Christum celebraret") und seine Leser vor Sünden warnen und zum Guten ermahnen wollte. Darauf nennt Le Nourry die beiden griechischen Handschriften der Testamente in der *Bibliotheca Regia* in Paris (jetzt Bibliothèque Nationale, gr. 2658 und 938),[50] wovon seiner Meinung nach die älteste aus dem 11. oder 12. Jahrhundert stammt;[51] ausserdem erwähnt er zwei Manuskripte der lateinischen

---

[49] In seiner Textausgabe *The Greek Versions of the Testaments of the Twelve Patriarchs*, Oxford 1908 (= Darmstadt/Hildesheim 1960, 1966[3]), setzte R. H. Charles die Passagen, die er als interpoliert ansah, in eckige Klammern.

[50] Vgl. Anm. 59.

[51] Diese Datierung ist richtig, vgl. H. Omont, *Inventaire sommaire des mss grecs*

Übersetzung in der *Bibliotheca Colbertina* und bringt endlich eine
Liste von 6 Editionen, darunter eine Ausgabe Paris 1541, die nicht
in Sinkers *Descriptive Catalogue of the Editions* (vgl. Anm. 28)
angegeben ist. Le Nourry endet: „Ob das fragliche Buch griechisch
herausgegeben ist, ist uns unbekannt [tatsächlich war dies 1694 noch
nicht der Fall]. Es ist freilich auch unwichtig, ob man dies weiss,
da derartige Bücher, die voll von Phantastereien und Altweiberfabeln
sind und von Widersprüchen gegen die heilige Schrift, niemals das
Tageslicht hätten sehen dürfen oder doch zu ewiger Finsternis ver-
dammt werden müssten". Wie hart sein Urteil auch sein mag, man
muss Le Nourry zugeben, dass er mehr als die andern Forscher
vor ihm versucht hat, seinen Standpunkt zu begründen und im
Zusammenhang damit konkret anzugeben, warum die Testamente
christlichen Ursprungs sind und was ihre Absicht ist.

Ohne wissenschaftliche Bedeutung ist der Hinweis auf die Testamente, den Henricus Ludolphus Benthem, Superintendent zu Bar-
dowick (1661-1723) in seinem *Engländischen Kirch- und Schulenstaat*,
Lüneburg 1695, gibt. Das Buch ist in niederländischer Übersetzung
1701 zu Utrecht erschienen. In einem Kapitel (VI, c. 17) über die
englischen Gelehrten von der ältesten Zeit an, erwähnt Benthem auch
Grosseteste und nennt dessen Übersetzung der Testamente, aber
ohne weitere Erläuterung; in einer späteren Ausgabe (Leipzig 1732,
S. 838) ist eine Notiz über Matthew Paris zugefügt, sowie mitgeteilt,
dass an dieser Stelle für Erwägungen über die Autorität der Testamente
nicht der rechte Platz ist.

Danach aber nimmt das philologische Interesse an den Testamenten
zu. 1698 erscheint die *editio princeps* des griechischen Textes, zugleich
mit den Abhandlungen von Grabe und Dodwell über dies Pseudoepigraphon. Das alles wird noch einmal von J. A. Fabricius im
Jahre 1713 (nochmals 1722) gedruckt, und in einer posthumen Ausgabe
von Grabe 1714. Aufmerksamkeit verdient aber noch ein höchstwahrscheinlich schon 1687, also vor diesem Wendepunkt geschriebenes
Kapitel über die Testamente, das 1708 anonym erschienen ist. Bevor
wir auf diese Veröffentlichung eingehen, wollen wir uns jedoch zuerst
dem Mann zuwenden, der die weitere Entwicklung der Erforschung
der Testamente entscheidend beeinflusst hat: Johannes Ernest Grabe
(1666-1711).

---

de la Bibl. Nationale III, S. 20, wo das Manuskript gr. 2658 ebenfalls dem 11. Jhdt.
zugeschrieben wird.

Es war Grabe, der 1698 den vollständigen griechischen Text der Testamente der Öffentlichkeit zugänglich machte. Nachdem er beinahe zehn Jahre lang Kirchengeschichte an der Universität Königsberg doziert hatte, war er 1694 unter dem Verdacht katholisierender Neigungen festgenommen und schliesslich ausgewiesen worden. 1697 ging er nach England und wurde Glied der anglikanischen Kirche. Im nächsten Jahr erschien sein *Spicilegium sanctorum patrum et haereticorum seculorum post Christum natum* I, Oxford 1698, in dem er u.a. den griechischen Text der Testamente nach einer ihm durch John Mill vermittelten Kopie der Handschrift in Cambridge herausgab.[52] Diese verglich er mit dem Manuskript Barocci 133 in der Bodleian Library zu Oxford und der lateinischen Übersetzung von Grosseteste, für die er zwei Handschriften, ebenfalls aus der Bodleian Library, benutzte. Er schickte der Ausgabe eine wichtige Praefatio voraus, in der die literarhistorischen Probleme der Testamente ausführlich behandelt wurden (S. 129-144). Ausserdem sind der Ausgabe zwei kürzere Abhandlungen des 1691 abgesetzten Oxforder Cambden-Professors für Geschichte Henry Dodwell (1641-1711) beigefügt, die eine über die *Tabulae coeli* aus T. Levi V,4, T. Aser II,10 und VII,5 (Der Ausdruck „tabulae coeli" wird als „lex in coelis archetypa" erklärt, das himmlische Vorbild des alten und neuen Bundes in Worten ausgedrückt und möglicherweise Teil des Henochbuches.), und die andere über die Chronologie der Erzvätergeschichte nach den Testamenten. Zu verschiedenen Stellen gibt Grabe selbst ausführliche Noten mit rabbinischem Vergleichsmaterial.

Das Wichtigste in der Einleitung von Grabe ist die neue Theorie, dass die Testamente ursprünglich eine hebräische, jüdische, vorchristliche Schrift gewesen sind, die ins Griechische übertragen und später durch einen Christen interpoliert wurde. Grabe nimmt nicht mit der Überlieferung an, dass die Testamente durch Chrysostomus übersetzt sind, sondern vermutet, dass dies zugleich mit den Büchern des Alten Testaments in der Zeit Ptolemäus' II. ins Griechische erfolgt ist. Offenbar hat er die Vorstellung, dass die Testamente spätestens ca. 300 v. Chr. geschrieben sind.

Dass die Testamente ursprünglich jüdisch sind, vermutet Grabe auf Grund von Passagen, wie T. Ruben VI,12, wozu er bemerkt, dass

---

[52] Sinker, a.a.O. (Anm. 43), S. viii, *sub* (1), meint, dass die von Grabe benutzte Kopie die jetzt in der University Library zu Cambridge bewahrte Handschrift, das zu den „Seller papers" gehört (Oo. VI. 91, 8), ist.

kein Christ jemals hätte schreiben können, dass Christus streiten
und in sichtbaren und unsichtbaren Kämpfen sterben würde. Auch
T. Sim. V,4-5 kann nicht christlich sein, da die Aussage, dass die
Juden, insbesondere die Nachkommen von Simeon, von Levi oder
dem Messias mit dem Schwert bekämpft werden sollten und dass
ihre Burgen durch Levi oder den Messias vernichtet werden sollten,
nicht christlich sein könne. Die dritte und letzte Passage, aus dem
Grabe auf ein jüdisches Originel folgert, ist T. Levi XVIII,6 : welche
Christen würden jemals behauptet haben, dass die Stimme, die bei
der Taufe Jesu vom Himmel kam, die von Abraham war?

Für das hohe Alter der Testamente beruft sich Grabe auf vier
Zeugnisse. 1. Epiphanius sagt in *De mensuris et ponderibus* 10, dass
dem Ptolemäus ausser den kanonischen Büchern des Alten Testaments,
auch 72 apokryphe Bücher zur Übersetzung zugesandt wurden.
2. Josephus teilt in *Contra Apionem* mit, dass seit Artaxerxes (also
nach ca. 450) eine Anzahl alttestamentlicher Bücher mit geringerer
Autorität geschrieben worden sind, wozu Grabe auch die „Patriarchae"
aus der Synopsis des Pseudo-Athanasius zählt. 3. Die „Patriarchae"
stehen in den alten Apokryphenlisten zwischen Schriften, die nach
Grabe's Auffassung zum grössten Teil vorchristlich sind. Dies ist ausser
in der eben genannten Synopsis, auch in der Stichometrie des Nicephorus, in *De LX libris et quinam extra illos sunt*, und im *Decretum
Gelasianum* der Fall.[53] 4. Schon Paulus zitiert in einem seiner ältesten
Briefe, I Thess. 2,16 (ἔφθασεν δὲ ἐπ᾽ αὐτοὺς ἡ ὀργὴ εἰς τέλος *textus
receptus* und Nestle) T. Levi VI,11 (ἔφθασε δὲ ἡ ὀργὴ κυρίου
ἐπ᾽ αὐτοὺς εἰς τέλος. Ms. *b* der Testamente).

Der jüdische und vorchristliche Ursprung der Testamente steht
damit nach Grabe fest. Christliche Interpolationen sieht Grabe nicht
so sehr in messianischen oder eschatologischen Passagen, die nach
seiner Meinung genügend Entsprechungen in der rabbinischen Literatur
haben, als eher in Ausführungen über christliche Themen, z.B. die
Gottheit Christi und über Paulus. Die christliche Interpolation stammt
aus der Zeit nach der Zerstörung Jerusalems, auf die in T. Levi XVI,4
und XV,1 angespielt wird. Auch wird in T. Beni. XI,4 die Apostel-

---

[53] Die richtige Lesart im *Decretum Gelasianum* lautet *Testamentum Job*; als Variante
erscheint : *Testamentum Jacob*. Grabe denkt, dass *Iob* lateinische Korruption von ιβ᾽
ist, das τῶν ιβ᾽ πατριαρχῶν gemeint haben soll. Grabe hat den Titel des Testaments
von Hiob irrtümlicherweise verändert, da er die Schrift nicht kannte. Anders steht
es bei Hugo von St. Victor, bei dem der Titel *Testamentum Job* korrekt überliefert
ist (vgl. Anm. 9).

geschichte genannt; also sind die Interpolationen jünger als Acta. Eine genauere Datierung der Interpolationen im ersten oder zweiten Jahrhundert n. Chr. hält Grabe nicht für möglich; auch der Stil weist nicht zwingend auf das erste Jahrhundert, wie Dodwell gemeint hat.

Schliesslich verwendet Grabe mehr als eine Oktavseite darauf, um auseinanderzusetzten, wie wertvoll vor allem die ethischen, aber auch die eschatologischen und historischen Teile der Testamente sind. Dazu gibt er eine Begründung seiner Edition.

Wenn auch Grabes Argumentation heute nur noch wenig Gültigkeit zuerkannt werden kann, so ist er doch der erste Gelehrte, der so argumentiert, dass der moderne Kritiker sich heute noch von ihm angesprochen fühlen kann. Diese Tatsache wird der Grund dafür sein, dass die Beschreibung der Forschungsgeschichte der Testamente immer wieder die Arbeit von Grabe zum Ausgangspunkt genommen hat und die ältere Kritik bis jetzt noch keine Beachtung gefunden hat. Auch hebt er sich wohltuend von der Geringschätzung ab, mit der die Testamente im 17. Jahrhundert behandelt wurden. Es wird darum kaum ein Zufall sein, dass gerade Grabe, der so genau beschreibt, worin er den Wert der Testamente sieht, grundlegend zu ihrer kritischen Erforschung beigetragen hat.

Derartiges Interesse, geschweige denn Respekt für die Testamente war auch in der Zeit vor und nach Grabe nicht selbstverständlich. Noch 1722 z.B. rezensiert der Hilfsbibliothekar der Leidener Universität Casimir Oudin das *Spicilegium* von Grabe mit der kritteligen Bemerkung, dass es „charactere nitido" gedruckt ist, aber dass Grabes Vorwort für ein „opus suppositum" wie die Testamente „nimiae prolixitatis" ist: „Haec opuscula enim [*Acta Pauli et Theclae* und *Testamenta XII Patr.*] apud eruditos nullius fidei vel ponderis sunt".[54] Damit wird Grabe indirekt die wahre Erudition abgesprochen.

Auch die Interpolationstheorie von Grabe fand keinen Beifall. Der Leidener Theologieprofessor Herman Witsius z.B. lässt es sich nicht entgehen, lange Abschnitte aus der Ausgabe der Testamente von Grabe auf Griechisch zu zitieren, wenn er in seinem Kommentar zum Judasbrief nach alter Gewohnheit die Testamente als Zeugnis für Henoch anführt. Aber unverkennbar lehnt er dessen Auffassungen über die Entstehung der Testamente ohne Namensnennung durch die Bemerkung ab: „auctorem fuisse Judaeum quendam, Christianae

---

[54] *Commentarius de scriptoribus ecclesiae antiquis*, Frankfurt am Main 1722, vol. I, Sp. 17.

fidei elementis tinctum, non sine ratione Viri Clarissimi Cavius &
Dodwellus opinantur".[55]

Völlig unbekannt ist die Ausgabe von Grabe noch 1706 dem Autor,
der in der Zeitschrift *Unschuldige Nachrichten, oder Sammlung von
alten und neuen Sachen*, Leipzig 1706, S. 769-772,[56] eine Mitteilung
über die Testamente macht. Er skizziert zunächst den Inhalt der
Schrift, wobei dreimal das Wort „sonderlich", zweimal „wunderlich",
zweimal „wunderbar" und ausserdem noch Vokabeln wie „erdichtet",
„falsch" und „absurd" vorkommen. Der Autor meint, dass das Buch
nur auf Lateinisch gedruckt ist, und seine Kritik gilt darum offensichtlich Grosseteste: „Der Stylus ist der Vulgatae ähnlich und mit
wunderlichen Wörtern angefüllt, als *impropitiabiliter*, &c. Die inflexion
spermam zeigt auch schlechte Griechische Gelehrsamkeit an". Darauf
endet das Ganze lapidar: „Das Original mag etwa im 6ten oder
7den Sec. nach Christi Geburt auffgesetzt seyn".

Vor dem Erscheinen der Textausgabe von Grabe hatte nicht nur
Thomas Smith den Plan gehabt, die Testamente auf Griechisch heraus-
zugeben, sondern auch der ungenannte Pariser Autor von zwei
„Discours" die erst in der *Bibliothèque critique, ou Recueil de diverses
pièces critiques, publiées par Mr. de Sainjore*, II (Paris-Amsterdam 1708,
S. 224ff.) publiziert wurden, die aber datiert sind „À Paris 1687".
Das Datum ist offenbar richtig, da der über die Testamente aus-
gezeichnet informierte Verfasser die 1698 erschienene Ausgabe von
Grabe und die Ausführungen von Le Nourry aus dem Jahre 1694
erst in den Fussnoten mitteilt. Der Anonymus schreibt, dass er von
der in der *Bibliotheca Regia* befindlichen griechischen Handschrift der
Testamente, die er in das zehnte Jahrhundert datiert, eine Abschrift
gemacht hat „dans le dessein de le donner au Public".

Aus dem Inhalt der *Bibliothèque critique* ergibt sich, dass der
Herausgeber M. de Sainjore niemand anders als Richard Simon ist.
Das in Wirklichkeit in Nancy gedruckte Werk wurde deswegen auch
auf Betreiben der Gesinnungsgenossen von Bossuet 1710 durch eine
Entschliessung des Conseil d'État mit Konfiskation und Vernichtung
gemassregelt.[57]

Simon beginnt mit einer eingehenden Darlegung der Einwendungen

---

[55] *Meletemata Leidensia*, Leiden 1703, S. 500-501.

[56] Ein Exemplar dieser Lieferung befindet sich in der U. B. Groningen.

[57] Jean Steinmann, *Richard Simon et les origines de l'exégèse biblique*, Paris 1960,
S. 364-365. Paul Auvray, *Richard Simon (1638-1712)*, Paris 1974, S. 145-150, 188.

derer, die die Testamente für Fabeln und betrügerische Fälschungen erklären und eine Ausgabe für überflüssig ansehen. Seine Replik lautet: „Il suffit que ces fables n'ayent point déplû aux anciens Écrivains Ecclesiastiques, pour qu'elles ayent leur utilité. Elles nous peuvent servir à entendre les ouvrages de ces anciens Écrivains".

Dass die Juden die Testamente verborgen gehalten haben sollen, wie das lateinische Kolophon und Matthew Paris meinen, und dass Grosseteste eine Expedition in Gang gesetzt habe, um eine Handschrift der Testamente aus Athen zu holen, ist reine Phantasie und „un conte de Moine", urteilt Simon kritisch, aber reichlich kategorisch.

Bemerkenswert ist die Auffassung Simons über die Entstehung der Testamente. Stilistisch sind, so sagt er, die Testamente so einheitlich, dass sie von einem Verfasser stammen müssen, und zwar von einem zum Christentum bekehrten Juden oder dem Mitglied irgendeiner Sekte. Über die Sekte, in der die Testamente entstanden sein sollen, sind vom 18. bis zum 20. Jahrhundert noch viele Hypothesen erstellt worden. Bei Simon aber ist der Gedanke an eine Sekte zum ersten Mal ausgesprochen. Er selber dachte jedoch angesichts der Entlehnungen aus dem Neuen Testament an eine Entstehung in einem christlichen Milieu, in dem sich jüdisch-hellenistischer Einfluss geltend macht. Diese Herkunft schlägt sich in der Lehre von den Geistern in den Testamenten nieder.

Mit der stilistischen und literarischen Einheit verbindet sich für Simon die Möglichkeit eines aramäischen Originals. Das Argument für diese Annahme ist für heutige Vorstellungen sehr schwach. Simon meint nämlich, dass in T. Napht. VI,1 ἐν τῇ θαλάσσῃ ἰάμμας gelesen werden muss, was seines Erachtens „sans doute" in Grossetestes Vorlage gestanden hat, als er „in mari jammae" übersetzte. Nun ist jamma die aramäische Vokabel für „Meer", das Wort bildet also eine Doublette neben θαλάσσῃ und ist offensichtlich aus dem Aramäischen in den griechischen Text gekommen und mit einer griechischen Erklärung versehen. Die Annahme von Simon ist unrichtig, da Grosseteste zwar „in mari jammae (oder: jamme)" übersetzt, seine griechische Vorlage aber über „das Meer von Iamnia" (ἐν τῇ θαλάσσῃ Ἰαμνίας) gesprochen hat. Jamnia ist ein Ortsname, der in den alttestamentlichen Apokryphen öfter vorkommt. Man muss allerdings einräumen, dass Simon Scharfsinn genug besitzt, um unmittelbar darauf zu bemerken, dass ein griechisch schreibender Verfasser natürlich auch ein aramäisches Wort aufgenommen haben kann, um seinem Erzeugnis ein echteres Aussehen zu verleihen. Somit ist Simon der

erste gewesen, der an die Möglichkeit gedacht hat, dass den Testamenten eine ursprünglich aramäische Schrift zugrunde liegt oder,
wie man damals noch sagte, eine chaldäische.[58] Es ist eine Ironie
des Zufalls, dass in Qumran heute zahlreiche mit dem griechischen
Text des T. Levi verwandte aramäische Fragmente zu Tage gefördert
sind, aber vom T. Napht., das Simon zu seiner anziehenden Annahme
anregte, bisher — soweit wir wissen — nur hebräische.

Auch darüberhinaus bringt Simon noch klärende Einsichten über
die Testamente, so dass er mit einigem Recht mit den folgenden
Worten enden kann : ,,Vous pouvez maintenant porter votre jugement
sur cette ancienne prière apocryphe qui a pour titre, *Le Testament
des douze Patriarches*. Si vous souhaitez lire l'Original, je vous
communiquerai la copie que j'ai écrite sur le beau Manuscrit de
la Bibliothèque du Roi".[59]

Zum Schluss sei noch beiläufig ein Abschnitt über die Testamente
in den *Historiae ecclesiasticae secundi seculi selecta capita*, Lipsiae 1711,
S. 42-45, von Thomas Ittig erwähnt.[60] Ittig weist die Testamente
dem zweiten Jahrhundert zu, zitiert in extenso das lateinische Kolophon
und Matthew Paris, erwähnt aber auch die Textausgabe und die
Interpolationstheorie von Grabe, sowie dessen unglückliche Konjektur
im *Decretum Gelasianum* (S. Anm. 53). Das ist alles nicht so wichtig
wie die Tatsache, dass Ittig der erste ist, der am Ende seines Kapitels
eine kurze bibliographische Übersicht über die Literatur, die die
Testamente behandelt, gibt. Hierbei zählt er auf : Wharton, Le Nourry,

---

[58] Doch hatte schon Jos. Scaliger das ,,Chaldäisch" richtig als Aramäisch bezeichnet.

[59] In der Bibliothèque Nationale liegt auch jetzt noch eine späte Abschrift des
von Simon in das 10. Jhdt. datierten Manuskript der Testamente. Das alte Manuskript
trägt jetzt die Signatur gr. 2658, die Abschrift gr. 938. Wenn die Datierung, die
für 938 gegeben wird, richtig ist, nämlich im 16. Jhdt. (H. Omont, *Inventaire sommaire
des mss grecs de la Bibl. Nationale* I, Paris 1886, S. 181), dann kann es sich dabei
nicht um die Abschrift Simons handeln. — Im selben Teil seiner *Bibliothèque critique*
behandelt Simon auch die *tabulae coeli* aus dem Test. Aser. In Teil III, Kap. III,
S. 53 befasst er sich ausserdem mit den Testamenten als Testimonium für Henoch.
Vgl. *Histoire critique du V.T.*, Nouvelle édition, Rotterdam 1685, p. 485 : ,,les mêmes
Juifs ont une infinité d'autres Traditions semblables [*sc.* semblables à celles concernant
Énoch] qu'ils attribuent à leur premiers Patriarches, sous le nom desquels leurs
Docteurs allegoriques et cabbalistiques ont ensuite publiés des livres qu'ils ont rempli
de rêveries. Ce qui n'empêche pourtant pas, qu'il n'y ait plusieurs vérités dans ces
mêmes Livres, qui ne peuvent être autorisées que par la Tradition; & il n'y a que
l'Esprit de Dieu qui puisse maintenant discerner le vrai d'avec le faux dans ces
sortes d'ouvrages".

[60] Fotokopien dieses seltenen Buches nach dem Exemplar der Stadtbibliothek
Antwerpen (K. 6391) verdanke ich Professor A. M. T. Welkenhuysen, Löwen.

Sainjore, Bebelius und die *Unschuldige Nachrichten*. Ein ebenfalls beschränkte Liste bietet J. A. Fabricius 1713, ganz am Ende seiner Ausgabe von Grabes Text in seinem *Codex Pseudepigraphus Veteris Testamenti*. Fabricius nennt: Sixtus Senensis, Bangius, Benthem, Sgambati und Miraeus. Auffallend ist nicht nur, dass die bibliographische Dokumentation über die Testamente am Anfang des 18. Jhdts. unvollständig war, — das ist auch die Ursache dafür, dass später das, was bis zu Grabes Zeit an den Testamenten gearbeitet worden ist, unbekannt geblieben ist, — auffallend ist auch, dass Ittig und Fabricius nicht einmal die wichtigsten Erforscher der Testamente aufgeführt haben: Drusius, Salianus, Selden, Heidegger und De Mey werden bei ihnen nicht genannt.

Ergebnisse

Die gegenwärtige Kenntnis von der vor Grabe an den Testamenten geübten literarhistorischen Kritik ist nicht nur sehr mangelhaft, sondern auch falsch.[61] Die bekannteste Auskunft darüber steht im ersten Paragraph der Einleitung zu R. H. Charles, *The Greek Versions of the Testaments of the Twelve Patriarchs*, Oxford 1908, unlängst dreimal in Neudruck erschienen (s. Anm. 49). Man liest darin u.a., dass Grosseteste die Testamente übersetzt hat „under the misconception that it was a genuine work of the twelve sons of Jacob".[62] Dies ist, wie aus der Weise, wie Grosseteste in einem Brief an König Henry III. eine Passage aus T. Juda XXI anführt und benutzt („Judas namque… ita ait:"; vgl. Anm. 2), hervorgeht, richtig. Man darf also Grosseteste tatsächlich zuschreiben, dass er die Testamente für ein echtes und authentisches Werk der Söhne Jakobs gehalten hat. Aber schon Grosse-testes Schüler Roger Bacon unterscheidet scharf zwischen Authentizität und inhaltlicher Richtigkeit. Für Bacon waren die Testamente „ignoti auctoris", „non habent certos auctores", „de auctoribus non est certum".

---

[61] Nicht mehr einsehen konnte ich: H. D. Slingerland, *The Testaments of the Twelve Patriarchs: A History of Research with Attendant Conclusions* (Diss. Union Theol. Sem., N.Y.) 1973. „Ch. I describes the beginnings of scholarly interest in the Testaments in the period from 1242 to 1781". Siehe *Diss. Abstr. Intern. A. Humanities*. 1973, S. 1355 A.

[62] Dieselbe Angaben macht Charles in *The Testaments… translated…*, London 1908, S. xviii und *The Apocrypha and Pseudepigrapha of the O.T. in English*, Oxford 1913, II, S. 283. Auch da führt er aus, dass Grosseteste die Testamente für „a genuine writing" der Söhne Jakobs hielt, und dass im Gefolge der Reformation die Bücher als christliche Fälschung abgelehnt wurden, sowie dass „in the course of four centuries only one voice was raised against this mistaken verdict".

Charles fährt fort: „The advent of the Reformation brought in
critical methods". Im Falle der Testamente aber ist es jedenfalls
nicht richtig, deren kritische Untersuchung den in der Reformations-
zeit aufblühenden kritischen Methoden zuzuschreiben. Einmal haben
die Testamente erst spät Gewinn aus den aufkommenden wissenschaftlichen Methoden gezogen. Schwach ist ihre Anwendung noch bei
Drusius, deutlichere Spuren finden sich erst zwanzig Jahre später
bei Salianus. Das ist bereits die Zeit der Synode von Dordrecht
(1619), und erst im letzten Viertel des siebzehnten Jahrhunderts
macht die Kritik an den Testamenten wieder Fortschritte. Erst um
die Jahrhundertwende erscheint die erste griechische Ausgabe. Ausserdem sind es nicht nur, selbst nicht in erster Linie, Protestanten
gewesen, die die Erforschung der Testamente gefördert haben. Zu
ihren Erforschern gehören auch der Jesuit Salianus, der einflussreiche
Dominikaner Sixtus Senensis, und das Beste ist erreicht durch den
katholisch beeinflussten zum Anglikanismus übergetretenen Grabe
und den Oratorianer Simon.

Die Impulse, die die Erforschung der Testamente angeregt haben,
waren dann auch nicht die spezifisch reformatorischen, sondern andere.
Das zeigt sich, wenn man die Reihe verdienter Kritiker kurz betrachtet.
Drusius wurde wegen seiner Lehre misstraut und darum der Auftrag,
die niederländische Bibelübersetzung des Marnix van St. Aldegonde
fortzusetzen, vorenthalten. Man sah ihn wohl als Krypto-Katholik an;
was ihn aber wirklich bewog, brachte er in der Vorrede zu seinem
Henoch (1615) zum Ausdruck: „Concedatur modo mihi aliqua *libertas
in exponendo textu...*". Heidegger wurde immer wieder des Cocceja-
nismus und Cartesianismus beschuldigt. Johannes de Mey hat sich
sein Leben lang gegen Anklagen wegen Heterodoxie verteidigen müssen.
Grabe wurde wegen seiner zweifelhaften Rechtgläubigkeit aus Königsberg verbannt. Die Bücher von Simon wurden verboten und vernichtet. So zeigt sich deutlich, dass die Entwicklung der Erforschung
der Testamente einer Anzahl freierer und offner Geister sowohl in
protestantischer wie katholischer Umgebung zu verdanken ist, die
bereit waren, auch ausserhalb des Kanons literarhistorische Erschei-
nungen positiv zu werten oder gar ethische Bedeutung zuzuerkennen.
Es war sowohl das freiere Interesse an der christlichen Tradition
im ganzen, als auch die historische Neugier der Aufklärung, die die
Erforschung der Testamente begünstigt hat.

Charles meint, dass die Testamente von der Reformation bis zu
seiner eigenen Zeit „for nearly four centuries" als christliche Fälschung

gebrandmarkt wurden. Eine Ausnahme macht er für Grabe (S. xxiii), konstatiert aber mit sichtlicher Enttäuschung: „Even Grabe, though he declared for a Hebrew original, advanced no linguistic arguments in support of his contention". In Wirklichkeit sind unseres Wissens die Testamente erst 1671 als christliches Pseudoepigraphon bezeichnet worden, nämlich durch Heidegger. Auch linguistische Argumente für ein hebräisches oder aramäisches Original waren durchaus schon früher angeführt worden, und zwar durch Sgambati und Simon. Aber nicht zu Unrecht hat hiergegen der lutherische Orientalist J. Wolfius, Schüler von Fabricius, in seiner *Bibliotheca hebraea* von 1715 eingewendet, dass, wenn Hebraismen auf ein hebräisches Original hinweisen sollten, das Neue Testament auf Hebräisch geschrieben sein müsste (Bd. I, S. 250).

Wie das wissenschaftliche Interesse für die Testamente der zwölf Patriarchen sich bis zum Beginn des 18. Jahrhunderts entwickelt hat, lässt sich abschliessend folgendermassen zusammenfassen.

Grosseteste (1242) verdanken wir es, dass in den viereinhalb Jahrhunderten, die noch vor dem Druck des griechischen Texts der Testamente verstreichen mussten, die Schrift in einer wörtlichen Übersetzung nach einer alten griechischen Handschrift weithin bekannt war. Die Authentizität der Testamente wurde bereits von Roger Bacon angezweifelt (1266). Sixtus Senensis (1566) bespricht das Problem nicht. Beide aber hielten die Testamente, ungeachtet ihrer Verfasserschaft, für eine zuverlässige Widergabe der letzten Worte von Jakobs Söhnen. Als erster gebraucht Sixtus Senensis die Testamente als Testimonium für Henoch und nennt die Zeugnisse für die Testamente bei Origenes und Prokop: in Hinsicht auf beide Angaben ist mancher spätere Gelehrte von ihm abhängig. Drusius (1595) nimmt an, dass die Testamente nur teilweise Unrichtigkeiten enthalten, und Salianus (1619) versucht festzustellen, was in dieser Schrift bei aller Unzuverlässigkeit noch haltbar ist: jedenfalls nicht viel von der Chronologie. Im Laufe des 17. Jahrhunderts spricht ein Gelehrter nach dem anderen seine Geringschätzung für die Testamente aus. Man bleibt von ihrem jüdischen und hebräischen Ursprung überzeugt. Johannes de Mey (1675) ist der erste, der sich herabsetzender Kritik enthält; ebenso wie Heidegger (1671) hält er die Testamente für das Werk eines Christen, und zwar, wie De Mey präzisiert, auf Griechisch. Caves Gedanke, dass der Verfasser ein zum Christentum übergetretener Jude war, hielt sich bis weit in das 18. Jahrhundert. Eine Ausnahme blieb die Hypothese von Grabe (1698), dass die Testamente von einem

Juden auf Hebräisch geschrieben waren, ins Griechische bereits im
dritten Jahrhundert v. Chr. übersetzt und im ersten oder zweiten
Jahrhundert n. Chr. durch einen Christen interpoliert wurden. Unabhängig von Grabe kam Richard Simon (1687; veröffentlicht 1708)
zu der Überzeugung, dass die Testamente in ihrer vorliegenden
griechischen Form sich durch ihre stilistische Einheit als das Werk
eines einzigen Verfassers erweisen; dieser gehörte zu einem juden-
christlichen oder sektiererischen Kreis. Der homogene Stil schliesst
trotzdem die Möglichkeit nicht aus, dass den Testamenten ein aramäisches Original zugrunde liegt.

Die ein wenig widersprüchliche Theorie von Simon, die mit einer
starken kompositorischen Selbständigkeit der griechischen christlichen
Textform rechnet und zugleich mit dem Bestehen eines aramäischen
Modells ist jetzt ganz und gar vergessen. Jedoch ist diese nicht
schlechter als die von Grabe, die immer noch genannt wird. Im
Gegenteil : das in Frage stehende Problem ist noch lange nicht gelöst,
aber man kan wohl sagen, dass die Lösung nicht weiter von Simons
Hypothese als von der von Grabe entfernt sein wird.

Namenregister
der wichtigeren Gelehrten,
die im vorstehenden Aufsatz behandelt werden

PART TWO

II

DIE TEXTÜBERLIEFERUNG
DER TESTAMENTE DER ZWÖLF PATRIARCHEN

HENK JAN DE JONGE *

I.

In der neueren Literatur über die Testamente der zwölf Patriarchen gehört es zur schönen Gewohnheit, jeder größeren Arbeit eine
Zusammenfassung der Geschichte des textkritischen Problems seit
Charles (1908) vorauszuschicken[1]. Diese Übersichten über Entwicklung
und Stand der Textkritik sind nicht nur zahlreich, sondern auch so
gelehrt, daß es unnötig und unmöglich scheint, daran im Jahre 1970
noch etwas zur Verbesserung hinzuzufügen. Lieber wenden wir uns
sofort zum eigentlichen Problem: welches sind die Beziehungen
zwischen den Zeugen, in denen der Text der Testamente uns vorliegt?

Der Zweck dieses Beitrages ist also, die Abhängigkeitsverhältnisse
zwischen den Handschriften[2], Exzerpten[3] und Übersetzungen[4] fest-

---

* Der Verfasser war ab September 1967 bis April 1970 als Assistent von Prof. M.
de Jonge (Leiden) im Dienst der *Niederländischen Organisation für Reinwissen-
schaftliche Forschung* (*Z. W. O.*), wo er mit den Vorarbeiten für eine textkritische
Neuausgabe der *Testamente der zwölf Patriarchen* beschäftigt war. Dank den Bemerkungen von Prof. M. de Jonge und Th. Korteweg (Leiden) konnte der Text
des vorliegenden Aufsatzes an mehreren Stellen berichtigt oder deutlicher gemacht
werden. Herrn Prof. de Jonge sei für sein allezeit freundliches und hilfreiches
Interesse Dank gesagt. — Lesarten, die vor eckigen Klammern ohne Angabe der sie
stützenden Zeugen angeführt werden, sind dem Text der Handschrift *b* (*ed.* M.
de Jonge, s. A. 1) entnommen.

[1] M. de Jonge, *The Testaments of the Twelve Patriarchs. A Study of their Text, Compo-
sition and Origin* (Diss. Leiden 1953), Assen ⟨1953⟩, pp. 13—16; id., *Testamenta XII
Patriarcharum, edited according to Cambridge Univ. Libr.* MS Ff 1. 24, fol. 203a—262b
(*Pseudepigrapha Vet. Test. Graece* I), Leiden 1964, pp. VII—XV; 1970², pp. VI
—XVII; Chr. Burchard, *Zur armenischen Überlieferung der Testamente der Zwölf
Patriarchen*, in: Chr. Burchard — J. Jervell — J. Thomas, *Studien zu den Testamenten
der zwölf Patriarchen*, BZNW 36, Berlin 1969, pp. 1—6; J. Becker, *Untersuchungen
zur Entstehungsgeschichte der Testamente der zwölf Patriarchen*, (*Arbeiten zur Ge-
schichte des antiken Judentums und des Urchristentums* VIII), Leiden 1970, pp. 7—16.

[2] *a.* Oxford, Bodleian Library, Baroccianus Gr. 133, ff. 182r.—205v., s. XIII;

b. Cambridge, University Library, Ff 1. 24, ff. 203r.—261v., s. X;

c. Città del Vaticano, Biblioteca Apostolica Vaticana, Vat. Gr. 731, ff. 97r.—166v.,
s. XIII;

d. Ibid., Vat. Gr. 1238, ff. 350r.—379v., s. XII;

e. Athos, Koutloumousiou 39, ff. 198r.—231r., s. XI;

zustellen. Alle griechischen Handschriften außer *h* sind aufs neue kollationiert[5]. Die Ergebnisse, die hier mitgeteilt werden, beruhen hauptsächlich auf Gesamtkollationen aller Varianten in allen Handschriften von vier Testamenten *(Rub., Levi, Zab., Beni.)*, also auf einem Drittel des Gesamtmaterials.

Nicht alle Beziehungen, die im folgenden nachgewiesen werden, waren bisher unbekannt. Speranskij[6] sah schon die Verwandtschaft zwischen der serbischen Übersetzung (Serb.) und *c*. Charles hat die Verhältnisse zwischen *c, h* und *i* dargestellt. Hunkin zeigte die Beziehungen zwischen *e, a* und *f*, und bewies die Abhängigkeit der Familie α von »β«. Burchard hat *l* mit *d*, und die neugriechische Übersetzung (Ngr.) mit *hi* verbunden. M. de Jonge hat gesehen, daß *m* zu *dl*

---

f. Paris, Bibliothèque Nationale, Fonds grec 2658, ff. lv.—71v., s. XI;

g. Patmos, Johanneskloster, 411, φφ. ροη΄r.—σκ΄v., s. XVI;

h. Sinai, Katharinenkloster, Gr. 547, ff.??, s. XVII;

i. Ibid., Signatur unbekannt, ff. lr.—?, bekannt bis f. 38r., s. XVII;

k. S. A. 3;

l. Athos, Laura 1132—I 48, ff. 204r.—276r., s. XVII;

m. Ankara, Türk Tarih Kurumu, Gr. 60, pp. 339—483, s. XVI.

Die Handschrift Athos, Laura 1403—K 116 konnte noch immer nicht bearbeitet werden [Siehe jetzt Kap. VII].

[3] *k*. Venezia, Biblioteca Marciana, Gr. 494, ff. 263r.—264v., s. XIII;

Fm*d*. *Fragmenta marginalia in d*, ff. 352r., 362v., 371v., 373r., s. XV; diese Fragmente hoffe ich baldigst veröffentlichen zu können, cf. H. J. de Jonge, *Les fragments marginaux dans le ms. d des Testaments des XII Patriarches, Journal for the Study of Judaism*, 2 (1971) [jetzt Kap. IV dieses Bandes].

n. M. Athos, Vatopediou 659, ff. 42r.—v.; 47r.—48r., s. XIV.

[4] Slaw.: die slawische Übersetzung von etwa 1200; *cf*. E. Turdeanu, *Les Testaments des douze Patriarches en slave, Journal for the Study of Judaism* 1 (1970), p. 165.

Serb.: die serbische Übersetzung, bekannt aus einer Handschrift des 16. Jhdt. S. E. Turdeanu, *art. cit.*, und M. Speranskij's Textausgabe in *Sbornik za narodni umotvorenija, nauka i kniźnina* 18, Sofia 1901, p. 242—251.

Ngr.: die neugriechische Übersetzung, bekannt aus einer Handschrift des 18. Jhdt. (Bukarest, Biblioteca Academiei Republicii Populare Romîne, Gr. 580 (341), cf. Chr. Burchard, *Neues zur Überlieferung der Testamente der zwölf Patriarchen, . . . eine unbekannte neugriechische Fassung*, NTS 12 (1965—1966), pp. 245—258).

Außer Betracht bleibt die lateinische Übersetzung, weil sie von *b* abhängig ist, und die armenische Übersetzung, weil die Untersuchung dieser Version noch nicht abgeschlossen ist. (Der Armenier läßt sich wahrscheinlich auf eine griechische Vorlage zurückführen, die im Stemma zwischen den Punkten 6 und 13 liegt.)

[5] Von der slawischen und serbischen Version hat E. Turdeanu (Paris) neue Kollationen gemacht. Ngr. war mir zugänglich in einem von der Bukarester Bibliothek freundlichst zur Verfügung gestellten Film.

[6] S. A. 4.

gehört. Turdeanu stellte die Zusammengehörigkeit der slawischen Version (Slaw.) und *af* fest. Diese Beziehungen wurden nachgeprüft und zum Teil präzisiert.

Andere Kombinationen hingegen bewahrheiteten sich nicht. In der Textgeschichte der Testamente haben β *(= aefbdg)*, γ *(= aef)* und δ *(= bdg)* nie als Familien existiert. Die übrigen Beziehungen, z. B. die zwischen *af* und α, und die verschiedenen Fälle von Kontamination, konnten erst jetzt neu gefunden werden. Endlich ließ sich die ganze Geschichte der Textüberlieferung in einem Stemma ausdrücken. Damit scheint mir der Weg zur Herstellung des Textes geebnet, obwohl die *constitutio*, u. a. wegen der anzunehmenden Kontamination, stellenweise unsicher bleiben wird[7].

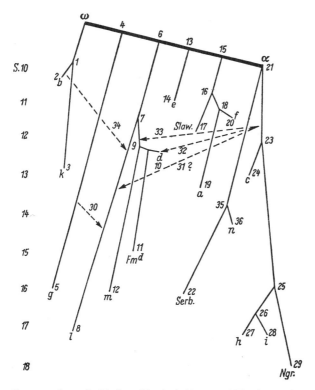

Stemma der griechischen Handschriften und Versionen der
Testamente der zwölf Patriarchen

---

[7] Dies ist namentlich der Fall, wenn die Lesung von *b(k)*, *b(k)g* oder *b(k)gl* der der übrigen Zeugen gegenübersteht.

II.

Die Überlieferungsgeschichte der Testamente läßt sich an Hand der folgenden Leitfehler und Überlegungen bis in Einzelheiten verfolgen. — Die im Stemma eingetragenen Zahlen sind die Nummern der Paragraphen, in denen der jeweilige Beweis für den Zusammenhang geführt wird.

1. Trennfehler von *bk* gegen *g ld(m) e af chi*, der die Möglichkeit, daß *g ld(m) e af chi* von *bk* abhängig sind, ausschließt: *T. Levi* XVIII, 9 *bk om.* τὰ ἔθνη πληθυνθήσεται — τῆς ἱερωσύνης αὐτοῦ *(m defic.)*. Dieser Fehler beweist keine Verbindung zwischen *b* und *k*, da es sich um ein Homoioteleuton handelt. Die Verwandtschaft zwischen *b* und *k* ist jedoch so eng, daß man *k* für abhängig von *b* gehalten hat[8]. Bekannt ist der Bindefehler dieser Handschriften in *T. Levi* IV, 4, wo beide υἱοί statt υἱοῦ (*g dm* τοῦ υἱοῦ) lesen.

2. Die Unabhängigkeit der Handschrift *b* gegenüber *k* geht nicht nur aus der Datierung, sondern auch aus der Eigenart beider Handschriften hervor: *k* bietet nur Exzerpte, *b* hingegen den vollständigen Text der Testamente.

3. Höchstwahrscheinlich kommt auch *k* neben *b* ein selbständiger Platz im Stemma zu. Mehrmals macht *b* Fehler, wo *k* mit den anderen Handschriften die richtige Lesart bewahrt hat. Nicht immer dürfen solche Fälle als Trennfehler zwischen *k* und *b* gelten. Die folgenden Fehler von *b* begegnen nicht in *k*. Ein Schreiber könnte sie jedoch bewußt gegenüber seiner Vorlage abgeändert haben: *T. Rub.* V, 7 κἀκεῖνοι (statt κἀκεῖναι *k g ldm e af chi*); *ibid.* ἐγρήγορες (statt ἐγρήγοροι *k g dm e af chi*; *l* ἐν ἐγρηγόρσει); *T. Sim.* VII, 2 οὕτως (statt οὗτος *k g ldm e af c*); *T. Levi* II, 9 διατί οὗτος (statt διατί οὕτως *k g l m e af*, *d defic.*, *chi* τί ἐστι ταῦτα οὕτως). Etwas schwieriger zu korrigieren sind *T. Zab.* X, 5 θεὸν ὑμῶν *(lectio facilior, b d h)*, wofür *k* θεὸν ἡμῶν liest (mit *g l m e f ci*), und *T. Beni.* IX, 5 ἔγνω, anstatt wovon *k* ἔγνων hat (mit *g ld e af*; *m ch* Ngr. *defic.*, *i*?). Daß aber *k* von *b* unabhängig ist, geht hervor aus Stellen wie *T. Rub.* III, 6 δωροληψίας *k dm e* Slaw.[9]; *T. Zab.* X, 1, wo nur *b* gegen *k ld e af chi* *(g m defic.)* ὑμῶν zufügt (nach ἀπολείπω), und vielleicht auch aus *T. Beni.* XI, 2, wo *b* mit *a* τῷ ἰσραήλ und ἀπ᾽ αὐτοῦ, aber *k* mit *g ld e f* τὸν ἰσραήλ und ἀπ᾽ αὐτῶν (*m chi*Ngr. *defic.*) liest.

4. Trennfehler von *g ldm e af chi* gegen *bk*, der die Möglichkeit, daß *bk* von *g ldm e af chi* abhängig sind, ausschließt: *T. Levi* VIII, 1

---

[8] M. de Jonge, *The Testaments* . . ., p. 20: »It is very likely, that *k* is directly or indirectly descended from *b*«. Cf. 3.

[9] Genauer: *k e* δωροληψίας, *dm* δωροληψείας ἢ προσωποληψίας, auch Slaw. setzt δωρο- voraus; *l af chi* δοσοληψίας. Nur *b* liest δολολειψίας, (*g defic.*).

g ldm e af chi ὅραμα statt πρᾶγμα *(bk)*. Mit Recht hat M. de Jonge[10] die Lesart ὅραμα als sekundäre Verbesserung betrachtet. Es lag nahe, daß nach der breiten Schilderung des ersten Gesichts von Levi (II, 3—V, 7) in die Eingangsformel des zweiten Gesichts (κἀκεῖ πάλιν εἶδον πρᾶγμα ὥσπερ τὸ πρότερον) πρᾶγμα in ὅραμα abgeändert wurde. Zu dieser leichten Abänderung trugen sowohl der Kontext, als auch die orthographische Ähnlichkeit von οΡΑΜΑ und πΡΑγΜΑ bei, ebenso die Spirantisierung und Auslassung von γ vor Nasalen in der Koinè[11]. Die Ursprünglichkeit von πρᾶγμα gewinnt an Wahrscheinlichkeit durch die Parallele ἔργον in *gr. Hen.* XXI, 2[12]. Die Stelle weist in ihrem apokalyptischen Zusammenhang und im Wortlaut große Ähnlichkeit[13] mit *T. Levi* VIII, 1 auf. Man vergleiche:

T. Levi VIII, 1—2	*gr. Hen.* XXI, 2
κἀκεῖ πάλιν εἶδον	κἀκεῖ ἐθεασάμην
πρᾶγμα *(bk)*	ἔργον
ὥσπερ τὸ πρότερον.	φοβερόν.
καὶ εἶδον . . .	ἑώρακα . . .

---

[10] *The Testaments*, p. 19.

[11] *Cf.* γίνεσθαι, γινώσκειν usw. — Die beiden letzten Argumente (orthographische Ähnlichkeit und Spirantisierung des Gamma) gelten natürlich auch *vice versa*.

[12] *Ed.* M. Black, *Apocalypsis Henochi Graece, et* Albert-Marie Denis, *Fragmenu͐ ᵖseudepigraphorum quae supersunt Graeca* (*Pseudepigrapha Veteris Test. Gr.* III), Leiden 1970, pp. 1—44.

[13] *gr. Hen.* XVII—XXXII erzählt die Reise Henochs durch Gegenden, wo ihm die Geheimnisse der Naturerscheinungen und der Himmelswelt enthüllt werden; er schaut den Verbannungsort der gefallenen Engel und die Wohnstätten der frommen und gottlosen Seelen. *T. Levi* II—VIII (mit einer Unterbrechung von VI—VII) berichtet die Reise Levis durch die Himmel und die Enthüllung ihrer Geheimnisse. Von den vielen formalen Elementen, die die beiden Berichte gemein haben, sei, außer dem im Text Erwähnten, noch folgendes angeführt:

T. Levi II, 9	*gr. Hen.* XXI, 4—5
καὶ εἶπον τῷ ἀγγέλῳ·	τότε εἶπον·
	διὰ ποίαν αἰτίαν . . .
διατί οὕτως;	καὶ διατί ὧδε . . .;
καὶ εἶπεν ὁ ἄγγελος	τότε εἶπεν μοι οὐρίηλ
πρός με·	XXV, 1 τί ἐρωτᾷς καὶ
μὴ θαύμαζε . . .	τί ἐθαύμασας . . . (*cf. Apk* 17 7)

Für den Ausdruck ἀνθρώπους ἀφανίσαντας τὴν ὁδὸν αὐτῶν (*T. Levi* II, 3) konnte Charles (*The Testaments of the Twelve Patriarchs translated from the Editor's Greek Text and edited, with Introduction, Notes and Indices*, London 1908, p. 26, n. 3) nur verweisen auf *Gen* 6 12 (*LXX*: κατέφθειρεν πᾶσα σὰρξ τὴν ὁδὸν αὐτοῦ ἐπὶ τῆς γῆς). Vergleiche aber *gr. Hen.* VIII, 2: ἠφανίσθησαν ἐν πάσαις ταῖς ὁδοῖς αὐτῶν oder, laut Syncellus' Exzerpten (Codex Paris., Bibl. Nat., Fonds grec 1711, p. 8): ἠφάνισαν τὰς ὁδοὺς αὐτῶν.

Trennfehler der Gruppe *g ld(m) e af chi* gegen *bk* begegnen auch in
T. Levi IX, 14, wo das ἀπαρχάς von *bk* in allen anderen Handschriften
durch Hinzufügung von τῷ κυρίῳ verdeutlicht wird[14]; und in *T. Zab.*
IV, 9, wo ziemlich ungeschickt καὶ ἐποίησαν οὕτως zugefügt ist (so alle
Handschriften außer *bk*; *cf.* IV, 13).

5. Trennfehler von *g* gegen *ldm e af chi*, der die Möglichkeit, daß
ldm e af chi abhängig von *g* sind, ausschließt: *T. Rub.* II, 2 ἑπτά —
III, 9 τοῦ πατρὸς ὑμῶν läßt *g* völlig aus. Dafür schreibt *g* lakonisch:
ἀρκεῖ μοι εἰς διδασκαλίαν ὑμῶν . . .

6. Trennfehler von *ldm e af chi* gegen *g*, die die Möglichkeit, daß *g*
von *ldm e af chi* abhängig ist, ausschließen: *T.Zab* III, 6 *b g* τοῦ φαραώ]
ld(m) e af c (e f + τοῦ) βασιλέως φαραώ, *hi* βασιλέα φαραώ *(k m defic.)*[15];
und *T.Zab.* X, 4 *b* ἐγώ, *g* ἐγώ τε] *ldm e af* τέως . . . (Genauer: *l* τέως ἐγώ,
dm τέως οὖν ἐγώ, *ef* τέως οὖν, *a* τέως δέ; *chi*, ganz frei, ἐγὼ δὲ νῦν).
Das τέως von *ldm e af* ist von ἕως γενεῶν in X, 3 veranlaßt.

7. Trennfehler von *ldm* gegen *e af chi*, die die Möglichkeit, daß
e af chi von *ldm* abhängig sind, ausschließen: *T. Zab.* V, 4 *b (k defic.)*
g e af chi διὰ ἰωσήφ, aber die Gruppe *ldm* erweitert den Text folgendermaßen: διὰ τὴν ἐν τῷ ἰωσὴφ γενομένην (*d* γεναμένην) παρὰ (*m* περὶ)
τῶν πατέρων αὐτῶν (*m* αὐτοῦ) παρανομίαν (*l* + καὶ ἀσπλαγχνίαν).
In *T. Levi* II, 1 fügen *ldm* τεκνία μου zu (vor ἐγώ). Statt ἀφανίσαντας
schreiben sie *T. Levi* II, 3 ἀφανεῖς ὄντας. In *T. Rub.* I, 2 lassen *ldm*
das Wort ἀρρωστοῦντι aus; dafür bieten sie ἀρρωστήσαντος γὰρ αὐτοῦ
in I, 1 nach αὐτόν. Hinter *T. Rub.* IV, 9 προσήνεγκε (*d* ἐπήνεγκε)
fügen *ldm* πρὸς φίλτρον αὐτῆς (*l* + τοῦ) διεγεῖραι zu.

8. Trennfehler von *l* gegen *dm*, der die Möglichkeit, daß *dm* von *l*
abhängig sind, ausschließt: *l* läßt *T. Beni.* II, 4—5 völlig aus. In *dm*
sind diese Stellen ungefähr in der Form, in der *b* sie bewahrt hat, überliefert[16].

9. Trennfehler von *dm* gegen *l*, der die Möglichkeit, daß *l* abhängig
von *dm* ist, ausschließt: *T. Rub.* III, 6, wo für δολολειψείας *(b)*,
δοσοληψίας *(l af chi)* oder δωροληψίας *(k e)* nur *dm* δωροληψείας ἢ

---

[14] Vollständigkeitshalber: *T. Levi* IX, 14*b* ἀπαρχάς] *ge* + τῷ κυρίῳ
                 ld praemitt. κυρίῳ
                 af + θυσίαν (*a* + τῷ) κυρίῳ
                 chi + εἰς θυσίαν (*i* + τῷ)
                      κυρίῳ τῷ (*i* καὶ) θεῷ
                      (*hi* + ἡμῶν).
               m om. ἀπαρχὰς καὶ πᾶσαν

[15] *Cf. T. Jos.* II, 1; VIII, 4; XIII, 5. Hier fehlt βασιλεύς vor φαραώ.

[16] Die Übereinstimmung von *dm* gegen *l* kann an dieser Stelle weder durch sekundären
Einfluß von *g* auf *l* (s. 30), noch durch sekundären Einfluß von α auf *dm* (s. 33) ver-
anlaßt sein. In *g* sind die beiden Verse nämlich bewahrt, und *c* Ngr. bieten eine freie
Redaktion.

προσωποληψίας bieten[17]. In *T. Rub.* III, 15 erweitern *dm* καὶ εὐθέως (so *b* [*k defic.*] *g l e f chi*, *a* κ. εὐθύς) zu εὐθέως δὲ ἄμα τὸ πρᾶξαί με τὴν ἀνομίαν ταύτην. Weitere Beispiele von Trennfehlern der Handschriften *dm* sind:

T. Rub. II, 4 σύστασις] *dm* + τοῦ ἀνθρώπου

T. Rub. III, 12 βδέλυγμα] *dm* + ἐνώπιον κυρίου

T. Levi II, 4 ηὐξάμην] *dm* ταῦτα θεωρῶν (*m* + καὶ) ηὐξάμην

T. Zab. II, 5 ἐβόμβει] *dm* ἐθαμβήθη

T. Beni. III, 4 αὐτόν[2]] *dm* + καὶ ἐρρύσατο αὐτὸν (*m om.*) ἐκ τῶν χειρῶν αὐτῶν.

Im übrigen sei darauf hingewiesen, daß die Unabhängigkeit der Handschrift *l* von *dm* sich nicht endgültig beweisen läßt. Die Handschrift *l* weist nämlich Spuren von Kontamination mit Texten, die *g* und *b* nahestehen, auf[18]. Wäre *l* von *dm* abhängig, so könnten die in *l* auf *dm* zurückgehenden Varianten durch Kontamination nach der Textform von *g* und *b* korrigiert sein. Dann wäre die Abhängigkeit der Handschrift *l* von *dm* an den korrigierten Stellen nicht mehr erkennbar, und *d* und *m* würden ihre gemeinsamen Varianten als scheinbare Trennfehler gegen *l* weiterführen.

Trotzdem ist es unwahrscheinlich, daß *l* von *dm* abhängt, und daß seine aus *dm* stammenden Fehler durch sekundären Einfluß von einem mit *g* oder *b* verwandten Text korrigiert sind. Durch Kontamination werden zwar häufig einzelne Wörter oder kleinere Wortgruppen geändert, gestrichen oder hinzugefügt, aber Umstellungen werden selten durch Kontamination übertragen. Auch das Rückgängigmachen von Umstellungen ist ein komplizierter Eingriff, mit dem man bei gewöhnlicher Kontamination nicht rechnen sollte. Z. B. ist in *T. Zab.* I, 6 καὶ ἔκλαιον πολλὰ ἐν κρυφῇ in *dm* an das Ende des Verses gestellt, und zwar in der Form ἔκλαιον οὖν (*m* μὲν) ἐγὼ (*m om.*) περὶ ἰωσὴφ ἡμέρας πολλὰς ἐν κρυφῇ. Dagegen hat *l* die Wortfolge von *b g e af chi* beibehalten. In diesem Falle ist es wahrscheinlich, daß *l* den ursprünglichen Zustand unmittelbar überliefert hat. Kaum ist in einer der Vorlagen von *l* der Text, wie er in *dm* noch vorliegt, durch ein mühseliges Verfahren an die Textform von *g* oder *b* angeglichen.

Vor allem lassen sich aus korrekten Lesarten — seien sie korrekt überliefert oder korrigiert — keine Folgerungen für Abhängigkeitsverhältnisse zwischen Handschriften ziehen.

10. Die Handschrift *d* ist von *m* unabhängig, was sich aus der Datierung beider Handschriften ergibt: *d* ist vor 1195 geschrieben, *m* gehört der zweiten Hälfte des 16. Jahrhunderts zu. Außerdem bietet *m* unzählige Sonderlesarten, darunter ungefähr 50 umfang-

---

[17] *Cf.* A. 9.

[18] S. 30 und 34.

reichere Verkürzungen, wovon etwa zehn sich über mehr als ein Kapitel erstrecken. Als Beispiel erwähne ich nur die erste größere Lücke. In *T. Sim.* fehlt V, 4 καὶ ἐν λευί — IX, 1 τὸν νόμον τοῦ πενθοῦς. Dafür findet sich ein Teil davon, VI, 1—VIII, 2, am Ende des *T. Levi*. Dort aber fehlt wieder das Stück *T. Sim.* VI, 2—VI, 5 und *T. Levi* XV, 2 ἐν αὐτοῖς κτλ. bis zum Ende des Testaments.

11. Die *Fragmenta marginalia in d* (Fm^d) weisen eine Textform auf, die eng mit *d* verwandt ist: nur *d* und Fm^d lesen in *T. Rub.* VI, 12, προσκυνῆσαι statt προσκυνήσατε; ebenso lassen nur sie in *T. Gad* VII, 7 οὖν weg, und ihre Lesart τὸν ἰούδαν καὶ λευίν in *T. Gad* VIII, 1 findet sich in keinem anderen Zeugen. Dennoch sind die Fragmente nicht (wenigstens nicht allein) von *d* abhängig. Mindestens viermal bieten sie einen weniger korrupten Text als *d*. In *T. Rub.* VI, 12 z. B. bewahrt Fm^d die Worte ὑπὲρ ἡμῶν ἀποθανεῖται, die *d* verloren hat. Selbstverständlich kann *d* nicht von Fm^d abhängen.

12. Trennfehler von *d* gegen *m*, die die Möglichkeit, daß *m* von *d* abhängig ist, ausschließen, sind z. B. die folgenden Auslassungen:

T. Rub. VI, 12   ὑπὲρ ἡμῶν ἀποθανεῖται] *d om.*
T. Levi XII, 5   καὶ ὀκτωκαίδεκα — τὸν συχέμ] *d om.*
T. Zab. VII, 1   ἐπ᾽ αὐτόν] *d om., k e af chi defic.*
T. Beni. II, 4   λέων] *d om., k l hi defic.*

13. Trennfehler von *e af chi* gegen *ldm*, die die Möglichkeit, daß *ldm* von *e af chi* abhängig sind, ausschließen, sind außerordentlich zahlreich. Hierher gehören die gemeinsamen Verkürzungen von *e, af* und *chi* in *T. Zab.* VI, 4—6; VI, 7; VII—VIII, 3; VIII, 6; IX, 5; IX, 6; und IX, 8.

Weitere Beispiele sind:

T. Levi III, 2   τῶν ἀνόμων]   *e af chi* τῶν ἀ̄ν̄ω̄ν̄ (= ἀνθρώπων)
T. Levi XV, 3   θεωροῦντες]   *e af chi* μισοῦντες
T. Beni. VII, 4 ἐπὶ τοῦ κατακλυσμοῦ] *e af c*Ngr. *om. (h defic., i ?)*
T. Beni. XI, 2   ἐπὶ γῆς]   *e af c om. (h*Ngr. *defic., i ?)*

14. Trennfehler von *e* gegen *af chi*, der die Möglichkeit, daß *af chi* von *e* abhängig sind, ausschließt: *T. Levi* XVIII, 5 τοῦ προσώπου — 6 ναοῦ τῆς δόξης *e om.* Ebenso läßt *e* in *T. Beni.* III, 4 καὶ ὁ θεὸς ἐσκέπασεν αὐτόν aus. Zu diesen Trennfehlern von *e* können auch die bekannten größeren Interpolationen in *T. Levi* II, 3; V, 2 und XVIII, 2 gerechnet werden.

15. Trennfehler von *af chi* gegen *e*, die die Möglichkeit, daß *e* von *af chi* abhängig ist, ausschließen:

T. Rub. IV, 6   ὄλεθρος] *af* Serb. *chi*Ngr. βόθρος (Serb. = »fosse«,
                                   »tombeau«, Turdeanu)

T. Levi VIII, 15   ἄφραστος] *af chi*Ngr. ἀγαπητή
ibid. 17   φυλαχθήσεται] *af chi*Ngr. ληφθήσεται
T. Zab. I, 3   ποίμνια] *af chi*Ngr. πρόβατα
ibid. VI, 3   ἡλίευον ἰχθύας] *af chi*Ngr. *om.*

An diesen Stellen bietet *e* die Lesart von *bk g ldm*.

Aufgrund der gemeinsamen Varianten von *af* und *chi* hat M. de Jonge gefolgert, »that *a* and *f* form a special group within γ with close relations with α«[19]. Wie sich aus seinem Schema ergibt, dachte er sich somit die Gruppe *af* auf irgendeine Weise von α abhängig oder beeinflußt. In Wirklichkeit jedoch stammen die gemeinsamen Varianten von *af* und α einfach aus ihren (ihrer) gemeinsamen Vorlage(n).

16. In seinem Aufsatz über die Textgeschichte der slawischen Übersetzung[20] kommt E. Turdeanu zu dem Schluß, »que S [= Slaw.] forme, avec les manuscrits *a* et *f*, une sous-division distincte dans le cadre du groupe *aef*«. Dieses Urteil beruht auf der textkritischen Analyse von etwa zehn Stellen in *T. Levi*[21]. Das schönste Beispiel liefert *T. Levi* VIII, 2[22] (τὴν μίτραν) τοῦ σημείου (so *bk g*), τοῦ σημέρου *(l)*, τοῦ σημείου *(dm e)*, τῆς κεφαλῆς *(chi)*] *af* τοῦ στηθίου, Slaw. »(la tiare) de la poitrine« (Turdeanu).

17. Daß die Gruppe *af* von Slaw. unabhängig ist, ergibt sich aus der Überlegung, daß eine Rückübersetzung aus dem Slawischen ins Griechische nie zu einer Textform hätte führen können, die den anderen originalgriechischen Texten so sehr ähnelt als die von *af*. Außerdem enthält schon die älteste slawische Rezension christliche Interpolationen, die in der griechischen Überlieferung unbekannt sind, z. B. am Ende von *T. Rub.* VI, 12.

18. Turdeanus Kollationen der slawischen *TT. Rub.* und *Zab.* erlauben die Folgerung, daß die Vorlage der slawischen Version zwar *af* besonders nahesteht, jedoch textgeschichtlich etwas älter als deren jüngste gemeinsame Vorlage ist. Den Durchschlag gibt die Feststellung, daß die slawische Übersetzung in *T. Zab.* II, 1 die Wörter μετ' ὀργῆς τοῦ ἀνελεῖν αὐτόν, καὶ πεσὼν ἐπὶ πρόσωπον ἰωσήφ voraussetzt. Dagegen sind diese in *af* durch Homoioteleuton verlorengegangen. In *T. Rub.* V, 3 las der Übersetzer von Slaw. nicht, wie *af,* ἐνσπείρουσαι,

---

[19] *The Testaments*, p. 18.

[20] S. A. 4. Der Autor hat mir das Manuskript seines Aufsatzes freundlicherweise überlassen. Alles, was hier über Lesarten von Slaw. gesagt wird, verdanke ich Herrn Turdeanu, der neue Kollationen der slawischen Übersetzung der *TT. Rub.* und *Zab.* angefertigt und zur Verfügung gestellt hat. *Art. cit.*, p. 160.

[21] Darunter die acht Stellen, aus denen M. de Jonge die Folgerung gezogen hat: »There does not seem to be any special relationship with either *a f* or *e*«, *The Testaments*, p. 22; *cf.* p. 136, Note 40.

[22] Vergleiche schon Charles (nach W. R. Morfill), *The Greek Versions* . . ., p. 42, Note 16: *af*, S[1] τοῦ στηθίου.

sondern ἐνσπείρουσι, wie *b(k) g l(dm) e chi* (*k defic.*, *d* ἐπισπείρουσι, *m* σπείρουσι). An derselben Stelle hat Slaw. für τῷ ἔργῳ (so *b d e c*) den Instrumentalis, statt des Akkusativs (wie *af* τὸ ἔργον, so auch *g m*; *hi* ἔργον, *l* εἰς ἔργον).

19. Trennfehler von *a* gegen *f*, die die Abhängigkeit der Handschrift *f* von *a* ausschließen, brauchen nicht angeführt zu werden, weil *f* (11. Jh.) sicher älter als *a* (13. Jh., ± 1270)[23] ist. Obendrein kann auf das Fehlen von *T. Beni.* III, 2 ὡς κἀμὲ οἴδατε — 3 φοβεῖσθε κύριον und von *T. Beni.* VII, 5 (völlig) in *a* hingewiesen werden.

20. Trennfehler von *f* gegen *a*, die die Möglichkeit, daß *a* von *f* abhängig ist, ausschließen: in *T. Levi* VIII, 4 läßt *f* ἤλειψέ με weg, ebenso in *T. Zab.* III, 5 οὐκ ἠθέλησαν und *ibid.* IV, 10 τοῦ πατρὸς ἡμῶν. Die Handschrift *a* hat alle diese Wörter erhalten.

21. Die serbische Übersetzung von *T. Rub.* I—V, 7 (bis einschließlich ἔτεκον γίγαντας) wurde 1901 von M. N. Speranskij veröffentlicht[24]. Er konnte sie damals nur mit den vier von Sinker[25] herausgegebenen griechischen Handschriften *(a, b, c, g)* vergleichen, und hat mit Recht festgestellt, daß Serb. am meisten mit *c* übereinstimmt. Charles hat Serb. nicht gekannt, hat aber zwei griechische Handschriften *(h, i)* mit *c* zu der Familie α zusammengefaßt. Dieser Familie hat unlängst Burchard die erstmals von ihm herangezogene neugriechische Übersetzung zugeordnet[26]. Auf Serb. hat erst Turdeanu[27] wieder aufmerksam gemacht. Den Zusammenhang zwischen Serb. und den anderen Zeugen der Familie α konnte ich nur dank seiner Auskünfte bestimmen[28]. Es stellte sich heraus, daß die griechische Vorlage des Serb. ein Stadium der Textüberlieferung der Familie α repräsentiert, das älter als die jüngste gemeinsame Vorlage von *chi*Ngr. ist. In den fünf Kapiteln, worin Serb. uns vorliegt, setzt diese Version sicher an 15 Stellen nicht die von *chi*Ngr. gebotene Variante, sondern den Text von *b(k) g d e af* voraus[29].

Die Zusammengehörigkeit von Serb., *c*, *hi* und Ngr. gegenüber *af*, *e* und allen anderen Handschriften erhellt z. B. aus ihrer Weglassung der Wörter ἀπὸ τοῦ βελίαρ in *T. Rub.* II, 2; τὸ ὄγδοον πνεῦμα in III, 7;

---

[23] »The MS is of the late 13th century, say about 1270«, N. G. Wilson (Oxford) brieflich 3. 7. 1969.

[24] S. A. 4.

[25] R. Sinker, *Testamenta XII Patriarcharum ad fidem codicis Cantabrigiensis edita; accedunt lectiones cod. Oxoniensis*, Cambridge 1869. Id., *Testamenta XII Patriarcharum, Appendix containing a collation of the Roman and Patmos MSS. and bibliographical notes*, Cambridge 1879.

[26] S. A. 4.

[27] S. auch M. Smith, in: *Interpr. Dict. o. t. Bible*, s. v. Testaments o. t. T. P., p. 576.

[28] Wir hoffen in einem speziellen Aufsatz auf Serb. zurückzukommen.

[29] Beispiele unter 23.

und παρὰ τῷ βελίαρ in IV, 7. Nach ἀνθρώπων in IV, 7 fügen die genannten Manuskripte καὶ πρόσκομμα τῷ βελίαρ (Serb. »et une pierre d'achoppement pour le diable« [Turdeanu]; Ngr. καὶ σκάνδαλον τοῦ διαβόλου) zu. Auch die Wörter ἵνα — κυρίου in VI, 4 haben sie verloren.

22. Trennfehler von Serb. gegen *chi*Ngr., die die Möglichkeit, daß *chi*Ngr. von Serb. abhängen, ausschließen, finden sich z. B. in *T. Rub.* II, 6 und V, 3. In *T. Rub.* V, 3 übersetzt Serb. μηχανῶνται mit »elles font l'amour avec« (Turdeanu), offenbar durch Verwechslung mit μοιχῶνται oder μοιχεύονται. In V, 5 ist δολιευομένη mit »devenue esclave« wiedergegeben (= δουλωμένη). Die noch in *c* vorhandenen Wörter II, 6 μεθ᾽ἧς — 7 γεύσεως sind in Serb. durch Homoioteleuton weggefallen. (*hi*Ngr. haben hier ein eigenes Homoioteleuton: sie lassen 6 πνεῦμα — 7 ἕκτον aus).

23. Trennfehler von *chi*Ngr. gegen Serb., die die Möglichkeit, daß Serb. von *chi*Ngr. abhängig ist, ausschließen, sind u. a. die folgenden Verkürzungen. In *chi*Ngr. fehlen die Wörter κλαύσας (I, 5); καί¹ — ὑμῖν (I, 6); τοῦ εἶναι (II, 3) — ὁράσεως (II, 4; Homoioteleuton); und πνεῦμα (III, 4). Serb. hat alle diese Wörter beibehalten. Die Zusammengehörigkeit von *chi* und Ngr., und besonders die von *hi* und Ngr., ist übrigens schon von Burchard³⁰ hinreichend bewiesen.

24. Trennfehler von *c* gegen *hi*Ngr., die die Möglichkeit, daß *hi*Ngr. abhängig von *c* sind, ausschließen, hat schon Charles aufgeführt³¹. Hier sei noch verwiesen auf *T. Rub.* I, 4, wo *h*³² mit *af* ἰδοὺ γὰρ ἐκλείπω ἀπὸ τοῦ νῦν ἐγώ (Ngr. δϊὰ τί [*sic MS.*] ἐγὼ ἀπὸ τοῦ νῦν λείπω) liest. In *c* ist dieser Satz verschwunden. Auch die Wörter διά — ἀναβῆναι ὕδωρ in *T. Zab.* II, 8 fehlen in *c*, aber *hi* lesen διὰ γὰρ τοῦτο ἐκώλυσε κύριος τοῦ μὴ ἀναβλῦσαι ὕδωρ, Ngr. ὅτι ἴσως διὰ τοῦτο ἐμπόδισεν ὁ κύριος νὰ μὴ ἀναβλύσῃ νερόν³³. In *T. Zab.* IX, 5 schließlich hat *c* καίγε πᾶν εἴδωλον προσκυνήσετε (so *b g l(d) e af h*; *d* καί statt καίγε; *k m defic.*) verloren. Aber *hi*Ngr. lesen noch καὶ τὰ εἴδωλα (Ngr. + νὰ) προσκυνήσετε.

25. Trennfehler von *hi*Ngr. gegen *c* brauchen nicht aufgeführt zu werden, weil *c* (13. Jh.) älter als *hi* (17. Jh.) und Ngr. (18. Jh.) ist. Bindefehler zwischen *hi* und Ngr. sind z. B.:

T. Zab. II, 5 *c* ἐβόμβει] *hi* ἔμφοβος ἦν, Ngr. εἰς πολὺν φόβον ἦτον
T. Zab. IV, 1 *c(= g ldm)* ἀδελφοί μου] *hi* ἀδελφοὶ αὐτοῦ, Ngr. ἀδελφοί του
T. Zab. IX, 8 *c* (διὰ τὸ ὄνομα αὐτοῦ) τὸ ἅγιον] *hi*Ngr. *(id.)* τὸ πανάγιον

---

³⁰ *Neues ...*, NTS. *St.* 12 (1965—1966) pp. 249—250.
³¹ Er hat sie aber falsch interpretiert: er hielt in solchen Fällen *hi* für korrumpiert durch Kontamination mit β. S. *The Greek Versions*, p. xx.
³² Nach Charles; *i* unleserlich.
³³ νερόν = Wasser.

26. Trennfehler von *hi* gegen Ngr., der die Möglichkeit, daß Ngr. von *hi* abhängig ist, ausschließt: *T. Zab.* III, 5:

b	*c*	*hi*	Ngr.
καὶ κύριος	καὶ ὁ κύριος	*om.*	ὁ κύριος
ὑπέλυσεν	ἐπέδυσεν		ὑπέλυσεν (= *b*!)
αὐτοὺς	αὐτοὺς		—
τὸ ὑπόδημα	τὸ ὑπόδημα		—
Ἰωσήφ.	ὃ ἐφόρεσαν		ἐκεῖνο ὅπερ ἐφόρεσαν
	κατὰ Ἰωσὴφ		ἐναντίον Ἰωσὴφ
	τοῦ ἀδελφοῦ		τοῦ ἀδελφοῦ
	αὐτῶν		τους.

Die Weglassung in *hi* beruht allerdings auf Homoioteleuton und schließt darum nicht die Möglichkeit aus, daß Ngr. von der jüngsten gemeinsamen Vorlage von *hi* abstammt. Darum notiere ich noch folgenden gemeinsamen Fehler von *hi* gegen Ngr.:

T. Zab. III, 6 *hi* βασιλέα] *c*Ngr. βασιλέως.

27. Trennfehler von *h* gegen *i*, der die Möglichkeit, daß *i* von *h* abhängig ist, ausschließt: *T. Rub.* I, 9 κυρίου — 10 ἔπιον fehlt in *h* durch Homoioteleuton (ἐνώπιον/ἔπιον). In *i* sind diese Wörter bewahrt. Außerdem ist *h* unvollständig.

28. Trennfehler von *i* gegen *h*: *T. Rub.* IV, 11 οὐδὲ ὁ βελίαρ — ὑμῶν fehlt in *i* durch Homoioteleuton.

29. Die Handschriften *h* und *i* können nicht von Ngr. abhängen, weil sie älter als Ngr. sind (S. unter 25). Darüber hinaus weist Ngr. zahlreiche Erweiterungen auf, die in *hi* nicht vorkommen.

Die bisher vorgelegte Anordnung des Materials zeigt die grundsätzlichen Zusammenhänge der handschriftlichen Überlieferung der Testamente. Der grundsätzliche Zusammenhang zwischen den Handschriften wird dadurch hergestellt, daß jedes der Manuskripte der Testamente nur von einer einzigen Vorlage abgeschrieben wird, die ihm den Hauptstrom der Tradition überliefert. Allerdings enthält nicht jeder uns bekannte Zeuge nur Lesarten, die aus dieser Vorlage erklärbar sind. Man muß mit dem gelegentlichen Einfluß anderer Handschriften rechnen. Solche sekundäre Überlieferung (Kontamination) konnte ich feststellen

in *l* aus einem mit *g* verwandten Text (30);

in *l* aus einem mit α verwandten Text (31) (?);

in *d* aus einem mit α verwandten Text (32);

in *dm* aus einem mit α verwandten Text (33);

in *l* aus einem mit *b(k)* verwandten Text (34).

30. Sekundärer Einfluß in *l* von einem mit *g* verwandten Text ist nachweisbar in:

T. Rub.	I, 7 ταῖς λαγῶσι	]	nur *g l* τοῖς λαγῶσι	
ibid.	IV, 4 παρέλθη	]	nur *g l* ἀπέλθη	
T. Levi	II, 2 ὡσεί	]	nur *g l a om.*	
ibid.	IV, 1 τῷ πάθει	]	nur *g l* τὸ πάθος	
ibid.	IX, 2 τῶν ὁράσεων	]	nur *g l* τῆς ὁράσεως	
ibid.	XIV, 6 διδάξητε	]	nur *g l* διαδέξη— (*g* διαδέξηται, *l* δια-	
			δέξησθε)	
T. Zab.	I, 1 μετὰ — Ἰωσήφ]		nur *g l om.*	
ibid.	II, 5 ἐβόμβει(*a*)	]	nur *g l* ἐμβόβη *(sic)*, (*b* ἐβόμβη)	

31. Sekundärer Einfluß in *l* von einem Text der Familie α zeigt sich vielleicht in:

T. Rub. I, 10 καὶ οὐ μὴ γένηται]   *c* οἷα οὐ γέγονεν, (*h* ἀνταμοιβὴ
γένοιτο), *i* οἷα μοι μὴ γένηται,
l οἷα μὴ γένηται

T. Rub. III, 6 δολολειψίας   ] *af chi*, *l* δοσοληψίας

Von den zahllosen Fällen in *T. Zab.* seien nur erwähnt:

I, 3 ἀγαθή	]	*chi* + γέγονα, *l* + ἐγενόμην	
I, 6 ὁμοῦ	]	*chi*, *l* om.	
II, 8 τοῦ ἀναβῆναι ὕδωρ]		*hi (c defic.)* τοῦ μὴ ἀναβλῦσαι ὕδωρ	
		l τοῦ μὴ ἀναβῆναι ὕδωρ	
IV, 5 περισχισ-	]	*chi* + τὸν χιτῶνα αὐτοῦ	
		l + τὸν ἑαυτοῦ χιτῶνα	
V, 1 εἰς ἄλογα]		*ci (h. om.)* ἐν ἀλόγοις ζώοις, *l* πρὸς τὰ ζῶα	
V, 5 παράλιον	]	*chi*, *l* τὴν παράλιαν[34]	

32. Sekundärer Einfluß in *d* von einem Text der Familie α macht sich bemerklich in *T. Levi* XIII, 8 ὅτι γενήσεται αὐτῷ αὐτή] *chi* ἐὰν γάρ τις φυλάξη ἑαυτὸν ἐκ τῶν πονηρῶν τούτων ἔργων (*c*)/ πράξεων (*hi*), τότε γενήσεται (*c* + ἐν) αὐτῷ σοφία. Unter dem Einfluß von α liest *d* ἐὰν δὲ φυλάξη ταῦτα, γενήσεται αὐτῷ ἡ σοφία. Ein weiteres Beispiel findet sich in *T. Levi* XIX, 3: für εἴπωμεν (so *b*; richtiger εἴπαμεν *e a*, oder εἴπομεν *l f*) lesen nur *chi* und *d* εἶπον (*chi* + αὐτῷ) οἱ υἱοὶ αὐτοῦ. In *T. Zab.* II, 9 lesen nur *chi* und *d* καὶ ἐποίησαν οὕτως statt καὶ ἐποίησε κύριος οὕτως[35].

---

[34] Mit diesen Varianten ist die Beziehung zwischen α und *l* noch nicht bewiesen; ich notiere sie nur, damit die Möglichkeit einer sekundären Beziehung zwischen α und *l* nicht übersehen wird.

[35] *Cf.* Charles, *The Greek Versions*, p. xxi: »*d* is a conflate text (*etc* . . .) Thus *d*, which is naturally related to *b* (. . .) shows many traces of the influence of α (. . .)«; Hunkin, *JThSt* 16 (1915), p. 82: »*d* is characterized by many conflate readings«; M. de Jonge, *The Testaments*, pp. 18—19: »We must therefore assume that *d*'s scribe [Warum dieser, und nicht der Schreiber einer der Vorlagen von *d*?], while copying a MS which belonged to the δ-group, was at the same time acquainted with a recension con-

33. Auf sekundären Einfluß in *dm* von einem Texte der Familie α darf man nur schließen, wenn *dm* Sonderfehler von α zeigt, die nicht in *e af* begegnen; sonst könnten diese Fehler auch auf die gemeinsame Vorlage von *ldm e af chi* zurückgehen und in *l* durch die unter 30 und 34 festgestellte Kontamination nach einem mit *g* oder *b* verwandten Text korrigiert sein. Die Lesarten, die *dm* mit *e* und *af chi* gemeinsam hat, stellen uns tatsächlich vor Probleme, gegen die kaum Kraut gewachsen ist. In *T. Aser* VI, 2 z. B. haben nicht nur *e* und *af chi*, sondern auch *dm* den Zusatz[36] ὅτι[37] καὶ πράσσουσι[38] τὸ κακὸν καὶ συνευδοκοῦσι[39] τοῖς πράσσουσι[38]. Wie ist die Interpolation in *dm* und ihr Fehlen in *l* zu erklären? Wenn sie auf die Vorlage von *ldm e af chi* zurückgehen sollte, wäre ihr Fehlen in *l* dem sekundären Einfluß eines *g*- oder *b*-Textes zuzuschreiben. Oder hat *dm* die Interpolation durch Kontamination aus α entlehnt? Denn auch auf eine gemeinsame Vorlage von *dm* hat α Einfluß ausgeübt[40].

Die folgenden Lesarten hat *dm* mit *chi* gemeinsam, nicht mit *e* oder *e af*. Sie beweisen also den Einfluß von α auf *dm*:

T. Rub.	III, 11	ἐνέπιπτον]	*chi f dm* ἂν ἔπιπτον
ibid.	IV, 1	προσέχετε]	*chi dm* + τέκνα μου (*c om.* μου), Serb. + »mes enfants« (Turdeanu)
ibid.	VII, 2	ἔθαψαν]	*chi dm* + αὐτόν
T. Levi	I, 2	ὤφθη]	*chi dm* ἀπεκαλύφθη
ibid.	II, 3	ἑώρων]	*chi dm* ἐθεώρουν
T. Zab.	I, 5	ἐπί[2]]	*chi dm om.*
T. Beni.	I, 6	υἱός — βενιαμίν]	*c*(Ngr.) *dm* βενιαμὴν (*c* —μὶν) ὅ (*dm* + —περ) ἐστιν υἱὸς ἡμερῶν. Ngr. βενιαμὴν τὸ ὁποῖον ὄνομα θέλει νὰ εἴπη υἱὸς ἡμερῶν.
ibid.	III, 1	οὐρανοῦ]	*c*Ngr. *dm* + καὶ τῆς γῆς

34. In den *TT. Rub., Levi, Zab.* und *Beni.* findet man auch mindestens 25 Stellen, an denen *b(k)* und *l* gegen alle übrigen Hand-

---

nected with the α- or γ-group«; Burchard, *Neues* ..., p. 246; »(*d* wechselt) gelegentlich von β zu α über«; Id., *Zur armenischen Überlieferung* ..., *BZNW* 36, p. 5, A. 29; *similia*.

[36] *Cf.* Röm. 1 32; Charles, *The Greek Versions*, pp. 178—179, n. 6; M. de Jonge, *The Testaments*, p. 19.

[37] *d* διότι, *m* διά τι.   [38] *m* πραττ-

[39] *m* συνοδεύουσιν.

[40] Noch schwieriger ist die lange Interpolation in *T. Aser* V, 1 zu erklären. Die Handschriften *dm* teilen sie mit *e, af,* und *chi*. Weil *l* IV, 4 bis einschließlich V, 1 (auch die Interpolation) wegläßt, ist nicht zu entscheiden, ob der längere Text von *dm* unter 6, 32 oder 33 aufgeführt werden müßte.

schriften zusammengehen. Dabei braucht man nicht immer an Kontamination zwischen *b(k)* und *l* denken. In solchen Fällen können gerade *b* und *l* die ursprüngliche Lesart bewahrt haben, z. B.:

T. Rub. II, 7 *bk l* αὐτοῖς] *d* αὐτῇ, *m e af chi* αὐτῷ, *g defic.*

T. Zab. II, 3 *b l* ἐπενέγκητε] *g dm* + ἐπ᾽ ἐμέ, *e af* + μοι, *chi* +
ἐν φόνῳ ἀδελφοῦ ὑμῶν; *l nihil addit,*
k defic.

T. Beni. IV, 4 *b l* ἀνδρεῖος] *g* ἀνδρείως, *dm* + ῇ, *e f c praemitt.* ῇ,
k a hi defic.

ibid. V, 1 *b l* ὑμῖν] *g d e af* μεθ᾽ ὑμῶν, *m* μεθ᾽ ὑμῶν, *c om.*,
Ngr. μαζί σας, *k hi defic.*

Auch können *b* und *l* unabhängig voneinander denselben Fehler haben, so vielleicht in *T. Levi* IV, 4, wo nur *b* und *l* (nicht *k*) den Artikel τῷ vor σπέρματι weglassen, analog dem Wortlaut des vorhergehenden Verses. (Die Anordnung des Textes dieser Verse bei M. de Jonge, *Testamenta . . .*, p. 12 ist lehrreich: auch in den Handschriften *b* und *l* stehen die Worte παντὶ σπέρματι von IV, 3 und von IV, 4 gerade untereinander, in *b* mit einer Zeile dazwischen).

Oft ist nicht leicht zu entscheiden, ob *b* und *l*, oder die anderen Manuskripte die richtige Lesart bieten; so in

T. Levi II, 3 *b l* ἐποιμαίνομεν] *ceteri* ἐποίμαινον; *k defic.*
ibid. II, 10 *bk l* σύνεγγυς] *g e af* σὺ ἐγγύς, *d* ἐγγύς, *m* συ
(alia linea) νικεῖς *(sic MS., pro*
συνοικεῖς? *Sed conservat* στήσει);
chi aliter, sed retinent ἐγγύς.

ibid. XIV, 2 *bk l* ἔσται] *ceteri* ἐστίν
T. Beni. III, 5 *b l* ὑπό[1]] *g* ἐξ, *dm e af c*Ngr. ἀπό; *k hi defic.*
ibid. III, 8 *b l* τοὺς ὑπηρε- *g e af c*Ngr. τοὺς ὑπηρέτας αὐτοῦ,
τοῦντας αὐτῷ⌋ *dm* τῶν ὑπηρετῶν αὐτοῦ πᾶσαν
δύναμιν; *k hi defic.*

ibid. X, 1 *b l* μορφήν] *g d e af* μόρφωσιν; *k m chi*Ngr. *defic.*

Aber an einzelnen Stellen scheint die Übereinstimmung zwischen *b* und *l* doch auf sekundären Einfluß von einem mit *b* verwandten Text in einer Vorlage von *l* hinzuweisen:

T. Levi III, 9 *b l* οἱ *(sic)* ἄβυσσοι] *g e hi* ἄβυσσοι, *k d af* αἱ ἄβυσσοι,
c ἡ ἄβυσσος, *m defic.*

ibid. XIV, 3 *bk l* οὐρανοῦ] *g m e af chi* ἰσραήλ, *d aliter: pro*
καθαρός — οὐρανοῦ: καὶ γὰρ αὐ-
τῷ ὡς φωστῆρές εἰσιν

35. Zum Abschluß nehme ich mit Genehmigung von Prof. M. de Jonge hier Gelegenheit, den Leser mit neugefundenem Textmaterial

bekannt zu machen. Am 11. August 1970 berichtete J. Paramelle vom *Institut de recherche et d'histoire des textes* in Paris über zwei im Katalog nicht erwähnte griechische Fragmente, die er in der Handschrift M. Athos, Vatopediou 659 (14. Jh.) festgestellt hatte, und zwar:

f. 42r.—v.: *T. Levi*   III, 1   ἄκουσον περὶ τῶν δειχθέντων σοι οὐρανῶν — 9 ἁμαρτάνουσι *(in margine)*;

f. 47r.—48r.: *T. Rub.* III, 6   μεθ᾽ἧς κλοπαὶ καὶ γριππιάσματα *(sic MS.)* — V, 7 καὶ ἔτεκον γίγαντας.

Durch das freundliche Entgegenkommen des *Institut* empfing M. de Jonge einen Mikrofilm der betreffenden Seiten. Es zeigte sich, daß die Fragmente, die beide von derselben Hand geschrieben sind, zu der Familie α gehören: in *T. Rub.* weist *n* — denn so werden diese Exzerpte hinfort bezeichnet werden — die unter 21 erwähnten, für α charakteristischen Lesarten auf. Die Anfangsworte von *T. Levi* III lauten: εὖρον ἐν τῇ διαθήκῃ λευὶ τοῦ πατριάρχου περὶ τῶν τριῶν οὐρανῶν ὧν ἔδειξε αὐτῷ ὁ ἄγγελος κυρίου τάδε ῥητῶς λέγων· (ἄκουσον κτλ. . .). Dadurch ist von vornherein klar, daß es sich auch hier um den α-Text handelt, denn nur in α ist von drei Himmeln die Rede, sonst überall von sieben. Vielleicht darf man folgern, daß beide Fragmente aus einer einzigen Quelle kommen. Jedenfalls ist ihr Text aufs engste verwandt mit Serb., repräsentiert also eine Überlieferungsphase von α, die älter ist als die jüngste gemeinsame Vorlage von *chi*.

Die folgenden Sonderfehler von Serb. finden sich jetzt auch in *n*:

T. Rub. IV, 2 τινι τῶν ἀδελφῶν μου *chi*]	Serb. »à mes frères« (Turdeanu)
	n τοῖς ἀδελφοῖς μου
ibid. IV, 4 ἔδειξέ μοι *omnes (exc. d)*]	Serb. »m'enseigna« (Turdeanu)
	n ἐδίδαξέ με
ibid. V, 4 ἐν σχήμασι πορνικοῖς τοῦτον πανουργεύεται *chi*]	Serb. »elles le trompent dans des images luxurieuses *et par des visions diaboliques*« (Turdeanu)
	n ἐν σχήμασι πορνικοῖς καὶ βλέμμασι σατανικοῖς τοῦτον καταπανουργεύονται
ibid. V, 5 δολιευομένη *b g l e af chi*]	Serb. »devenue esclave« (Turdeanu)
	n δουλωμένη (*cf.* unter 22)

Darüber hinaus brechen beide Texte, *n* und Serb., genau an derselben Stelle im *T. Rub.* V, 7 ab: γίγαντας ist bei beiden das letzte Wort.

Auch in *T. Levi* zeigt *n* eine ältere Textform als *chi*: das zweite σοί in III, 1 *(ch, i aliter)* hat *n* noch nicht, und statt αὐτῶν in III, 5 und III, 8 *(chi;* III, 8 *hi* αὐτῷ) liest *n* richtig αὐτόν, wie *af*.

36. Die Frage, ob Serb. von *n* abhängig ist, muß negativ beantwortet werden. (Die Abhängigkeit der Handschrift *n* von Serb. ist ausgeschlossen, schon weil *n* älter ist als Serb.) Das Fehlen von *T. Rub.* I—III, 6a in *n* kann allerdings aus folgenden Gründen nicht als Beweis für die Unabhängigkeit des Serbiers von *n* beigebracht werden: Für die fehlende Passage *T. Rub.* I—III, 6a würden genau zwei Seiten in *n* ausreichen. Der heutige Text fängt mitten im Satz oben auf f. 47r. an, während die vorhergehenden Blätter unbeschrieben sind (f. 45v., 46r. und 46v.). Es ist daher wahrscheinlich, daß die Anfangsseite von *T. Rub.* verlorengegangen und beim Zusammenbinden des Codex durch weiße Blätter ersetzt ist. Das verlorene Blatt könnte aber noch vorhanden gewesen sein, als die serbische Übersetzung angefertigt wurde.

Dennoch ist es klar, daß Serb. nicht von *n* abhängt, denn in den folgenden Fällen folgt er nicht der Sonderlesart von *n*, sondern bietet den Text wie auch andere Zeugen ihn noch bewahren:

T. Rub.	III, 8 νουθεσίας]	*n* νομοθεσίας, Serb. = *bk ldm e af (chi* νουθεσίαν)
ibid.	III, 13 ἀκάλυφος]	*chi* ἀκάλυπτος, *n* ἀκατάληπτος, Serb. »non-couverte« (Turdeanu)
ibid.	V, 7 ἐπιθυμοῦσαι]	*n* μὴ ἐπιθυμοῦσαι, Serb. = *bk g dm e af chi (l defic.)*

Das textgeschichtliche Stadium, für das Serb. und *n* unsere Zeugen sind, ist in *T. Rub.* I—III, 6a nur von Serb. vertreten, in *T. Levi* III, 1—9 nur von *n*. Beide haben also ihren Wert.

III.

Die Ergebnisse der vorliegenden textgeschichtlichen Arbeit an den Patriarchentestamenten lassen sich folgendermaßen zusammenfassen.

1. In der Geschichte der Textüberlieferung der Testamente hat es die Familie β nie gegeben[41]. Die bisherige Gruppe β *(bk g ldm e af)* ist

---

[41] M. de Jonge urteilte noch anders; *Testamenta XII Patriarcharum . . .,* 1964[1], p. XIII und 1970[2], p. XV: »Dr. Charles rightly distinguished between two groups of MSS: *chi* (= α) and *b d g a e f* (= β)«. Burchard konnte noch schreiben: »Geblieben ist Charles' Gruppierung der Zeugen in vier Textformen, die zu zwei Familien α *(c, hi)* und β *(bdg* A, *aef* S) zusammentreten«, *Zur armenischen Überlieferung,* p. 2; aber der Unterschied zwischen α und β, und überhaupt die Voraussetzung einer Familie β = *b k g l d m e a f* gegenüber α = *chi*, wird in der Textkritik der Testamente von nun an keine Rolle mehr spielen dürfen.

keine wirkliche Familie, erstens, weil die älteste Spaltung der Überlieferung gerade zwischen *bk* und allen anderen Handschriften liegt, zweitens, weil sie in Wirklichkeit die ganze Überlieferung, auch die Familie α, umfaßt. Das Siglum β wäre am besten zu ersetzen durch ω (= Archetypus der ganzen Textüberlieferung).

2. Familie α (jetzt = *n* Serb. *chi* Ngr.) ist nicht nur, wie J. W. Hunkin[42] richtig erkannt hat, wenig mehr als eine späte und freie Überarbeitung einer Handschrift des mit »β« angedeuteten Texttyps; sondern einfach die Rezension eines Textes, von dem sonst nur noch die gemeinsame Vorlage von Slaw. und *af* abhängt (im Stemma: Punkt 15).

3. Das von M. de Jonge eingeführte Siglum γ muß wieder eliminiert werden, weil »γ« nicht mehr nur *e*, Slaw. und *af* umfaßt, sondern auch die ganze Familie *n* Serb. *chi* Ngr. Auch M. de Jonge's Siglum δ (für *bk g d*) bezeichnet keine wirklich einheitliche Gruppe, weil die Hauptspaltung der Überlieferung zwischen *bk* und *gd* liegt, und überdies auch *e af n chi* und die serbische und neugriechische Version von der gemeinsamen Vorlage von *g d* abhängen.

Somit kann Charles' Gruppierung der Zeugen in zwei Familien α und β nicht länger beibehalten werden.

4. Auch hängt *b* nicht, wie in Hunkin's graphischer Darstellung[43], von einer mit *g* gemeinsamen Vorlage ab, die ihrerseits wieder von einer mit *d* gemeinsamen Vorlage abhänge, sondern:

5. Der Entwicklungsgang der uns bekannten und rekonstruierbaren Überlieferung der Testamente der zwölf Patriarchen verläuft auf folgende Weise: wir müssen mit einem einzigen Archetypus der gesamten Tradition (ω) rechnen, der im Laufe der Zeit zum Hyparchetypus der Familie α depraviert. Die vorliegenden Handschriften und Übersetzungen sind von verschiedenen Hyparchetypen abhängig, die einzelne Stadien der Entwicklung darstellen; *bk* als vom ältesten Stadium abhängig entstammen dem Archetypus selbst. Danach sind aus den jeweiligen Entwicklungsformen des Archetyps nacheinander entsprossen: eine (die) Vorlage von *g*, eine (die) Vorlage von *ldm*, (eine/die Vorlage von) *e*, und eine (die) Vorlage von Slaw. *af*. Vom jüngsten Hyparchetypus (α) lassen sich zwei Handschriftengruppen ableiten: *n*Serb. und *chi*Ngr. — Daneben zeigen die Handschriften *ldm* sekundäre Beeinflussung aus verschiedenen Richtungen.

Für Einzelheiten sei auf das Stemma verwiesen.

---

[42] *JThSt* 16 (1915), p. 89.
[43] Op. cit., p. 97.

III

THE EARLIEST TRACEABLE STAGE OF
THE TEXTUAL TRADITION OF THE
TESTAMENTS OF THE TWELVE PATRIARCHS

HENK JAN DE JONGE

The textual tradition of the Greek pseudepigraphical writing *The Testaments of the Twelve Patriarchs* rests on twenty-six witnesses.* Eight out of these twenty-six depend exclusively on one or another surviving exemplar of the Greek text. A textcritical reconstruction of the *Testaments* has therefore to be based on the testimony of eighteen witnesses, viz. :

11 MSS. containing a continuous Greek text (*a*, *b*, *c*, *d*, *e*, *f*, *g*, *h*, *i*, *l*, *m*);[1]
3 MSS. containing excerpts from the Greek text (*k*, *n*, Fm^d);
4 translations made after the Greek (Arm., Slav., Serb., Ngr.).

As two witnesses, *b* and *k*, show peculiar errors in common as against all the other witnesses, these other witnesses can not possibly derive from *bk*. Nor can *bk* derive from any of the other witnesses, since all witnesses except *b* and *k* exhibit common errors as against *bk*. Thus the primary split in the textual tradition of the *Testaments* is into two branches or families :[2]

---

* I am grateful to H. E. Gaylord who checked the English of this article.

[1] For a descriptive list of the MSS. to which these sigla refer, see *ZNW* 63, 1972, pp. 27-8, in this volume pp. 45-46.

[2] For the discussion on stemmatic 'Zweispaltigkeit', see J. Bédier, 'La tradition manuscrite du "Lai de l'Ombre"', *Romania* 54, 1928, pp. 161 ff. and 321 ff.; J. Andrieu, 'Principes et recherches en critique textuelle', *Mémorial des Et. Lat. offert à J. Marouzeau*, Paris 1943, pp. 458 ff.; J. Fourquet, 'Le paradoxe de Bédier', *Publ. de la Fac. des Lettres de l'Univ. de Strasbourg*, fasc. 105, Mélanges 1945 II (Et. littér.), Paris 1946, pp. 1 ff.; P. Maas, *Textkritik*, Leipzig 1960⁴, pp. 29-30; J. Irigoin, 'Stemmas bifides et états de mss.', *Revue de philologie* 80 (3d Series, 28), 1954, pp. 211 ff.; A. Castellani, *Bédier, avait-il raison?* (Discours Universitaires, N.S. 20), Fribourg (Switzerland) 1957; S. Timpanaro, *Die Entstehung der Lachmannschen Methode*, Hamburg 1971², Anhang 3, 'Zweigeteilte Stemmata und Kontamination', pp. 115-50; *idem*, 'Ancora su stemmi

family I, consisting of the witnesses *b* and *k*;

family II, comprising all the other witnesses: *glmd*Fm^*d* Arm. *e*
Slav. *af* Serb.*nchi*Ngr. Within family II, *gldm*Fm^*d* and Serb.-
*nchi*Ngr. (= α) form 'sub-families'. (See diagram).[3]

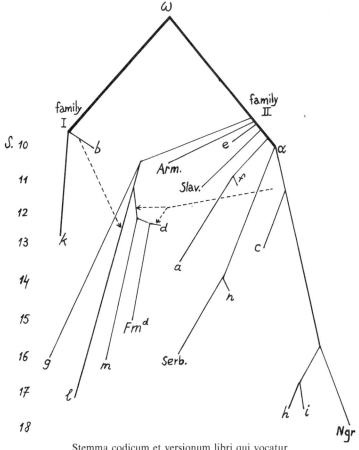

Stemma codicum et versionum libri qui vocatur
Testamenta duodecim Patriarcharum
(cf. n. 3)

bipartiti e contaminazione', *Maia* 17, 1965, pp. 392-9; W. Hering, 'Zweispaltige Stemmata. Zur Theorie der textkritischen Methode', *Philologus* 111, 1967, pp. 170-185; A. Kleinlogel, 'Das Stemmaproblem', *Philologus* 112, 1968, pp. 63-83.

[3] This stemma differs on three points (*g*, Arm. and Slav.) from the one I published in 1972. I willingly agree with Th. Korteweg that *g* has to be connected with the group *lmd*, and that Slav. has to be detached from *af* and inserted between *e* and *af* (see Korteweg's contributions to this symposium, Ch. IX and XI). On Arm. see M. de Jonge in Ch. VIII.

It follows that, in establishing the text of the *Testaments*, it is only by comparing the readings of family I with those of family II that one can try to restore the archetype[4] ω of the whole tradition.

It will be obvious that the reconstruction of the archetype is far from being a mechanical operation.[5] Where both families agree, usually one has the text of the archetype; but where they do not agree, either or neither may have the text of ω. Especially at this point the textual critic of the *Testaments* has to take into account all relevant external and internal evidence which is available. Not only here indeed his method will be eclectic.[6]

In many cases it is not easy to choose between the reading of family I and that of family II. To quote only a few examples:

T. Levi	IX,5	καταλῦσαι	fam. I]	καταμεῖναι	fam. II
T. Jud.	XXIII,5	ἐν ἀγάπῃ	fam. I]	ἀναγάγῃ/-ει	fam. II
T. Iss.	IV,5	πορισμόν	fam. I]	περισπασμόν	fam. II
T. Iss.	VII,3	ἐπόθησα	fam. I]	ἐπεθύμησα	fam. II

But the difficulty of deciding in such cases is not the only circumstance warning against optimism as to the degree of reliability which one can attain in reconstructing ω, let alone in establishing the original text of the *Testaments*, which is something different. Another, even more serious problem is that in a great many of instances the readings of the hyparchetypes of family I and of family II cannot be reconstructed with certainty. As for family I, this uncertainty is due to the hiatusses in *k*. In family II it is a result of contamination (in *l* from a MS. related to *b*, and in *d* and *dm* from MSS. related to *a*), and of the divergencies between the readings of different witnesses. At times these divergencies are considerable and their development cannot be determined.

---

[4] I use the term archetype in the sense of last common source of the surviving tradition ('le-plus-proche-commun-ancêtre-de-la-tradition', as Dain termed it).

[5] Cf. P. Maas, *Textual Criticism*, Oxford 1958, p. 6: 'We have here variants, between which it is not possible to decide on the lines of our procedure hitherto'.

[6] The geneaological method *as a whole* primarily consists in judging variants and marking them either as (separative or conjunctive) errors, or as correct readings. The decision whether a reading is an error or not, often requires a cautious weighing of all kinds of evidence. This reminder has become necessary, it seems, since recent writers on the *Testaments* have recommended internal criticism and eclecticism as methods different from a consistent stemmatic procedure — whereas these are just components of it.

Here it should also be pointed out that in the ninth century or even earlier the size of the *Testaments* seems to have been reckoned at 5100 *stichoi*, whereas the last common source of all witnesses known today can only have contained *c.* 2600 *stichoi*, hardly more than half of the number recorded in Nicephorus' *Stichometry*.[7]

In the light of all this it may be a significant fact that no witness of the *Testaments* is earlier than the tenth century, which means that the whole surviving MS. tradition, without exception, may derive from one ninth- or tenth-century minuscule codex.

The question whether the archetype of the *Testaments* has been a minuscule or a majuscule codex, is of extreme importance for an evaluation of the reliability of the text reconstructed on the basis of the surviving witnesses. The degree of reliability which can be attained by such a reconstruction does not seem to worry many readers of the *Testaments*. The critic who cares for the trustworthiness of his knowledge, however, has to form a clear idea concerning the textual reliability of the documents on which his knowledge depends. Since texts are the foundation of all philological investigation, the least possible doubt should remain as to how far they are reliable.

If then the archetype of the *Testaments* was a MS. in minuscule script, our knowledge of the text does not reach back beyond the ninth century.[8] In that case the whole surviving MS. tradition is dependent on only one single majuscule codex of uncertain date. All other majuscule copies in which the text of the *Testaments* must have circulated during the first millennium of our era would have perished without leaving any trace, i.e., without contributing to our

---

[7] On the *Stichometry* of Nicephorus, see J. Leipoldt, *Geschichte des n.t.lichen Kanons* I, Leipzig 1907, p. 100: "Das Verzeichnis geht in der vorliegenden Form nicht auf Nicephorus zurück, sondern muss um die Mitte des neunten Jahrhunderts in Jerusalem entstanden sein. Es ist aber immerhin möglich, dass der Grundstock von Nicephorus herrührt. Vielleicht ist aber auch Nicephorus nur der Bearbeiter älterer Vorlagen gewesen. In einer Beziehung erinnert die Stichometrie des Nicephorus sogar an den Kanon des Euseb von Cäsarea...". Cf. also Th. Zahn, *Geschichte des N.t. Kanons* II, Erlangen-Leipzig 1890, pp. 295-301.

[8] The only thing we know about the wording of the text in earlier centuries is that the words ἧπαρ πρὸς θυμόν and νεφροὺς εἰς πανουργίαν in *T. Napht.* II,8 were already extant in a copy of the *Testaments* used by Jerome: 'in libro quoque Patriar-charum... ita inveni, ut quomodo *fel ad iracundiam* sic *renes ad calliditatem* et ad astutiam sint creati'. (E. Schürer, *Gesch. d. Jüd. Volkes*[4], III, p. 353). But Jerome's quotation arouses doubts as to the textual reliability of the words which the surviving MSS. present between the two Greek parts of the sentence just quoted.

knowledge of the history of the text, and without removing any of our doubts about the reliability of its reconstructed archetype.

Of course it detracts from the textual trustworthiness of any ancient Greek writing, when its archetype turns out to have been a minuscule copy and its majuscule tradition proves to have perished without any progeny except the one MS. which was the result of transliteration. In the case however of a popular book like the *Testaments of the Twelve Patriarchs*, of which any exemplar may have been an individual recension, the disappearence of the majuscule tradition amounts to as much as a disaster. For we cannot assume that the uncial MS. which was transliterated in the ninth or tenth century, on which all the surviving witnesses depend, has been selected because of the purity of its text. If the scribe who transliterated the *Testaments* would have had the option of different MSS. — which is by no means probable —, he would not have known how to make the right choice.

If on the other hand the archetype of the *Testaments* has been a majuscule codex, then it is likely to have been earlier than the tenth century, and perhaps much earlier. But in that event one may also draw another conclusion, one of much greater importance in fact. In case the archetype was a majuscule copy, the surviving MS. tradition can only be split into two families if the *Testaments* have been transliterated at least twice from majuscule script into minuscule script.

In theory both transliterations might have been executed on the basis of one and the same majuscule model.[9] But in certain instances of double transliteration one branch of the tradition has been proved to derive from the transliteration of a different uncial book than the rest of the tradition. This is, for instance, the case with Plato.

'In the tradition of Plato one manuscript (Vienna, supp. gr. 39) differs greatly from all others in its errors, and it is difficult to believe it derived from the same ninth-century exemplar; it may derive from the transliteration of a different uncial book, so that at least two old books would seem to have survived the dark ages. A confirmation of this is that when a Greek text has been translated into an Oriental language at an early date, perhaps the fifth century, the readings which are characteristic of the Oriental translation may occur also in a small group of the Greek manuscripts. This is true of the Armenian version

---

[9] This possibility, which is generally disregarded, was brought to my notice by G. J. Wieberdink, of The Hague, who has investigated the textual tradition of some Hippocratic writings.

of some of Plato's dialogues, the Arabic version of Aristotle's *Poetics*, and,
if the example of a patrictic text may be admitted here, of the Syriac translation
of St. Gregory of Nyssa's *de virginitate*.[10]

Accordingly, it is generally supposed that if a Greek text has been
transliterated twice, two different uncial copies have served as models.

'S'il y eut pour un texte deux, trois et même quatre translittérations, c'est
qu'elles furent exécutées dans des centres indépendants les uns des autres, et
souvent à des dates éloignées; c'est le cas pour Sophocle. ... Des *Discours* de
Démosthène, de l'*Anabase* de Xénophon, nous avons deux translittérations, qui
nous donnent deux textes parfois difficilement réductibles l'un à l'autre'.[11]

Now it makes a considerable difference for the date of the archetype
of a text, whether its surviving MSS. descend from one uncial copy
or from two. For if a MS. tradition rests on *two* uncial copies dating
from, e.g., the early middle-ages, the archetype dates with more
probability back to late antiquity than in the case that all known MSS.
derive from *one* single early-medieval codex in uncial writing. And as,
ceteris paribus, an archetype dating from, e.g., Jerome's time claims
more confidence regarding the condition of its text than one from
the time of John of Damascus, it adds to the textcritical reliability
of a reconstructed text, if its transmission can be traced back to
more than one uncial copy.

A certain *terminus ante quem*, then, for an archetype is supplied
by variants which can only have arisen from misreadings of majuscule
script: e.g. between E, Θ, O, and C, and between A, Λ, and Δ.[12]

When we turn now to the *Testaments of the Twelve Patriarchs*,
a fine specimen of the first kind of misreading can be registered
in *T. Dan* VI, 6. There the patriarch says: "And it shall be in the
time of the lawlessness of Israel, that the Lord will depart from
them. He will go over to nations, ἐπὶ ἔθνη, that do his will".[13]
Thus family II. In lieu of ἐπὶ ἔθνη, *b* has ὄπισθε, which makes the

---

[10] L. D. Reynolds, N. G. Wilson, *Scribes & Scholars, A Guide to the Transmission of Greek & Latin Literature*, Oxford 1968, p. 52; 1974², p. 53.

[11] A. Dain, *Les manuscrits*, Paris 1964, p. 130.

[12] P. Maas, *op. cit.* (see n. 5), p. 36. For the groups of letters liable to be confused with each other in Greek uncial script, see B. A. van Groningen, *Traité d'histoire et de critique des textes grecs* (Verh. der Kon. Ned. Akad. van Wetensch., Afd. Lett., N.S., LXX, no. 2), Amsterdam 1963, pp. 88-89 and the literature quoted there.

[13] As far as possible I use the English translation of R. H. Charles, *The Testaments of the Twelve Patriarchs* (Translations of Early Documents, Series I, Palestinian Jewish Texts, pre-Rabbinic), London 1917.

sentence incomprehensible : μετελεύσεται ὄπισθε ποιοῦντα τὸ θέλημα αὐτοῦ. For ὄπισθε ποιοῦντα *k* reads ἔμπροσθεν ποιούντων, which is obviously an attempt to improve the sense and the syntax of the corrupted sentence as given by *b*. How to account for ὄπισθε in *b*? That the most plausible explanation is that it is a transcriptional error, follows from a comparison of the words ἐπὶ ἔθνη (or ἔθνει, as it is written in *g*) and ὄπισθεν written in uncials :

$$\text{ΕΠΙΕΘΝΕΙ or -ΝΗ}$$
$$\text{ΟΠΙΣΘΕΝ.}$$

To my mind there is no better explanation for the reading of *b* (ὄπισθε) than that the scribe of one of its ancestors has misread the majuscule script of his model. The reading of family II on the other hand reflects a correct transliteration. Consequently, two different transliterations underlie the textual tradition 'of family I and that of family II.

Misreadings of the same character account for the variants of family I and family II in several other places. So in *T. Jos.* VII, 1. There family II reads : "But still, ἔτι δέ, her heart was addicted to licentiousness ...". Instead of ἔτι δέ, *b* has ὅτι δέ : "But because her heart etc.". As a result of this mistake *b* also omits the conjunction καί which links the sentence quoted above with what follows : "*and* sighing deeply she became downcast". As a matter of fact the mistake may also have been made the other way around. In that case ὅτι (*b*) has been misread to ἔτι (family II) and καί has been added. It is difficult to decide which reading is at the root of the corruption, and which is the result of it, but in any event the corruption is due to misreading of majuscule script. Either ΕΤΙ has been read as ΟΤΙ, or ΟΤΙ as ΕΤΙ.

To a similar mistake *b* owes its reading Βησσους, at least the final sigma of this name, in *T. Jud.* VIII, 2. For here it is clear that not family II, but *b* is at fault. In *b* Judah's wife ("Shua" in Gen. 38,2) is constantly called Βη(σ)σουε, except in the passage under consideration, where her name is Βησσους. In family II her name ends in -σουε, not only in *T. Jud.* VIII,2, but also in X,6; XIII,3; XVI,4 and XVII,1. The reading Βησσους of *b* in *T. Jud.* VIII,2 is best explained as a faulty transcription of ΒΗΣΣΟΥΕ, i.e. as a misreading of majuscule script.

Confusion of the majuscules Ε and Ο has also played a part in the development of the text in *T. Iss.* IV, 5. Here a description is given of how a single-hearted man behaves :

"wrath overmastereth not his wit,
envy melteth not his soul,
neither doth his mind run covetously upon gain".[14]

In *b* (*k defic.*) the last line runs: οὐδὲ πορισμὸν ἐν ἀπληστείᾳ
ἐννοεῖ. The word πορισμός means, in this context, "gain". But
instead of πορισμόν all witnesses of family II have περισπασμόν,
"occupation", usually "toiling occupation", "worry" (e.g. Ecclesi-
astes I, 13 LXX, and especially II,26, cf. *T. Gad* VII,6; in Epict.
III,22,72 περισπασμός is connected with ἀσχολία). The verb ἐννοεῖν,
"think of", here — as often — in the sense of "intending to do,
or to bring about" fits somewhat better with "gain" than with "toiling
occupation", I think, and the same is true for the words ἐν ἀπληστείᾳ,
"in insatiate desire, greediness". But on the other hand the transcriptional evidence is more in favour of περισπασμός. Not so much
on account of the confusion of E and O, which may have worked
in either direction, but because of the close similarity of Π and M
in certain types of uncial script. "Il faut se rappeler qu'à partir du
moment où le tracé de l'écriture [onciale grecque] prit un caractère
cursif, la lettre *mu* se confondit avec la lettre *pi*".[15] Accordingly,
the combinations -CΠ- and -CM- in the word περιCΠαCMος may
have resembled each other very much. This may have caused a *saut
du même au même*, as a result of which the letters -CΠA- were
omitted. This explanation presupposes however that the mistake was
made by a scribe who copied the *Testaments* after an examplar in
uncial script.

Several variant readings have been induced by confusion of A, Δ,
and Λ. A curious instance of this error occurs in *T. Zeb.* I, 1.
According to *b* (*k defic.*), Zebulun spoke his last words to his sons
"*thirty-two* years after the death of Joseph", μετὰ λβ' ἔτη κτλ.
According to family II he did so "*two* years after the death of
Joseph" (μετὰ δύο ἔτη).[16] As early as 1698 J. E. Grabe has observed

---

[14] After the sixteenth-century translation of Arthur Golding, of which I use a copy
of the edition Glasgow 1684.

[15] A. Dain, *Les manuscrits*, Paris 1964, p. 131.

[16] In a foot-note to his German translation in *Jüdische Schriften aus hellenistisch-
römischer Zeit*, III, Gütersloh 1974, J. Becker states: "*bg*: 32". This is incorrect:
in *g* (and in *l*) the words μετά — Ἰωσήφ are missing. Becker has copied the error
from Charles' textcritical apparatus, though he could have observed that Charles'
note 9 contradicts his note 8. Apparently Becker's textual criticism dispenses with
collations.

that the reading δύο of witness *a* should be preferred to the reading λβ' of *b*. In a note he pointed out that "thirty-two" is an error for "two": "male XXXII. pro duobus annis positi sunt". The same conclusion had already been drawn by H. Dodwell,[17] who had examined the chronological information contained in the *Testaments*: "rectius in Graeco 2 annis post mortem Josephi, quam in Latino 32".[18] That the reading λβ' cannot be right, may appear from the following calculation. Joseph died at the age of 110 (Gen. 50,22). Zebulun died when he was 114 (*T. Zeb.* I,1). If Zebulun's death is dated thirty-two years after that of Joseph, the latter would have been born 110 + 32 — 114 = 28 years earlier than Zebulun. But this would contradict Gen. 30, 19-24, where Joseph is supposed to be born later than Zebulun was. If on the contrary Zebulun died only two years after Joseph, the latter would have been born two years after Zebulun. This is a disparity in age between Joseph and Zebulun which is prefectly in keeping with the chronological implications of Gen. 30, 19-24.

How can the lambda have entered into the text? The answer is obvious: it is no more than the repetition of the last letter of the preceding word μετA. It may be clear that the dittography could not simply result in AB', for in that case the interval between Joseph's and Zebulun's death would amount to 1002 years. Yet the mistake is best explained as occasioned by misreading of uncial script.

The same applies to a variant reading in *T. Levi* VI,1. Here it is said that the mountain Aspis, on which Levi saw his vision of the heavens, was near Gebal, to the south of "Abila". The latter geographical name is given by *b* as Ἀβιλα (*k defic.*). Family II reads Ἀβιμα.[19] The variation can be explained in three different ways. Either (1) αβιΛA (*b*) is a haplography of αβιMA misread as αβιΛΛA. Or (2) αβιMA (family II) is a dittography of αβιΛA. Or (3) the primitive reading was αβιΛΛA, and *b* gives a haplographic spelling

---

[17] On Dodwell, see our study "Die Patriarchentestamente von Roger Bacon bis Richard Simon", in this volume pp. 3-42, esp. 32-36.

[18] H. Dodwellus, "Tabula Chronologica contracta de annis Patriarcharum", in Grabe's edition, and in J. A. Fabricius, *Codex Pseudepigraphus V.T.*, I, Hamburg 1722², p. 753.

[19] Thus *g e af*. In *ldm* the two consonants have been transposed. This secondary error may have been induced by the close similarity of bèta and mu in older minuscule script. But it can also have arisen spontaneously: transposition of letters is very common. In *chi* any equivalent to "to the south of Abila" is missing.

-ΛΑ for -ΛΛΑ,[20] whereas family II presents the common misreading of -ΛΛ- as -M-.[21] Whatever may be the error, it was made by a scribe who copied from an uncial.

In *T. Jud.* III,7 the "King of all the kings" whom Jacob slew is called Βεελισα, thus *b* (*k defic.*). According to family II his name was Βεελισαδ, though the final dental is written -τ by *ld*, and -θ by *af chi*. The shorter form ending in -α (*b*) may be an attempt at de-barbarising the giant's name. But it is very possible as well that -A is a haplography of -AΔ, misread as -ΑΑ- — if indeed the reverse is not the case.

If in majuscule script a lambda is followed too closely by an iota the combination may look like the letter nu, especially in majuscule script of a sloping type (ΛΙ ∞ N). Thus in the MSS. of 2 Peter ii.18 οΛΙγως alternates with οΝτως.[22] The reverse of this error has occurred to the scribe of some 'ancestor' of *b*. When he had to copy, in *T. Jos.* XV,3, that Joseph desired greatly, πάΝυ, to weep, he wrote down that he desired again, πάΛιν, to weep. Obviously the scribe who made this error availed himself of a model in majuscule script. Family II has remained free from the error in question.[23] The difference between the readings ΛΗστεύοντα of *b* and ΝΗστευοντα of family II in *T. Ash.* IV,3 must have arisen from a similar oversigt.

Confusion of gamma, iota and tau is usually considered as due to misreading of uncial writing.[24] Yet some caution should be exercised as to this inference. Iota and tau could almost as easily be confused in minuscule writing as in majuscule writing; this is reflected in the many instances of confusion of καί and κατ(ά) definitely of recent date. To quote some examples from only one Testament:

---

[20] The reading -ΙΛΑ for -ΙΛΛΑ is not even a textcritical haplography, but only an orthographical variant. In Greek MSS. the letters for liquids between vowels, especially -λ- and -μ-, are often arbitrarily written single or double.

[21] "If two lambdas were written too close together they could be taken as the letter mu, as has happened at Rom. vi.5, where most MSS. have ΑΛΛΑ ('but') but others have AMA ('together')", B. M. Metzger, *The Text of the N.T.*, Oxford 1968², p. 187.

[22] Metzger, *loc. cit.*

[23] Πάλιν *b* (*k* defic.)] πάνυ *gdm e af ch*, *l om.*, *i incertae lectionis*.

[24] See e.g. B. A. van Groningen, *Traité* (see n. 12), p. 88: "Dans la majuscule on a souvent confondu... I, Γ, et T". On p. 89 Van Groningen points out that especially on papyrus I and T were liable to confusion. Cf. also Dain, *op. cit.*, (n. 15), p. 47.

T. Levi   IX,2 κατά   ] καί *d solus.*

          IX,9 καὶ ἔλεγεν] κατέλεγεν *f solus.*

          XIV,7 καὶ κατά   ] κατά *df,* καί *m.*

          XIV,8 καταπαίξετε] καὶ καταπαίξεται *k solus.*

          XIX,2 κατά   ] καὶ κατά *chi.*

And when in the course of time more and more majuscule forms, among these that of the gamma, crept into the minuscule script and showed themselves side by side with their purely minuscule equivalents,[25] the gamma, too, could give again occasion to confusion with tau and iota. An example of such a recent confusion may be found in *T. Jos.* XII,2 :

γῆς *b, k defic., gldm e af c* (*i incertae lectionis*)] τῆς *h solus.*

Nevertheless a number of variants induced by confusion of gamma, iota and tau may be due to misreading of majuscule writing. For that reason I signalise here three cases in which the reading of family I (in each case = *b*) stands against that of family II.

T. Sim. VIII,4 τῇ (Αἰγ.)   ] γῇ *d e,* τῇ γῇ *l af chi, gm defic.*

T. Jud. I,6   καὶ εὐοδούμενος] κατευοδούμενος *gdl e af chi,*

                                καταιδούμενος *m.*

T. Jos. XIII,8 τῆς (Χαν.)   ] γῆς *gldm e af ch, i incertae lect.*

Finally I cannot refrain from recording a most curious instance of confusion of Π and Γ. Most readers of the Greek Testament will remember the alternative readings in 2 Peter ii.13, where αΠαταις ("deceptions", thus Codex Sinaiticus) stands against αΓαπαις ("love meals", thus Codex Vaticanus). The corruption dates back to the second or third centuries A.D. Much the same transcriptional error disfigures — or rather : adorns — the text of *T. Jud.* XXIII,5. There Juda foretells his sons that in the last times the Lord will visit them with mercy and, according to *b*, with love, εναγαΠη, (to deliver them) from the captivity of their enemies. According to all other witnesses, however, the Lord will visit them with mercy and will bring them up, αναγαΓη, from captivity among the gentiles. I suspect the reading of *b* to be grammatically too unwieldy to be right. But whatever may have been the original reading, there is

---

[25] E. M. Thompson, *Handbook of Greek and Latin Palaeography*, London 1906, p. 161.

a great chance that the corruption has arisen from the misreading of uncial script.

Presumably there are more divergencies between the text of family I and that of family II which can be traced to different interpretations of uncial characters.[26] But among the thirteen instances mentioned so far there may be one that convinces the reader. And one convincing instance suffices to warrant the conclusion that the transliteration underlying *bk* is another than that or those on which the text of all other witnesses rests.

Incidentally it may be observed, that the variant readings mentioned need not have arisen at the very moments of transliteration. Misreading of majuscule script has caused errors as long as majuscules have been copied. A transcriptional error committed by a scribe of e.g. the fourth century may have been copied in the sixth and eight centuries, and thus have been adopted in the copy that happened to serve as basis for transliteration. Mistakes due to misreading of uncials may date back, therefore, to the oldest stages of textual transmission, as is plain from the variant readings of the New Testament referred to above. On the other hand mistakes of this type may have been produced until the ninth century. As a result, the uncial exemplars which were transliterated must have contained each its own reservoir of scribal errors due to misreading of uncials, dating from different stages of the tradition. It is owing to this that one finds the mu confused one time with the double lambda, another time with the pi. These confusions with letters of rather different appearence go back to distinct stages of the tradition. To the errors already extant the scribes who executed the transliteration may have added some others, but this cannot be ascertained.[27]

The variant readings discussed above seem to justify the supposition that the *Testaments of the Twelve Patriarchs* have been transliterated at least twice from majuscule into minuscule writing. From this it follows that the archetype of the textual tradition of the *Testaments* must be earlier than the ninth century.

I have not found a clue for establishing whether the two trans-

---

[26] E.g. *T. Gad* IV,5 μῖϹΟϹ ΕΝεργεῖ *b*, *k defic.*] μῖϹΟϹ ϹυΝεργεῖ *gdm e af chi, l contaminatus legit ut b*.

[27] Somewhat too optimistic on the other hand is Dain's judgment: "On devra admettre, en effet, qu'on ne commit qu'exceptionnellement des fautes de lecture de ce genre au moment même de la translittération, cette opération ayant été, en principe, un travail critique". (*Op. cit.*, see n. 15, p. 131).

literations have been executed after one examplar or after two. If one accepts the assumption generally made — for which there is indeed much to be said — that in case of two transliterations they were effectuated "dans des centres indépendants les uns des autres, et ... à des dates éloignées", there is some likelihood that two different uncial codices underlie the surviving MS. tradition, and that the archetype dates back to late antiquity.[28] But this is no more than a vague sort of general probability.

It is true that the reader of the *Testaments* need no longer feel bound to suspect their reconstructed text of being later than the ninth century (what had never been proved so far). But on the other hand he cannot be sure either that their text dates back beyond the Middle Ages. It need not be remembered again that prior to the ninth century the copies of the *Testaments* may have differed as widely from each other as they did after that century. One cannot but draw the conclusion, that there are no longer grounds for excessive pessimism[29] as to the degree of reliability one can hope to attain in reconstructing the text of the *Testaments*. Yet an archetype of which no more can be said than that it is prior to the ninth century cannot warrant the reconstructed text to be congruent in all details with the authentic ancient Christian recension of the book.

I may be allowed to add some remarks to this conclusion.

(1) At one or two places the text of the *Testaments* turns out to be corrupt in all witnesses without exception. This is the case, e.g., in *T. Zeb.* IV,1.[30] Such corruptions affecting the whole tradition can be taken as conjunctive errors of all witnesses. They prove that

---

[28] One would be tempted to locate this archetype in the famous library at Caesarea. The basis of this library, built up by Pamphilus (d. 309) and specialised in Christian literature, had been the works left by Origen. Origen is the earliest known reader of the *Testaments* (Schürer, *loc. cit.*, see n. 8). The second father to quote the *Testaments*, Jerome, tells himself that he has done research in the library at Caesarea. (He consulted Origen's *Hexapla* there). At Bethlehem he was constantly adding to his store of books. Perhaps he has disposed of a MS. of the *Testaments* copied from that in the library at Caesarea.—All this is possible, but no more than that.

[29] I admittedly shared this pessimism with only a very few readers of the *Testaments*, but it is hardly likely that their optimism rests on better grounds than my pessimism did.

[30] I propose to read the sentence as follows: Μετὰ ταῦτα ἔλαβον ἐσθίειν ἐκεῖνοι. For ἔλαβον ἐσθίειν, cf. Euripides' *Cyclop* 561 ὅπως λήψει πιεῖν. The confusion of λαβ- and βαλ- is one of the most common in Greek MSS. In copying the *Testaments* scribes have gone so far as to replace the name of Βάλλα with that of Λαβάν (*T. Rueb.* III,13 Βάλλα]Λαβά *i*; *T. Napht.* I,12 Βάλλαν]Λάβαν *a*).

the whole MS tradition derives from one single archetype in which
the corruptions at issue already figured. In case all witnesses can
be traced back to a single archetype, some critics speak of the tradition
as being "closed".[31] Others however reserve the term "closed" for
traditions springing from one transliteration and from one minuscule
archetype.[32] Only if more transliterations have to be postulated, they
consider the tradition as open. The reason for this is that, if a text
has been transliterated twice, the archetype does claim to be earlier
than the ninth century, but cannot be dated more exactly. In that
case it is impossible to mark the place of the archetype in a genealogical
table or stemma of which one axis expresses the progress of time.
Nor can one draw the lines suggesting the dependence of the hyparchetypes on the archetype.[33] As a result the top of the stemma
is missing, or, to put it less awkwardly, the tradition is open. The
tradition of the *Testaments*, then, is closed in the sense that it can
be traced back to a single archetype; but it is open in the sense
that the archetype, apart from being prior to the ninth century,
cannot be dated with any precision.

(2) The main inference drawn so far from the alternative readings
in which family I stands against family II, is that the textual tradition
of the *Testaments* goes back to two distinct transliterations. But the
evidence seems to confirm at the same time that the tradition is
split into two and no more than two branches or families: that
of *bk* and that of all other witnesses.

True, it is possible that in all thirteen instances which I adduced,
b(k) are at fault. It would follow, first, that in none out of those
thirteen instances the reading of the remaining witnesses can be taken
for an indication of a common source on which *bk* do not depend,
and second, that *gldmeafnchi* do not constitute a family. But if it
be supposed that *gldmeafnchi* form no family opposed to *bk*, one
has to presume that groups like *gldm* and *eafnchi* (or worse: *gldm*,
eaf and *nchi*) go back to distinct transliterations: distinct not
only from that to which we owe *bk*, but also from each other.

---

[31] Reynolds-Wilson, *op. cit.* (n. 10), ed. 1968, p. 144; 1974², p. 193, cf. p. 248,
first paragraph.

[32] Dain, *op. cit.* (n. 15), pp. 130 and 132.

[33] The obvious solution, to my opinion, is that stemmas be provided with a
simple marginal chronological scale that indicates the centuries (s. X, s. XI, s. XII, etc.)
only for those events in the textual history concerned which are datable. Where no
chronological information is supplied in the margin, the stemma should be supposed
to imply nothing as to the chronology of the textual history.

In theory the possibility cannot be excluded that *gldm* and *eafnchi* do go back to two different transliterations. But this possibility can only be substantiated by a list of alternative readings of *gldm* and *eafnchi*, which must have resulted from misreading of uncial writing, — in the way I have demonstrated above for *bk* as against all other witnesses.

As a matter of fact I have deemed it my duty to look for such readings as might prove that *eaf* etc. represent another transliteration than *gldm* do. But so far I have not found any of them.

As long as no differences between *gldm* and *eafnchi* are found which are definitely due to misreading of uncial script, the supposition that *gldm* and *eafnchi* represent different transliterations remains without any foundation. As things are one cannot but assume that *gldmeafnchi* go back to a single transliteration.

Now going back to a single transliteration means nothing less than deriving from a single minuscule codex. And witnesses deriving from a codex on which other witnesses are independent, form what in textual criticism is termed a family. The conclusion is inescapable that *gldmeafnchi*, together with the Armenian, Slavonic and Serbian translations, form a family deriving from a single ninth- or tenth-century minuscule codex.

(3) Still, the minuscule codex referred to in the end of the preceding paragraph has another surprise in store for the critics of the *Testaments of the Twelve Patriarchs*. It provides the inevitable *terminus post quem* for the Armenian translation. This translation cannot possibly be earlier than the ninth century.

(4) Nothing is known with certainty of the circumstances under which the transliterations of the *Testaments* have been undertaken. But there are signs that at least one of the two, *viz.* that to which *b* and *k* owe their text, has been accomplished at Constantinople.

As for *b*, this witness is contained in a tenth-century codex. In an earlier article I have shown that this codex is very likely to have belonged to the library of Michael Choniates, metropolitan of Athens from 1182 A.D. From Choniates's letters we know that he had been collecting books ever since his studies at the Patriarchal Academy [34]

---

[34] See on this institution F. Fuchs, *Die höheren Schulen von Konstantinopel im Mittelalter* (Byzantinisches Archiv 8), Stuttgart 1926, repr. Amsterdam 1964, pp. 47-48, and Τ. ᾽Α. Γριτσοπούλου, Πατριαρχικὴ Μεγάλη τοῦ Γένους Σχολή, τόμ. Α᾽, (Βιβλιοθήκη τῆς ἐν ᾽Αθήναις Φιλεκπαιδευτικῆς ῾Εταιρείας 37), ᾽Αθῆναι 1966.

at Constantinople. On his elevation to the bishopric at some distance from the capital, he took his library with him. Though the possibility cannot be excluded that Michael Choniates acquired his codex containing, among other writings, the *Testaments of the Twelve Patriarchs*, when already residing at Athens, there is a reasonable chance that he brought it with him from Constantinople.

It should be observed that *b* has not directly been copied from a MS. in uncial script. In fact, several errors of *b* are best explained as arisen from misreading of minuscule script. In *T. Dan* IV,3, e.g., *b* reads κινεῖσθε in lieu of μὴ κινεῖσθε as correctly preserved in all other witnesses. The error of *b* would seem to indicate that the mu of μή has been misread as a kappa — an obvious and common confusion in early minuscule hands — and that this induced a *saut du même au même* resulting in the omission of μή. In certain minuscule hands the alpha and the omega bear a striking resemblance to each other. In *T. Zeb.* IX,6 this has occasioned a *saut du même au même* in the word κακωθήσεσθε, which in my opinion is the correct reading. The witnesses *c* and *d*[35] have the lipography καθή-σεσθε, independently of *b* that has καθίσεσθε. The reading ἔσται ὡς of *bk* in *T. Dan* VI,6 looks much like a transcriptional error for ἔσται ἴσος as given by other MSS. If so, the error is most likely due to the misreading of a minuscule exemplar, in which a sigma and an omicron, written too close together, could easily be taken for an omega closed at its top.

Apparently, *b* is not the 'autograph' of the man who executed the transliteration. Still there is some reason to suppose that this 'autograph', too, has been extant somewhere in the capital and has proliferated there. For when about 1250 the monastery of Prodromos-Petra at Constantinople procured or acquired a MS. of the *Testaments*, its text (*k*)[36] happened to be very closely related to that of Choniates's copy. True, this may be no more than a coincidence. But it may also indicate that Constantinople had something like a local text of the *Testaments*, emanated from a local transliteration brought about during

---

[35] As *hi* and Ngr. present the reading of the majority of the MSS., the reading of *c* is not distinctive of α. It cannot be ascertained, therefore, whether the agreement between *c* and *d* at this place is due to contamination or not (*k m defic.*).

[36] On the provenance of MS. Marc. gr. 494 (*k*) from the Prodromos-Petra monastery in Constantinople, see our note "Additional notes on the History of MSS. Bibl. Marc. gr. 494 (*k*) and Cambridge Univ. Libr., Ff. 1.24 (*b*)", Ch. VI in this volume.

the Photian Renaissance. As is well-known there are grounds for thinking that the process of transliterating Greek literature originated as a whole in the capital.

The hypothesis that *b* and *k* represent a Constantinopolitan transliteration, distinguished from that accomplished somewhere else on which all other witnesses depend, would perfectly account for the MS. tradition of the *Testaments* being bifurcate.

To preserve myself from launching wilder conjectures than I have made so far, I close at this point. Some observations on the bifurcate character of the transmission of the text of the *Testaments*, will be added in an appendix to this paper. Here I confine myself to sum up the main conclusions reached in the above.

(1) The *Testaments of the Twelve Patriarchs* have been transliterated twice from majuscule into minuscule writing. One transliteration is represented by *bk*, the remaining witnesses reflect a different transliteration.

(2) The archetype or last common source of the surviving textual tradition was a MS. in uncial script, earlier than the ninth century; it cannot be dated more precisely, however.

(3) A faithfully established text of the *Testaments* need no longer be suspected of representing no more than the capriciously corrupted text of some indeterminate ninth- or tenth-century minuscule. Still one cannot be sure that the reconstructed text dates back beyond the Middle Ages. Such a gap of centuries separating the original ancient Christian book from its reconstruction, inevitably impairs the reliability of the reconstruction, even if it is the best obtainable.

(4) The witnesses *gldmeafnchi* seem to go back to a single transliteration and consequently constitute a family undependent of *bk*. This confirms the hypothesis, grounded till now on textcritical evidence only, that the textual tradition of the *Testaments* is split into two families : that of *bk* and that of all remaining witnesses.

(5) If conclusion 4. holds good, the Armenian translation cannot be earlier than the ninth century.

(6) Perhaps the transliteration to which *b* and *k* owe their text has been effectuated at Constantinople.

APPENDIX

THE RELATION BETWEEN *bk* AND ALL OTHER WITNESSES

That the textual tradition of the *Testaments* is split into two branches
and "die älteste Spaltung der Überlieferung gerade zwischen *bk* und
allen anderen Handschriften liegt", was one of the conclusions of an
article which I wrote in 1970, and which was published in *ZNW* 63
of 1972 (in this volume pp. 45-62). In 1974, J. Becker criticised my
position in the introduction to his German translation of the *Testaments*
(see n. 16); he has not presented, however, the single argument which
would disprove my thesis, i.e. that the determinative errors upon
which my argument is based are not in fact errors but original
readings. Moreover, his own translation reflects and confirms time
and again my view on the relation between *bk* and the other witnesses — as I shall demonstrate presently.

§1.

First of all it should be clear once and for all that in textual
criticism no group of witnesses can be called a family, unless they
share one or more errors not occurring in other witnesses. I say
errors, not readings. For only common errors are the indication of
a common ancestor, whereas correct readings may occur in any
witnesses, without indicating anything about their relationship. For
that reason good readings are worthless for the determination of
relationships between witnesses. B. is astray, therefore, in defining
a family as "ein Sammelbecken für konstitutive Gemeinsamkeiten",
whatever precisely that may be. Neither common features in general,
nor common readings, nor the mere fact that witnesses "gemeinsam
stehen gegen" other ones, but exclusively common errors prove
that witnesses belong to a family.

In the article referred to above I adduced three conjunctive errors
of the witnesses *gldm e af chi* which, if they are really errors,
necessarily prove that these witnesses derive from one common source.
Otherwise it is impossible to explain how a corruption that is not
likely to arise more than once, occurs in more than one witness.
At the same time these corruptions prove that *bk* form a group
independent from *gldm e af chi*; for how could *bk* be free from
the errors occurring in witnesses on which they depend? The three
corruptions I pointed to were the following:

(1) *T. Levi* VIII,1 πρᾶγμα *bk*] ὅραμα *gldm e af chi*. In my opinion it can be argued that πρᾶγμα (*bk*) is the correct reading, and that all other witnesses present here a *lectio facilior* dictated by the apocalyptic context. In support of the reading πρᾶγμα (*bk*) I cited *Henoch graece* XXI,2 ἔργον, to which I now add a parallel from the *Visions*(!) of Hermas 12, 1 : Κυρία, μεγάλως καὶ θαυμαστῶς ἔχει τὸ πρᾶγμα τοῦτο. If πρᾶγμα is the correct reading, *gldm e af chi* are at fault and — barring unforeseen circumstances — derive from a common source on which *bk* cannot be dependent. — Though I think that there is a good case for the correctness of πρᾶγμα (*bk*), I admit that no one could be blamed for thinking differently. In B's translation the passage in question reads : '... sah ich wiederum einen Traum'. This implies that B. accepts the reading ὅραμα as original. Accordingly, B. cannot be expected to regard the reading of *gldm e af chi* as evidence for a common source from which *bk* are independent. In both following instances, however, he can.

(2) *T. Levi* IX,14 ἀπαρχάς *bk*] + τῷ κυρίῳ *omnes ceteri* (for details, see above, p. 50, n. 14). B's translation does not render the words added in all witnesses except *bk*. In a foot-note B. justifies his translation of *bk* as follows : "So *bk*. Alle anderen : + dem Herrn (Einfluss aus Vers 13)". Consequently, B. agrees with me that from a textcritical point of view the addition in *gldm e af chi* is an error. But the obvious conclusion which B. should draw as well is, that *bk* cannot depend on the common source of all other witnesses, and thus, that *bk* and *gldmeafchi* form two independent families. From B.'s preference for the reading of *bk* it follows, that the textual history of the *Testaments* is bifurcate, an early split separating *bk* and all other witnesses. The same conclusion may be drawn from the third example.

(3) *T. Zeb.* IV,9 οὗτος *b*] + καὶ ἐποίησαν οὕτως *omnes ceteri*. B.'s translation is a rendering of the shorter text in *b*. In a foot-note B. states : "Alle ausser *b* fügen an : Und sie taten so. Der Satz nimmt Vers 13b vorweg und steht vor Vers 10-12 zu früh". So according to B. himself, *b* preserves the original text, and all other witnesses are faulty. Now it is impossible that the error at issue has been made more than once. It must come from a common source. Consequently, B. will have to admit that *gldmeafchi* constitute a family to which *b* is not related.

In view of B's decisions on the variants 2. and 3. discussed above, he cannot avoid postulating a family *gldmeafchi* = family II, clearly distinguished from *bk* = family I by the errors he himself has detected. Possibly he could not accept this conclusion on the authority of only two errors in *gldmeafchi*. But fortunately it appears from his translation that he has found a great many other separative errors of *gldmeafchi* as against *bk*. In at least twenty other instances, which will be listed below, B. is of the opinion that *gldmeafchi* present a common corruption of the text correctly preserved by *b(k)*.

§ 2.

B. states that I have a high estimation of the value ("Hoch-schätzung") of *bk*. However, this more accurately reflects his own inclination. I have found only two or three readings of *bk* which I would favour over those in family II and I have stated only that the α-text is a late and free recension of the text as presented by the prototype of *af*. Apart from this evaluation of α, I have not expressed any general preference for any family or any witness, but exclusively for certain readings. B. seems to be under the misconception that, if *b* and *k* are regarded as a family opposed to all other witnesses, their text is generally superior to that of the remaining witnesses. But this does not follow at all. In all individual instances of *bk* deviating from *gldmeafnchi* one has to decide which branch of the tradition preserves the authentic (or at least: the least corrupt) reading, and in most of these instances the reading of *bk* proves to be inferior to that of *gldmeafnchi*. I am not even sure now that all three examples of common errors in *gldmeafnchi* mentioned above in §1 still hold (in *T. Zeb.* IV,9, e.g., M. de Jonge rightly prefers the longer text, see Ch. X in this symposium), though I do think that there are three other errors common to *gldmeaf(n)chi* (two decisive separative errors of *gldmeafchi*, proving that *bk* cannot depend on *gldmeafchi*, are mentioned by Th. Korteweg in Ch. XI, p. 171, n. 20.). If accepting three readings of *bk* as correct amounts to "Hoch-schätzung" of these witnesses, what are we to say of B. himself, who at least twenty-two times has preferred the text of *b(k)* to that of all or most other witnesses? It may be worth while to list here the readings in *b(k)* which B. authorises, and to oppose them to those of the other witnesses which he rejects, as at least a number among these compel B. to admit, firstly, that *gldmeafchi* derive from a common source on which *bk* do not depend, and secondly, that the group of witnesses formerly designated with the siglum β must be dissolved into two independent families : *bk* (family I) and *gldmeaf*, now linked with the group α (family II). In a third paragraph I shall have to say a few words on the authorship of this theory. The list I append here does not pretend to be exhaustive.

T. Levi IX,14	(*vide supra*, p. 81).
T. Zeb. IV,9	(*vide supra*, p. 81).
T. Sim. III,1	τέκνα *b*, Becker "Kinder"] + μου *gldm e af hi, c. om., k sua sponte ut gldm etc.*
T. Sim. IV,6	καί² *solus b, k deficit*, Becker "und (ehrte)"] *gldm e af chi om.*
T. Levi IX,1	ἀνέβημεν *bk*, Becker "zogen"] ἀνέβην *gldm af chi*, ἀνέβαινον *e*.
ib. XVII,2	*asyndetice* ἐν (τῷ πρ. Ἰωβ.) *b, k defic.*, Becker "Im"] καὶ ἐν *g e af chi, dm defic., l contaminatus ut b*.
T. Jud. XXIV,3	πορεύσεσθε *b*, Becker "werdet wandeln"] πορεύεσθε *gld e, afchi defic., k sua sponte ut gld e, m sua sponte ut b*.
T. Zeb. V,5	ἐν τῇ Χαναάν *b, k defic.*, Becker "in Kanaan"] εἰς γῆν Χαναάν *gl*, ἐν γῇ Χαναάν *dm e af* Slav. *chi*.
T. Dan II,4	*asyndetice* διά *b, k defic.*, Becker "Durch"] καὶ διά *gld e af chi, m defic.*
T. Gad I,5	πατέρα αὐτοῦ *b, k defic.*, Becker "seinem Vater", *adnotans* : "So *b*, A. α, β-*b* : unserem (Angleichung an Vers 6)"] πατέρα ἡμῶν *gldm e af chi*.
T. Gad V,2	τὸ μῖσος *b, k defic.*, Becker "den Hass", *adnotans* : "So nur *b*. ...*b* wird im Recht sein : διάβολος haftet nur in der ehedem selbständigen Ueberlieferung TN 8, 4.8 fest im Textbestand..., und τὸ διαβολικόν wird unter Einfluss aus Vers 1 entstanden sein."] + τοῦ διαβόλου *gldm e af*, + τὸ διαβολικόν *chi*.
T. Gad V,5	ἐννοιῶν *b*, k *defic.*, Becker "Gedanken" *numero plurali (cur non* "in seinem Denken" *num. sing.?)*] ἐννοίας *gdm e af ch, i lectionis incertae, l def.*
T. Ash. II,8	καὶ πορνεύει *b, k defic.*, Becker "und treibt Hurerei"] *asyndetice* πορνεύει *gdm e af chi, l contaminatus ut b*.
T. Ash. III,1	ὅτι *b, k defic.*, Becker "denn"] + καί *gldm e af*, + κύριος *chi, l contaminatus ut b*.
T. Jos. XII,1	κατ' ἐκεῖνον *b, k defic.*, Becker : "In jener (Zeit)"] + δέ *gdm af ch, praem.* καί *l, e sua sponte ut b, i defic.*
T. Benj. III,1	Καί¹ *b, k defic.*, Becker "Und (jetzt)" (*cur non* "Nun denn" = νῦν οὖν *g c?*)] *omnes ceteri om., l hi defic.*
T. Benj. IV,5	συνεργεῖ *b, k defic.*, Becker "gibt er Hilfe"] συντρέχει *omnes ceteri* (συντρέχειν = "jems. Partei nehmen"), *m a chi defic.*

T. Benj. IX,2	μονογενοῦς *bk*, Becker "Einziggeborenen", *adnotans* "So *b* ..."] + προφήτου *gld e af*, + υἱοῦ αὐτοῦ *c, hi defic.*
T. Benj. X,4	ἐποίησαν *bk*, Becker "taten"] ἐποίησε(ν) *omnes ceteri, m hi defic.*
T. Benj. X,10	ἀδελφοὺς αὐτῶν *bk*, Becker "ihre Brüder"] αὐτὸν ἀδελφούς *g*, ἀδελφοὺς αὐτοῦ *l*, ἀδελφοῦ αὐτῶν *ef*, ἀδελφὸν αὐτῶν *a, m chi defic.*
T. Jud. III,7	Βεελισᾶ *b, k defic.*, Becker "Belisa", *adnotans* : "Alle verschiedenen Namensformen in den MSS. sind wohl corr aus *bă͏ᵉăl šijlō*, d.h. Herr von Silo ..."] Βεελισάς *g*, Βελιάτ *d*, Βελισάβετ *l*, Βεηλισάδ *e*, Βελισάθ *af chi*.
T. Levi VI,1	Ἀβιλᾶ *b, k defic.*, Becker "Abila", *adnotans* : "Die Ortsbestimmung fehlt in α. Da die Hauptstadt Abila der Tetrarchie Abilene geographisch abwegig ist, ist eine Identifizierung nicht möglich"] Ἀβιμᾶ *g e af*, Ἀμιβᾶ *ldm, chi om*.

§ 3.

According to B., I have tried, "offenbar ohne Kenntnis von Hultgårds Arbeit ... ein Stemma für G (= the Greek witnesses) zu erstellen". But in the first place I am not at all interested in a stemma. The only thing I have tried to do is to establish the interrelationships between witnesses. The diagram which I added has no value in itself. It is intended only to be a summary of my conclusions and an aid for the reader. Criticism, however, should be levelled at my argumentation, not at the diagram.

Secondly, how could I have known in 1970 Hultgård's dissertation of 1971? And that I wrote the article to which B. refers in 1970, is clear enough from its second sentence.

Now B. states that Hultgård has proposed to dissolve the family formerly designated as β in various smaller groups. In order to prevent Hultgård from being charged with a theory which he did not develop, I cannot refrain from inserting at this place the postscript which I wrote on the appearance of Hultgård's dissertation, but was suggested, from various sides, not to publish.

"Nachtrag. Nach Abschluss des Manuskripts erschien die Dissertation von A. Hultgård, *Croyances messianiques des Test. XII Patr. Critique textuelle et commentaire des passages messianiques* (maschinenschr. Dissert.), Uppsala 1971. Der erste Teil des ersten Kapitels (S. 1-21) handelt vom griechischen Text der Testamente, speziell vom "groupement des manuscrits grecs". Jedoch, was H. seine Methode nennt (l'éclectisme, S. 5), ist bei ihm nichts als Willkür. Ich verstehe nicht, warum man, wenn sich das Abhängigkeitsverhältnis zwischen den Zeugen grössten-

teils einwandfrei aufzeigen lässt, auf die feste Grundlage der genealogischen
recensio verzichten soll. H. beschuldigt die genealogische Methode, "par le moyen
de la critique externe" zu operieren (S. 8), aber seine "critique interne" besteht
darin, dass er beliebig ausgewählte Lesarten zur Grundlage seiner Überlegungen
macht. [See now above n. 6]. Ich hätte die Darstellungen H.'s mit Stillschweigen
übergangen, wenn er nicht unerwarteterweise zu einigen Ergebnissen gekommen
wäre, die mir bekannt vorkamen : "Résumons... Il n'est plus exact de parler
de deux groupes (familles) qui s'opposent : α et β. α = c h i est certainement une
famille et selon toute vraisemblance également les mss d l m". (S. 21). Diesen
Schluss nun kann H. unmöglich aus seinen eigenen Analysen gezogen haben.
Er entnimmt ihn — wie er selber mit Recht in einer Fussnote angibt — einem
Vortrag, den M. de Jonge September 1970 zu Uppsala gehalten hat. In diesem
Vortrag [see now *Svensk Exegetisk Årsbok* 36, 1971, pp. 77-96] hat M. de Jonge
mit meiner Genehmigung auf das Manuskript meiner Arbeit "Die Textüberlieferung...". Bezug genommen. Nur daher kommt die auf den ersten Blick
befremdende Übereinstimmung der von H. erzielten Resultaten mit den meinen.
Dass H. selber mit diesen Ergebnissen nocht nicht völlig vertraut ist, erhellt
daraus, dass er fortfährt : "Un groupement à part est constitué par les mss *b* d g
k l (m)" [my italics], obwohl die älteste Spaltung gerade zwischen *bk* und *gldm*
liegt!".

§4.

There are eleven other instances of confusion, misrepresentation
and misconception in B's section of three and a half pages on the
textual criticism of the *Testaments*. One of them I should like to
correct here. In B's opinion my stemma is "zu einfach angesichts
der komplizierten Textgeschichte. Dies betrifft ... vor allem auch die
angenommene allzu gradlinige Rückführung der Hyparchetypen". As a
matter of fact there may lie an inlimited number of copies between
the different points of the tradition where splits occurred, and between
the final points of splitting and the surviving witnesses. But as far
as the textual transmission of the *Testaments* is concerned, it is
methodically impossible to prove that there have existed more intermediate copies than I have marked in my earlier stemma with the
numbers 1, 4, 6, 7, 9, 13, 15, 16, 18, 21=α, 23, 25, 26, and 35,
to which can be added the last common source of d and Fm^d and
the last common source of Arm. and e Slav. *af* α. There is no
evidence to prove that more than sixteen intermediate copies existed,
except the one or two uncial codices underlying the transliterations
to which family I and family II owe their texts. Contamination
can be established in *l, d,* and *m.* But further complications

in the textual history of the *Testaments* cannot be demonstrated. I cannot rid myself of the impression, therefore, that the alleged complexity of this history is little more than an excuse for arbitrariness.

IV

LES FRAGMENTS MARGINAUX DANS LE MS. *d*
DES TESTAMENTS DES XII PATRIARCHES

H. J. DE JONGE

Le moine copiste qui vers l'an 1195 [1]) dans un des monastères de l'Italie méridionale [2]) achevait [3]) le manuscrit que nous désignons

[1]) A la fin du *T. Beni.*, *f.* 379 v., directement au dessous de la dernière ligne, on trouve la date ἔτει ,ςψγʹ (= 1194/5). F. C. CONYBEARE, qui a été le premier à rendre accessible le texte de *d*, n'a pas manqué de noter cette date; vide 'The Testaments of the XII Patriarchs', *Jew. Quat. Rev.* 13 (Jan. 1901), p. 258; p. 274. Pour son édition critique des *Test. XII Patr.*, CHARLES n'a pas voulu se fier aux collations de *d* publiées par CONYBEARE, mais a préféré se référer à des photos. C'est pourquoi cette souscription lui a échappé, et qu'il a fait de *d* un ms. du XIIIᵉ siècle. Il fut suivi en cela par plusieurs autres savants. Selon CONYBEARE, *art. cit.*, p. 258, la note ἔτει ,ςψγʹ est de la main du (dernier) copiste du ms. C'était également l'opinion de K. et S. LAKE (vide infra). G. GARITTE (vide n. 2) croit que la datation est d'une main différente des trois qui se sont partagé la transcription du texte. Comme CONYBEARE, GARITTE voit dans la date en question l'indication de l'année où le ms. a été terminé. Quoi qu'il en soit, nous avons ici un *terminus ad quem*. Une belle reproduction de la feuille avec la date se trouve dans l'œuvre de K. et S. LAKE, *Dated Greek Minuscule MSS. to the year 1200*, VIII, *MSS. in Rome*, Part II, Boston-Massachusetts 1937, Plate 600.

[2]) Le ms. vient probablement de Calabre. Dans son excellente description du *Vat gr.* 1238, 'Deux mss. italo-grecs, (Vat. gr. 1238 et Barber. gr. 475)', dans *Misc. G. Mercati* III (Studi e testi 123), C. d. Vaticano 1946, 16-40, G. GARITTE parle aussi de l'histoire et de la provenance de notre ms. (p. 17-19). Les souscriptions, l'écriture et l'ornementation l'ont mené à la conclusion que le *Vat. gr.* 1238 est d'origine italo-grecque. Une indication supplémentaire, qui semble confirmer la provenance italienne de *d*, pourrait être tirée d'une des variantes dans le texte des *Test. XII Patr.*, que nous nous permettons de signaler ici. On sait que jusqu'au XIVᵉ siècle certaines églises de Calabre ont résisté à la latinisation progressive de leur province ecclésiastique. Or, dans cette lutte de langues le scribe grec de *d* a, lui aussi, dû faire une concession. En copiant le *T. Juda*, où Juda raconte, en VII, 3, que, faisant la guerre à une ville des Cananéens, il sut ouvrir de nuit τὰς πύλας de la ville, notre scribe écrit qu'il ouvrit τὰς πόρτας! — Evidemment cet erreur est imputable à un relâchement de l'attention chez le scribe, que chaque lecteur des *res gestae* de Juda — sans doute le passage le plus fastidieux des *Testaments* — lui pardonnera volontiers. Mais le latinisme n'en est pas moins significatif, quoiqu'on puisse nous objecter à bon droit — comme l'a fait J. SMIT SIBINGA — que dans le grec du moyen-âge le mot πόρτα n'est point rare; cf. Car. DU FRESNE, dom. DU CANGE, *Glossarium ad scriptores mediae & infimae graecitatis* ..., Lugduni 1688, s.v. πόρτα: ... Occurrit passim; et E. A. SOPHOCLES, *Greek Lexicon of the Roman and Byzantine Periods*, s.v. πόρτα: ... = πύλη. Dans la langue parlée grecque d'aujourd'hui πόρτα est le mot usuel pour „porte".

aujourd'hui par la signature *Vat. gr.* 1238 et, dans la critique textuelle
des *Test. XII Patr.*, par le sigle *d*, n'a pas fait son travail pour rien.
Les marges du manuscrit conservent toujours les traces de plusieurs
lecteurs qui se sont intéressés aux dernières paroles des fils de Jacob,
telles qu'ils les trouvaient transmises dans ce manuscrit-ci.

Apparemment ces lecteurs ne se sont pas seulement intéressés aux
passages christologiques dont, au cours du livre, une trentaine avait
été indiquée en marge par un τοῦ χριστοῦ [1]). Parmi eux on rencontre
aussi le pessimiste qui, en lisant les trois premiers chapîtres du *T. Rub.*,
a noté en marge κατὰ τοῦ ἀνθρώπου (II, 2), κατὰ τοῦ ὕπνου (III, 4),
κατὰ τῶν γυναικῶν (III, 10) [2]). Pour un autre lecteur de *d*, les
Testaments formaient une source de renseignements sur l'histoire
sainte: c'était lui qui, s'étonnant d'un passage corrompu (*T. Levi*
XII, 3) d'après lequel les fils de Μεραρί (*d* Μεθαρή) ne s'appelaient
pas Μοολὶ καὶ 'Ομουσί, [3]), mais Μααλή, Μωυσὴ καὶ 'Ααρῶν, a ajouté
la note marginale: ὁ πατὴρ τοῦ μωύσεως μεθαρή (*f*. 357 r.).

Mais il va sans dire que maint lecteur des *Testaments* contenus
dans le *Vat. gr.* 1238 a été captivé surtout par les prophéties messianiques qu'il y trouvait. Aussi la lecture de ces passages a stimulé
l'un d'entre eux à en comparer le texte avec celui d'un autre manuscrit,
ce qui l'a incité à récrire quatre passages de teneur prophétique dans
les marges du manuscrit *d* [4]). C'est à ces passages que nous voudrions
prêter quelque attention dans ces pages.

Les passages qui nous intéressent se trouvent aux *ff*. 352 r., *marg.
sup.*; 362 v., *marg. sup.*; 371 v., *marg. inf.* et 373 r., *marg. inf.* Leur texte

---

[3]) Avant de copier le *Test. de Job* et les *Test. XII* Patr. (*ff*. 340 r.-379 v.), le
même scribe avait déjà écrit le texte des *ff*. 206 r.-216 v., 249 r.-260 v., et 277 r.-330 v.
(livres historiques de l'A.T.). Deux autres copistes sont responsables du reste
de ce ms. (GARITTE, *art. cit.*, p. 17).

[1]) D'une main qu'on peut identifier avec celle du scribe du ms. lui-même. De
la même main sont les indications marginales τῆς θεοτόκου (*f*. 377 r., *T. Jos.* XIX, 8)
et παῦλος (*f*. 379 v., *T. Beni.* XI, 2). De plus, le scribe du ms. a utilisé les marges
onze fois pour y apporter des corrections ou un ὡραῖον (*f*. 356 r., *T. Levi* IX, 14)
etc.

[2]) A la même main sont dues les notes marginales: ἄρτος ἐπιθυμίας (I, 10),
περὶ τῶν ἑπτὰ πνευμάτων (II, 2) et ἔτι περὶ πνευμάτων (III, 3).

[3]) Ainsi *b*. Cf. Ex. 6, 19 et 20 LXX.

[4]) Peut-être la note marginale θεὸν καὶ ἄνθρωπον qui se lit au verso du *f*. 353
(*T. Sim.* VII, 2) a été écrite par la même main. Comme cette citation du *T. Sim.*
ne présente pas de variante, nous la laisserons de côté. Noter cependant que le
thème de cette note correspond à celui des quatre textes marginaux qui sont le
sujet de cet article.

est assez difficile à déchiffrer. L'écriture est une cursive peu soignée, fourmillant d'abréviations, et certainement d'une main exercée. L'encre avec laquelle les additions ont été écrites est d'une teinte brune pâle et irrégulière, çà et là un peu plus noire, mais presque jamais aussi foncée que celle du texte principal [1]).

Chacun des quatre fragments se termine par la traduction latine, écrite par la même main, des premières paroles.

Pour la datation de ces additions marginales, nous avons jugé sage de consulter Mgr. P. CANART de la Biblioteca Apostolica Vaticana. Abstraction faite des additions latines, il aurait daté l'écriture grecque soit du XIVe, soit du XVe siècle; mais l'écriture latine n'est pas antérieure au milieu du XVe siècle, et serait plutôt de la fin du XVe ou du début du XVIe [2]). Comme le codex a appartenu à la collection de manuscrits que le Cardinal Bibliothécaire Antoine CARAFA (mort le 14 janvier 1591) légua à la Bibliothèque Vaticane [3]), les textes marginaux dans le *Vat. gr.* 1238 ont été écrits un siècle à peu près avant que le manuscrit ne fût incorporé dans la bibliothèque pontificale. Malheureusement on ne sait qu'imparfaitement quelle a été l'histoire du manuscrit entre 1195 et 1591....

L'étendue de ces passages étant assez restreinte, nous croyons pouvoir donner ici leur texte intégral. Nous écrivons *plene* les abréviations et les contractions, normalisons l'orthographe, l'accentuation et la ponctuation, et nous ajoutons les numéros des paragraphes d'après l'édition de Charles.

I. *f.* 352 r., *marg. sup.*: *T. Rub.*

VI, 8 αὐτὸς γνώσεται νόμον κυρίου καὶ [*nonnulla desunt*] θυσίαν ὑπὲρ παντὸς ἰσραήλ, μέχρι τελειώσεως τῶν χρόνων τῶν ἀρχόντων καὶ ἀρχιερέων θεοῦ, ὃν κύριος [*spatium 2 litt.*; *omitt. vv.* 9-11 ἰούδαν; *sequuntur reliqua v.* 11:] διότι αὐτὸν κύριος ἐξελέξατο βασιλεῦσαι πάντων λαῶν. 12 καὶ προσκυνῆσαι τῷ σπέρματι αὐτοῦ, ὅτι

---

[1]) Ces renseignements sont dus à Mlle Jacqueline BURGERS (Leiden), qui au cours de 1969, lorsque nous ne connaissions les *marginalia* de *d* que d'un microfilm mal lisible, a bien voulu consacrer plusieurs heures précieuses de son séjour à Rome à l'examen du *Vat. gr.* 1238. Qu'elle en soit ici cordialement remerciée.

[2]) A l'amabilité de Mgr. P. CANART nous ne devons pas seulement ces communications sur la datation des *marginalia* dans *d* (lettre du 16 XI 69) et l'autorisation d'en faire état dans cette publication (*id.* du 25 I 70), mais encore la faveur et le plaisir d'avoir été pilotés par lui à travers la Bibliothèque Vaticane, le 10 VII 1970. Qu'il trouve ici réitérée l'expression de notre reconnaissance.

[3]) *Vat. gr.* 1218-1287. Cf. GARITTE, *art. cit.*, 17; Rob. DEVREESSE, *Les mss. grecs de l'Italie méridionale, histoire, classement, paléographie* (Studi e testi 183), C. d. Vaticano 1955, p. 18, 19, 40; id., *Le fonds grec de la Bibliothèque Vaticane des origines à Paul V* (Studi e testi 244), *ibid.* 1965, p. 482.

ὑπὲρ ὑμῶν ἀποθανεῖται ἐν πολέμοις ὁρατοῖς τε καὶ ἀοράτοις, καὶ ἔσται ἐν ἡμῖν βασιλεὺς αἰώνιος: *quis noscet legem domini et sacrificia pro omni israel* [1])

II. *f.* 362 v., *marg. sup.*; *T. Juda*

XXIII, 5 καὶ ἐπισκέψεται [*MS.* -ψηται] ἡμᾶς κύριος ἐν ἐλέει [*om.* καὶ ἐν ἀγάπῃ — XXIV, 1 εἰρήνη; *sequuntur reliqua v.* 1 *etc.*] καὶ ἀναστήσεται ἄνθρωπος ἐκ τοῦ σπέρματός μου, ὅς ἐστι κλάδος θεοῦ τοῦ ὑψίστου, ὡς ἥλιος δικαιοσύνης, συμπορευόμενος τοῖς υἱοῖς τῶν ἀνθρώπων ἐν πραότητι καὶ δικαιοσύνῃ, καὶ πᾶσα ἁμαρτία οὐχ εὑρεθήσεται ἐπ' αὐτῷ. 2 καὶ ἀνοιγήσονται ἐπ' αὐτῷ οἱ οὐρανοὶ καὶ [*nonnulla desunt*] ἐκχεεῖ πνεῦμα χάριτος ἐφ' ὑμᾶς ἐν εὐλογίᾳ: *visitabit nos dominus in misericordia* [2])

III. *f.* 371 v., *marg. inf.*; *T. Gad*

VII, 7 ἐξαρεῖται [*sic MS.*] τὸ μῖσος ἀπὸ τῶν ψυχῶν ἡμῶν, καὶ εἰρήνη ἔσται εἰς ἀλλήλους ἐν εὐθύτητι καρδίας. VIII, 1 [*om.* εἴπατε — ὅπως] τιμήσατε τὸν ἰούδαν καὶ λευίν, ὅτι ἐξ αὐτῶν ἀνατελεῖ κύριος, σωτὴρ τοῦ ἰσραήλ: *aufferte odium ab animabus vestris* [3])

IV. *f.* 373 r., *marg. inf.*; *T. Aser*

VII, 3 [*om.* ἕως οὗ] ὁ ὕψιστος ἐπισκέψηται τὴν γῆν, καὶ αὐτὸς ἐλθὼν ὡς ἄνθρωπος μετὰ ἀνθρώπων ἐσθίων καὶ πίνων [*nonnulla desunt*]. οὗτος σώσει τὸν ἰσραὴλ καὶ πάντα τὰ ἔθνη, θεὸς εἰς ἄνδρα ἀποκρινόμενος. 4 εἴπετε οὖν τοῖς τέκνοις ὑμῶν μὴ ἀπειθεῖν αὐτῷ: *altissimus visitabit terram et ipse veni* [4])

Posons d'abord la question suivante. D' après quel principe ces passages ont-ils été choisis? En comparant les phrases latines qui

---

[1]) Conybeare, *Jew. Quat. Rev.* 13 (Oct. 1900), p. 115, et Charles, *The Greek Versions* . . . , pp. 13-14, passent ce texte marginal sous silence.

[2]) Conybeare, 'The Testament of Job and the Testaments of the XII Patriarchs according to the Text of Cod. Vatican. Graecus, 1238', *Jew. Quat. Rev.* 13 (Oct. 1900), p. 125, signale que „against αἰῶνος as a scholion is written in upper margin in a later hand. Begins thus: καὶ ἐπισκέψηται κ̄ κ̄ς οι ελ. down to π̄ν̄α χάριτος ἐφ' ἡμῖν ἐν εὐλογίᾳ, also something illegible [à savoir l'addition en latin] in the side margin". La transcription de Conybeare est défectueuse. Charles ne dit rien sur ce *marginale*. — Les paroles ὅς ἐστι κλάδος θεοῦ τοῦ ὑψίστου reflètent *T. Juda* XXIV, 4, mais la leçon κλάδος au lieu de βλαστός ne se trouve dans aucun autre ms. Les deux mots apparaissent ensemble: *Vita Aesopi* G 99 κλάδους ἢ βλαστούς.

[3]) Conybeare, *art. cit.*, p. 266, note que le ms. *d* „om. καὶ ἀγαπήσατε τὸ τέκνοις ὑμῶν in ch. η' per homoiotel. A later hand adds the words in lower margin". Il ne donne pas de transcription. Charles, *op. cit.*, p. 170, n. 40: Καὶ ἀγάπη εἰς ἀλλήλους . . . καρδίας are added by a later hand at foot of page in *d*".

[4]) Conybeare, *art cit.*, p. 267: „Note that in a scholion on the christological passage in ch. ζ' beginning ἕως οὗ ὁ words ὕψιστος κ.τ.λ. as far as ὑποκρινόμενος already given in the text of the MS., are repeated in the lower margin in a somewhat later hand. There is no trace of erasure in the text. The scholion may come from a copy in which the text itself omitted the christological passage," — une explication qui n'explique pas pourquoi cet extrait figure dans la marge du ms. *d*, où ce passage christologique ne manque pas du tout. Charles n'en dit rien.

terminent les quatre textes cités avec les passages correspondants
dans la traduction latine des *Test. XII Patr.* faite, en 1242 (?), par Rob.
GROSSETESTE [1]), on constate, à côté de ressemblances frappantes, des
divergences remarquables. Que le lecteur juge lui-même:

Fragm. marg. in d	GROSSETESTE
I.	(FABRICIUS, p. 531)
quis *noscet legem domini et*	quoniam ipse *noscet legem domini et*
sacrificia pro	(*dividet judicia et*) *sacrificia pro*
omni israel	*omni israel*
II.	(FABRICIUS, p. 616)
visitabit nos *dominus*	*visitabit* vos *dominus*
in misericordia	*in misericordia*
III.	(FABRICIUS, p. 686)
aufferte odium ab animabus vestris	*auferte* igitur *odium ab animabus vestris*
IV.	(FABRICIUS, p. 696)
altissimus visitabit *terram*	*altissimus* visitaverit *terram*
et ipse veni	*et ipse veni(ens)*

Le texte latin des *marginalia* dans *d* ne semble donc pas dériver directement d'une copie de la traduction de GROSSETESTE.

Le résultat est cependant tout autre, si l'on consulte les extraits de
la traduction de GROSSETESTE que VINCENT DE BEAUVAIS (c. 1190-

---

[1]) Faute d'une édition critique de la traduction de GROSSETESTE, on se sert
du texte publié par J. E. GRABE dans son *Spicilegium Ss. Pp.* I, Oxonii 1698[1]
(inaccessible pour nous), réédité par J. A. FABRICIUS, *Codex Pseudepigraphus
V.T.*, Hamburgi-Lipsiae 1713, p. 519-748 = I[2], Hamburgi 1722. (Dans MIGNE,
PG 2, Parisiis 1886, col. 1038-1150, le texte latin a été emprunté à Andr.
GALLANDIUS, *Vet. Patr. Biblioth.* ... I, Venetiis 1765, qui à son tour a reproduit
le texte latin recensé de GRABE, *Sp. Ss. Pp.* I, Ox. 1714[2]). Pour la datation de la
traduction de GROSSETESTE, cf. S. H. THOMSON, *The Writings of Robert Grosseteste,
Bishop of Lincoln 1235-1253*, Cambridge 1940, p. 42, qui renvoie à Matth. PARIS,
vide p. 25, n. 1.— A la liste de mss. de la traduction latine de GROSSETESTE, THOMSON,
op. cit., p. 43-4, se laissent ajouter: Düsseldorf, Landes- und Stadtbibliothek,
B 112, 3°, *s.* XIV-XV; *ibid.*, B 120, 3°, *a.* 1347 (ces deux mss. m'ont été signalés
par W. BAARS, Leiden); Kiel, Univ.-bibl., Bordesholmer Hss. 48, 2°, *f.* 31v.-43r.,
s. incerti; Liège, Bibl. de l'Univ., 354 C (jadis 349; l'ancien n°. 184 = 293 B selon
la numérotation actuelle), *f.* 242v.-243r., *s.* XV, (recension courte; le nombre VII
au lieu de XII dans le titre indiqué par M. GRANDJEAN, *Biblioth. de l'Univ. de
Liège, Catalogue des mss.*, Liège 1875, p. 221, n. 349, cf. la Table alphabétique *s.v.
Testamenta VII Patr.*, est dû à une erreur); *olim* Padova, v. J. P. TOMASINUS,
Bibliothecae patavinae manuscriptae publicae et privatae, Udine 1639, p. 26, *sub* 'Mss...
qui in Bibl. S. Ioan. in Viridario Patavii asservantur', (*ad dextrum latus, plut.* XXVI);
mais qu'est devenue cette collection?; Bruges, Biblioth. Publ. 162 C, *ff.* 27-38,
s. XIII. Sans aucun doute la liste est encore loin d'être complète.

1264) a insérés dans son *Speculum historiale* ¹), et qui maintes fois ont
été copiés indépendamment de cet œuvre. Là, les phrases correspon-
dantes apparaissent sous la forme suivante:

I.   (*Cap.* CXXV)   *Quis noscet legem domini et (dividet in iudicium et) sacrificia*
                        pro omni israel
II . (*Cap.* CXXVII)   *Visitabit* vos *dominus in misericordia*
III. (*Cap.* CXXVIII)   *Auferte odium ab animabus vestris*
IV. (*Cap.* CXXIX)   *Altissimus visitabit terram et ipse veni(ens)*

De toutes les différences signalées plus haut, il ne reste que le pronom
vos (fragm. II) pour lequel le texte marginal de *d* donne *nos* — con-
formément au texte grec qui précède: ἐπισκέψεται ἡμᾶς ²).

Mais ce qui plus est, dans la recension des *Testaments* qui figure
dans le *Speculum historiale*, les trois premières des phrases latines que
nous venons de citer constituent précisément les paroles initiales des
Testaments auxquels elles appartiennent ³). Par conséquent, trois des
quatre textes marginaux de *d* débutent au même point que les extraits
du *Speculum*. De plus, les fragments grecs III et IV s'arrêtent au même
mot que les *Test.* Gad et *Aser* dans la recension du *Speculum*, le *Test.*
Gad se terminant par ... *quoniam ex ipsis orire faciet dominus salvatorem*
israhel, et le *Test.* *Aser* par ... *dicite ergo vestris ut non discredant ei*. Et à
quatre mots près, le fragment grec I couvre parfaitement le *Test.* *Ruben*
de Vincent, ce dernier conservant encore les paroles ... *et mortuus est*
ruben, qui manquent dans la marge de *d*. Enfin, le *Speculum*, aussi bien
que le fragment grec I, supprime *Test.* *Ruben* VI, 9-11 ἰούδαν, ce qui
a été indiqué dans le *Speculum* par les paroles *Et post pauca*, dans le
texte grec du fragment I par un petit espace.

Jamais les *marginalia* de *d* ne dépassent les bornes mises par le texte
du *Speculum*. Dans la plupart des cas, les *incipit* et les *explicit* des
fragments grecs correspondent à ceux des *Testaments* du *Speculum*.
Dans le *Test. Rub.* les deux témoins ont en commun une omission.
Cela suffit pour justifier la conclusion que le choix et l'étendue des
textes marginaux grecs qui accompagnent les *Test. XII Patr.* dans le
Vat. gr. 1238 ont été déterminés par la recension latine des *Testaments*

---

¹) Vincentius Bellovacensis, *Speculum historiale*, [*sine loci, anni et typogr. nota,*
sed impr. Argentorati apud Joh. Mentelin, c. 1473]. *lib.* II, *cap.* CXXV-CXXIX.
Est-ce que Vincent de Beauvais a compilé lui-même les *Testaments* pour les
insérer dans son histoire universelle? Nous n'osons pas l'affirmer, mais cela nous
parait bien probable.
²) Sauf *d* et son texte marginal, tous les mss. grecs ont ici ὑμᾶς. En lisant
vos, de Beauvais et Grosseteste conservent la lecture de leur modèle *b*.
³) La quatrième est précédée par le texte de *T. Aser* VII, 2.

que Vincent de Beauvais a insérée dans son *Speculum historiale*. —
À en juger d'après l'introduction qui précède sa sélection des passages
des *Testaments*, Vincent de Beauvais semble être intéressé surtout
par les *apertissimae atque pulcherrimae de christo prophetiae* qui se lisent
dans les *Testaments* [1]) .C'est par ce même intérêt que s'est laissé mener,
consciemment ou inconsciemment, le scribe des *marginalia* de *d*.

Tout cela ne concerne cependant que l'aspect extérieur des textes
qui nous occupent. Ce qui nous intéresse ici est de savoir quelle est
la place que ces fragments tiennent dans l'histoire de la tradition
textuelle des *Test. XII Patr.*, mises à part leurs phrases finales en latin,
qui ont été copiées directement d'un témoin de la version latine brève
des *Testaments*. L'influence de la recension latine insérée dans le
Speculum, se retrouve-t-elle dans les détails de la forme textuelle des
additions marginales de *d*? Voilà ce qu'on pourrait être tenté de
supposer, vu le rapport entre les extraits du *Speculum* et les *marginalia*
de *d* établi ci-dessus.

Ce qui est certain, c'est qu'avec aucun des témoins grecs des
Testaments le texte des fragments marginaux de *d* ne montre une
affinité aussi étroite qu'avec *d*. Seuls *d* et ses *marginalia* ont les
variantes suivantes:

T. Rub.	VI, 11	πάντων τῶν λαῶν	] [2]) *d* Fm[d] [3]) πάντων λαῶν (=*a*)
ibid.	12	προσκυνήσατε	] *d* Fm[d] προσκυνῆσαι
ibid.		ὁρατοῖς καί	] *d* Fm[d] ὁρατοῖς τε καί
T. Juda XXIII, 5		ὑμᾶς	] *d* Fm[d] ἡμᾶς (*v.i.*, p. 95)
ibid.	XXIV, 2	ἐκχέαι - καὶ αὐτός	] *d* Fm[d] om. (*hmt.*)
T. Gad	VII, 7	οὖν	] *d* Fm[d] om.
ibid.	VIII, 1	ἰούδαν καὶ τὸν λευίν	] *d* Fm[d] τὸν ἰούδαν καὶ λευίν

---

[1]) *Lib.* II, *cap.* CXXV *De Testamento ruben & symeon. Extant autem testamenta
.xii. patriarcharum in quibus sunt apertissime atque pulcerrime de christo prophetie.
quas nuper* [il y a deux ans à peu près] *transtulit magister robertus grossum caput,
lincoliensis episcopus de greco in latinum, ideoque hic eas inserere placuit. Testamentum
ruben. Quis noscet* ... (*etc.*). Le texte qui, soit comme colophon, soit comme
avant-propos, accompagne les *Test. XII Patr.* dans une grande partie de la tradition
manuscrite et imprimée occidentale, en latin et en traduction, (*incipit: Haec
abscondita et celata fuerunt per longa tempora*), et qui remonte au XIIIe siècle (témoin
le ms. London, B. M., Royal 4. D. VII, *s.* XIII[m]), parle de *manifestas de christo
prophetias quae in his scripturis inveniuntur*, et un peu plus loin de *manifestae ac
expressae prophetiae quae in hoc libello inveniuntur*. L'histoire de l'origine de la traduction latine des *Test.*, racontée par Matthaeus Paris dans son *Historia maior* ....,
Tiguri 1589, p. 577, est en grande partie dépendante de ce colophon. Aussi
Paris ne manque pas de faire mention des *prophetias de Salvatore in eis contentas*.

[2]) Les *lemmata* seront pris du ms. *b*.

[3]) Fm[d] = *Fragmenta marginalia in d*

On voit bien par cette liste qu'il existe un rapport évident entre *d*
et les fragments conservés dans ses marges.

Reste à préciser en quoi ce rapport consiste: dépendance de *d* à
l'égard de Fm*d*, dépendance de Fm*d* à l'égard de *d*, ou bien dépendance
des deux à l'égard d'un intermédiaire commun. De ces trois possibilités, la première n'entre pas en ligne de compte: il va sans dire que
le texte de *d* qui couvre le texte complet de douze *Testaments* et qui
a été écrit avant 1195, ne peut pas être dépendant des textes frag-
mentaires qui ont été apportés dans ses marges vers la fin du XVe
siècle. Ni la seconde, car plusieurs passages qui sont omis dans *d* sont
présents dans les fragments marginaux, tandis qu'une addition propre
à *d* ne se retrouve point dans la marge:

T. Rub.	VI, 12	ὑπὲρ ἡμῶν ἀποθανεῖται	] *d om.*, *sed* Fm*d* ὑπὲρ ὑμῶν ἀποθανεῖται
T. Juda XXIV, 2		ἐκχέαι πνεύματος εὐλο-γίαν πατρὸς ἁγίου	] *d om.*, *sed* Fm*d* *retinet* ἐν εὐλογίᾳ
T. Gad	VII, 7	καὶ ἀγαπᾶτε ἀλλήλους ἐν εὐθύτητι καρδίας	] *d om.*, *sed* Fm*d* καὶ εἰρήνη ἔσται εἰς ἀλλήλους ἐν εὐθύτητι καρδίας
T. Aser	VII, 4	ὑμῶν	] *d* + τοῦ ἐντείλασθαι αὐτοῖς Fm*d* *nil add.*

De ces variantes de *d* et Fm*d* il ressort que les textes marginaux n'ont
pas été copiés du texte proprement dit du *Vat. gr.* 1238. De même
il est clair qu'aux trois premiers endroits cités, où il s'agit d'omissions
dans *d*, le texte grec des fragments n'a pas été influencé non plus par
le texte latin des *Testaments* recueilli dans le *Speculum historiale*. En
effet, les paroles omises par *d* se lisent chez VINCENT DE BEAUVAIS
comme suit:

T. Rub.	VI, 12	*pro nobis morietur*
T. Juda XXIV, 2		*ad effundendum spiritus benedictionem patris sancti*
T. Gad	VII, 7	*et diligite ad invicem in rectitudine cordis*

Ce que les fragments de *d* ont en commun avec ces leçons latines,
s'explique aussi bien de la tradition grecque. Là où les *marginalia* de
d comblent les lacunes de *d* lui-même, on ne trouve pas d'erreurs de
traduction, qui, en général, sont l'indication unique permettant de
conclure qu'un texte a été traduit. Bref, il n'y a pas lieu de supposer
que dans les additions marginales de *d* les paroles qui manquent dans
d ont été suppléées du latin.

Nous ajoutons que dans le reste du texte des fragments marginaux
de *d* l'influence de la version latine est, là aussi, absente, ou presque.

Si l'on dresse la liste des leçons par lesquelles ces textes se distinguent du reste de la tradition grecque des *Testaments*, il apparaît qu'aucune de ces variantes n'est imputable à l'influence du texte latin, excepté les deux suivantes: par l'omission du pronom ὑμῖν (*d e af hi*) ou ἡμῖν (*m c*) après ἀνατελεῖ dans *T. Gad* VIII, 1 le *marginale* de *d* retourne, soit spontanément, soit sous l'influence du texte latin [1] (*quoniam ex ipsis orire faciet dominus salvatorem israhel*), à la leçon originale attestée par *bk g l*, qui n'ont, eux non plus, le pronom. Dans *T. Aser* VII, 4 le texte marginal de *d* est le seul témoin grec qui supprime ταῦτα s'approchant en cela au texte latin:

Fm*ᵈ*

εἴπετε οὖν τοῖς τέκνοις ὑμῶν
[*om.* ταῦτα] μὴ ἀπειθεῖν αὐτῷ.

Speculum historiale:

dicite ergo vestris
ut non discredent ei

Mais c'est tout. L'inverse se produit, une fois, dans *T. Juda* XXIII, 5, où le scribe du texte marginal, ou celui de son modèle, en ajoutant la phrase finale en latin, ne s'est pas tenu au texte latin tel que nous le lisons chez VINCENT DE BEAUVAIS (*visitabit vos*), mais a adapté son addition au texte grec qu'il venait de copier (*visitabit nos*, ἐπισκέψεται ἡμᾶς). Voilà toutes les interférences entre le texte grec des additions marginales dans *d* et celui de la traduction latine [2]. Inutile, du reste, d'énumérer ici les autres leçons particulières des fragments: elles n'ont en soi aucune valeur.

Retournons à la question de la relation entre le texte de *d* et celui de ses *marginalia*. Ces derniers fournissent, comme nous l'avons déjà constaté, un texte qui s'approche plus de *d* que d'aucun autre témoin des *Testaments*. A certains endroits cependant, où le texte des *marginalia* est moins lacuneux que celui de *d* sans être complété à l'aide de la traduction latine, il reflète un stade de la tradition textuelle des *Testaments* antérieur à celui attesté par *d*. Ainsi, la conclusion s'impose que le texte de *d* et celui de ses *marginalia* descendent, indépendamment l'un de l'autre, d'un intermédiaire commun qui ne nous était pas connu jusqu'à ce jour. C'est là qu'est toute la valeur de ces bribes retrouvées dans les marges de *d*. Elles font voir que, dans l'évolution du texte des *Test. XII Patr.* à l'intérieur de la famille constituée

---

[1] L'on se souviendra que la traduction latine a été faite d'après le ms. *b*. Un tel retour du texte marginal de *d* à *b*, par l'intermédiaire du texte latin, n'a donc rien d'étonnant.

[2] A part ce que nous avons dit plus haut sur la relation entre l'étendue des extraits des *Testaments* dans la version latine brève et de ceux qui figurent dans les marges de *d*.

jusqu'ici par les manuscrits *l-dm*, le texte de *d* n'est issu du dernier ancêtre commun de *d* et *m* que par l'intermédiaire attesté par *d* et ses fragments marginaux [1]).

Cette note était destinée à faire connaitre les quatre petits morceaux de texte qui garnissent les marges encadrant le texte des *Test. XII Patr.* dans le *Vat. gr.* 1238. Ces fragments, datant de la seconde moitié ou de la fin du XVe siècle, contiennent le texte de quelques passages christologiques pris des *Test. Rub.*, *Juda*, *Gad* et *Aser*. Le début et la fin de la plupart de ces extraits coincident avec ceux des *Testaments* abrégés correspondants, tels qu'on les trouve dans le *Speculum historiale* (c. 1244?) de VINCENT DE BEAUVAIS. Dans la délimination de ces passages, le scribe qui les a choisis s'est évidemment conformé à la recension brève dans laquelle la traduction latine des *Testaments* faite par GROSSETESTE (1242?) a bientôt circulé. De cette recension courte viennent également les phrases latines qui ont été ajoutées à chaque fragment. Le texte grec cependant, qui est en étroite parenté avec celui de *d*, ne révèle presque aucune influence du texte latin, ni du texte principal de *d*. Les fragments marginaux dans le manuscrit *d* méritent donc d'être reconnus comme témoin indépendant, apportant, par conséquent, quelque lumière sur l'histoire de la famille des manuscrits *l-dm*. Désormais on sait, d'une part, que le manuscrit *d* n'a pas été copié directement du dernier intermédiaire commun des deux manuscrits *d* et *m*, d'autre part, que les nombreuses lacunes qu'on trouve dans *d* n'ont pas défiguré toutes les copies qui le séparent du dernier hyparchetype qu'il a en commun avec *m*, enfin, que pour un certain nombre de fautes qui semblaient particulières à *d*, ce n'est pas le scribe de *d* qui en est responsable. Quelque restreinte que soit cette réhabilitation du moine copiste qui vers l'an 1195 dans un des monastères de l'Italie méridionale achevait le manuscrit que nous désignons aujourd'hui par la signature *Vat. gr.* 1238, elle nous parait bien valoir la peine d'un article modeste. Ceux qui s'occupent des *Test. XII Patr.* ne seront pas tous réhabilités avant huit cent ans.

---

[1]) *m*: Ankara, Türk Tarih Kurumu, gr. 60, pp. 339-483, *s.* XVI; en dehors des passages attestés par les additions marginales de *d*, aucun témoin n'est plus apparenté à *d* que *m*.

V

LA BIBLIOTHEQUE DE MICHEL CHONIATES ET LA TRADITION OCCIDENTALE DES TESTAMENTS DES XII PATRIARCHES

H. J. DE JONGE

Vers 1200 un étudiant anglais, originaire de Basingstoke, décida de compléter la formation qu'il avait probablement reçue à Oxford en faisant un voyage d'études qui devait le mener dans les principaux foyers de culture du continent[1]. Il s'arrêta longtemps à Paris. Mais son désir d'apprendre devait le pousser plus loin encore de son pays natal, et c'est ainsi que nous le trouvons finalement à Athènes, la μητρόπολις τῶν ὁποδήποτε φιλολόγων πόλεων καὶ σοφίας τροφός[2].

Parmi les rares données que nota le chroniqueur[3] de Basingstoke l'année de sa mort (1252), on trouve la charmante anecdote suivante:

„Quaedam puella, filia archiepiscopi Atheniensis, nomine Constantina, nondum vicesimum agens annum, virtutibus praedita, omnem trivii et quadrivii noverat difficultatem; unde alteram Katerinam, vel Katerinam, consuevit dictus magister J[ohannes de Basingstokes] jocose, propter suae scientiae eminentiam, appellare. Haec magistra fuit magistri J[ohannis] et quicquid boni scivit in scientia, ut saepe asseruit, licet Parisiis diu studuisset et legisset, ab ea mendicaverat. Haec puella pestilentias, tonitrua, eclipsim, et quod mirabilius fuit, terrae motum praedicens, omnes suos auditores infallibiliter praemunivit."[4]

---

[1] Pour la bibliographie ancienne sur John de Basingstoke, exclusivement basée sur Matt. Paris (v.n. 3), voir Ul. Chevalier, *Répertoire des sources historiques du moyen age*, II, Paris 1907, col. 2362, *sub nomine* Jean de Basingstoke. Informations plus complètes dans J. C. Russell, *Dictionary of Writers of Thirteenth Century England, Being Special Supplement No. 3 to the Bulletin of the Institute of Historical Research* 1936, réimpr. Londres 1967, pp. 54-5.

[2] Michael Choniatès, *Eisbaterios,* éd. Sp. Lampros, Μιχαὴλ 'Ακομινάτου τοῦ Χωνιάτου τὰ σωζόμενα, Athènes 1879-80 = réimpr. Groningue 1968, I, p. 94 l. 7-8.

[3] Mattaeus Paris(iensis, Monachus Sancti Albani), *Chronica Majora*, éd. H.R. Luard, Londres 1872-83. Voir pour Paris († 1259) comme historien Ch. Gross, *The Sources and Literature of English History from the Earliest Times to about 1485,* London 1915[2], pp. 384-5: „Matthew Paris is commonly regarded as England's greatest medieval historian..." Paris utilisa deux chroniques plus anciennes, mais à partir de 1235 „[he] carried the story to 1259. ... Much of the author's information was gathered from eye-witnesses of the events narrated." Pour Paris voir également le *Dictionary* (v.n.1) de Russell, pp. 83-4. S.H. Thomson critique certains détails dans l'histoire de Basingstoke écrite par Paris dans *The Writings of Robert Grosseteste, Bishop of Lincoln 1235-1253,* Cambridge 1940, p. 102.

[4] Paris, éd. Luard, V, 1880, pp. 286-7. Luard lit *Parisius* au lieu de *Parisiis.*

La rencontre de cette jeune Athénienne a été apparemment un
des plus précieux souvenirs que notre étudiant anglais ait gardés
de son voyage; le chroniqueur insiste sur le fait qu'à plusieurs
reprises Basingstoke lui a raconté cet épisode („quod mihi, haec
scripturo, familiariter consuevit enarrare".)

Il est regrettable que le récit, du moins la version qu'en donne
le texte cité, ne soit pas en tous points digne de confiance. Nous
n'avons pas l'intention de contester à John de Basingstoke des
entretiens édifiants avec une personne aussi jeune qu'instruite.
Mais il est impossible que cette Constantina ait été la fille de
l'archevêque d'Athènes, comme le prétend le chroniqueur. L'archevêque en question ne peut avoir été autre que le dernier
métropolite orthodoxe d'Athènes avant l'invasion des Francs en
1204, c'est-à-dire le célèbre Michel Choniatès[5]. Or celui-ci écrit
dans une de ses lettres πατὴρ οὐκ ἐγενόμην[6].

Mais même si la chronique fait erreur quant au lien de parenté
entre Constantina et l'archevêque, il importe de signaler que,
dans le compte-rendu de ses rencontres à Athènes, Basingstoke ne
manque pas de nommer l'archevêque. Il serait en effet inimagi-
nable que le jeune savant anglais ne soit entré en contact avec le
grand philologue qu'était l'archevêque d'Athènes[7]. Car c'est
seulement dans le milieu de Michel Choniatès, résidant à l'Acropole, que vivait encore une culture susceptible d'intéresser Basingstoke, un certain culte des lettres et de la philosophie, un hu-
manisme avant la lettre. En dehors de ce cercle régnait la décadence spirituelle que déplorait si vivement cet archevêque érudit.

A cette époque Athènes était devenue une ville sans aucune
importance culturelle[8]. Au point de vue économique elle était
supplantée par Corinthe et Thèbes, et elle n'avait aucun dévelop-
pement industriel. L'extension de la grande propriété foncière et
les lourds impôts byzantins avaient appauvri la population tout
entière et en particulier les monastères. Les habitants de la ville et
des monastères enduraient de cruelles privations et la pauvreté
entraînait avec elle le dépeuplement. Dans ces conditions, depuis
longtemps déjà, il n'y avait plus de place à Athènes pour
l'enseignement, la science, les activités littéraires et philosophiques. Maintes fois Michel Choniatès s'est plaint de la décadence

---

[5] c.1138-1222. G. Stadtmüller, *Michael Choniates* (Orientalia Christiana XXXIII, 2,
1934). L.D. Reynolds-N.G. Wilson, *Scribes and Scholars* . . . Oxford 1968, p. 62.

[6] Lampros, *op. cit.*, I, χθ'. F. Gregorovius, *Geschichte der Stadt Athen im
Mittelalter*, Stuttgart 1889, I, p. 234; Dresde 1927, p. 156; Stadtmüller, *op.cit.*, p. 159.

[7] Gregorovius, *op.cit*, 1889, p. 234; 1927, p. 157-8.

[8] Pour la suite voir les ouvrages cités de Gregorovius et de Stadtmüller.

spirituelle de l'antique Athènes. A propos de sa métropole, jadis ἡ μήτηρ τῶν σοφῶν, il écrit qu'à son époque elle σπανίζει φιλοσόφων ἀνδρῶν[9]. Le Péripatos et le Lycée ont totalement disparu et les moutons broutent dans les ruines de la Stoa poikilè[10].

Le seul lieu où fussent encore pratiquées les études littéraires et philosophiques était la résidence du métropolite. Nous savons par ses lettres que le fait de disposer du Parthénon encore intact comme cathédrale n'était à ses yeux qu'une maigre compensation à l'absence d'un cercle un peu plus important de lettrés et d'érudits. Nous savons que ses livres étaient sa grande consolation, car sa vaste bibliothèque était à la fois son orgueil et son bien le plus précieux.

Les lettres de Michel lui-même nous renseignent assez bien sur sa collection de livres[11]. Comme étudiant déjà à l'Ecole du Patriarcat à Constantinople, et comme disciple d'Eustathe[12] il réunissait πολλὰ καὶ παντοῖα βιβλία[13]. Lorsqu'en 1182 il accéda à l'épiscopat, il emporta sa bibliothèque à Athènes. L'on ignore si avant sa venue il y avait déjà une bibliothèque épiscopale dans cette ville. Pendant son séjour à Athènes il étendit considérablement sa bibliothèque tant en achetant qu'en recopiant lui-même des livres. Il y a donc lieu d'admettre que, lorsque, après la conquête d'Athènes par les Francs en 1204, Michel dut partir en exil, la bibliothèque qu'il laissait sur place comprenait les éléments suivants:

1. les livres que Michel avait réunis avant 1182 à Constantinople et emportés à Athènes;
2. les livres achetés à Athènes après 1182 et ceux qui lui furent offerts;
3. les ouvrages que lui-même avait composés ou recopiés soit à Constantinople, soit à Athènes;
4. enfin, peut-être, des livres qui se trouvaient déjà avant 1182 dans la bibliothèque épiscopale.

Cette bibliothèque, probablement conservée à l'Acropole[14], peut-être même dans les murs du Parthénon[15], John de Basing-

---

[9] Ed.Lampros, II, 11, 5-6.
[10] Ed. Lampros, I, 160, 1-5.
[11] Pour les détails mentionnés ici, cf. Σπ. Λάμπρος, Περὶ τῆς βιβλιοθήκης τοῦ μητροπολίτου Ἀθηνῶν Μιχαὴλ Ἀκομινάτου (1182-1205), Ἀθηναῖον 5 (1877), 354 ss.
[12] Stadtmüller, op. cit., p. 139-40.
[13] Ed. Lampros, II, 295, 20-1.
[14] Lampros, art. cit., p. 355.
[15] Lampros, art. cit., p. 355. Le Parthénon était alors église de la Théotokos.

stoke doit l'avoir vue lors de sa visite à Athènes. C'est longtemps
après son retour en Angleterre qu'il a fait part de ses découvertes
à un savant ami, Robert Grosseteste, à partir de 1235 évêque de
Lincoln:

> „magister J[ohannes de Basingstokes] intimaverat episcopo Lincolniensi
> Roberto, quod, quando studuit Athenis, viderat et audierat ab peritis
> Graecorum doctoribus quaedam Latinis incognita. Inter quae reperit duo-
> decim patriarcharum, filiorum videlicet Jacob, testamenta."[16]

Le chroniqueur ajoute d'emblée:

> „Unde idem episcopus misit in Graeciam, et cum ea habuisset, transtulit
> de Graeco in Latinum, et quaedam alia."

Il doit cependant s'être écoulé bien des années entre le retour de
Basingstoke et l'expédition ordonnée par Grosseteste. C'est seulement pendant l'épiscopat de Michel Choniatès, c'est-à-dire
jusqu'en 1204, qu'il peut y avoir eu à Athènes un climat
scientifique de quelque importance. Le voyage de Basingstoke à
Athènes doit donc avoir eu lieu avant 1204. Le voyage en Grèce
d'un groupe de savants anglais envoyés dans ce pays par Grosseteste pour y acquérir des ouvrages n'existant pas en latin, ne peut
se situer avant 1235, l'année où Grosseteste est devenu évêque[17].
Jusqu'ici rien ne porte à croire que Grosseteste ait entrepris des
traductions avant de devenir évêque[18]. S'il est vrai qu'il faut
établir un rapport entre la traduction des *Testaments* et les
projets de conversion des Juifs en Angleterre[19], et que cet
ouvrage devait servir à prouver que les Juifs étaient dans l'erreur,
et cela sur la base des prophéties de leur propre littérature,

---

Lampros renvoie à Ad. Michaelis, *Der Parthenon* (texte), Leipzig 1871, p. 47: „An der
einen Seite des Altars wurden in der Wand vier mit Marmorplatten verschliessbare
Schränke für das Kirchengeräth(σκεύη)und die Bücher angebracht", cf.n.172: „. . . Vgl.
auch den Kapuziner P. Alexis bei Laborde, *Athènes* I, [que nous n'avons pu consulter]
108 Anm.: qu'il y a d'un costé deux armoires lesquelles sont ouvertes, et de l'autre
costé deux qui ne le sont pas et qu'on ne veut pas ouvrir, parce que c'est une tradition,
qu'après que les Turcs se furent rendus maîtres de ceste ville, ceux qui ouvrirent les
autres, devinrent aveugles. On dit qu'on n'y trouva autre chose que des livres."

[16] Paris, éd. Luard V, 1880, pp. 284-5.

[17] La date du voyage en Grèce de Basingstoke que donne M. Cantor, *Vorlesungen
über Geschichte der Mathematik* II, Leipzig 1892, p. 90 („um 1240") ne peut se
rapporter qu'à l'expédition ordonnée par Grosseteste; Cantor l'a calculée prenant pour
point de départ la date traditionelle de la traduction latine des *Testaments,* l'année
1242. La confusion entre les deux voyages en Grèce, celui de Basingstoke vers 1204, et
celui des *exploratores* de Grosseteste, se constate également chez J.E. Sandys, *A
History of Classical Scholarship* I, Cambridge 1906², p. 422-3, et chez J.W. Thompson,
The Medieval Library, New York 1957, 286, cf. 322-3. Voir aussi p. 112, note.

[18] Thomson, *op. cit.* (n.3), p. 49.

[19] L.M. Friedman, *Rob. Grosseteste and the Jews,* Cambridge Mass. 1934, p. 8.

Grosseteste ne peut pas s'être intéressé aux *Testaments* avant 1231[20].

Il doit donc s'être écoulé une trentaine d'années entre le séjour de Basingstoke à Athènes et le fait signalé ci-dessous:

„[Grosseteste] usque in Graeciam misit diligentissimos exploratores, ut exemplar scripti memorati [sc. Test. XII Patr.] non soliciti de expensis quas abundanter ei invenerat reportarent."[21]

L'on sait que cette entreprise fut couronnée de succès. Car les *exploratores* envoyés par Grosseteste ont su mettre la main sur un manuscrit des *Testaments* et l'emporter en Angleterre où il put servir de base à la traduction latine que Grosseteste fit des *Testaments:*

„Venerabilis igitur Episcopus, ut memoriam lucidissimarum prophetiarum, ad robur fidei Christianae perpetuaret, Anno Christi M. cc. xlii. e Graeco in Latinum, in quibus idiomatibus peritissimus habebatur, transtulit evidenter, de verbo in verbum, ac fideliter, adiuvante Magistro Nicolao Graeco, Rectore Ecclesiae de Dachet, Clerico domini Abbatis de sancto Albano, quo sic luculentae prophetiae, quae in hoc scripto, luce clarius, coruscant, in maiorem confusionem Iudaeorum & omnium haereticorum & inimicorum Ecclesiae gloriosius prorumpant."[22]

Il est parfaitement établi que le manuscrit qui servit à Grosseteste de base pour sa traduction est le ms de Cambridge, University Library Ff 1.24, ff.203a *sqq*, désigné par *b* dans la critique textuelle des *Testaments;* on y trouve des notes marginales de la main de Grosseteste. Il suffit au lecteur de consulter la première reproduction dans *Robert Grosseteste...*[23], de S.H. Thomson pour s'en convaincre.

Le manuscrit que Grosseteste fit venir de Grèce est-il toutefois identique à celui que Basingstoke avait vu dans la bibliothèque de Michel Choniatès et dont il avait parlé à Grosseteste? On est en droit de formuler quelque réserve à l'endroit de cette identification car il s'était écoulé plus de trente ans entre le séjour de

---

[20] Pour la date de la lettre de Grosseteste à Margaret de Quinci, veuve du comte de Winchester, à propos des Juifs, v. Friedman, *op. cit.* (n. 19), p. 12.

[21] Emprunté au colophon qui accompagne la traduction de Grosseteste déjà dans des mss du 13e siècle (par ex. Londres, B.M., Royal 4.D.VII; Bruges, Bibl. Publ. 162C). Nous citons d'après l'édition latine de Haganoae 1532.

[22] Pour le colophon v.n. 21. Nicolas Grecus n'est pas un inconnu, cf. Russell, *Dictionary* (n.l.), p. 89. Id., Preferments and Adiutores, *HTR*, 26, 1933, pp. 169-70. Pour complément de littérature v. D.A.Callus, *Robert Grosseteste, Scholar and Bishop*, Oxford 1955, p.40.

[23] *Op. cit.*, (n.3.), vérifié et confirmé par R.W. Hunt dans: Callus, *op. cit.*, (n.22), p. 134-5.

Basingstoke et le voyage des envoyés de Grosseteste. Il y a
pourtant de sérieuses raisons d'admettre que le codex découvert
par ces Anglais est bien l'exemplaire signalé par Basingstoke.

En premier lieu, Basingstoke doit avoir donné des indications
précises sur l'endroit où il se souvenait avoir trouvé cet ouvrage,
et c'est là qu'il aura envoyé tout d'abord les *exploratores*. Rien
n'indique que Basingstoke — devenu entretemps archidiacre de
Leicester, fonction occupée jusqu'en 1232 par Grosseteste lui-
même — aurait pris part à cette expédition[24]. Les renseignements
qu'il a fournis auront été d'autant plus détaillés.

Ensuite, l'occupation de l'Acropole par les Francs n'a connu ni
violence ni pillage. La forteresse s'est rendue sans résistance[25].
La bibliothèque a été épargnée du moins lors de ces événements.

C'est en partie grâce à cela que, par la suite, Michel Choniatès a
encore pu récupérer dans son lieu d'exil plusieurs ouvrages de son
ancienne bibliothèque[26] et nous savons donc qu'ils ont survécu à
la prise d'Athènes en 1204. Nous connaissons le sort ultérieur de
certains de ses livres et il existe dans les bibliothèques de
l'Europe occidentale des livres dont on pense qu'ils ont appartenu à Michel[27]. C'est un fait que la prise de Constantinople,
dans la même année, eut des conséquences infiniment plus
désastreuses pour les bibliothèques qui s'y trouvaient[28]. Il y a
lieu d'être reconnaissant à Michel pour chacun des livres qu'il a
sauvés en les emportant à Athènes.

En troisième lieu, la politique suivie par les Francs en ce qui
concerne les livres du métropolite a été assez bénéfique pour ces
ouvrages, contrairement à ce qu'on pense généralement. Ils n'ont
pas pillé la bibliothèque épiscopale[29] (ils n'étaient pas capables
de lire ces livres![30]), ne les ont pas vendus à des prix déri-
soires[31], mais ils ont veillé dessus comme le dragon sur la Toison
d'or ou les Hespérides sur les pommes d'or. Ces comparaisons et

---

[24] La remarque de Thomson, *op. cit.* (n.3), p. 42 „. . . is in all probability the
copy brought to England *b y B a s i n g s t o k e*" n'est donc pas fondée.

[25] Gregorovius, *op. cit.* 1927, p. 197. La mise à sac de l'église dont parle Ad.
Michaelis, *op. cit.*, pp. 363-4 ne concerne pas une dévastation lors de la prise de la cité,
mais l'usage que les Francs firent par la suite des trésors d'église. On retrouve le texte
de la *Monodie* citée par Michaelis dans Lampros éd.I, p. 357, 1. 17 sqq.

[26] Lampros, *art. cit.*, pp. 357-8.

[27] Lampros, *art. cit.*, p. 362-3: Paris, B.N., gr. 1234.

[28] Reynolds-Wilson, *op. cit.*, p. 62.

[29] C'est ce que dit Gregorovius 1927, p. 199.

[30] Même pas en traduction, d'après Michel Choniatès lui-même, cité par Lampros,
art.cit., p. 356; cf. Lampros éd. II, pp. 295-6.

[31] C'est ce que dit Stadtmüller, *op. cit.*, p. 183 („verschleuderten").

d'autres encore sont de la veine de Michel lui-même[32]. Ce qui
inspirait aux Francs cette vigilance, ce n'était certes pas le respect
de cette illustre bibliothèque qui dépassait leur entendement,
mais tout l'argent qu'ils escomptaient en retirer; ils n'étaient
disposés à la vendre qu'à prix d'or. Ce qu'ils firent du riche
trésor de l'église révèle la même préoccupation: ils le fondaient
pour en faire de l'argent[33]. Aussi lorsqu'un jeune ami de Michel
nommé Bardanès, réussit à extorquer quelques livres au cerbère
de l'Acropole pour les envoyer à leur propriétaire légitime,
l'archevêque exilé à Céos, celui-ci incite son ami à essayer de
récupérer encore d'autres livres, à n'importe quel prix, mais de
χρυσὸν ἐγχέειν au monstrueux gardien: Ταύτῃ γὰρ καὶ μόνῃ τῇ ὕλῃ
τὰ τοιαῦτα κήτη ἁλώσιμα[34]. Il est bien évident que cet état de
choses, bien qu'il ait été à déplorer pour Michel, a dû favoriser la
préservation de la collection. Il est vrai qu'un certain nombre de
livres se sont trouvés dispersés encore avant la mort du métropolite[35]. Il va sans dire que les acheteurs étaient seulement
disposés à payer cher les ouvrages qu'ils jugeaient de grande
valeur, c'est-à-dire ceux qui présentaient un intérêt scientifique,
tels que les ouvrages d'Euclide, de Théophylacte, d'Aristote et de
Galien[36]. Mais qui aurait été disposé à dépenser beaucoup
d'argent pour un exemplaire des *Testaments des XII Patriarches*
ou pour un des autres textes transmis dans le même manuscrit, tels que le livre des *Chroniques*, l'obscur *Commonitorium*
d'un Joseph, compilateur chrétien parfaitement inconnu, une
énigme de l'empereur Léon VI, le Sage, un poème sur Lazare et le
mauvais riche? Il ne s'est probablement pas présenté d'acheteur
pour ces ouvrages jusqu'au jour où les envoyés de Grosseteste
,,non soliciti de expensis quas abundanter ei invenerat" vinrent
chercher le manuscrit des *Testaments* et le trouvèrent à l'endroit
signalé par Basingstoke.

Un quatrième point, c'est que même si le manuscrit en
question ne se trouvait plus à l'Acropole au moment où les
envoyés anglais y arrivèrent, il doit avoir été possible de le
trouver chez son nouveau propriétaire. L'on sait que Michel,
ayant appris dans son exil qu'un manuscrit de Théophylacte
qu'il avait lui-même recopié avait échoué chez l'abbé d'un

---

[32] Lettre à Bardanès, éd. Lampros II, p. 242.
[33] Gregorovius 1927, p. 199. Stadtmüller, p. 183.
[34] Ed. Lampros II, p. 242.
[35] Lampros, *art. cit.*, pp. 356 sqq.
[36] Michel possédait e.a. ces auteurs.

monastère près d'Athènes, lui écrivit pour le prier de le lui rendre
[37]. Il est donc vraisemblable que les *diligentissimi exploratores*
de Grosseteste aient pu, le cas échéant, retrouver en dehors de
l'Acropole le livre qu'ils cherchaient.

En cinquième lieu, comme seule la résidence épiscopale n'avait
pas été atteinte par la décadence culturelle générale à cette
époque, il est déjà probable *a priori* qu'un livre vieux de trois
siècles et rapporté d'Attique peu après 1235, provient directement ou non de la très riche bibliothèque du métropolite[38]. La
bibliothèque de Michel mise à part, on n'aura guère pu trouver en
Attique que des écrits liturgiques ou bibliques[39]. On ne voit
donc pour un livre tel que celui rapporté d'Athènes par les
Anglais qu'une seule origine plausible: la bibliothèque de l'archevêque.

Sixièmement, ce dernier argument a plus de poids encore si
l'on considère qu'en effet Basingstoke avait parlé des *Testaments*
qui figuraient dans cette bibliothèque.

Il est donc hautement probable que le manuscrit rapporté de
Grèce par les envoyés de Grosseteste est vraiment identique à
celui que John de Basingstoke avait vu trente ans auparavant dans
la bibliothèque de Michel Choniatès.

Nous avons déjà admis plus haut que cette fameuse bibliothèque comprenait: 1. les livres réunis à Constantinople jusqu'en
1182; 2. ceux acquis à Athènes après 1182; 3. les ouvrages
composés ou recopiés par le métropolite; 4. peut-être des livres
se trouvant déjà dans la bibliothèque épiscopale d'Athènes avant
l'arrivée de Michel Choniatès. Comme le ms. Cambridge Univ.
Libr. Ff. 1. 24 date du dixième siècle, il ne peut appartenir au
troisième groupe. Restent les trois autres possibilités: il est
malheureusement impossible d'établir où il se trouvait avant
d'appartenir à Michel, de sorte que la partie la plus ancienne de
l'histoire de cet important manuscrit reste dans l'ombre[40]. Tout

---

[37] Ed. Lampros II, p. 254, 10 sqq.

[38] Il ne faut pourtant pas se faire d'illusions sur ce qu'on entendait à l'époque par
une grande bibliothèque: une bibliothèque privée, même importante, ne devait pas
compter plus d'une centaine d'ouvrages à cette époque.

[39] L'inventaire des biens de l'église en Attique dressé peu après 1204 à l'intention du
pape, nous apprend avec précision quels couvents appartenaient au diocèse de Michel;
c'etaient 4 *abbayes* et 16 *monastères* (Stadtmüller, p. 153). Aucune mention de
bibliothèques appartenant à ces couvents. Pour l'inventaire, v. Migne, *PL* 215, 1559-62.

[40] Mise en garde contre des données pouvant prêter à confusion sur l'histoire la plus
ancienne de ce ms. (les deux dernières pages) voir R.W. Hunt, „The Library of Robert
Grosseteste", dans: D.A. Callus (éd.), *Robert Grosseteste, Scholar and Bishop*, Oxford
1955, pp. 134-5.

au plus peut-on, sans trop de risques d'erreurs, établir la liste
suivante d'anciens *possessores:*

?	—	1204	Michel Choniatès, métropolite orthodoxe d'Athènes;
1204	—	1206	Othon de la Roche, seigneur d'Athènes[41] ;
1206	—	?	Bérard, archevêque latin d'Athènes;
c. 1235	—	1253	Robert Grosseteste, évêque de Lincoln;
1253	—	?	bibliothèque du monastère des Frères Mineurs d'Oxford[42] .

Il ne nous est pas possible, malheureusement, de retrouver la
trace de ce manuscrit dans les dixième, onzième et douzième
siècles.

Cependant dès le milieu du treizième siècle ce codex connaît
une faveur et une influence particulières. La traduction latine des
Testaments faite par Grosseteste (c. 1242) et l'abrégé qu'en a fait
peu après Vincent de Beauvais (1253?) nous restent dans plus
de 80 mss[43], et dans un nombre inconnu d'éditions
imprimées[44]. A son tour la version latine a servi de base pour les
traductions en français, allemand, néerlandais, anglais, danois,
bohémien, anglo-normand[45]. L'histoire des *Testaments* en
traduction néerlandaise sera le sujet d'une étude particulière en
préparation. Nous nous bornons ici à noter que, en néerlandais,
les *Testaments* ont été traduit deux fois du latin et peut-être une

---

[41] A moins que l'on ne préfère considérer la bibliothèque de Michel comme faisant
partie des biens de l'église qui échurent à l'église latine lors de l'arrivée des croisés à
Athènes.

[42] R.W. Hunt, *op. cit.* (n.40), pp. 130-32. On sait qu'au 16e siècle l'archevêque
Matth. Parker († 1575) était propriétaire de ce codex.

[43] La liste de mss de cette traduction dressée par S.H. Thomson, *op. cit.* (n.3), p.
43-4, a reçu un complément dans l'étude 'Les fragments marginaux dans le ms. *d* des
Test. XII Patr'., *J.S.J.* 2 (1971), p. 23, n. 1 [Chap. IV, p. 91, n. 1]. Le ms. *'olim
Padova'* qui s'y trouve cité est manifestement celui que Thomson a déjà signalé comme
le ms Venezia, Bibl. Naz. Marciana, lat. VI, 81. Quant à la datation du ms Vat. gr.
1238 discutée au. p. 87 de ce recueil, n. 1, il semble avoir échappé à l'auteur que
d'après J. Irigoin la souscription de Vat. gr. 1238 donnant la date 1195 a été recopiée,
v. 'Les premiers mss grecs écrits sur papier et le problème du bombycin', *Scriptorium*, 4
(1950), p. 200, n. 2. — L'extrait de Beauvais est daté en 1253 par Callus, o.c., p. 61.

[44] Des listes de ces éditions chez R. Sinker, *A Descriptive Catalogue of the Editions
of the Printed Text of the Versions of the Testamenta XII Patriarcharum*, p. 5-6; L.
Baur, *Die philosophischen Werke des Robert Grosseteste, Bischofs von Lincoln*,
Münster i.W., 1912, p. xi; v. aussi Thomson, *op. cit.* (n.3), p. 42.

[45] Voir les listes de Sinker, *op. cit.* (n. 44), p. 6-27 et Thomson, *op. cit.* (n. 3); p. 42,
dernière note. Pour les éditions néerlandaises la liste de Sinker est très incomplète;
d'autre part, plusieurs des éditions qu'on y trouve citées n'ont jamais existé.

fois du français. Jusqu' à nos jours jamais du grec. De ces versions
néerlandaises nous connaissons trois ou quatre manuscrits et plus
de 30 éditions imprimées, dont la plus ancienne semble être
parue en 1541 et la dernière date de 1679.

Toute la tradition occidentale des *Testaments* remonte à un
seul manuscrit grec, celui préservé de l'anéantissement par —
selon notre hypothèse — Michel Choniatès, signalé par John de
Basingstoke et traduit par Robert Grosseteste. On sait à présent
que c'est précisément ce manuscrit qui représente le stade le plus
ancien que l'on connaît de la tradition textuelle grecque[46]. C'est
donc grâce à Michel, John et Robert, que les *Testaments* ont été
lus en Europe occidentale dès le treizième siècle dans une forme
textuelle relativement fidèle. Au dixseptième siècle on lisait à
Amsterdam un texte des *Testaments* moins corrompu qu'au
Mont Sinaï! [47]

---

[46] ,,Die Textüberlieferung der Testamente der zwölf Patriarchen'', *Zeitschrift für die
neutestamentliche Wissenschaft* 63 (1972), p. 27-44 [Chap. II dans ce recueil].
[47] Ms Mont Sinaï, Sainte Catherine, gr. 770 (jadis 547), et le ms *i* de R.H. Charles,
(*The Greek Versions of the Testaments of the Twelve Patriarchs*, Oxford 1908 =
Darmstadt 1960, 1966³, p. xii).

VI

ADDITIONAL NOTES ON THE HISTORY OF
MSS. VENICE BIBL. MARC. GR. 494 (k) AND
CAMBRIDGE UNIV. LIBR. Ff. 1.24 (b)

HENK JAN DE JONGE

I. *Venice Marc. Gr. 494 (k)*

Witness *k* of the *Testaments* is contained in Cod. Marc. Gr. Z. 494 (= 331). This codex dates as a whole from the middle of the thirteent century. Its folios are of Oriental paper, without watermarks. Two hands can be distinguished, that of ff. 1-246r., and that of ff. 246v.-319.

The text of the *Testaments* contained in this codex has neither directly, nor indirectly been copied from that in MS. Cambridge, Univ. Libr. Ff. 1.24. The latter MS. was either in Athens or in England when *k* was written, so that *k* can hardly have been copied directly from it. But even indirect dependence is excluded by such readings as discussed in *ZNW* 63 (1972), p. 30, paragraph 3 (see now p. 48 in this volume), to which may be added :

> *T. Levi* VIII,5 ἐψώμισεν *b i*] + με *k g e af c*, + μοι *h, ldm aliter*.
> *T. Levi* XIV,1 γενήσεται *b gdm hi*] γενήσεσθε *k l e af c*.
> *T. Jud.* XXIV,3 πορεύσεσθε *b m, lectio facilior!*] πορεύεσθε *k g ld e, af chi defic*.

The MS. contains on the recto of the first folio the following inscription in iambic verses (the poetic character of the inscription is usually disregarded) :

> ἡ βίβλος αὕτη τῆς μονῆς τοῦ προδρόμου
> τῆς κειμένης ἔγκηστα [= ἔγγιστα] τῆς Ἀετίου [a cistern] ·
> ἀρχαϊκὴ δὲ τῇ μονῇ κλῆσις Πέτρα.

According to this ex-libris,[1] the MS. has belonged to the library

---

[1] On this traditional ex-libris of the monastery Prodromos-Petra, and on the library of this monastery in general, see Ἑλένη Δ. Κακουλίδη, "Ἡ βιβλιοθήκη τῆς μονῆς Προδρόμου-Πέτρας στὴν Κωνσταντινούπολη", Ἑλληνικά 21 (1968), pp. 3-39. The Venetian codex Marc. gr. 494 (= *k* of the *Testaments*) is dealt with on pp. 12-13; see also p. 32.

of the monastery Prodromos-Petra at Constantinople.[2] As the books
surviving from any one medieval library are not numerous as a rule,
it is exceptional that twenty-eight have come down to us from this
monastery (N. G. Wilson). The list of these twenty-eight books, now
scattered all over Europe, has been drawn by Heleni Kakoulidi
(see n. 1). N. G. Wilson thinks that so many books remain from
Prodromos-Petra because the monastery had a school attached to it,
which may have had its own scribal tradition.[3] But whether the MS.
under consideration has been written in the monastery where it turns
up first or not, cannot be ascertained.

In the fifteenth century we find the codex in the possession of
no less a person than Cardinal Bessarion. Educated at Constantinople,
and having been for some time an abbot of one of the monasteries
in the capital, Bessarion came to Italy in 1438 as a participant in
the Council of Florence. More or less disappointed in the results
of the council, he took up residence at Rome. He was the owner
of the largest and most important library of Greek books collected
in Italy in the fifteenth century, amounting to some five hundred
volumes by the end of his life. "He had not always been a keen
collector, since he had relied on the book trade in Constantinople
as an adequate source of supply; but one of his letters states that
the fall of the Greek empire in 1453 made him form the plan of
building as complete a collection as possible of Greek books, in the
intention of placing it eventually at the disposal of those Greeks
who survived the fall of the empire and reached Italy. This statement
of his plans shows one of his main reasons for presenting his
collection during his own lifetime (1468) to the city of Venice to
form the basis of a public library, for it was in Venice that a high
proportion of Greek refugees tended to congregate".[4]

The original inventory of the books which Bessarion bequeathed
to Venice has been published by H. Omont, "Inventaire des manuscrits
grecs et latins donnés à Saint-Marc de Venise par le cardinal Bessarion

---

[2] This monastery was founded c. 500 A.D., but very little is known of its history
prior to the twelfth century. A detailed report on its origin, history, location, housing
and library has been given by R. Janin, *La géographie ecclésiastique de l'empire
Romain* I, Le siège de Constantinople et le patriarcat œcuménique, tome III. Les
églises et les monastères, Paris 1953, pp. 435-443.

[3] N. G. Wilson, "The Libraries of the Byzantine World", *Greek, Roman, and
Byzantine Studies* 8 (1967), p. 64.

[4] L. D. Reynolds, N. G. Wilson, *Scribes & Scholars*, Oxford 1968, p. 126; 1974[2], p. 134.

(1468)".[5] The description of entry 89 in this list runs as follows:
"Item multa multorum doctorum, id est expositio super Lucam,
carmina Theologi cum expositione, Dionysius Areopagita cum expositione, theologia Damasceni, expositio in Apocalypsim, et alia multa,
in papyro". This succinct table of contents suffices to identify the
codex described as Marc. Gr. 494.

Another inventory, drawn up when the books were transported
to Venice in thirty cases or chests, has been published by Lami in
1740 and reprinted in Migne, *P.G.* 161, col. 701-714 : *Tabula librorum ...
quos ... cardinalis Nicaenus ... dono dedit ... ducali Venetiarum dominio :
qui reconditi (prout Roma transmissi fuerant) in capsis XXX commendati
fuere ...*. The list is itemized according to the contents of each chest.
"In capsa signata Q, ponderis librarum 240, sunt libri infrascripti :
... Expositio in Lucam : Carmina Nazianzeni cum expositione Dionysii
Areopagitae, cum expositione theologica Damasceni. Expositio in
Apocalypsim, et alia multa, in papyris". (Col. 709). Thus the book
arrived in the library where it is preserved up to the present day.[6]

The *Testaments* occupy in this codex the folios 263r.-264v., no more
than four pages. Owing to this their occurrence in the MS. seems
not to have been registered until 1740, when the MS. was described
in the catalogue by A.M. Zanetti and A. Bongiovanni, *Graeca D. Marci
Bibliotheca codicum manuscriptorum per titulos digesta ...*, Venice 1740,
p. 258 : "Codex CCCCXCIV in folio, chartaceus, foliorum 320. saeculi
circiter XIII". But even here the *Testaments* are only mentioned
cursorily, as something quite accidental. For whereas the titles or
authors of other writings contained in the MS. are capitalised, the
Testaments are dealt with as an appendix to the preceding title :
"subsequuntur Testamenta filiorum Jacob". As is well known the
Venice codex was first used for the textual criticism of the *Testaments
of the Twelve Patriarchs* in 1927 by M. R. James, who published
a (rather faulty) transcript from the text of Marc. Gr. 494 in *The
Journal of Theological Studies* 28 (1927), pp. 337-348. For the new
critical edition in preparation I have made fresh collations from
photographs. (In December 1973 I had the pleasure of seeing the
MS. in Venice).

For the edition and criticism of other texts Marc. Gr. 494 has
been utilised earlier, so for the New Testament. F. H. A. Scrivener,

---

[5] *Revue des bibliothèques* 4 (Paris 1894), pp. 129-187. Entry 89 appears on p. 152.

[6] For particulars on other inventories, see Omont, *art. cit.*, p. 136, n. 2.

A Plain Introduction to the Criticism of the N.T., Cambridge 1883³, designates it as nr. 466 (p. 226) and gives a short description in which the MS. is dated as fifteenth-century. Scrivener has also payed attention to the ex-libris of the Prodromos monastery (he records the occurrence of the same inscription in minuscules 87 and 178 and refers to Montfaucon, *Palaeogr. graeca*, pp. 59, 110, 305). The codex is also registered, as a rule with some descriptive notes, in the following lists of N.T. MSS.: C.R. Gregory, *Die griechischen Handschriften des N.T.*, Leipzig 1908, p. 69, no. 598 (cf. p. 306); *idem, Textkritik des N.T.*, Leipzig 1909, p. 206, no. 598 (with inter alia the note: 'G. 6. März 1886'); H. von Soden, *Die Schriften des N.T. in ihrer ältesten erreichbaren Textgestalt...*, I. Teil, I. Abt.: Die Textzeugen, Göttingen 1911, p. 260 (here Marc. Gr. 494 is listed as witness of Nicetas's catena on Luke) and p. 285 (here as witness of the commentary on Revelation by Andrew of Cappadocia); K. Aland, *Kurzgefasste Liste der gr. Handschriften des N.T.*, Berlin 1963, p. 92, no. 598. Especially for Nicetas's catena on Luke the codex has been studied by J. Sickenberger, *Die Lukaskatene des Niketas von Herakleia* (T.U., N.F. 7,4), Leipzig 1902, pp. 61 f. For his research into the text of Revelation, H.C. Hoskier, too, made use of Marc. Gr. 494: *Concerning the Text of the Apocalypse* I-II, London 1929, I, p. 667, no. 204). Josef Schmid in his model critical edition of the commentary on Revelation by Andrew of Cappadocia has duly collated and utilised the text of Marc. Gr. 494; for his description of the MS. and a discussion of the Prodromos ex-libris, see his *Studien zur Geschichte des griechischen Apokalypse-Textes*, 1. Teil: Der Apokalypse-Kommentar des Andreas von Kaisareia. Einleitung, München 1956, pp. 39-40.

I have not traced the part played by Marc. Gr. 494 in the criticism of other writings contained in it. But there is a description of the MS. in Joh. Koder-Jos. Paramelle s.j., *Symeon le Nouveau Théologien, hymnes 1-15*. Introduction, texte critique et notes; traduction (Sources chrétiennes 156), Paris 1969, pp. 23-24, cf. p. 44. —J. Darrouzès, *Nicétas Stethatos, Opuscules et lettres*. Introduction, texte critique, traduction et notes (Sources chrétiennes 81), Paris 1961, p. 19, n. 1 mentions and quotes the colophon "au dessous des *Hymnes* de Syméon le Nouveau Théologien (d. 1052) édités par Nicétas". (fol. 291v.). Further references to Marc. Gr. 494 are to be found in A. Kamkylis, "Eine Handschrift des Mystikers Symeon (Cod. Paris. Suppl. gr. 103), *Scriptorium* 22, 1968, pp. 21-22, in

Bibliotheca Hagiographorum graecorum III, 1957, p. 64, *sub* no. 2360, and in J. W. Wevers, *Septuaginta. Vetus Testamentum Graecum...*, *I, Genesis*, Göttingen 1974, preface.

A photographic reproduction of fol. 268r. is found in H. Hunger, *Byzantinische Geisteswelt von Konstantin dem Grossen bis zum Fall Konstantinopels*, Baden-Baden 1958 = repr. Amsterdam 1967, Plate 5 : Symeon Neos Theologos, *Hymnos* 6 (cf. p. 148 top).[7]

II. *Cambridge University Library Ff. 1.24 (b)*

Witness *b* of the *Testaments* is contained in Cambridge, Univ. Libr., MS. Ff. 1.24, fol. 203a-261b. The provenance of the codex has been dealt with in "La bibliothèque de Michel Choniatès et la tradition occidentale des *Testaments des XII Patriarches*", *Nederlandsch Archief voor Kerkgeschiedenis* 53 (1973), pp. 171-180 (in this volume Ch. V). How the text of the *Testaments* transmitted in this MS. was translated into Latin and became the object of scholarly interest, has been sketched in "Die Patriarchentestamente von Roger Bacon bis Richard Simon" (in this volume Ch. I). The following notes are only supplementary, and do not aim at completeness.

In 1253 the MS. came into the possession of the Friars Minors at Oxford along with other books left them by Grosseteste. Three hundred years later it turns up in the library of Matthew Parker, Archbishop of Canterbury, together with, *inter alia*, a beautiful Greek Psalter with Canticles, now no. 480 in the library of Corpus Christi at Cambridge. The MS. in the Univ. Libr., now Ff. 1.24, is referred to in a note (of Parker's time?) on a slip of vellum pasted in the beginning of the Corpus Psalter : "Hic liber script per eu qui sc. ypomnisticon grece", whereas a note on a fly-leaf at the beginning of the Testaments MS. in the Univ. Libr. intimates that "Hic liber script. per eum qui scripsit psalterium parvum Grecum". (Cf. J. Rendel Harris, *The Origin of the Leicester Codex of the N.T.*, London 1887, pp. 20-21). According to M. R. James, "Greek Manuscripts in England before the Renaissance", in *The Library*, 4th series, 7, 1927, pp. 337ff., esp. 341-343 and 350, Parker saved the MS. containing the *Testaments* from some monastery at Canterbury, possibly St. Augustine's.[8]

---

[7] The above survey does not in the least claim to be exhaustive.

[8] Ff. 1.24 figures as item 5 in the list of "Manuscripts owned by Parker, and not at Corpus Christi" in M. R. James, *A Descriptive Catalogue of the MSS. in the Library of Corpus Christi College, Cambridge*, I, Cambridge 1912, p. xxiii. I have

As early as 1600 Cambridge Univ. Libr. Ff. 1.24 figures in a catalogue of the "Bibliotheca Publica" of Cambridge University, *viz.* in [Th. James], *Ecloga Oxonio-Cantabrigiensis, ... continet Catalogum confusum Librorum Manuscriptorum ... Academiarum Oxoniae & Cantabrigiae ...*, London 1600. Under the heading "Libri omnes subsequentes, ex dono Beatissimae memoriae, Reverendissimi in Christo Patris Mathiae Parkeri Archiepiscopi, in cista quadam intra Bibliothecam inclusi, diligentissime custodiùntur" (p. 67), one finds, as no. 243, the title *Liber Paralipomenon, & Testamentum 12. Patriarcharum, Graece.* The latter work is called "Testamentum 12. *Prophetarum*" (my italics) in the table of contents appended to the main title of the codex. James's catalogue was reprinted by E. Bernard, *Catalogi librorum MSS. Angliae et Hiberniae in unum collecti* I, Oxonii 1697, Pars altera, see p. 171, no. 2423. 243.

Almost from the very moment (1575) that the codex entered into Cambridge University Library, it has been common knowledge in England that a Greek copy of the *Testaments of the Twelve Patriarchs* was available in that library. This was due to its mention on the title-page of the English translation of the *Testaments*, of which at least thirty editions appeared before 1700, the first being of London 1575 or 1576. (Cf. R. Sinker, *A Descriptive Catalogue of the Editions of the Printed Text of the Versions of the Testamenta XII Patriarcharum*, Cambridge-London 1910, pp. 6-14). The title of these editions unvaryingly intimates that this is an English translation by A.G. (= Arthur Golding), after Grosseteste's Latin version from the Greek, "*To the Credit whereof, an ancient* Greek *Copy, Written in* Parchment, *is kept in the University Library of* Cambridge". (The citation is from a copy of the edition Glasgow 1684). To my knowledge the first scholar to refer to the Cambridge MS. of the *Testaments* in scientific literature was J. de Mey, professor of theology at the Athenaeum Illustre in Middelburg (1675) (see "Die Patriarchentestamente von Roger Bacon etc.", p. 28-29). De Mey's information

---

not been able to consult M. R. James, *Sources of Archbishop Parker's MSS.* (Cambridge Antiq. Soc.) cited by E. A. Savage, *Old English Libraries*, London 1911 = repr. New York-London 1970, p. 70, n. 3, nor M. R. James, *Archbishop Parker's MSS.*, 1899, cited *ibidem*, p. 288. In Savage's own account of the history of Cambridge Univ. Libr. MS. Ff. 1.24 (*op. cit.*, p. 220), the widespread error is repeated that "the manuscript was brought home by John of Basingstoke". The same mistake is made by M. Cantor, J. E. Sandys and J. W. Thompson, cf. "La bibliothèque de Michel Choniatès ...", p. 174, n. 17; in this volume, p. 100, n. 17. See p. 115, *Addendum 1.*

came, however, from the title-page of some edition of the English version.

As the source of Joseppus's *Hypomnesticon biblion* the Cambridge MS. has been used, copied or studied by: Patrick Young, *Clementis ad Corinthios Epistola Prior*, Oxonii 1633, fol. N2r. (Young quotes Joseppus "quem nos ex codice MS. Cantabrigiensi descriptum habemus"); John Selden, *De anno civili veterum judaeorum*, cap. viii, in: *Opera omnia*, Vol. I, Pars I, col. 28 (Selden quotes from a "MS. in Bibliotheca Colleg. Benedict. Cantabrigiae"); Jean B. Cotelier, *SS. Patrum qui temporibus apostolicis floruerunt*, Paris 1672 (only accessible to me in J. Clericus's re-edition, Amsterdam 1724, volumen primum, p. 452) (in a note on *Const. Apost.* VIII, 76, where a canon of biblical books is given, Cotelier cites "Ex Josephi Commentario, Cap. 158", in Latin and Greek, from "Membranae Regiae Cod. 22"; but he mentions also the Cambridge MS.); Thomas Gale, *Iamblichi Chalcidensis de Mysteriis liber*, Oxford 1678, p. 215, (Gale states that copies of the *Hypomnesticon* are in the possession of J. Crojus and Cambridge Univ. Libr.; he himself uses a copy from the Cambridge MS., cf. p. 29 above, n. 43); Is. Vossius, *De Sibyllinis... oraculis*, Oxford 1679, p. 18 (Vossius says that the *Hypomnesticon* "in multis reperitur Bibliothecis"); G. Olearius, *Observationes sacrae ad Ev. Matth.*, Leipsic 1713, p. 72 (mentions Vossius's and Cave's view that Joseppus should be identified with Joseph Tiberiensis, a converted Jew mentioned by Epiphanius, and says that he has borrowed a copy from I. Laughton, professor at Cambridge). I have not found a copy of the Berlenburg Bible of 1742, of which vol. 8 must contain "Josephi Gedächtnis-Büchlein" (according to E. Hennecke, *Handbuch zu den Neutestamentlichen Apokryphen*, Billige Ausg., Tübingen 1914, p. 8). That the Cambridge MS. cannot be earlier than the ninth or tenth century was pointed out by C. F. Boernerus in his re-edition of Jac. le Long's *Bibliotheca sacra*, Leipsic 1709, p. 354. Until that time it has been generally accepted on the authority of Parker that the MS. dated from the seventh century. This erroneous date has been maintained in the *Catalogue of the MSS. preserved in the Library of the University of Cambridge* II, Cambridge 1857, p. 313, where the MS. is described by F. J. A. Hort. The correction of the date on fol. [A7]r. in the same volume of the *Catalogue* was overlooked by H. Usener, *Rheinisches Museum* 28 (1873), pp. 430-433.

The Greek text of the *Hypomnesticon* was first edited by J. A.

Fabricius in his *Codex Pseudepigraphus Veteris Testamenti* II, Hamburg 1723 (it covers the second half of the volume). The edition, provided with a Latin translation, is based on a transcript of Gale's copy (see above) and on Boernerus's copy from the Cambridge MS. In his dedicatory letter and in several of his critical notes (see esp. that to chap. CXX, p. 247), Fabricius refers to earlier writers dealing with the *Hypomnesticon*. Fabricius's edition has been reprinted in Migne, *P.G.* 106, col. 16-176.

More information on Joseppus's *Hypomnesticon* and the MSS. in which it has been circulating may be found in J. A. Fabricius, *Bibliotheca Graeca*, ed. G. C. Harles, V, Hamburg 1796, p. 60 (on Gale's copy); VIII, p. 349; and XI, Hamburg 1808, p. 51 (on the date of the Cambridge MS., on excerpts made from the Cambridge MS. by J. Chr. Wolfius, and on the copies used for Fabricius's edition). The only special study devoted to the *Hypomnesticon* in recent times (apart from articles in encyclopedias) is J. Moreau, "Observations sur l'Ὑπομνηστικὸν βιβλίον Ἰωσήππου", *Byzantion* 25-27, 1955-1957, pp. 241-276; p. 242, n. 1: "Le codex est écrit en belle minuscule, avec d'assez nombreuses formes onciales. Mais il serait difficile, sur la base de ce critère, de dater le ms. avec plus de précision... Un coup d'œil sur l'écriture suffit à démontrer l'inanité de la légende attribuant l'acquisition du ms à l'évêque Théodore, mort en 690, qui l'aurait apporté en Angleterre... Une copie du *Cantabrigiensis*, faite au XVIIIᵉ s., se trouve à la Bibliothèque Universitaire d'Utrecht (H. Omont, *Centralblatt für Bibliothekswesen*, 1887, p. 210)". See p. 115, *Addendum 2*.

The folios 1-103 of the Cambridge MS. contain the LXX text of the two books of Chronicles. A collation of this portion of the MS. has been published in Brian Walton's *Biblia sacra polyglotta* VI, London 1657, pp. 121-123. A fresh collation, made by Rob. Holmes, was used for the edition of Chronicles in Rob. Holmes-Jac. Parsons, *Vetus Testamentum Graecum* II, pars septima, Oxford 1817. The MS. is quoted as no. 60. The 'Praefatio', fol. *9F, sub no. 60, gives a brief description of the codex ("jampridem in Bibliis Polyglottis Waltoni, sed testante Holmesio minus accurate, collatus..."). I have not been able to consult Rob. Holmes, *The second annual Account of the Collation of the MSS. of the Septuagint Version*, 1790, p. 36, quoted by Rahlfs, see below.

The Cambridge MS. figures in the following lists of LXX witnesses. H. B. Swete, *An Introduction to the Old Testament in Greek*, Cambridge 1914, p. 155, no. 60. A. Rahlfs, *Verzeichnis der griechischen Handschriften des Alten Testaments...*, Berlin 1914, pp. 41-42. A. E. Brooke-N. McLean, *The Old Testament in Greek*, Vol. II, Part III, I and II Chronicles, Cambridge-London 1932, p. v. and Leslie C. Allen, *The Greek Chronicles* (Suppl. to V.T.), Leiden 1974, p. 4, Ch. III, and p. 85.

I have not been able to consult J. O. Halliwell, *The Manuscript Rarities of the University of Cambridge*, 1841, p. 140, mentioned by Rahlfs (but had the privilege of inspecting the MS. in June 1973).

Photographs of the Cambridge MS. figure in S. H. Thomson, *The Writings of Robert Grosseteste, Bishop of Lincoln 1235-1253*, Cambridge 1940, Plate I.

Addendum 1. ad p. 112, n. 8: MS. Cambridge Univ. Libr. Ff. 1.24 is also mentioned in Roberto Weiss, 'The Private Collector and the Revival of Greek Learning', in: F. Wormald, C. E. Wright (edd.), *The English Library before 1700*, London p. 126: 'Grosseteste's Greek MSS.... were left by him to the Grey Friars of Oxford. Three of them still survive. The Cambridge Univ. Libr. possesses Grosseteste's copy of the Testaments of the Twelve Patriarchs...'.

Addendum 2. ad p. 114: The Utrecht MS. of Joseppus referred to by Moreau is: Utrecht, Univ. Libr. MS. 17 = 1 C 7. See the *Catalogus codicum manu scriptorum Bibliothecae Universitatis Rheno-trajectinae*, Utrecht-The Hague 1887, I, p. 4: 'In fronte legitur: "Descr. Cantabrigiae a. 1706 ex cod. membr. Biblioth. publ. qui olim fuit... Parkeri...".'

Addendum 3. ad p. 113-4: For Gale's copy of Joseppus' *Hypomnesticon*, now Cambridge, Libr. of Trinity College, MS. O.4.24, see M. R. James, *The Western MSS. in the Libr. of Trinity College...* III, Cambridge 1902, pp. 274-5, no. 1255, *sub* 2. James points out that this copy seems to have been written by Patrick Young; cf. p. 29 in this volume, nn. 42 and 43.

VII

THE RELATIONSHIP BETWEEN MS. ATHOS LAURA I 48 (*l*) AND MS. ATHOS LAURA K 116

H. W. HOLLANDER

During a visit to Mount Athos in 1970 A. Hultgård succeeded in photographing the until that moment unknown text of the Testaments of the Twelve Patriarchs in MS. Athos Laura K 116. The report of his visit and the result of his analysis of the text of a number of passages in this MS. can be found in his doctoral dissertation.[1]

The new MS. proves to be narrowly related to MS. Laura I 48, known under the siglum *l*. In the passages he investigated Hultgård found only very few differences, and on the basis of these variants he concluded that MS. I 48 is a copy of MS. K 116. On p. 3 of his book he notes the following variants :

	K 116	I 48
T. Levi XIV,1	χεῖρας ἐπιβάλλοντες	χεῖρας ἐπιβάλοντες
T. Juda XXIII,5	τῶν ἐχθρῶν ὑμῶν	τῶν ἐχθρῶν ὑμᾶς -ῶν (corr.)
T. Zeb. IX,8	λυτρώσεται	λυτρώσηται
T. Dan V,12	τῆς νέας ιλημ	τῆς νέας ιηλ
T. Dan V,13	συναναστραφόμενος	συναναστρεφόμενος
	αἰχμαλωσίαν αἰχμαλωτισθήσεται	αἰχμαλωτισθήσεται
T. Levi IV,5	οἱ (corr.) ὁ καταρώμενοι	οἱ καταρώμενοι

I 48 must be the copy of K 116, according to Hultgård, because : "on a corrigé ὑμᾶς (T. Juda XXIII:5) sur ὑμῶν de K 116 et par mégarde (homoioarkton?) omis αἰχμαλωσίαν dans T. Dan V:13. De plus, la correction de K 116 dans T. Lévi IV:5 se trouve acceptée par I 48". To this it must be remarked, however, that these minimal differences do not allow us to draw such a definite conclusion. It is purely arbitrary to suppose that in T. Jud. XXIII,5 where I 48 has a double reading, ὑμᾶς was corrected in I 48 after the

---

[1] A. Hultgård, *Croyances Messianiques des Test. XII Patr. Critique textuelle et commentaire des passages messianiques*, Uppsala 1971, pp. 1-4.

ὑμῶν in K 116, but that the correction οἱ found next to ὁ in K 116 in T. Levi IV,5 is not secondary but original. It is possible that in T. Dan V,13 αἰχμαλωσίαν was omitted because of *hma* in I 48, but a secondary addition in K 116 cannot be excluded.

For the purpose of the preparation of the *editio maior* it was necessary to make a complete collation of MS K 116 against I 48. A. Hultgård made this possible by kindly putting photographs of the entire MS. at our disposal.

The result of our investigation may be summed up as follows.

Theoretically the narrow relationship between the two MSS. can be explained in three ways : *a*) I 48 is directly dependent on K 116, *b*) K 116 is directly dependent on I 48, *c*) I 48 and K 116 go back to a common ancestor.

Ad a) It is impossible that I 48 is dependent on K 116.

(1) A number of omissions because of *hmt* in K 116 are not found in I 48. They are ἰδού... ὑμῖν in T. Rub. I,6[2]; the entire verse T. Jud. IV,2; λύπη... καὶ οἱ ἐν[2] in T. Jud. XXV,4; καὶ ἐπιστρέψει ὑμᾶς εἰς τὴν γῆν ὑμῶν in T.N. IV,3.

(2) In K 116 we find a number of variants which must be regarded as secondary. In T. Iss. VII,9 it reads ὕπνον ἀναπαύσεως ἕως τὴν κοινὴν ἀνάστασιν in stead of ὕπνον αἰώνιον; in T. Jos. XX,4 ἐν εἰρήνῃ ὕπνου ἕως τῆς ἀναστάσεως again for ὕπνον αἰώνιον. In both cases I 48 sides with the rest of the Greek MSS.[3]

Ad b) There are a number of arguments which make it likely that K 116 is dependent on I 48.

(1) In T. Dan V,6 the words τῷ Λευὶ ὑπακούσονται have been eraded in I 48; they are still faintly visible under the ἐπαναστήσονται which has been put at their place. This correction is taken over by K 116. A similar case is T. Dan VI,2; here the correct reading παραιτουμένῳ is deleted in I 48 and replaced by περιέχοντι, taken over by K 116 as ὑπερέχοντι. It is possible, of course, to suppose that in these cases I 48 and K 116 go back to a common « Vorlage »; in that case I 48 must have used this « Vorlage » plus a good manuscript, and have followed the reading of the good manuscript first, but rejected it afterwards. It is much simpler to suppose that

---

[2] Omission by *hmt* is likely, because both MSS. omit καί at the beginning of this verse.

[3] In T. Jos. XX,4 *c* reads ὕπνῳ καλῷ in stead of ὕπνον αἰώνιον.

the scribe of I 48 took the initiative for the changes, and that his readings were taken over by the scribe of K 116.

(2) In T. Jos. V,2 we find the word αἰδέσθητι twice. In I 48 it occurs at the end and the beginning of two successive pages. In K 116 it is also repeated but there no special situation can account for the repetition. Also here it is very likely that K 116 followed I 48.

(3) In I 48 there are no omissions because of *hmt* or *hma* over against K 116.[4]

Ad c) In favour of the hypothesis that I 48 and K 116 go back to a common ancestor a few rather weak arguments may be adduced.

(1) In T. Levi V,5 K 116 adds σου after δέομαι, together with *dmchi*. In T. Jud. XII,9 I 48 is the only MS. that adds καί after τελεσκομένην. In both cases K 116 may be thought to have preserved the common « Vorlage » over against I 48.

(2) A text-critically very difficult situation is found in T. Jos. III,3.[5] The correct reading will be λόγους πατρός μου Ἰακώβ. Already in a stage before *b* a scribe must have written πατέρων inadventently, and corrected his mistake afterwards without crossing out πατέρων. I 48 reads λόγους πατρός μου Ἰακώβ, whereas K 116 has λόγους πατέρων μου Ἰακώβ. These readings can be explained by assuming the reading with both πατέρων *and* πατρός in the common ancestor (comp. *b*). Alternatively we may suppose that in copying I 48 the scribe of K 116 made the same mistake as the scribe in the stage before *b*, with the difference that in K 116 πατρός was no longer preserved.

The arguments mentioned ad c) are not conclusive, whereas those mentioned ad b) are very strong. The most likely theory, therefore, is that K 116 is dependent on I 48.

A. Hultgård adduces, however, yet another argument in favour of his theory of dependence of I 48 on K 116. On p. 4 he writes: "A partir de ces exemples et de *la datation signalée dans le catalogue*

---

[4] For αἰχμαλωσίαν in T. Dan V,13 see above.

[5] *b*   reads... λόγους πατέρων πατρός μου Ἰακώβ
     g   reads... λόγων   πατέρων μου πατρὸς Ἰακώβ
     d   reads... λόγων   πατρός μου Ἰακώβ
     eaf read ... λόγων   πατέρων μου
     c   reads... λόγους   πατρός μου
     hi   read... λόγους πατέρων μου
     km abs.

(curs. H.W.H.), il paraît certain que K 116 est l'original et I 48 la copie". According to this catalogue [6] I 48 is dated in the XVII th century and K 116 in the XVI th, and if these dates are correct dependence of K 116 on I 48 must be excluded. But first Hultgård himself remarks: "Nous ne savons pas sur quoi s'appuie la datation des deux MSS. par *Lauriotes* et *Eustratiades*" [7] so that we cannot regard these dates as absolutely binding. And secondly Hultgård tells us of both MSS.: "...la graphie indique la même époque, environs, XVIᵉ-XVIIᵉ siècles". [8]

Given these uncertainties our conclusion, reached on the basis of text-critical argumentation still stands. [9] One should keep textual criticism separate from codicology. In the case an earlier date for K 116 is proved beyond doubt, we shall have to assume a common ancestor with a text identical—or practically identical—with that of I 48; as yet this is a superfluous hypothesis.

---

[6] Spyridon Lauriotes-S. Eustratiades, *Catalogue of the Greek Manuscripts in the Library of the Laura on Mount Athos*, with notices from other Libraries (*Harv. Theol. Studies XII*), 1925.

[7] *Op. cit.*, p. 3 n. 2. He continues, however: "...mais on doit vraisemblablement faire crédit à la datation conventionnelle".

[8] *Op. cit.*, p. 3.

[9] In his *Die Testamente der zwölf Patriarchen* (Jüdische Schriften aus hellenistisch-römischen Zeit, Bd. III Lief. 1), Gütersloh 1974, J. Becker comes to the same conclusion. On p. 18 he writes: "Zwei MSS. befinden sich in der Bibliothek von Laura (Athos). Von ihnen hat Burchard eines (*l*) näher untersucht und exemplarische Lesarten veröffentlicht. Darüber hinaus hat Hultgård nachgewiesen, daß das andere Laura-MS. eine Kopie des eben genannten MS. ist". Hultgård maintains the opposite theory; in misreading his statements Becker has, by chance, hit upon the right solution!

VIII

THE GREEK TESTAMENTS OF THE TWELVE PATRIARCHS AND THE ARMENIAN VERSION

M. DE JONGE

1. Introduction

In recent years our knowledge of the Armenian version of the Testaments of the Twelve Patriarchs has increased considerably. In his edition of the Testaments of 1908 [1] R. H. Charles mentioned 12 manuscripts of which he used 9. In 1969 C. Burchard [2] published a list of 45 MSS. in various libraries (2 of which in the Library in the Convent of St. James in Jerusalem), and in the same year M. E. Stone published the Armenian text of the Testament of Levi [3] on the basis of 8 MSS. in the Jerusalem library.[4] A year later he announced that he had been informed of the existence of three more copies in New Julfa.[5] This brings the grand total of known MSS. to 54.

The majority of these MSS. have not yet been studied. M. E. Stone's edition gives the fullest possible survey of MS.-material for one Testament only, using the 8 Jerusalem MSS. and Charles' notes in the apparatus to his edition. C. Burchard only gives a useful list of variants in Test. Reuben and Test. Benjamin taken from the

---

[1] *The Greek Versions of the Testaments of the Twelve Patriarchs*, Oxford 1908 (reprint Oxford-Darmstadt [3]1966).

[2] "Zur armenischen Überlieferung der Testamente der Zwölf Patriarchen", in C. Burchard-J. Jervell-Joh. Thomas, *Studien zu den Testamenten der Zwölf Patriarchen* (*B.Z.N.W.* 36), Berlin 1969, 1-29. This article is dated 1963/4; it was reworked in July 1967.

[3] *The Testament of Levi*. A First Study of the Armenian MSS. of the Testaments of the XII Patriarchs, in the Convent of St. James, Jerusalem, Jerusalem 1969. See also the review by C. Burchard in *J.B.L.* 89, 1970, pp. 160-162 and L. Leloir in *R.Q.* VII 3 (no. 27) 1970, pp. 441-449 (who also discusses *B.Z.N.W.* 36).

[4] In an Appendix on pp. 166-188 he gives the text of the Testament of Reuben, Simeon and Levi in the Calcutta MS., listed by Burchard as no. 28.

[5] In his review of *B.Z.N.W.* 36 in *J.B.L.* 89, 1970, pp. 487f. See also his "Methodological Issues in de Study of the Text of the Apocrypha and Pseudepigrapha" in *Proceedings of the Fifth World Congress of Jewish Studies 1969*, Jerusalem 1971, pp. 211-217.

important MS. Erewan 1500.[6] On the basis of his hypotheses concerning the possible relationships between MSS. (mainly based on his observations in connection with the text of Joseph and Aseneth,[7] a writing often appearing in Armenian codices together with the Testaments) and his suggestions with regard to future study, A. Hultgård[8] studied MSS. Erewan 1500, 346, 353, 354 and Vienna (Library of the Mechitarists) 706.[9] He gives a considerable number of variants, taken from these MSS. limiting himself, however to the "messianic" passages discussed in his dissertation.[10]

Our knowledge is, therefore, still far from complete. And although some important preliminary conclusions can be drawn—it is abundantly clear that the results of my own discussion of A in 1953[11] and of that of J. Becker in 1970[12] based on Charles' variants are only partly tenable—it is, at the same time, clear that new evidence may come to light in the study of the many MSS. of which we only know the existence. Therefore M. E. Stone is at the moment stimulating research of these MSS. by various scholars, starting from the collation of a number of sample passages.[13] It is hoped that on the basis of these collations a definite decision can be made with regard to the MSS. on which a future edition of the Armenian version is to be based.

Awaiting the results of this further research it may be useful to sum up briefly what has been found so far and to ask what the contribution of the Armenian evidence to the reconstruction of the Greek text is likely to be. The answer given to this question is decisive for the publication of the new edition based on all available Greek evidence which is about to be completed.

---

[6] *Op. cit.*, p. 25f.

[7] See his *Untersuchungen zu Joseph und Aseneth* (*W.U.N.T.* 8), Tübingen 1965.

[8] In his dissertation *Croyances Messianiques des Test. XII Patr.* Critique textuelle et commentaire des passages messianiques, Uppsala 1971.

[9] Burchard, *op. cit.*, p. 12 gives it the number 705.

[10] Though we must be grateful for Hultgård's efforts to supplement the available evidence, the restriction of his information to passages which were not selected because of their importance for textual criticism, remains a serious drawback.

[11] *The Testaments of the Twelve Patriarchs*. A Study of their Text, Composition and Origin, Assen 1953, pp. 23-34.

[12] *Untersuchungen zur Entstehungsgeschichte der Testamente der Zwölf Patriarchen* (*A.G.J.U.* 8), Leiden 1970, pp. 9, 12f., 44-68. Becker knows Burchard's study, but as this contains only few actual variant readings it does not really influence his analysis.

[13] See his "The Jerusalem Manuscripts of the Testaments of the Twelve Patriarchs", in *Sion* 1970, pp. 1-7 and "Methodological Issues" (see note 5 above), pp. 213-216.

2. *The relationships between the Armenian MSS.*

R. H. Charles divided the Armenian MSS. into two groups, A^α and A^β, each representing a different type of text. He even tried to establish exact genealogical relationships between the MSS. belonging to each of these two groups. C. Burchard observed agreements between Charles' classification and his own results with regard to the classification of MSS. which contain both the Armenian version of Joseph and Aseneth and that of the Testaments. On the basis of this he was able to predict the affinities of the Armenian text of the Testaments in MSS. of which he had studied the Joseph and Aseneth text. At the same time he could point to MSS. which did not (yet) fit into the system. In this way he was able to spot MS. Erewan 1500 and point to a number of clearly important and original readings in that manuscript; Hultgård, following his suggestions, made a more extensive study of this MS. (calling it A^z) as well as of other MSS. singled out by Burchard. Of these MS. Erewan 353 ($= A^v$) proved to be the most valuable.

Burchard refused however, to set up a stemma. In his review of M. E. Stone's study he sums up his own position as follow: "By and large our views seem to converge. All extant MSS. appear to derive from a common origin. If later influence from the Greek is present, it has yet to be detected. A^α is a deliberate reworking of the text. The A^β MSS. only form a group when contrasted with A^α. Viewed by itself, A^β disintegrates into a series of distinct manuscript families. The one or ones represented by $A^{cd.efg}$ (MSS. used by Charles, d.J.) NOPQRT (MSS. used by Stone, d.J.) seem to be the largest; most of the MSS. that have not yet been studied will no doubt belong here. Further investigation is needed to establish their interrelationships and to determine their value for reconstructing the original A".[14]

M. E. Stone's book is valuable because it gives a consistent analysis of a considerable uninterrupted portion of the Armenian text and new MS. evidence. Six of the Jerusalem MSS. belong to the A^β-group, one to A^α. The eighth is the most important and by far the oldest manuscript: no. 1925, the so-called Bible of Erznka, written in 1269. Stone gave it the siglum A^m. His results are conveniently summed up in his paper "Methodological Issues in the Study of the Text of

---

[14] *J.B.L.* 89, 1970, p. 362.

the Apocrypha and Pseudepigrapha"[15] : "After the investigation of
the Jerusalem manuscripts for the *Testament of Levi*, a third textual
type can be added to the two recognized by CHARLES, i.e., the Bible
of Erznka, called *M*. This is a long text, in this respect similar
to *Beta*. Yet it contains many Greek readings not preserved in *Alpha*
and *Beta*. ... When the three textual types, *Alpha*, *Beta* and *M*, are
compared with the Greek, we find cases in which each of them
agrees with the Greek against the other two. This implies that none
of them is the direct ancestor of any other and apparently *M*, the
ancestor of *Beta*, and the ancestor of *Alpha* might be described as
sister text forms, each bearing independent witness to *Armenian".

A. Hultgård[16] supplements this picture : A^m is closely related to A^v,
so that we should speak of the text-type A^{mv}. A^z represents an
independent text-type, closely related to A^α, just as according to
Stone's investigation $A^{m(v)}$ is closely related to A^β. Moreover all
superior readings of A^α (over against A^{mv} and A^β) seem to be
shared by A^z. Hultgård does not pay special attention to the relationships between the MSS. within the two groups A^α and A^β,
nor does he define the relationship between the prototype of A^β and
that of A^{mv}. He contents himself with the statement "... les groupes A^α
et A^β n'ont fourni, du moins pour les passages étudiés, avec certitude
aucune leçon primitive qui ne se retrouve pas dans A^z ou A^{mv}
également". This clearly provides insufficient support for his suggestion
"Même si la base du texte étudié est étroite il nous paraît que
le texte de la version arménienne se laisse établir seulement à l'aide
de A^{mv} et A^z".[17] However reliable A^{mv} and A^z may be, it seems
to be safer to follow Stone's proposal to try to supplement the
available evidence and to complete the picture of the (possible)
interrelationships before selecting the MSS. one wants to use as
primary witnesses.

A second question requires a short discussion here : that of secondary
Greek influence on the development of the Armenian MS. tradition.
M. E. Stone accurately sums up the general opinion when he writes :
"It should be added that the Greek readings found in each of these
three textual types, as far as they are distinctive, all seem to go back
to the same branch of the Greek textual tradition. This apparently

---

[15] See note 5 above, p. 216.
[16] See *op. cit.* (note 8), pp. 22-37.
[17] *Op. cit.*, p. 36.

implies that there has been no second contact between any given branch of the Armenian tradition and the Greek and that (at least theoretically) all the variants within the Armenian are probably to be regarded as inner-Armenian".[18] In a note he points to some cases in *Test. Levi*, where variants of Armenian appear to be reflected in the variants of Greek. He adds that "no pattern or consistent constellation of these variants appears in the manuscripts and the text studied so far, and they are not all sure examples".[19] The present author, after study of the variants and Stone's notes on them, would like to comment that these cases are, indeed, either not certain or represent parallel developments in Armenian and Greek—after all there are obvious ways of solving difficulties! M. E. Stone's additional warning that more evidence may come to light which will compel us to alter our opinion is, of course, apposite. Yet he is right in concluding that "any such second contact will be of very minor proportions and of little influence on the Armenian text".

Obviously, a number of uncertainties remain. Yet it is, so far, unlikely that the general picture of the situation with regard to the Armenian version will be altered considerably in the course of future research. We are on reasonably safe ground and are able to proceed to the next important group of problems : those centering around the relationships between the Armenian and the Greek.

3. *The relationship between the Armenian version and the Greek MSS.*

Here we find agreement between Burchard, Stone and Hultgård on two matters. First, the study of the new manuscripts, particularly A^m, A^v and A^z, has shown that many variants noted in Charles' edition are inner-Armenian variants and do not represent differences between the prototype of the Armenian version and the Greek. The Greek text from which A derives will not have been so very different from the Greek manuscripts in our possession. Burchard's conclusion is right : "Ursprünglich dürfte A eine bessere und voll-ständigere Übersetzung gewesen sein, als $A^{Charles}$ erkennen lässt, wenn man auch Freiheiten und Kürzungen zugestehen muss, und zwar je weiter man nach hinten kommt, desto mehr".[20] Stone's and Hultgård's investigations have corroborated this.

---

[18] "Methodological Issues", p. 216.

[19] See n. 17 on the page just mentioned. The cases are A^β III,9, V,6, VI,9, XVIII,5,9 and A^α XIX,2. A similar case is found in A^β II,3.

[20] *Op. cit.*, p. 27.

Burchard is also right, when he criticizes my comparison of A with a MS. like d^{21}. This is unfair "wenn man die zahllosen Eigenheiten dieser kapriziösen Handschrift bedenkt". Our new evidence does, indeed, lead to the conclusion that the prototype of A and the Greek before A must have been "better" than our MS. *d*.

The second question is, what place should be assigned to A between the various Greek MSS. It is generally assumed that A shows the type of text found in *b d g k* (*l*). Burchard formulates the problem correctly when he writes : "Wie sich die Vorlage des Armeniers zu den übrigen Handschriften ihres Texttyps *bdgkl* verhielt ist neu zu untersuchen".[22] Stone concludes that A^β and A^m "are substantially like the Greek, and in particular like Greek *b* and *d*".[23] Hultgård concludes : "La version arménienne se rattache au groupement constitué pas les mss. *b d g k l*, et parmi ceux-ci on trouve les contacts les plus précis avec mss. *d* et *g*".[24]

None of these authors could use the material collected at Leiden for the new *editio maior* of the Testaments; nor did they know H. J. de Jonge's attempt to reconstruct a stemma for the Greek MS.-tradition.[25] A new attempt to define A's relationship with the Greek MSS. seems, therefore, to be called for.

First, in Test. Zebulun A joins *eafchi* in giving the short text in chapters VI-IX. Below [26] I shall argue that this short text is secondary; consequently, we are here confronted with a "Bindefehler" between A and *eaf chi* against *bkgldm*. Consequently, A would have to be placed off the main line at some point after no. 6 in the stemma.

Secondly, a comparison of A and G in Test. Levi[27] allows the following further conclusions :

a) A cannot be dependent on *af chi* because it does not share a number of secondary readings in these MSS.

| VIII,15 ἄφραστος | + A] ἀγαπητός | *af chi.* |
| VIII,17 ἀρχιερεῖς | + A] ἱερεῖς | *af chi.* |

---

[21] In *The Testaments* (see note 11), p. 30f.

[22] *Op. cit.*, p. 27.

[23] *The Testament of Levi* (see note 3), p. 163.

[24] *Op. cit.*, p. 36.

[25] "Die Textüberlieferung der Testamente der zwölf Patriarchen", *Z.N.W.* 63, 1972, pp. 27-44; see now chapter II above. The stemma is found on p. 47.

[26] See section 5.

[27] For this testament we have now Stone's edition and Hultgård's detailed notes on II 10-11; IV 2-6; XVI 3-5 and XVIII.

VIII,17 φυλαχθήσεται   + A] ληφθήσεται *af chi*.
XI,2   Γηρσάμ² ... γράφεται + A] om.   *af chi*.

In all these cases the variants are peculiar to *af chi* and does A support
the other Greek MSS.

b) In the cases just mentioned *e* does not support the reading of
af chi. It does join them, however, in two cases, where A, again,
gives the reading of the other Greek MSS.

III,2 ἀνόμων rel G, A] ἀνῶν = ἀνθρώπων *eaf chi* + fragment *n*
XV,3 θεωροῦντες (ὁρῶντες *ld*) rel G; who will see you A] μισοῦντες
                                                          eaf chi.

Consequently A cannot be dependent on *eaf chi* either and in the
stemma reconstructed by H. J. de Jonge its most likely place would
seem to be, before no. 13, i.e. before the point where *e* branches
off from the main line.

c) A does not share any of the special *b(k)* readings, as IV,4
ἀποσκολοπίσαι; πρᾶγμα in VIII,1; τῇ ἱερατείᾳ in XVIII,1; the
omission of τὰ ἔθνη ... τῆς ἱερωσύνης αὐτοῦ by hmt. in XVIII,9.
At the same time *b(k)* do not show acquaintance with any of the
special readings in A and I have not been able to find any other
case where a special relationship between *b(k)* and A has to be
assumed.

The same applies to *g*. A does not share *g*'s omissions in XI-XII,4
and XVIII,1 and *g* does not follow A in its special readings. The
two cases where *g* and A show agreement do not prove anything.
In V,5 *g* reads and A presupposes καί in stead of ἵνα; the change
from hypotaxis to parataxis in both witnesses may have been fortuitous.
Moreover the spelling ἐπικαλέσομαι (*kgldec*) may have suggested
that this verb should be taken as future. In XII,6 A reads "you are,
my sons, three families". Stone remarks here that A^m (and the edition
of Yovsepiʽancʽ in 1896) read the singular of the noun.[28] It seems
hazardous, therefore, to assume that A follows *g*'s reading τρεῖς γενεαί
over against the τρίτη γενεά in the other MSS. I have not found
other examples of agreement between *g* and A over against all others.

With regard to *ldm* it is clear that A does not share secondary
readings in this group of MSS. In VIII,5. e.g., *ldm* have the (obviously

---

[28] See his note on p. 102 of his edition. A^α is incomplete and can be explained
as a corruption of A^β—see Stone in his note on p. 153.

wrong) reading ὕψωσεν (+ με *m*) in stead of *bk g eaf c* ἐψώμισέν με (μοι *h*, om. *b i*). A reads "fed me". In XI,7 the awkward, but clearly original καὶ τρεῖς ἔτεκε of *b* (*k g* def.) is changed into καὶ προσθεῖσα ἔτεκε in *ldm*. A follows here *eaf chi* in substituting the ordinal number for the cardinal, an obvious correction which does not prove any special relationship between A and these MSS. The few arguments which are found between A and *ldm, dm, l, m, d* are all fortuitous.[29]

On the basis of the evidence produced so far, and of H. J. de Jonge's stemma, the most obvious place for A is off the main line at some point between no. 6 and no. 13. We have to ask, however, in what respect Th. Korteweg's further observations on the relationships between *g, l, d* and *m* affect our present study of A.[30] Working on this problem Th. Korteweg and the present author made a few interesting observations; unfortunately they are nearly all concerned with texts for which only the Armenian evidence in Yovsepiˈancˈ's unsatisfactory edition and Charles' apparatus was available. The nature of the variants makes it unlikely, however, that more up-to-date evidence will invalidate the conclusions reached so far.[31]

Mostly A does not share special readings in *gdm* (T.S. VII,2; T. Jud. XIII,3; T.D. IV,4, V,6; T.N. I,6; T. Jos. VI,6 XVI, 6); in all these cases *gdm* are obviously secondary. There are also a

---

[29] In XII,7 *ldm* and A (A^α om. the whole verse) speak of 110 years in stead of 118. We may suspect here influence of Gen. L,22,26, which mentions this figure in connection with Joseph's age when he died. The original text refers to Levi's age at Joseph's death (see my *The Testaments*, p. 113). A comparable case is found in IX,6 where *bg* (*k* defic.) read ἔδειξε together with *chi* against *ldm eaf* ἐδίδαξε, A^β "had taught me" A^α "was teaching me". A few words later all Greek witnesses read ἐδίδασκέ με (μοι) in IX,7. A^α reads "he would teach me", but A^β "he would show me". The Armenian verbs are similar. So in IX,6 there was either a corruption in the Armenian, or a confusion between ἔδειξε and ἐδίδαξε in *ldm eaf* and A's "Vorlage". As to *dm*, the addition of ἐκαλεῖτο *d*, καλεῖται *m* in VI,1 is as intelligible as the parallel addition in A (A^α, however, "I called"). It does not prove any connection. Nor does the equally understandable addition ταῦτα ποιήσετε in *dm* after οὐ μόνον δέ in XIV,7, which is also found in A. In IV,3 only *l* A have φωτιεῖ σε and its equivalent in stead of φωτιεῖς (see on this reading Stone's note on p. 69); in VIII,5 *m* A read ἅγιον (so also *h*, cf. *i*) in stead of ἅγια ἁγίων, connecting it with οἶνον; and in XIV,6 the name "Israel" (*b*: Jerusalem) is omitted in *d* A. None of these parallels can be explained as "Bindefehler"; they may all be fortuitous. The same is true of incidental parallels between *e* and A in VII,1; X,2; XI,1; (perhaps) XVII,11.
[30] See chapter XI in this volume and the new stemma given on p. 64.
[31] M. E. Stone kindly checked the text of the passages concerned in MSS. A^mvwxyz.

few agreements between A and *gdm* (T.L. XIV,4b; T. Jos. XIII,2, XIV,2; T.B. II,1), but in none of these cases the element of chance can be excluded.

Very interesting are the cases where A agrees with *gldm*.

T.R. IV,4 οὖν *b*]   μετανοῶν   *gld* + A (litt. ἐν μετανοίᾳ)
            τέκνα μου   *m*
            ἕως ἐννοιῶν *eaf n* Serb.
            ἕως νῦν   *chi*

Here A + *gld* (temporarily deserted by *m*) may well have the right text over against *b* and *eaf n* Serb. and *chi*.

T.L. XIV,4a (τὸ φῶς)   *bk i* τοῦ νόμου   *g m eaf ch*
            τοῦ κόσμου   τοῦ κόσμου νόμου   *l*
                              τοῦ κόσμου καὶ τοῦ νόμου *d*
            (τὸ δοθὲν) *bk af* ὑμῖν   *gldm e*
            ἐν ὑμῖν   om   *chi*

According to Stone A$^\beta$ (A$^\alpha$ absent) reads: "and the light which is given through the law to you for illumination and to everyman" —presupposing a text which reads τοῦ νόμου and ὑμῖν. The textual situation is very complicated, but it may not be too rash to assume that the introduction of τοῦ κόσμου in various ways in various MSS. is secondary. This would imply that A's translation in fact agrees with the Greek text underlying *gldm* and *e* which is very likely original.

T.N. V,8 (ὅτι ἤμην) ἐκεῖ που *b*] ἐν κήποις   *gldm*
                              παρὼν ἐκεῖ *eaf*
                              παρεκεῖ   *chi*

At first sight *b* seems to give the *lectio difficilior* compared to that of *gldm* which is presupposed in A ("in (the) garden(s)"). On the other hand there is only superficial agreement between *b* and *eaf*, *chi* and it is also possible that *gldm* A represent the original reading, variously corrupted in *b* and the other MSS.

T.A. VI,6 παρακαλέσει *B*] παρακαλοῦντα   *gld(m)*
                            παραμυθεῖται   *eaf*
                            καὶ εἰσφέρει   *chi*

A reads "the comforter (of his life)", very much like the reading found in *gld(m)*. This agreement may be fortuitous; the readings found in *b*, *eaf*, *chi* are harsh and introduce a change in subject which is avoided by introducing a participle in the accusative(*gld(m)*) or a substantive (A).

T. Jos. XIV,5 οὐκ ἔστι *b*]   + ἔθνος *g* (sic! corr. of the foll. word)

+ ἔθος   *dm*

+ νόμος *l*

+ τοῦτο *c*

A reads "law", either presupposing the reading of the prototype of *gdm l*, or independently adding a suitable substantive.

T.B. VII,4 ἐν τοῖς ἑπτακοσίοις ἔτεσιν *b f*]   ἐν τοῖς ἑπτὰ κακοῖς   *glm*

ἐν τοῖς ζ′ οὖν κακοῖς *d*

ἐν τοῖς ἑπτακοσίοις *e*

ἐν τοῖς ἑπτά   *a*

ἐν πᾶσι τοῖς κακοῖς *c*

A presupposes here clearly the *gl(d)m*-reading. Again the textual situation is very complicated; some might prefer the *b f* reading as the *lectio difficilior*, but it is also possible to explain the readings in *b, e, a, f,* (*c*) as independent corruptions of the *gl(d)m*-text, in *b,* (*e*) and *f* influenced by the first half of the verse. In that case A would join *gl(d)m* in preserving the right text.

Extremely difficult is T.Z. IV,1. Here *gldm* read :

g   μετὰ δὲ τὸ βάλλειν αὐτὸν   εἰς τὸν λάκκον, ἤρξαντο ἐσθίειν οἱ ἀδελφοί μου

l καὶ   μετὰ τὸ βληθῆναι τὸν Ἰωσὴφ   ἐν τῷ λάκκῳ, ἤρξαντο ἐσθίειν οἱ ἀδελφοί μου

d ἀλλὰ τότε γὰρ μετὰ τὸ βληθῆναι αὐτὸν εἰς τὸν λάκκον, ἐκάθησαν ἐσθίειν οἱ ἀδελφοί μου

m   μετὰ γὰρ τὸ βληθῆναι αὐτὸν   εἰς τὸν λάκκον, ἔλαβον ἐσθίειν οἱ ἀδελφοί μου

b and *eaf* have a much shorter text : μετὰ ταῦτα ἔβαλον (ἔβαλλον *ef*) ἐσθίειν ἐκεῖνοι, and *chi* (obviously secondarily) read : μετὰ τὸ πραθῆναι αὐτόν, ἐκάθησαν οἱ ἀδελφοί μου (αὐτοῦ *hi*) ἐσθίειν καὶ πίνειν.

A, which may be retranslated καὶ ὅτε ἔβαλον (τὸν) Ἰωσὴφ εἰς τὸν λάκκον, ἤθελον ἐσθίειν, is clearly nearest to the prototype of *gldm*. It may represent, however, an incependent correction of the *b eaf*-reading which is possibly a corruption of the original μετὰ ταῦτα ἔλαβον ἐσθίειν ἐκεῖνοι.[32]

In none of these cases of agreement between *gldm* and A we may

---

[32] See H.J. de Jonge *ad loc.* in M. de Jonge, *Testamenta XII Patriarcharum*, Leiden ²1970, and pp. 145f. and 169f. below. Alternatively, we might conjecture an original reading μετὰ ταῦτα ἔβαλον αὐτὸν εἰς τὸν λάκκον καὶ ἔλαβον ἐσθίειν ἐκεῖνοι independently shortened by *homoioteleuton* in *b* and *eaf*, and with different stylistic improvements preserved in *gldm* and A.

with any certainty speak of a "Bindefehler". In some instances the agreement may be fortuitous, in others *gldm* A may represent the reading of the main stream of the textual tradition, which under these circumstances represents the earliest accessible text.[33]

There does not seem to be sufficient reason, therefore, to assume a special relationship between A and *gldm*; until new evidence is brought to bear upon this question the most likely place for A in the stemma is still off the main line at some point between no. 6 and no. 13.

4. *"Original" readings in A*

Having thus assigned to A a possible place amongst the other witnesses, we must ask what its value will be for the reconstruction of the text. Hultgård is right in insisting that A's evidence will have to be taken seriously (even) in cases where A differs from all Greek MSS. "Dans ces cas on doit prendre au sérieux la leçon de A en regard de celle de G".[34] Of course every serious textual critic will weigh the evidence and not count it; still it should be clear that A does not stand over against G. Its Greek prototype is one of the more important Greek witnesses, playing its part in the reconstruction of the oldest attainable form of text. Considering its position in the stemma, it is a priori unlikely that it will have preserved many original readings not preserved in any other MS.

Yet this is what Hultgård claims. Referring to the selected messianic passages which he discusses in his book, he says: "Le résultat est

---

[33] In any case the earliest accessible text will be represented in A where it sides with *b + g*, *l* or *dm*. See e.g. the interesting cases which occur in Test. Asher V,1 and VI,2, where both times *bg* A (the second time supported by *l*, the evidence of which lacks entirely in the first case) are still free from the additions annotated in the apparatus of the *editio minor*. Other examples are T. Jos. I,3 ἐπλανήθην *bgl* A] + ἀλλ᾽ἔμενον *dmeafch*; T. Jos. IV,7 ἐσιώπησε *bgl* A] (ἀντ)εφιλονείκει rel. (whereas *dm* are conflate); T. Jos. XIV,2 με *bchi* A] ἡμᾶς rel.; T. Jos. XX,1 τὴν ἐπαγγελίαν *bk* A S₁ (cf. *d*)] τὰς ἐπαγγελίας rel. (where Th. Korteweg conjectured: γῆν ἐπαγγελίας). We have been able to find only two clear instances where A sides with (nearly) all others against a reading of the prototype of *gldm*. Both cases are found in Test. Sim., in both cases only *gl* represent what seems to be the reading of the prototype. T.S. II,9 ἐγχρῄζοντα *b eaf* (cf. *chi*) and χρεώδη *dm*] ἐγχειρίζοντα *gl*. A reads "necessities". T.S. IV,2 τῆς πράσεως Ἰωσήφ *b e c* (*af hi*)] τοῦ κακοῦ *g*; τῆς κακώσεως τοῦ Ἰωσήφ *l*; παρὰ πάντας εἰς τ. Ἰ. *d*; παρὰ πάντα τῆς πράσεως τοῦ Ἰ. *m*.

[34] *Op. cit.*, pp. 36f.

que dans beaucoup de passages la version arménienne a conservé le texte primitif vis-à-vis de la tradition grecque. Nos conclusions seront donc que A est un témoin indispensable pour l'établissement du meilleur texte des Test. XII".[35]

We shall check his results for Test. Levi II,10-11, IV,2-6; XVI,3-5; XVIII where we can compare his notes with the text and the notes in Stone's edition, and those for Test. Joseph XIX where we also have new evidence presented by Stone[36]. The number of cases where A is thought to be original is not impressive and Hultgård's argumentation hardly inspires confidence.

In II,9b A is retranslated into Greek as ὅτι ἐὰν ἔλθῃς ἐκεῖ. H. connects it with vs 10, like καὶ ἐν τῷ ἀνέλθειν σε ἐκεῖ in chi, because A chi leave out the following ὅτι. The various readings in rel. G are explained as corruptions of the text presupposed for A's Greek prototype.[37] It is very likely, however, that the corruption is found in A and chi; it is improbable that the author of the Testaments located not only Levi's priestly activity, but also his revealing of God's mysteries to men and his announcement of the coming saviour, in heaven.[38] In vs 10c of the same chapter H. prefers A's reading, which in retranslation runs περὶ λυτρώσεως τοῦ Ἰσραήλ, to the τοῦ μέλλοντος λυτροῦσθαι τὸν Ἰσραήλ of G. The reason is that G is influenced by the wording of Lk XXIV,21. A far more plausible explanation is, that A just chose a free rendering and did not translate a different text. After all vs 11 is not omitted! Nor is it likely that for the translator in A there was much difference between salvation and "the one who will come to save". There is no difference in Luke (cf. XXIV,21 with I,68, II,38 and XXI,28), and though the LXX prefers the expression ὁ λυτρούμενος σε to ὁ μέλλων λυτροῦσθαι it is clear that the saving Lord will also grant salvation in the future—see, e.g., Is. XLI,14 and XLIV,22-24. We shall be wise to keep the problem of the Jewish or Christian origin of the Testaments out of our textcritical considerations, here and elswhere.

In XVI,3 Hultgård omits ὡς νομίζετε, in his view a marginal gloss; he thinks that the original text is reflected in A^α which omits

---

[35] Op. cit., p. 37.
[36] See the article mentioned in note 13, pp. 4-6.
[37] Hultgård, op. cit., pp. 40f.
[38] See chapter XV "Notes on the Testament of Levi II-VII" in this volume, esp. pp. 249f.

this phrase.[39] This is an impossible theory: A^mv and A^z have here the text of the best Greek MSS.[40] and if A^α does not give this text it must have abbreviated the text, as it often does. In XVI,5b H. superfluously adds ὑμᾶς after ἐπισκέψηται because A has an object after this verb as well as after the following προσδέξηται (connected with the former through καί).[41] It is surely not necessary to suppose that the Greek prototype had a double ὑμᾶς over against all other extant MSS.[42] In the same verse Hultgård omits καὶ ὕδατι as an interpolation without textual evidence,[43] once again mixing up textual criticism and considerations concerning the earlier stages of transmission of the text.

In XVIII,6c Hultgård uses e and A for a fantastic reconstruction of the text.[44] The Greek MSS. except e read ὡς ἀπὸ (ἐπὶ g) Ἀβραὰμ πατρὸς (+ καὶ chi) Ἰσαάκ. e reads ὡς ἀπὸ πατρὸς Ἀβραὰμ καὶ Ἰσαὰκ καὶ Ἰακώβ. A evidently read (or had before it a text with) πρός instead of π̄ρ̄ς̄ and one may reasonably ask whether πρός or π̄ρ̄ς̄ was the original Greek reading. H., however, takes the π̄ρ̄ς̄ of e, changes it into πρός, assumes a corruption because he cannot accept the double ἀπὸ πρός and so ends with the "original" reading ὡς πρὸς Ἀβραὰμ καὶ Ἰσαὰκ καὶ Ἰακώβ: his argumentation being that the reconstructed text, (nearly) preserved in e, gives a much better sense than that found in the other Greek MSS. or A.

Equally unacceptable is H.'s reading (πνεῦμα συνέσεως καὶ) γνώσεως with A in stead of ἁγιασμοῦ in XVIII,7.[45] Here his argument is that A conforms to Is XI,1ff and that ἁγιασμοῦ is an unnecessary repetition of the ἁγίασμα in the previous verse. These may well be the two reasons for the obviously secondary alteration in A!

I could mention more examples of less importance in the Test. Levi- passages discussed by Hultgård, and also cases where he uses A

---

[39] *Op. cit.*, pp. 40f.

[40] Hultgård even supposes that the present in A^mv and the aorist in A^z reflect a similar difference between the Greek MSS., but change in forms in A just as easy as it is in Greek. Hultgård rightly rejects the readings found in A^β and chi as secondary.

[41] *Op. cit.*, p. 43.

[42] The Armenian translator obviously wanted to give a shorter text than the Greek MSS. give.

[43] A^α omits ἐν πίστει καὶ ὕδατι, together with chapters XVII and XVIII. In XVIII,7 Hultgård (*op. cit.*, p. 116) omits ἐν τῷ ὕδατι on the basis of the evidence of e alone.

[44] *Op. cit.*, p. 115.

[45] *Op. cit.*, p. 116.

as supporting evidence where it agrees with individual Greek MSS. The instances given may have shown, however, that Hultgård over-estimates the value of the Armenian version and that, in fact, he uses textual criticism too often to support theories for which textual evidence cannot be adduced or is irrelevant.

We now turn to Test. Jos. XIX where there is also J. Becker's opinion [46] to be considered. Very briefly the situation with regard to A's large addition in vss 3-7 (see Charles' retranslation) and its abbreviations in vss 8-12 may be summed up as follows :

a) Stone's new information [47] concerning A^m and Hultgård's notes [48] with information on A^v and A^z give a fuller and better, but not really different picture of A's text in this chapter.

b) Hultgård's arguments in favour of the originality of vss 3-7 in A are : The Greek abbreviates because it wants to go on to the Christian passages further on in the chapter; something is required between vs 2 and vs 8.[49] And next, the Armenian gives a text which is often obscure; who would have inserted such an unintelligible pericope? H.'s hypothesis is just as probable or improbable as that of Becker who assumes that A (or its Greek prototype) wanted to fill the gap between the exile (end of vs 2) and the new era of salvation (vss 8ff).

c) The decisive indications against A's originality in vss 3-7 are to be found in vss 8-9, as Becker has recognized. In vs 9 A has very awkwardly introduced the animals figuring in the previous verses into a text which spoke of angels and men and the whole of the earth.[50] A's text in vs 8 is equally impossible : In the midst of the horns

---

[46] See his *Untersuchungen*... (mentioned in note 12), especially pp. 57-66. Compare also my *The Testaments* etc. (see note 11), pp. 28f., 33, and pp. 226-228 below.

[47] See note 13.

[48] *Op. cit.*, pp. 163-172.

[49] He shows that in 2^c A agrees with *d* in adding ὕστερον or something equivalent. According to him *d* would have preserved here a trace of the original text. In my opinion the additions will have originated independently as attempts to make the text easier and smoother.

[50] Charles gives here as retranslation of the reading of the majority of the MSS. οἱ ἐλαφοί; A^{mv} read "the three harts". The A^a MSS. have variants of A^z's reading "the three horns". "Harts" occur as symbol of the twelve tribes in vss 2-4 and are therefore superfluous besides the bulls which represent the twelve tribes in vss. 5-7. Also if we, with Hultgård, prefer A^z's reading "the three horns", we notice an attempt in A to combine material from vss 2-7 with vss 8ff—in the latter case the reference is to vss 5-7 alone, but equally strained.

there appears a virgin, although, according to vs 6, another horn had sprung up there already. At the right of the lamb born from this virgin not only" all the beasts" (so also G) but even "all the reptiles" are seen rushing against it. Why "at the right"? Hultgård thinks of an internal Armenian corruption and changes into the "at the left" of the Greek, the left being the "sinister" side. But this is as much as admitting that the Armenian text is confused, because in G it is the lion who appears at the lamb's left side.[51]

d) With regard to the Levi-Judah-passage in vss 11-12 both Becker and Hultgård (in general) prefer the A-text to that of the Greek MSS., trying to find textcritical support for their "traditionsgeschichtliche" ideas. Hultgård regards φυλάξατε τὰς ἐντολὰς κυρίου καί which is not found in A as a stereotyped addition in G; Becker rightly hesitates.[52] Next, these two scholars give the names of Levi and Judah in this order, following *c* A against the others who mention Judah first. *c* and A are supposed to represent here the pre-Christian stage of the text. This argument is textcritically unsound. In two other cases, T.D. V,10 and T.G. VIII,1, the order Judah/Levi is found, without variants either in A or in any of the Greek MSS. Moreover in both cases a sentence follows with ἀνατελεῖ and σωτήριον (T.D. V,10) or σωτῆρα (T.G. VIII,1 MS. *b*; σωτήρ (+ gen.) (*l*)*dm eaf*; σωτηρία *kg chi*). The variety among the Greek MSS. in the latter case (and in T.N. VIII,2b) shows that there is no reason to prefer the A-text which presupposes the impersonal ἡ σωτηρία to the personal σῴζων in G.[53] The author of the Testaments adopted here traditional L.J. material to the preceding verses 8-10.[54] A omits vs 12a, probably because of *homoioarkton*; in any case the fact that this clause reminds of Dan. III,33, VII,14 (Theod.) is no argument for a later addition.[55]

---

[51] Charles wrongly puts ἐξ ἀριστερῶν in his text, but he gives the translation "on his right" in his commentary *The Testaments of the Twelve Patriarchs*, London 1908. J. Becker in *Die Testamente der zwölf Patriarchen* (*Jüdische Schriften aus hell. röm. Zeit* III 1) Gütersloh 1974, p. 129, note a on vs 10, suspects an omission in A after "on his right" (comp. Charles in his commentary).

[52] See his translation mentioned in note 47, p. 130, note a on vs 11.

[53] So J. Becker, *Untersuchungen...*, p. 58 and Hultgård, *op. cit.*, p. 169. See also my remark on T. Levi II,10 above p. 131.

[54] Particularly to vs 8, a verse which also J. Becker regards as Christian : "Der Vers ist eindeutig christlich überarbeitet. Seine ursprüngliche Gestalt ist schwer, wahrscheinlich überhaupt nicht mehr rekonstruierbar" (*Die Testamente...* see note 51), p. 129, note b on vs 8.

[55] The reading of *k* παρασαλεύεται (παρασαλεύσεται *ab*) should here, however,

Our investigation of the A-text in T. Jos XIX corroborates the conclusion formulated after the analysis of a number of Hultgård's arguments in favour of A in Test. Levi. Nowhere in this chapter is it clear that A has preserved the original text.[56]

5. Conclusion; some additional remarks
on the date of the Armenian version

As our analysis proceeded it has become abundantly clear that A is a useful witness to the Greek text, mainly because of its supporting evidence. The constitution of the Greek text on the basis of the extant MSS. need not be postponed until the oldest attainable A-text has been reconstructed. It is not likely that our knowledge of this Armenian text will necessitate us to revise our opinion on the earliest accessible Greek text considerably, though, of course, at a later stage the full Armenian evidence will have to be evaluated with regard to its importance for the constitution of the Greek text.

---

be preferred as *lectio durior* to the more common παρελεύσεται found in *g ld ef c* (and Dan. VII,14 Theod.).

[56] In his translation with commentary of 1974 (see note 51) J. Becker tries to defend the originality of the very short A-text in T. Benj. XI (cf. his *Untersuchungen ...*, pp. 49-51). Against this may be remarked : a) Also A read κληθήσομαι in its "Vorlage" (see Stone, *Sion* 1970, p. 6 for A^m and Burchard, *B.Z.N.W.* 36, p. 26 for A^z). The reading κληθήσεται in *gl* and (practically) all other MSS. of A is not a *lectio difficilior* but an attempt to connect the beginning of this chapter with "Israel" mentioned in T. Benj. X,11. A's short text is either the result of a deliberate policy —A often gives a shorter text, particularly at the end of the individual testaments and throughout in this last testament—or it arose by an incidental mistake. A scribe's eye may have wandered from ἐργάτης κυρίου to ἀγαπητὸς κυρίου; with the intermediary words the reference to Paul in vss 1-2ª disappears, and vss 2ᵇ-5 become superfluous. The full Greek text, both in vss 1-2a and in vss 2b-5 gives clearly a picture of Paul, in agreement with other early Christian references (see my *The Testaments*, p. 34 and p. 122). It is not easy to see what the function of the short A-text of vss 1-2a, if original, could have been and how it would have led to the G-text which is found in all Greek MSS., except *c* and *NGr*. *c* goes its own way in vs 2a, reading ἐκ τοῦ σπέρματος Ἰούδα καὶ Λευί, transposed after ἀγαπητὸς κυρίου, while *NGr* reads ἐκ τοῦ σπέρματός μου together with the other Greek MSS. without transposition. *c* and *NGr* go back to a text which was broken off by accident. *NGr* ends the Testaments with a short doxology after γένος δίκαιον which replaces ἀγαπητὸς κυρίου [...] ποιῶν εὐδοκίαν ἐν στόματι αὐτοῦ in *c*. In this MS. these are the last words except a clearly conventional closing chapter (plus ending) which has little in common with the text of T. Benj. XII in the other MSS. *c* nor *NGr* really support A's short text.

This links up with Burchard's conclusion in 1969 :[57] "Lesarten,
die der griechischen Überlieferung überlegen wären, sind allerdings
in grösserem Umfang nicht zu erwarten". He adds, however : "Der
Hauptwert der Übersetzung liegt in ihrem Alter. Sie bedeutet soviel
wie eine mittelgute Handschrift der insgesamt besten Gruppe (*bdgkl*)
aus dem 6. oder 7. Jh. bedeuten würde. Das heisst, der Armenier
macht den aus den griechischen Zeugen zu gewinnenden Text nicht
besser, wohl aber älter und sicherer".

Burchard arrives at this date for A on the ground of his "impression" of the language. "Sie (i.e. die Daten, d.J.) sind nicht viel
mehr als Umschreibungen des Eindrucks, dass A ein gutes, wenn
auch nicht mehr ganz frühes Altarmenisch spricht. Dieser Eindruck
ist aber wohl richtig ....[58] Stone agrees with him [59] without any further
argumentation. We should remark, however, that Burchard knows
of no older MSS. than S. Lazarro 346 (A^a), writen in 1220, Jerusalem
1925 (A^m) of 1269 and Erewan 1500 (A^z) of 1282/3. As oldest external
evidence he mentions the "Arrangement of Holy Writings" of Johannes
Sarkawag of Hałbat, probably to be dated around 1085.[60] The
Armenian translation must, therefore, at the latest, have been made
in the XIth century.

Can be really go back much earlier? Here it may be significant
that A gives a shorter text in Test. Zebulun, together with *eaf chi*
and the Slavonic version over against the other Greek witnesses.
In *eaf chi SA* the text of VI,4 up to VIII,3 inclusive is missing, with
the exception of two little sentences πέντε ἔτη ἡλίευσα in VI,7 and
τὸ θέρος ἡλίευον καὶ ἐν χειμῶνι ἐποίμαινον μετὰ τῶν ἀδελφῶν μου
in VI,8. Next, a number of phrases in VIII,4-6 and in IX,5,6,8 are
wanting.[61] The omissions (or additions) cannot be accidental; either
the shorter or the longer text is the result of deliberate recension.
It is clear that the stemma the Leiden team has been working with
requires that the shorter text is secondary. At some point between
the "Vorlage" of *gldm* and the "Vorlage" of A (itself branching off
from the main line before *e*, as we have shown) the text must have

---

[57] *B.Z.N.W.* 36, p. 28.

[58] *Op. cit.*, p. 15.

[59] *The Testament of Levi*, p. 3; *J.B.L.* 89, 1970, p. 487.

[60] *Op. cit.*, pp. 13f. Johannes died in 1129—see also H. Thorossian, *Histoire de
la littérature Arménienne*, Paris 1951, pp. 131f.

[61] Charles' evidence is for ch. IX corroborated by Stone's collation in *Sion* 1970,
pp. 3f. and for IX,8 by Hultgård's information, *op. cit.*, pp. 88f.

been shortened deliberately. In another paper in this volume I have tried to prove that this is, in fact, the case.[62]

The most important arguments may be summed up as follows:

a) The longer text in VIII,4-6 gives a picture of Joseph which agrees with that found in T. Sim. IV,4 and other descriptions of "the good man" in the Testaments. Moreover, Joseph's ἔλεος and εὐσπλαγχνία, and his lack of μνησικακία reflect God's attitude as described in T.Z. IX,7 (in *all* MSS.).

b) The longer text in VIII,4-6 serves as a transition between the exhortations in VIII,1-3, and new exhortations in IX,1-3, but because of the agreements just noted there is no reason to assume secondary addition under the influence of that section.

c) VIII,1-3 follows the description of Zebulun's activities as a fisherman. In the shorter text this description serves only as a transition from the story which tells how Joseph was treated by his brothers I,5-IV,13 (leading to the parenetic passage V,1-4), to the account of Joseph's treatment of his brothers in VIII,4. In the longer text Zebulun as a fisherman gives abundant evidence of his εὐσπλαγχνία and ἔλεος.[63] It may well be that the scribe responsible for the abbreviation of the text found the examples given too extravagant, and regarded the references to Zebulun's compassion for Joseph in I,5-IV,13 quite sufficient biographical illustration. It must be asked, however, whether he did not do his work too thoroughly with regard to the exhortations concerning compassion and mercy. Not only *b*, but also *ef* S, belonging to the MSS. with the shorter text, indicate the theme of this testament as περὶ εὐσπλαγχνίας καὶ ἐλέους. In the shorter text this theme is treated very briefly, in V,1,3 and in IX,7. In the account of what happened to Joseph at Dothan we find an appeal for mercy by Joseph in II,2 and a description of Zebulun as σπλαγχνιζόμενος ἐπὶ Ἰωσήφ in IV,2 (cf. I,6 and II,4). This makes it likely that the original author always intended to add some more examples connected with Zebulun's life as a fisherman and Joseph's reception of his brothers in Egypt, after the exhortations concerning compassion and mercy in V,1-4.

d) From the point of view of unity and composition the shorter text is "better" than the longer one. The longer text has two bio-

---

[62] See chapter X "Textual criticism and the analysis of the composition of the Testament of Zebulun", esp. pp. 149-152.

[63] On the larger and shorter text in ch. IX see the paper just mentioned, p. 151f.

graphical sections (the first one very complex) followed by two parenetic sections; the shorter text has only one of each. In both forms of text a new theme, that of unity, is introduced at the end. The shorter text can easily be explained as an abbreviated form of the longer. It is not clear why and how the longer text may have originated if the shorter is original. If we assume—as we should, I think [64]—that the Testaments are the result of compositional activity of an author, or group of authors, who wanted to use all material available, we have to expect a number of unevennesses in the original text. Consequently efforts to produce a more coherent and unified text are likely to be secondary.

Now, if the shorter text is the result of deliberate recensional activity, how old is it? The oldest Greek witness for the shorter text is the XIth century MS. *e*. The Greek evidence would be satisfactorily explained by the theory that some time in the Xth or XIth century a scribe deliberately abbreviated the then current text of the main stream of the tradition. If we accept the external evidence for A's date, the presence of the short text in the Armenian version fits into this picture very nicely.

In fact, if H. J. de Jonge's conclusions in his study "The earliest traceable stage in the textual tradition of the Testaments of the Twelve Patriarchs" [65] are sound, the Armenian translation is very unlikely to be earlier than the IXth century. We should be cautious, therefore, to put the Armenian translation in the VIth or VIIth century on the basis of the impression made by its language alone. Surely the possibility may not be excluded that some scribe at a later date deliberately used classical or classicizing language for a writing like the Testaments which purported to come from ancient times. What we really need is unequivocal early external evidence for A.

Postscript. After this chapter was written M. E. Stone published two further contributions to the study of the Testaments. In "The Armenian Version of the Testaments of the Twelve Patriarchs: Selection of Manuscripts", *Sion* 49, 1975 (forthcoming) he outlines his plan for an *editio minor* on the basis of A^z, A^{mv}, a selection of

---

[64] See particularly my discussion in the paper on T. Zebulun with J. Becker who defends the originality of the shorter text, and at the same time explains the origin of the Testaments as a process of gradual growth.

[65] See chapter III above.

MSS from family A^α, and a few MSS belonging to A^β. In his *The Armenian Version of the Testament of Joseph* published as vol. 6 in the S.B.L. Texts and Translations-series (= Pseudepigrapha Series no. 5), Missoula 1975, he gives an edition and translation of this one testament prepared along the lines indicated in his Sion-article.

Dr Stone informed me in August 1975 of the discovery of yet four further MSS. in the Treasury of the Cathedral of St. James in Jerusalem.

IX

THE SLAVIC VERSIONS

H. E. GAYLORD, jr. and TH. KORTEWEG

In a recent article E. Turdeanu has reexamined the Slavic versions of the *Testaments* and their treatment in the edition of Charles in 1908.[1] That article points out very well both the shortcomings of Charles' citations and the state of research of the earliest Slavic translation. His conclusions are as follows :

(1) For further work the full text of the Moscow Historical Archives MS. no. 279-658 should be examined. This is a copy of a lost 12th century MS. which represents the best available textual basis. At present we have only citations of this MS. (MS. A in Turdeanu) in the edition of another MS. of the long recension by N. S. Tichonravov.[2] One should add that a full review of all available MSS. would be in order here. Because of their number this would be a major enterprise.[3]

(2) The citations in Charles' edition of the Greek text are very inaccurate. Charles worked from a Greek retroversion by Morfill. This retroversion was not based on the superior MS. A, and Turdeanu has cited many examples of errors in the retroversion and its use by Charles. The classic abuse by Charles is his distinctions on the basis of the use of the article when in Slavic languages such an article does not exist with a noun. H. E. Gaylord has examined several more sections in which even on the MS. Morfill was using the citation is very faulty. Charles' references to the Slavic cannot be relied upon but must be checked at all times at least against the published transcriptions and citations.[4]

---

[1] E. Turdeanu, "Les Testaments des Douze Patriarches en Slave", *Journal for the Study of Judaism* I (1971), pp. 148-184.

[2] Pamjatniki otrecennoj russkoj literatury I (1863); cf. Turdeanu, *o.c.*, p. 166.

[3] An extensive listing of the Slavic MSS. of the *Testaments* can be found in A. I. Jacimirskij, *Bibliograficeskij obzor apokrifov v juznoslavjanskoj i russkoj pismennosti* (1921), pp. 141-165.

[4] *O.c.*, pp. 157f. and, in fact, *passim*.

This is particularly clear in the many cases where Charles in his apparatus notes agreements between *b* and S. S, as a rule, is closely related to *e* and *af* (see below) and agreements between *b* and S would have to be explained by contamination. However, examination of some twenty instances of special *b* S-readings in Charles' edition showed that in only one case agreement between these two witnesses really exists, i.e. in *T. Zeb.* IV,9 where *b* and S omit καὶ ἐποίησαν οὕτως. This is a clear instance of *homoeoteleuton* and consequently there is no conjunctive error. Of the other instances the following examples may be given :

T. Jud. XXV,2 ἐλαία *b* σελήνη *ceteri*; S has "moon" (contra Charles p. 103, n. 30).

T. Dan III,4 διὰ τῆς δυνάμεως καὶ τῆς βοηθείας *b* ἀπὸ τῆς βοηθείας *ceteri*; S agrees with the other witnesses (contra Charles p. 134, n. 17).

T. Dan V,2 ἡδονήν *b* μῆνιν *ceteri*; S "hatred" (the verb from this root translates μηνίειν; contra Charles p. 136, n. 15).

T. Dan VI,2 τῆς βασιλείας τοῦ ἐχθροῦ *bg* τῆς βασιλείας τοῦ θεοῦ *ceteri*; S reads "kingdom of God" (contra Charles p. 140, n. 9).

T. Jos. XIX,2 τῇ γῇ *bk*; εἰς πᾶσαν τὴν γῆν *ceteri*; S has "to all the earth" (contra Charles, p. 209, n. 7).

T. Benj. X,10 ἀπατήσασιν *bg*; ἀποστήσασιν *d* ἀπιστήσασιν *eaf*; S reads "to be unfaithful" (contra Charles, p. 230, n. 59).

One could multiply these examples, but the exercise is not worthwile. Probably Morfill's working Greek text for comparison was the then current edition of the *Testaments* by R. Sinker, based on *b*. The unusually high number of mistaken agreements between *b* and S may be due to the (not always detected) influence of the Sinker-text on Morfill's retranslation.

(3) In Slavic languages there are two translations, one of which is contained in two versions. The second translation, a Serbian fragment containing only *T. Reuben* I-V, does not come from a complete translation,[5] but seems to come from an excerpted collection also standing behind the Greek MS. *n*.[6] Its text belongs to the text type α among the Greek MS. (sub)families. The earlier complete translation comes down in a "long" and a "short" version. These

---

[5] Cf. Turdeanu, *o.c.*, pp. 181 ff.

[6] *Ibid.*; H. J. de Jonge, "Die Textüberlieferung der Testamente der Zwölf Patriarchen", Z.N.W. LXIII (1972), pp. 36 ff. In this volume ch. II, pp. 54 ff.

are not independent translations but derive from a single translation. This situation is parallel to that in the Slavic version of III *Baruch*. There a long-standing dispute over the question of independent translations in "long" and "short" versions can now finally be settled on the basis of new MS. evidence which proves that only one translation was made but that its transmission has led to widely differing readings and vocabulary and extensive redactional activity. In the forthcoming critical edition of this work H. E. Gaylord has discovered that often the earliest Slavic translations of the pseudepigraphical writings were highly literal and based upon good Greek MSS., but that later transmission has led not only to textual corruption but, at times, also to summarizing and extensive reworking.

(4) In his article and in collations, which he made for M. de Jonge, Turdeanu has shown that the first Slavic translation was based upon a Greek MS. closely related to the Greek MSS. *eaf.*[7] Proceeding from a remark by M. de Jonge in 1953[8] he tries to determine whether there is a special relationship with *e* or with *af.* He checks a number of instances taken by M. de Jonge from Charles' apparatus and concludes that there is no relationship between *e* and S; S forms with *af* "une sous-division distincte dans le cadre du groupe *aef*". This statement is taken over by H. J. de Jonge[9] without further comment, although it clearly contradicts his own reconstruction of the textual tradition of the *Testaments* in which *eaf* belong by no means to a "groupe".

On closer examination we find that in all the examples, save one, which Turdeanu brings to illustrate the close relation of S to *af*, the agreement is in fact with *af* α. These examples consequently do not tell us anything about a special relationship between S and *af*. The single exception is *T. Levi* VIII,2 where the distribution of variants is as follows : τοῦ σημείου *bgde* του στηθίου *af* τῆς κεφαλῆς α; "de la poitrine" S. Here too the reading τοῦ στηθίου may well be not just peculiar to *af* S but go back to the common ancestor of *af* α, τῆς κεφαλῆς being an obvious correction of τοῦ στηθίου rather than of τοῦ σημείου which we find in *bgde*. Thus, so far, no unique readings of S with *af* have been established.

To determine the precise relationship of the Slavic version one

---

[7] Turdeanu, *o.c.*, pp. 158 ff.
[8] *The Testaments of the Twelve Patriarchs*, Assen 1953, p. 22.
[9] *O.c.*, p. 35; see p. 53 above.

would need the full available MSS. evidence, especially that of MS. A. However, on the basis of the published evidence the following suggestions can be made : There is no doubt that S does not belong to family I (*bk*). Nor does it, within family II, belong to the sub-family *gldm*. In the stemmatic division between (*g*)*ldm* and *eaf* α S agrees with *eaf* α in all four examples mentioned by H. J. de Jonge in Chapter II under no. 13. Of the disjunctive errors between *e* and *af* α, offered by H. J. de Jonge under no. 15 S agrees with *af* α in three cases (*T. Reub.* IV,6; *T. Levi* VIII,15, 17). One case, *T. Zeb.* I,3 is ambiguous, but in *T. Zeb.* VI,3 S clearly does not side with *af* α : Here *b* reads ἡλίευον ἰχθύας, *gldm* read ἁλιεύων ἰχθύας, *e* ἁλιεύων, S has "fishing" and *af* α omit the phrase. The conclusion from this evidence is that the Greek MS. behind this Slavic translation should be placed at a point in the major stemmatic line of family II between *e* and *af*.[10]

At this point the necessary steps to take for the understanding and use of the Slavic version are clear. A full examination of MS. A and other unpublished MSS. should be undertaken. This could help us to get a clearer picture of the Greek MS. tradition at the stage of the Greek MSS. *e* and *af*. Although S is therefore of relatively little value for the reconstruction of the oldest attainable Greek text, further study of it could bring us useful information regarding the use of pseudepigraphical writings in Christian and particularly in eastern Christian churches. Turdeanu has mentioned the anti-Jewish polemical interpolations found in the Slavic MSS. with the exception of MS. A. Preparation of a critical edition would provide the materials for redactional criticism of these activities and should be illuminating for the history of medieval social and religious history as well.

---

[10] Charles, in his discussion of the Slavic on p. XVIII of his edition, is misinformed concerning the agreements of S with α against *eaf*. The example of *T. Levi* IX,1 is ambiguous as is that of *T. Levi* XII,1. In *T. Gad* I,4 S could translate either phrase, and in the citation of MS. A we find the missing clause from *T. Levi* IX,11. Thus no agreement of S with α against *eaf* has yet been shown.

X

TEXTUAL CRITICISM AND THE ANALYSIS
OF THE COMPOSITION OF THE TESTAMENT OF ZEBULUN

M. DE JONGE

The main purpose of this article is to provide information about
the new critical edition of the Testaments of the Twelve Patriarchs
which is being prepared by a small team in the University of Leiden.[1]
It uses the material which this team has at its disposal[2] and builds
on the results of earlier investigation.[3] First a number of individual
passages of textcritical importance are analysed; next the problem
of the relationship between the longer and the shorter text in the
second half of Test. Zebulun is discussed at some length.

The results reached in this first part of the article ask for a
discussion of a question of a more general nature. Are there parallel
developments in the history of the text during the period which we
are able to investigate with textcritical methods and during the period

---

[1] The present author wishes to express his gratitude for the suggestions and criticisms
of his assistants while the material for this article was collected and after the present
text had been drafted.

[2] A survey of available material and a list of the sigla used are given on pp. VII-XV
of the present author's "editio minima", *Testamenta XII Patriarcharum* edited according
to Cambridge University Library MS. Ff. 1.24 fol 203a-261b, with short notes (*Pseudepigrapha V. T. Graece* I), Leiden ²1970. To the textual witnesses mentioned in this
edition the following should now be added : some fragments (Test. Reub. III,6b-V,7a;
Test. Levi III) in MS. Athos Vatopedi 659, discovered by J. Paramelle of the
"Institut de Recherche et d'Histoire des Textes" in Paris (= *n*), and the MS.
Athos Laura K 116 photographed by A. Hultgård, Uppsala. Photographs of the text
of the Testaments in this MS were kindly put at my disposal by dr Hultgård;
further investigation proved that K 116 is very likely a copy of MS. Laura I 48
(= MS. *l*; contra A. Hultgård's provisional conclusion in his *Croyances messianiques
des Test. XII Patr.*, Critique textuelle et commentaire des passages messianiques,
diss. Uppsala 1971, pp. 3-4). For further details see the articles mentioned in note 3.

[3] See H. J. de Jonge, "Les fragments marginaux dans le MS. d des Testaments
des XII Patriarches", *J.S.J.* 2, 1971, pp. 19-28 [now chapter IV]; *idem*, "Die Textüberlieferung der Testamente der Zwölf Patriarchen", *Z.N.W.* 63, 1972, pp. 27-44 [now
chapter II] and H. W. Hollander, "The relationship between MS. Athos Laura I 48 (*l*)
and MS. Athos Laura K 116" [chapter VII].

before, especially during the earliest stages of transmission? The second part of this article makes an attempt to answer this question for Test. Zebulun and for the Testaments of the Twelve Patriarchs as a whole. It is hoped that the considerations put forward here may of some use to students of other pseudepigrapha.

I. 1. *Some textcritically interesting passages in Test. Zebulun*

a) In III,5 *b* reads καὶ κύριος ὑπέλυσεν αὐτοὺς τὸ ὑπόδημα Ἰωσήφ. Instead of the genitive Ἰωσήφ *l eaf c* S read the expression ὃ ἐφόρεσαν κατὰ Ἰωσὴφ τοῦ ἀδελφοῦ αὐτῶν. This whole clause is absent from *k g dm hi*, in *k* and *m* as part of larger omissions, characteristic for these MSS. In vs 4 *g* adds ὃ ἐφόρεσεν after ὑπόδημα; the rest of this verse and verse 5 are omitted. As will be shown below (see II,4) *g* rewrites chapter III (and the end of chapter II) completely; omission through homoioteleuton cannot be excluded, however. In any case the scribe of *g* must have had before him a text like that given by *l eaf c* S. In *d hi* the second half of vs 5 is omitted; if these MSS. knew a text like that in *l eaf c* S, this omission can be explained by homoioteleuton. We may add that, according to R. H. Charles,[4] the Armenian version presupposes the Greek text ἃ ἐφόρεσαν κατ' αὐτοῦ, and conclude that in this case *b* stands over against all other textual witnesses known to us.[5] It is clear that the longer text of the other MSS. tries to explain and correct the unclear genitive in *b*.[6] We have to assume that *b* gives the most original reading.

b) In IV,1 *b* reads μετὰ ταῦτα ἔβαλον ἐσθίειν ἐκεῖνοι. This reading is unintelligible, but it is presupposed by all other MSS.[7] *eaf* give direct support to *b* (with minor alterations in *e* and *f*: (*f* + καὶ) μετὰ ταῦτα ἔβαλλον (*a*: ἔβαλον) ἐσθίειν ἐκεῖνοι), the other MSS. attempt to contruct a better sentence through various more or less radical corrections.

---

[4] R. H. Charles, *The Greek Versions of the Testaments of the Twelve Patriarchs*, Oxford, 1908.

[5] Of course nothing certain can be said of *k* and *m*.

[6] Compare the somewhat vague use of the genitive in IV,10 where τὸν... χιτῶνα τοῦ πατρὸς ἡμῶν must mean: "the coat which our father had given to Joseph". (*l* changes this expression into τὸν... χιτῶνα τοῦ Ἰωσὴφ ὃν ἐνέδυσεν αὐτῷ ὁ πατὴρ ἡμῶν! IV,9 speaks of τὸν χιτῶνα Ἰωσήφ).

[7] *k* is (again) absent.

g : μετὰ δὲ τὸ βάλλειν αὐτὸν εἰς τὸν λάκκον, ἤρξαντο ἐσθίειν
        οἱ ἀδελφοί μου

l : καὶ μετὰ τὸ βληθῆναι τὸν Ἰωσὴφ ἐν τῷ λακκῷ, ἤρξαντο
        ἐσθίειν οἱ ἀδελφοί μου

d : ἀλλὰ τότε γὰρ μετὰ τὸ βληθῆναι αὐτὸν εἰς τον λάκκον,
        ἐκάθησαν ἐσθίειν οἱ ἀδελφοί μου

m : μετὰ γὰρ τὸ βληθῆναι αὐτῶν εἰς τὸν λάκκον, ἔλαβον ἐσθίειν
        οἱ ἀδελφοί μου

chi : μετὰ δὲ τὸ πραθῆναι αὐτόν, ἐκάθησαν οἱ ἀδελφοί μου (*hi* :
αὐτοῦ) ἐσθίειν καὶ πίνειν. The expression ἐκάθησαν ἐσθίειν is clearly
secondary, and derived from Gen. XXXVII,25; one should note the
agreement between *d* and *chi* which is found very often in cases
where those MSS. have secondary readings. Equally secondary is
the ἐσθίειν καὶ πίνειν in *chi* as compared with the simple ἐσθίειν
in the other MSS. μετὰ δὲ τὸ πραθῆναι (*chi*) is clearly impossible
in this context. The readings of *gldm* are to be explained as
corrections of μετὰ ταῦτα ἔβαλον; these MSS. choose another form
of the verb βάλλειν, and *m* uses the expression ἔλαβον ἐσθίειν
besides. The scribe of this manuscript may have given an important
clue for the reconstruction of the original text; if in *m* ἔβαλον
became ἔλαβον, in *b* an original ἔλαβον may have been changed,
erroneously, into ἔβαλον. A similar transposition occurs elsewhere
in MSS. of the LXX and the N.T.[8] Therefore H. J. de Jonge suggested
the conjecture ἔλαβον in the apparatus of the second edition of my
editio minima.[9] In any case *b* is, again, nearest to the original.

c) In IV,9 *b* and the Slavonic version omit the clause καὶ ἐποίησαν
οὕτως at the end of this verse, possibly because of hmt. and independently, the proceeding sentence ending with οὗτος (*chi* <). The
longer text is clearly original.[10]

d) In VIII,6 the full reading καὶ τὴν ψυχὴν ταράσσει καὶ τὴν
ὕπαρξιν ἀφανίζει *l*, *eaf*, S, A^z is probably original.[11] MSS. *b*

---

[8] See the examples mentioned by G. Mussies, *The Morphology of Koine Greek
as used in the Apocalypse of John. A Study in Bilingualism* (*Suppl. to N.T.* 27),
Leiden 1971, p. 33, note 2. See also Mark XIV,65.

[9] See note 2. In a letter to the present author dated 12.10.1971 he points to
the expression ὅπως λήψῃ πιεῖν in Euripides, Cycl. 561 and to expressions like
ἤνεγκεν φαγεῖν John IV,33; προσήνεγκαν ἐμφαγεῖν καὶ πιεῖν in Xenophon, Cyr. 7,1,1;
εὕρωμεν φαγεῖν in Epictetus III,19,5.

[10] See further II.1 below.

[11] *k* and *m* are absent.

and *g* omit here καὶ τὴν ὕπαρξιν ἀφανίζει, over against *d* which
omits καὶ τὴν ψυχὴν ταράσσει. The reading of *chi* is clearly secondary
and dependent on that found in *l eaf*. By changing τὴν ὕπαρξιν
into τὸ πρόσωπον *chi* introduce the notion of a parallelism existing
between the inner and the outer man (see also T.N. II,6). One should
note that *l* agrees here with *eaf*. This is not the case at the end
of this verse where the clause ὁ γὰρ μνησίκακος σπλάγχνα ἐλέους
οὐκ ἔχει is not found in *eaf chi* A S. These witnesses give the
shorter text whereas the longer one is found in the other manuscripts.
This variant will be dealt with below (see I.2b).

e) In IX,8 the textual situation is very complicated. Apart from
two instances connected with the problem of the shorter and the
longer text in this testament (see I.2c below) we find a great number
of variants at the end of this verse. Also here *eaf chi* S A (acc.
to Charles) give a text which is shorter than that found in the
other MSS., but in this case it must be explained as the result of
a mechanical error; we have here another clear example of omission
because of homoioteleuton. *bk* read καὶ ὄψεσθε θεὸν ἐν σχήματι
ἀνθρώπου, ὃν ἂν ἐκλέξηται κύριος (*k* καὶ ἡ) Ἰερουσαλὴμ ὄνομα
αὐτῷ. *b* is clearly corrupt and *k* attempts to produce a somewhat
better reading trough the change of κ̅ς̅ into κ´η. In *g* we find a
more drastic and therefore more effective alteration: καὶ ὄψεσθε
κύριον ἐν σχήματι ἀνθρώπου, ὃν ἂν ἐκλέξηται κύριος, ἐν Ἰερουσαλὴμ διὰ τὸ ὄνομα αὐτῷ. If we compare this with the reading found
in *eaf chi* S: καὶ ὄψεσθε κύριον (*chi*: αὐτὸν) ἐν Ἰερουσαλὴμ διὰ
τὸ ὄνομα αὐτοῦ (*chi*: + τὸ (*hi* παν-) ἅγιον) it becomes clear that
this shorter text is the result of an erroneous omission of the words
after κύριον till κύριος inclusive.[12] It is interesting to note the solution
for the difficulties in this passage which is found in *ldm*: καὶ ὄψεσθε
κύριον (*l*: θεόν, cf. *bk*) ἐν Ἰερουσαλὴμ (< *l*) ἐν σχήματι ἀνθρώπου
καὶ κληθήσεται τὸ ὄνομα αὐτοῦ (< *l*) μεγάλης βουλῆς ἄγγελος
(cf. Is IX,6). It is clear that this wealth of variant readings can
only be explained if we assume that a text like that found in *b*
stood at the beginning of the textual tradition known to us. The *b*-text
is evidently not in order, and because of the expression ἐν σχήματι

---

[12] A is retranslated into Greek by Charles as καὶ ὄψεσθε κύριον ἐν Ἰερουσαλήμ.
Already N. Messel, "Über die textkritisch begründete Ausscheidung vermutlicher
christlicher Interpolationen in den Testamenten der Zwölf Patriarchen", *Festschrift
W. W. Baudissin B.Z.A.W.* 33), Giessen, 1918, pp. 355-374 pointed out that the shorter
text is here the result of an omission because of hmt. (p. 366).

ἀνθρώπου it must be christian. Because of the parallel expressions
in Test. Levi X,5 ὁ γὰρ οἶκος ὃν ἂν ἐξελέξηται κύριος, Ἱερουσαλὴμ κληθήσεται and T.L. XV,1 διὰ ταῦτα ὁ ναός, ὃν ἂν ἐκλέξηται
κύριος, ἔρημος ἔσται...[13] we may suppose that the original text
read ἐν οἴκῳ or ἐν ναῷ after ἀνθρώπου. Omission of ἐν ναῷ through
parablepsis could occur very easily (ἀνουεννναωοναν).[14]

f) In the discussion of these five passages the conclusions reached
by H. J. de Jonge in his article "Die Textüberlieferung der Testamente
der Zwölf Patriarchen" (see chapter II) were not referred to explicitly.
It is good to note, however, that some of his more important results
are confirmed by the analysis given above and that none of them
are contradicted by it. I should like to draw attention to the following
points :

(1) All extant witnesses to the text go back to one archetype.
Nearest to this archetype are *b* and *k*, then *g*, *l* and *dm*, *e*, *af* and
chi (+ *n*, Serb, New Greek).

(2) This archetype can only be reconstructed on the basis of
numerous decisions pro and contra variants in individual cases. It is
clear, however, that this eclectic procedure will have to take stemmatic
relationships into consideration. Because secondary influence cannot
be excluded the exact relationships between *b*, (*k*), *g*, *l* and *e* which
stand nearest to the archetype remain uncertain. We may say, however,
that the readings of these MSS. will have to be considered carefully
in all cases, whereas variants in *dm*, *af*, *nchi* will usually be of
secondary importance only.

(3) In this connection the problem of the relationship between
the longer and the shorter text in Test. Zeb. is of primary importance.
The longer text is found in manuscripts which stand nearest to the
archetype : *bk gldm*, the shorter text in *eaf chi* with S (which
usually joins *af*) and also A (very important for the determination

---

[13] Neither in Test. Levi X,5 nor in Test. Levi XV,1 we find variants which can
possibly be original.
[14] W. A. van Hengel, "De Testamenten der twaalf Patriarchen op nieuw ter sprake
gebragt", *Godgeleerde Bijdragen* 34, 1860, pp. 881-970 proposes ἐν τῷ τόπῳ ᾧ ἂν
ἐκλέξηται κύριος because of Deut. XII,5,11,14,18,26 and other instances in Deuteronomy (see p. 940, n. 6). See also M. de Jonge, *The Testaments of the Twelve Patriarchs.
A Study of their Text, Composition and Origin*, Assen 1953, p. 154, n. 261, where
Justin, Dial. XL,4 is referred to. In this passage it is said that at the second advent
the Jews will see the Christ in Jerusalem : ...ὅτι ἐν τῷ αὐτῷ τόπῳ τῶν Ἱεροσολύμων
ἐπιγνώσεσθε αὐτὸν τὸν ἀτιμωθέντα ὑφ' ὑμῶν.

of the place of the Armenian version in the stemma). At a certain moment in the process of the transmission of the text either a number of additions were made or a number of passages were omitted deliberately. In either case we must speak of recensional activity. If the stemma given in ch. II and modified in ch. III is right, the longer text is more likely to be original than the shorter one, and the latter may be properly called the shorter recension. In this case we must assume that at a point between the "Vorlage" of *gldm* and (the "Vorlage" of) *e* the text was shortened deliberately. In the following section we shall try to prove that this must have been the case.

I. 2. *The longer and the shorter text in Test. Zeb. V-IX*

a) The text of VI,4 up to VIII,3 inclusive is not found in *eaf chi* S A with the exception of two little sentences, πέντε ἔτη ἡλίευσα in VI,7 and τὸ θέρος ἡλίευον καὶ ἐν χειμῶνι ἐποίμαινον μετὰ τῶν ἀδελφῶν μου in VI,8. In this shorter text Zebulun's activities as a fisherman are not supplemented with references to his εὐσπλαγχνία and his ἔλεος for his fellow-men in distress. The longer text mentions Zebulun's compassion several times (VI,4,(5), VII,1,4) and states with some emphasis that God will treat a man in the way he treats his fellow-man (VI,6); if one has compassion one may expect to receive compassion, also at the end of days (VIII,1-3). Consequently Zebulun admonishes his sons to show compassion (VII,2-3, VIII,1). The contents of the longer text link up with V,1-4 where the same exhortations and the same reference to God's compassion and mercy are found (in *all* witnesses to the text!), connected with the history of the selling of Joseph by his brothers. This is recorded in I,5-IV,13, where Zebulun's attitude towards his brother is characterized as σπλαγχνιζόμενος (IV,2; cf. I,6, II,4 and Joseph's appeal for mercy in II,2).

The fact that the longer text in VI,4-VIII,3 agrees with the contents of the preceding sections of Test. Zeb. is, in itself, not yet an argument in favour of the originality of this text. The possibility remains that a later redactor wanted to use the story of Zebulun the fisherman as an illustration for the main theme of exhortation in this testament and adapted it accordingly. Moreover, if we opt for the longer text we have to explain why this text was shortened.

b) Next there are a number of smaller variants in VIII,4-6. In VIII,4 all manuscripts characterize Joseph's attitude towards his brothers

with the words οὐ μνησικάκησεν. In *b g l* (*d*)[15] we read also
ἐμὲ δὲ ἰδών, ἐσπλαγχνίσθη. In this way VIII,4 is connected with
the directly preceding verses 1-3. The same is true of VIII,6 (end)
where *b g d l* (*k* and *m* are absent) read ὁ γὰρ μνησίκακος σπλάγχνα
ἐλέους οὐκ ἔχει.[16] The fact that the words ἀμνησίκακοι γίνεσθε
in VIII,5 are not found in *l eaf chi* S A will have to be explained
otherwise. Here we may suppose an omission in order to avoid
the duplication with καὶ μὴ λογίζεσθε ἕκαστος τὴν κακίαν τοῦ
ἀδελφοῦ αὐτοῦ at the end of this verse.[17]

With regard to the variant in VIII,4 we should note the striking
agreement between the longer text and Test. Sim. IV,4: Ἰωσὴφ δὲ
ἦν ἀνὴρ ἀγαθός, καὶ ἔχων πνεῦμα θεοῦ ἐν ἑαυτῷ, εὔσπλαγχνος καὶ
ἐλεήμων, οὐκ ἐμνησικάκησέ μοι, ἀλλὰ καὶ ἠγάπησέ με, ὡς τοὺς
ἄλλους ἀδελφούς (so in all manuscripts with some unessential variants).
Moreover it agrees with the description of God himself in Test.
Zeb. IX,7 (in all manuscripts with some secondary variants): ὅτι
ἐλεήμων ἐστὶ καὶ εὔσπλαγχνος, μὴ λογιζόμενος κακίαν τοῖς υἱοῖς
τῶν ἀνθρώπων. Also elsewhere in the Testaments ἔλεος and εὐσπλαγχνία are characteristic for God's acts and the behaviour of
"the good man".[18] The longer text of VIII,4 (and that of VIII,6)
goes perfectly not only with Test. Zebulun but also with the whole
of the Testaments and there is no reason to assume secondary addition
under the influence of the preceding section.

If we suppose that the shorter text is the result of a deliberate
abbreviation, it will strike us on closer examination that Zebulun's
activities as fisherman are still described as lasting five years, until
the time Joseph's brothers went to Egypt (VI,3 and 5); immediately
after that we are told what happened after they arrived there. In this
way the story telling how Joseph was treated by his brothers (I,5-IV,13),

---

[15] In *k and m* these words are omitted as part of larger omissions; *d* rewrites
the text, but presupposes the reading found in *b g l*.

[16] Test. Zeb. VIII,6 is a typical transitional verse. In the shorter text it introduces
the exhortations on the necessity to avoid dissension in IX,1-4. In the longer text
it also gives a conclusion of the preceding admonitions; here ἀμνησικακία serves
as a connecting link between σπλαγχνίζομαι and the following.

[17] *k and m* are absent here; *l* supports *eaf chi* A S but reads μνησικακίαν in
stead of κακίαν in the concluding sentence.

[18] See Test. Benj. IV,1f. (cf. Test. Benj. IV,4; V,4; Test. Jud. XVIII,3; Test.
Issach. V,2; Test. Asher II,5-7) and Test. Issach. VI,4; Test. Dan V,9; Test. Napht.
IV,3; IV,5; Test. Asher VII,7.

leading to the parenetic passage V,1-4, is connected with the account of Joseph's treatment of his brothers (VIII,4, cf. Test. Sim. IV,4, T. Jos. XVII,4), leading to new exhortations in VIII,5 and VIII,6-IX,4. In the shorter text the biographical account in V,5-VI,3, 7a, 8 serves only as a connecting link between two Joseph stories; at the same time a number of somewhat extravagant examples of Zebulun's εὐσπλαγχνία and ἔλεος are omitted.

In this way omission can be explained satisfactorily. The scribe who was responsible for this, however, seems to have done his work too thoroughly with regard to the exhortations concerning compassion and mercy. It is important to note that not only *b* but also *ef* S indicate the theme of this testament as περὶ εὐσπλαγχίας καὶ ἐλέους and mention these words in the title.[19] In the shorter text found in *ef* S this theme is treated only very briefly, in V,1 and 3f. (cf. IV,2) and in IX,7; this can hardly be original. Also for this reason omission is more probable than addition.

c) Finally we have to discuss a number of variants in IX,5f. and in IX,8. Also here *eaf chi* S A give a shorter text than the other manuscripts. In the case of the variants in IX,5 and IX,6 it is difficult to make a definite choice. In IX,5 the words ἐν ἐσχάταις ἡμέραις ἀποστήσεσθε are not found in the manuscripts just mentioned. It is possible that they were omitted because they stand in between the warnings against divisions in Israel and the following of two kings on the one hand and the preceding parenetic passage on dissension in IX,1-4 (introduced by the transitional verse VIII,6) on the other.[20] Why in IX,6 the expression καὶ ὀδύναις ψυχῆς was added or omitted after ἐν πάσαις ἀσθενείαις καὶ θλίψεσι is not clear; perhaps it was omitted because the connection between external oppression and internal anguish may have seemed strange here.[21]

---

[19] See further *g* περὶ ἐλεημοσύνης; *l* περὶ εὐσπλαγχνίας; *d* περὶ εὐσπλαγχνίας καὶ ἐλεημοσύνης; *m* περὶ εὐσπλαγχνίας καὶ περὶ ἐλέους. *a* gives nothing more than the name of the patriarch in the titles of all Testaments, just like *chi* which add Jacob's name and that of the mother of the patriarch, and indicate the patriarch's number among the sons of Jacob.

[20] This clause is a stereotyped phrase in the "Sin-Exile-Return-pattern". See on this pattern M. de Jonge, *The Testaments of the Twelve Patriarchs* (n. 14), pp. 83-86 and J. Becker, *Untersuchungen zur Entstehungsgeschichte der Testamente der Zwölf Patriarchen* (*A.G.J.U.* 8), Leiden 1970, pp. 172-177. The closest parallel is found in Test. Dan V,4.

[21] It is remarkable that *l* substitutes καὶ δουλείαις for καὶ ὀδύναις ψυχῆς.

More important are the first two variants in IX,8 (for the third see I.1e above). The first to be discussed is a long passage found in *bk gldm* only. In *b* it reads as follows :[22] (φῶς δικαιοσύνης) καὶ ἴασις καὶ εὐσπλαγχνία ἐπὶ ταῖς πτέρυξιν αὐτοῦ. Αὐτὸς λυτρώσεται πᾶσαν αἰχμαλωσίαν υἱῶν ἀνθρώπων ἐκ τοῦ Βελίαρ, καὶ πᾶν πνεῦμα πλάνης πατηθήσεται. In the first clause there is a clear reference to Mal. III,20a (IV,2a) : καὶ ἀνατελεῖ ὑμῖν τοῖς φοβουμένοις τὸ ὄνομά μου ἥλιος δικαιοσύνης καὶ ἴασις ἐν ταῖς πτέρυξιν αὐτοῦ whereas the φῶς δικαιοσύνης in the shorter text provides only a vague hint in this direction (cf. also Test. Levi XVIII,4; Test. Jud. XXIV,1). The καὶ εὐσπλαγχνία added after ἴασις is remarkable; it fits very well into this testament. The second clause has a clear parallel in Test. Dan V,11 καὶ τὴν αἰχμαλωσίαν λάβῃ ἀπὸ τοῦ Βελίαρ ψυχὰς ἁγίων[23] and the third in Test. Levi XVIII,12 καὶ ὁ Βελίαρ δεθήσεται ὑπ᾽ αὐτοῦ, καὶ δώσει ἐξουσίαν τοῖς τέκνοις αὐτοῦ τοῦ πατεῖν ἐπὶ τὰ πονηρὰ πνεύματα and Test. Sim. VI,6 τότε δοθήσονται πάντα τὰ πνεύματα τῆς πλάνης εἰς καταπάτησιν (cf. also Lk X,19f).

In the longer text of IX,8 we find, therefore, a number of motifs which are entirely in keeping with the rest of this testament and with the Testaments as a whole. If these clauses are additions they are very subtle additions (see especially the expansion and adaptation of the reference to Mal III,20 which is at the most only vague in the shorter text!). Omission is much more likely because of the general tendency to omit and to abbreviate in *eaf chi* A S. Directly after this part of IX,8 the shorter text goes on with καὶ ἐπιστρέψετε ἐπὶ τῆς γῆς ὑμῶν *e* (*af* S : ἐκ τῆς γῆς ὑμῶν; *chi*, A—acc. to Charles— εἰς τὴν γῆν ὑμῶν), a clear repetition of the καὶ ἐπιστρέψει ὑμᾶς in IX,7. *bk g l* clearly have a more difficult reading καὶ ἐπιστρέψει πάντα τὰ ἔθνη εἰς παραζήλωσιν αὐτοῦ.[24] The latter manuscripts are more likely to represent the original text than the former.

---

[22] Some secondary variants are not taken into account. We should note, however, *gldm*'s ἐν (ταῖς πτερ.) in stead of ἐπί, as in Mal. III,20a LXX.

[23] In Test. Dan V,11 this is followed by καὶ ἐπιστρέψει καρδίας ἀπειθεῖς πρὸς κύριον, cf. Test. Zeb. IX,8 καὶ ἐπιστρέψει πάντα τὰ ἔθνη etc. (see below). Compare also M. de Jonge, *The Testaments of the Twelve Patriarchs* (n. 14), p. 91.

[24] *m* omits the entire clause; *d* combines two readings ἐπιστρέψει ὑμᾶς εἰς τὴν γῆν ὑμῶν καὶ ἔθνη εἰς παραζήλωσιν. The difficulty of the *bkgl*-text lies in the construction ἐπιστρέψει εἰς παραζήλωσιν, where παραζήλωσις must have the meaning of "zeal for" in stead of "jealousy", "emulation"—see the Dictionaries of Liddell-Scott-Jones and Lampe.

II. *Textual criticism and the analysis of earlier stages in the transmission of the text*

(1) Textual criticism cannot provide information about the time prior to the archetype (or archetypes) from which all extant witnesses are descended in one way or another. Before we are able to analyse the earlier stages in the transmission of the text we must, however, know where to work back from; reconstruction of the archetype(s) is very important, even if complete reconstruction is often impossible. Some examples taken from the preceding sections may illustrate this.

If in IV,9 the clause καὶ ἐποίησαν οὕτως belongs to the text, it must be a redactional remark which serves as a temporary conclusion, in the same way as IV,13 gives the final conclusion of the story of the selling of Joseph. It is possible that the omission of these words is not due to a mechanical error but to a deliberate attempt to avoid duplication with the latter verse. However this may be, IV,9 end and IV,13 are redactional remarks [25] and we may ask whether the man who composed this story did not add vss 10-12 only at the last moment. Something similar must have happened in chapter III where the Joseph-story is interrupted by an account about the sandals which the brothers bought for themselves with the money they received for Joseph (III,1-3); this account is followed by a second one about the reception of the brothers in Egypt, which may be called a super-midrash (III,4-7). [26] Here there are no textual variants to draw attention to these elements in the composition; in IV,9 there is one, but textual criticism can do no more than supply arguments in favour of the originality of an unevenness in the text.

In the same way the position of VIII,6 as transitional verse between the exhortations concerning εὐσπλαγχνία and ἔλεος and the warnings against dissension is brought out much more clearly in the (original) longer text than in the shorter recension. In the latter only τοῦτο (referring to vs 5) is left as an introduction to the following phrases (see I.2b).

Finally the analysis of the textual history of the last sentence

---

[25] One should note the transition to the third person plural in IV,9 and IV,13.

[26] So already E. J. Bickerman, "The date of the Testaments of the Twelve Patriarchs", *J.B.L.* LXIX, 1950, pp. 245-260, on p. 248. See also M. de Jonge, *The Testaments of the Twelve Patriarchs* (n. 14), p. 100 and J. Becker, *Untersuchungen zur Entstehungsgeschichte der Testamente der Zwölf Patriarchen* (n. 20), pp. 206f.

in IX,8 makes clear that the earliest text of Test. Zeb. which is accessible to us by textcritical methods is Christian. Of course it is possible to regard ἐν σχήματι ἀνθρώπου as the result of interpolation or redaction, but no textcritical arguments can be adduced in favour of that theory.

(2) The direct contribution of textual criticism to the analysis of the history of the transmission of Test. Zebulun in the period prior to the origin of the earliest accessible written text is very small. Also its indirect contribution may not be overrated. From the analysis of the relationship between the longer and the shorter text in Test. Zebulun, which was given above, it is clear that copyists—or at least one copyist—regarded the connection between a biographical account and the following exhortations as secondary. They(he) gave the biographical sketch but omitted the exhortations; also the opposite is conceivable though less likely in the present case. This leads us to inquire into the nature of the connection between the story told in I,5-IV,13 and the exhortations following in V,1-4, especially because we have noticed that the story itself gives only slight points of contact for these exhortations (see I.2a).

J. Becker [27] who explains the longer text as the result of addition, regards V,1-4 as added by a later redactor, whose work did not leave any traces in the extant textual witnesses. According to him neither V,1-4 nor chapter III belong to the "Grundstock" of the testament. Originally VIII,4 followed IV,13 after a short intermezzo on Zebulun the fisherman. The exhortations in VIII,5-IX,3, given at the end, were originally the only parenetic passage in Test. Zebulun. It is impossible to discuss Becker's analysis in detail here. It is important to note that he regards the longer text as a redaction of the shorter one, both in the case of chapters VI-VIII where there are textual variants and in the case of I,5-V,4 where there are none. If we assume, however, that the shorter text in chapters VI-VIII is the result of recension, we shall look for another theory to explain the early history of the origin and transmission of I,5-V,4, even though textual criticism will never be able to provide compelling arguments for or against theories concerning that earlier history.

My main objection against Becker's explanation is that he ascribes

---

[27] For his literary-critical and traditio-historical analysis of Test. Zebulun one should consult section III,5 "Die Abschiedsrede in Test. Seb." on pp. 203-213 of his book.

to successive stages of redaction what can quite well be ascribed to one redactor who composed the testament using different material from different sources. If in the longer text of chapters VI-VIII exhortations concerning compassion and mercy were connected with a short biographical sketch of Zebulun as a fisherman, also in V,1-4 similar exhortations may have been connected with the story of the selling of Joseph right from the beginning! The excursus in III,1-3 may have been added by the same redactor, as a footnote at ἕως οὗ ἐπώλησαν αὐτὸν τοῖς Ἰσμαηλιταῖς. III 4-7 present more difficulties : here οἱ ἀδελφοὶ Ἰωσήφ are introduced in the third person plural. Zebulun did not share in the blood-money received for Joseph, but he could not pose as an outsider in an account of the journey to Egypt and of the humiliations experienced there. Yet is not necessary to conclude that this part of the story is an addition from a later hand. Also the redactor responsible for the composition of the testament may have used and incorporated additional material; in any case in vs 8 the story changes over again to the first person plural.[28]

If we assume that the Testaments are the result of compositional activity of one man or a limited number of people within a short period of time, we may also expect some unevennesses in the final text. Zebulun's attitude against Joseph is characterised as ἄγνοια in I,5; this does not exclude exhortations at the end of the Joseph-story which are orientated differently. If V,4 refers back to III,2 this does not imply that V,1-4 must have been added later; it shows the ability of the redactor to combine material of different provenance and different orientation to a more or less coherent whole.[29] In the same way the transition from V,4 to V,5 is clearly redactional, but not necessarily the work of a later redactor. Zebulun's activity as a fisherman is introduced and at the same time V,5b emphasizes

---

[28] Only *chi* read ἐνεδείξαντο (cf. *d* : ἐνεδειξάμεθα); *g* omits this verse but avoids the use of the third person in the preceding verses (see further II,4 below). J. Becker, *op. cit.* (n. 20), pp. 206f, wrongly asserts that VIII,4 is incompatible with chapter III. The latter chapter does not tell us anything about Joseph's personal attitude towards his brothers. The discrepancy between Test. Zeb. III,4-7 and Test. Jos. XI,2-XVI,6 cannot be denied, but need not be explained by the assumption that Test. Zeb. III was added later. A "composing redactor" may very well have used different midrashic material in different ways in different places; logical consistency may not be expected from him.

[29] J. Becker regards the use of the third person plural with οἱ δὲ ἐμοὶ υἱοί in V,4b as incompatible with the situation of a testament. He overlooks the fact, however, that this verse ends with the words ὡς οἴδατε.

that he continued unhurt where many were distressed, just like his sons over against the sons of his brothers in V,4. Finally, the coexistence in one testament of two different sets of exhortations (about compassion and about unity) does not compel us to regard either the one or the other as a later addition.

(3) What is the possible contribution of the analysis of the earlier stages in the history of the text to textual criticism? Let us start, again, with two examples taken from Test. Zebulun. In IX,5-7 we find a Sin-Exile-Return-passage :[30] vs 5 speaks of "sin" (especially about dissension), vs 6 deals with "exile" and distress connected with it, vs 7 mentions "return". Next there is a new start (again μετὰ ταῦτα...) at the beginning of the complicated vs 8. J. Becker who follows the shorter text in vs 8[31] regards this verse as a parallel to vs 7 which disturbs the line of thought and removes it as a later Jewish addition. He does not explain, however, why this gloss was added. This theory of duplication can only be maintained on the basis of the shorter text, for in the longer text the events of vs 8 can be put after those mentioned in vs 7 without much difficulty.[32] In any case the analysis of the composition of these verses, and a theory of the origin of this text connected with it, do not provide any useful textcritical arguments, and Becker, therefore, rightly separates his textcritical analysis and the literary-critical and traditio-historical approach in this case.

In his discussion of the problem of the shorter and the longer text in chapters VI-VIII, however, he is less cautious. In his textcritical treatment of this section of Test. Zebulun on pp. 23 f. of his book[33] his main argument in favour of the shorter text is that all supposed additions want to portray Zebulun as an example of compassion whereas in the immediate context other problems are more important.

---

[30] See note 20 above.

[31] He chooses the reading ἐπιστρέψετε εἰς τὴν γῆν ὑμῶν in chi, (d), (e). See op. cit. (n. 20), pp. 211-213.

[32] The S.E.R.-pattern is repeated in a very short form. The element of "sin" is mentioned in vs 9a, that of "exile" very shortly in ἀπορριφήσεσθε, and "return" is implied in ἕως καιροῦ συντελείας. According to the longer text αὐτόν in vs 9 refers to θεὸς ἐν σχήματι ἀνθρώπου in vs 8. A comparable repetition is found in Test. Napht. IV,4-5 and Test. Asher VII,5-7. Especially in Test. Asher VII (see also vs 3!) the parallellism with the longer text of Test. Zeb. IX is striking.

[33] He discusses Test. Zeb. VI-VIII within the framework of section I,2a which gives "fundamental considerations regarding the relations between α and β". This way of stating the problem is no longer adequate.

In VIII,5f. the point of the original exposition is formulated quite clearly.[34] The proof for VIII,5f. as the original point of the original exposition is given much later, on pp. 203-213 of Becker's book. The most important elements of his argumentation were given in the previous section (see II.2 above); here it is important to note that the theory of secondary addition of V,1-4 is said to be supported by the fact that exhortations of the same type were added later in chapters VI-VIII.[35] This means that Becker is guilty of circular argumentation. His use of textcritical arguments in support of his analysis of the earliest stages in the history of the text cannot be objected to, as long as we see clearly that such textcritical arguments can never be compelling. At closer inspection, however, his textcritical arguments are not textcritical at all; they, in turn, depend on his views on the earliest stages of the text.

(4) This does not mean, of course, that there may not have been parallel developments in the period before and the period after the origin of the archetype. Only, textual criticism cannot tell us anything about the transmission of the written text before that archetype. J. Becker reminds us of R. Bultmann's opinion that no distinction can be made between the literary and the pre-literary stages in the transmission of the Synoptic Gospels, and he concludes that also in the case of the Testaments there is a transition from (what he calls) "traditio-historical growth" to "the stage of textual criticism".[36] In saying this he forgets, however, that in the case of the history of the text of the Gospels we have very early documents, but that those are lacking for the Testaments of the Twelve Patriarchs. Moreover, the distinction literary/pre-literary does not coincide with that between the text which can be reconstructed with textcritical methods and that which cannot. Our oldest Greek manuscript of the Testaments dates from the Xth century and there is no evidence

---

[34] See p. 24: "Alle genannte Zusätze haben im Übrigen ein gemeinsames Thema. Sie wollen das Erbarmen Sebulons als Vorbild herausstellen, haben aber für dieses Thema im unmittelbaren Kontext keinen Anhaltspunkt und stehen zum Ziel des ursprünglichen Textes (8,5f.) in Konkurrenz".

[35] See p. 208: "Auch in T. Seb. 6,4-6.7b; 7,1-8,3.6b (nur bg) und 8,4b ist Tugendparänese zum Thema 'Erbarmen' sekundär nachgetragen, so dass—wenn auch 5,1-4 herausgestellt ist—T. Seb. keine Paränese mehr zum Thema 'Erbarmen' enthält".

[36] See p. 24: "D. h. grundsätzlich: traditionsgeschichtliches Wachstum geht im Stadium der Textgeschichte weiter".

to date the archetype much earlier.[37] The question whether we may assume a preliterary stage in the development of the present Testaments (here we should emphasize : not of specific elements, but of the whole conception of twelve testaments) cannot be answered affirmatively with any certainty; it is of secondary importance for the present line of argument. We should remember, however, that there is a great interval between the earliest literary stages and the stage which can be reconstructed with the help of textual criticism.

Medieval copyists of the Testaments will have read and copied them in a way which differs completely from the treatment given to them by those who used and copied them in the first stages of transmission. The XVIth century scribe of manuscript *m* omits long passages (e.g. Test. Zeb. II,9 ἕως οὗ-III,7 ἔμπροσθεν αὐτοῦ with the exception of III,6a καὶ γὰρ ἐλθόντες ἐν Αἰγύπτῳ; IV,5 ὅτι ἐπράθη-13 end; VIII,4-IX,7); sometimes he gives a brief summary of the passages omitted (e.g. in a part of the description of Judah's war in Test. Jud. II-IX). There are also smaller abbreviations (Test. Zeb. VI,5; VI,7f; VIII,3). This copyist did not want to transmit the whole text but omitted the less interesting or less important parts. His criteria were subjective and necessarily bound up with the requirements of his readers.

The scribe of manuscript *k* (XIIIth century) is much more radical; he gives extracts, some very long (as in the case of the Testaments of Reuben, Simeon, Levi and Benjamin), some only very short. Mostly he refers to the exhortations in the testament (generally indicating the theme very briefly) and concentrates on the passages at the end of the individual testaments which he regards as announcements of the coming of the Christ. This may be illustrated by his extracts from Test. Issachar and Test. Zebulun : ε̄ διαθήκη,

---

[37] See H. J. de Jonge in chapter III. The Armenian version is dated, for linguistic reasons, in the VIth or VIIth century (see C. Burchard, "Zur armenischen Überlieferung des Testamente der Zwölf Patriarchen", in C. Burchard-J. Jervell-J. Thomas, *Studien zu den Testamenten der Zwölf Patriarchen*, B.Z.N.W. 36, Berlin 1969, pp. 1-29, especially p. 27 and M. E. Stone's recension of this book in *J.B.L.* 89, 1970, pp. 487f.). The question remains to be seen whether the analysis of the relationship between the longer and the shorter text given above, which led to the conclusion that A too gives a secondary text does not compel us to adopt a later date. If there are really unquestionable arguments in favour of an early date, the conclusion must be that our archetype is much earlier than could be deduced from the situation of the Greek manuscripts. See further chapter VIII.

ἀντίγραφον Ἰσάχαρ· οὗτος οὐδέν τι περὶ τοῦ χριστοῦ ἐφθέγξατο
and : ἕκτη διαθήκη ἀντιγράφου ζαβουλών, ἐν ᾗ μετὰ πολλὰς παραι-
νέσεις πρὸς τοὺς υἱοὺς αὐτοῦ, εἶπε καὶ περὶ τοῦ χριστοῦ ταῦτα·
(here follows T. Zeb. VIII,1 - X end).

Another interesting case is that of manuscript g (XVIth century).
It omits the explanation of Zebulun's name in Test. Zeb. I,3; its
scribe did this on purpose because in Test. Issachar the whole
passage I,2b ἐν μισθῷ - II,5 end is omitted and in Test. Naphtali
we find τῆς παιδίσκης ῥαχιήλ, ὄγδοος υἱὸς τῷ Ἰακὼβ τῷ πατρί
in stead of the long exposition in I,6-12. The copyist who wrote g
obviously was not interested in such explanations of names. Next
it is interesting to see that g's scribe abbreviated and polished the
long story of the selling of Joseph and the excursus on the blood-money
in Test. Zeb. II-IV. The explanation of the fact that the pits were
dry is omitted in II,7-9; in III,1 ἐγὼ οὐκ ἐκοινώνησα is replaced
by the much stronger μὴ γένοιτό μοι κοινωνῆσαι. In III,4f. the text
is shortened (see I.1a above) and besides that the first person plural
is used consistently in III,6f. Apart from III,7 οὐ μόνον-αὐτῷ the
whole of III,8 is omitted. Finally, in IV,3 it is said that Zebulun
was told to watch Joseph.

Next, g omits two lists of spirits in Test. Reub. II,2-III,9 and
substitutes the significant remark ἀρκεῖ μοι εἰς διδασκαλίαν ὑμῶν.
A similar omission and a similar remark are found in Test. Naphtali.
In stead of II,2-8 we read καὶ ἐποίουν τὰς ἐντολὰς αὐτοῦ κατὰ
τάξιν, καὶ ἕτερα τινα πολλὰ φυσιογνωμικά (sic!). After that the
copyist continues with καὶ ὑμεῖς πάντα τὰ ἔργα ὑμῶν ἐν τάξει ποιεῖτε
τὰ ἀγαθὰ ἐν φόβῳ θεοῦ κτλ. in vs 9.

It is clear that later copyists omitted those parts of the text which
they regarded as inessential, irrelevant or uninteresting without hesitation. It is equally clear that the latest stages in the transmission
of the text show a tendency towards abbreviation.[38] The developments
in the history of the text prior to the archetype need not be (quite)
parallel to those in the period during which our extant manuscripts
were written and they may have shown points of agreement with
phenomena in the earliest stages of transmission of the text. Only

---

[38] One should not forget the many omissions in the Armenian version, see
M. de Jonge, The Testaments of the Twelve Patriarchs (see n. 13), pp. 26-28 and the
remarks on A's omission of statements about "the nations" in J. Jervell, "Ein
Interpolator interpretiert", B.Z.N.W. 36 (see n. 36), pp. 30-61, espec. pp. 39-40.

the recensional activities during the period of the manuscripts known
to us, however, can be analysed by the textual critic and only these
can be compared with developments which must be examined with
the help of literary-critical, form-critical, "redaktionsgeschichtliche"
and other traditio-historical methods. In this comparison we shall
have to proceed with extreme caution.

FURTHER OBSERVATIONS
ON THE TRANSMISSION OF THE TEXT

TH. KORTEWEG

1. *Introduction*

H. J. de Jonge's article „Die Textüberlieferung der Testamente der zwölf Patriarchen", originally published in the *Zeitschrift für die neutestamentliche Wissenschaft* of 1972 and now reprinted as the second chapter in this volume,[1] was based on a considerable part of the material assembled for the new *editio maior*. It tried to define the relationships between the various witnesses to the text as exactly as possible. The results, represented graphically in a *stemma codicum*,[2] were intended to serve as a working-hypothesis which would facilitate to some degree the constitution of the text that was to follow.

While the latter was in progress, H. J. de Jonge's theory was subjected to constant scrutiny and it is the present writer's duty to report on this investigation. His remarks will not affect the method which was used. As often elsewhere, so in text-critical matters, hardly any mere theoretical argument is likely to be entirely satisfactory. That means that the only way for a hypothesis to prove its value is by explaining in the most convincing manner the facts that present themselves, without at the same time being seriously contradicted by those that it fails to account for. If the present interest in the Testaments continues, the last word on this subject will not be spoken within the near future. In the meantime I should like to offer here some observations which, though not involving fundamental criticism of H. J. de Jonge's results, may nonetheless supplement them in a way that will lead us finally to some more general reflections.

2. *The possibility of a special relationship between* gldm

a) In order to prove that *ldmeafchi* go back to a common ancestor H. J. de Jonge adduced a number of conjunctive errors in these MSS.,

---

[1] See pp. 45sqq. above.

[2] See p. 47 above.

that is to say errors which, in his eyes, cannot have originated independently and therefore must derive from a lost original which he marks as no. 6 in his stemma. Another set of conjunctive errors of *ldmeafchi* also includes *g* and make it necessary to assume the existence of an even earlier, likewise lost original from which both *g* and the ancestor of *ldmeafchi* derive (no. 4 in the stemma). In this situation there is clearly no place for conjunctive errors of *gldm* only, because they would have to be traced back to the hyparchetype of *gldmeafchi* as a group and in that case it would be impossible to explain how *eafchi* could have preserved the original text.

There are, however, a number of common readings in *gldm* which probably are conjunctive errors. If this claim can be substantiated, H. J. de Jonge's stemma should be corrected as follows :

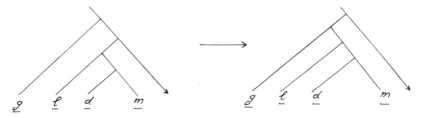

In support of this suggestion we will now draw up a list of the most interesting cases, where *gldm* coincide against all other witnesses, adding a few comments as to their value as evidence of a common original. The list will show a relatively large number of variants only attested by *gdm*, while *l* agrees more or less with *b*. In these cases we shall have to assume secondary influence of a MS. related to *b* on *l*,[3] the *gldm*-reading still being represented by *gdm*. Next, we find instances where *gl* seem to give the *gldm*-reading, whereas *dm* are secondarily influenced by the α-text.[4] Making allowance for these special cases the following list may be offered :

T. Sim. II,9 ἐγχρῄζοντα *beaf* χρῄζοντα *chi*] ἐγχειρίζοντα *gl* (χρεώδη *dm*; cf. α). Secondary influence of *g* on *l*, though not necessarily present, cannot be excluded. The same applies to

T. Sim. IV,2 τῆς πράσεως (τοῦ) Ἰωσήφ *bmeafchi* εἰς τὸν Ἰωσήφ *d*] τοῦ κακοῦ *g* τῆς κακώσεως Ἰ. *l*.

---

[3] So H. J. de Jonge, *art. cit.* under no. 34.

[4] So H. J. de Jonge, *art. cit.* under no's 32 and 33. The present correction of the stemma seems to render the hypothesis of secondary influence of *g* on *l* (H. J. de Jonge, under no. 30) unnecessary though it cannot be excluded in every case.

T. Levi I,1 συναντήσει *ceteri*] συναντήσεται *gdm.*

T. Levi XIV,4 θέλοντες *bleaf* θέλετε *chi*] θελήσετε *gdm.*

T. Jud. VI,4 πόλις *ceteri*] + αὐτῶν *gld* (*m defic.*).

T. Jud. VII,10 ἐγένετο *ceteri*] γέγονεν *gd* γεγόνασιν *l* (*m defic.*).

T. Jud. VIII,2 εἶδον Βαρσὰν (Βαρσαβά *eaf*) βασιλέα *bleaf* (*chi aliter*)] ἰδὼν (+ με *d*) Βαρσὰ (-ν *d*) βασιλεύς *gd* (*m defic.*).

T. Jud. XII,2 Ἀμορραίων *ceteri*] Ἀμορραίοις *gdm.*

T. Jud. XIII,3 οὐκ ἠπάτησέ με *ceteri* (*chi aliter*)] οὐκ ἥττησέ με ἄνθρωπος ἢ εἰς χρυσὸν διερρέθιζον οὐδὲ εἰς *g* οὐκ ἠπάτησέ με ἄνθρωπος ἐν χρυσίῳ καὶ (ἢ *m*) ἀργυρίῳ οὐδέ *dm*. It is difficult to imagine that the readings of *g* and *dm*, which betray influence from the context, originated quite independently.

T. Jud. XVIII,1 βίβλοις *beaf*] βίβλῳ *gld* (*m defic.*)

T. Zeb. I,2 (καὶ) εἶπεν αὐτοὺς *ceteri*] καλέσας (+ γάρ *m*) αὐτοὺς (τοὺς υἱοὺς αὐτοῦ *dm*) εἶπεν αὐτοῖς *gdm*. A comparable case is found in *T. Gad* I,1 where καλέσας has been added in *gd* (*m defic.*), see also *T. Benj.* I,2.

T. Zeb. IV,1 μετὰ ταῦτα *beaf* (*chi aliter*)] μετὰ (+ δέ *g* + γάρ *m*) τὸ βάλλειν (βληθῆναι *ldm*) αὐτὸν (τὸν Ἰωσήφ *l*) εἰς τὸν λάκκον (ἐν τῷ λάκκῳ *l*) *gldm*. Especially if one compares the evidence of A (= Armenian version) one might surmise the reading of *gldm* to be nearer the original than that of *beaf*. In that case it would, of course, no longer prove any family-relationship. On balance, however, I feel reasonably sure that the corrupted text of *beaf* with its ἔβαλον in stead of ἔλαβον lies at the origin of the readings of both *gldm* and A and that we have here a conjunctive error of *gldm*, though perhaps not of *gldm* A.

T. Zeb. IX,5 βασιλεῦσιν *ba* βασιλείαις *efch*] βασιλεῖς *gld* (*m defic.*).

T. Dan IV,4 ἐρεθισθέν (ἐρέθισεν *l*) *ceteri*] ῥηθέν *gdm.*

T. Dan VI,9 μετάδοτε καὶ (δέ *h*) ὑμεῖς (+ ταῦτα *l*) τοῖς τέκνοις ὑμῶν (+ αὐτῶν *a* + αὐτά *ef*) *bleafchi*] καὶ ὑμεῖς τοῖς τέκνοις ὑμῶν ἀναγγείλατε *g* καὶ ὑμεῖς ποιεῖτε, ἀναγγείλατε δὲ αὐτὰ (< *m*) καὶ τοῖς τέκνοις ὑμῶν *dm*.

ibidem ἔστι γὰρ ἀληθὴς καὶ μακρόθυμος *ceteri*] ἐν πᾶσι γὰρ ἀληθὴς καὶ μακρόθυμός ἐστι *g* ἔστι ἀληθὴς καὶ μακρόθυμος ἐν πᾶσι *dm*.

T. Napht. I,6 Βάλλας *ceteri*] Βάλλας (+ τῆς παιδίσκης Ρ. *g*) ὄγδοος υἱὸς τῷ Ἰακὼβ τῷ πατρί μου (Ἰ. τῷ π.μ. υἱὸς ὄγδ. *dm*) *gdm.*

T. Napht. VI,1 σὺν αὐτῷ *ceteri*] μετʼ αὐτοῦ *gldm*. Here it is not so easy to decide which reading is original. The same has to be admitted of

T. Gad I,1 ἅ *ceteri*] ὅσα *gldm*, although ἅ seems to be slightly more difficult.

T. Ash. VI,6 παρακαλέσει *b* παραμυθεῖται *eaf* καὶ εἰσφέρει *chi*] παρακαλοῦντα *gldm*. Since the agreement between *b* and *eaf*(*chi*) seems to point to an indicative in the archetype, the reading of *gldm* has to be taken as secondary here. On the other hand, the attestation of παρακαλεῖν in both *b* and *gldm* has to be taken into account. So *b*'s reading may well be nearest to the original and something like ὅς may have to be supplied before it.

T. Jos. VI,6 δι᾽ ἀγγέλου *ceteri*] < *gdm*. The omission may admittedly be a case of *homoeoteleuton*.

T. Jos. XIII,2 ὃ λέγεις *ceteri*] τί λέγεις *gdm*.

T. Jos. XIII,4 ἐπίστευσεν αὐτῷ *ceteri*] + ὁ Πεντεφρής *gdm*.

T. Jos. XIII,7 λέγω *ceteri* (*ch exc.*)] εἶπον *gldm*.

T. Jos. XIV,2 φυλακισθῆναί με *b* ἡμᾶς φυλακισθῆναι *l* φυλαχθῆναι ἡμᾶς *eaf* φυλαχθῆναί με *ch*] ἐν (< *d*) φυλακῇ βληθῆναι ἡμᾶς *gdm*. This seems to be a particularly clear case of a *gldm*-reading being represented by *gdm* while *l* shows secondary influence of a MS. related to *b*.

T. Jos. XVI,6 ἵνα μὴ ἐτασθῇ (αἰκισθῇ *leaf* αἰσχυνθῇ *c*) ὁ εὐνοῦχος *bleafc*] ἵνα μὴ καταισχύνω τοὺς εὐνούχους (τοὺς συνδούλους μου μήτε μὴ αἰκισθῇ ὁ εὐν. *d* τοὺς ἀδελφούς μου [cf. XI,2] μήτε μὴ αἰκισθῇ ὁ εὐν. *m*) *gdm*.

T. Benj. I,2 φιλήσας *ceteri*] καλέσας *gldm* (*cf. T. Zeb.* I,2; *T. Gad* I,1).

T. Benj. IV,4 τῷ ἀσθενεῖ *bef* τῷ ἀσθενοῦντι *c*] τὸν ἀσθενῆ *gld* (*m defic.*). The dative undoubtedly presents here both the correct and the more difficult reading.

As was already indicated in some cases, not all of the instances quoted above are equally conclusive. It is nevertheless clear that quite a few readings emerge that are most readily explained by taking them to be common errors of *gldm* that have sometimes disappeared either from *l* or from *dm* through contamination. To select only some of the more convincing examples, I might point to the change of the construction in *T. Jud.* VIII,2, to the addition of ἐν πᾶσι in *T. Dan* VI,9 and to such readings as βασιλεῖς (*T. Zeb.* IX,5), παρακαλοῦντα (*T. Ash.* VI,6), (ἐν) φυλακῇ βληθῆναι ἡμᾶς (*T. Jos.* XIV,2) and καλέσας (*T. Benj.* I,2). Moreover, once a single case of conjunctive error has been granted, even instances which, if taken separately, may seem rather ambiguous, acquire considerable value as cumulative evidence. For this purpose the present list may even be supplemented with some other variants of *gldm*, omitted above because of their more doubtful character :

T. Sim. VII,2 ὡς ¹... ὡς ² *ceteri*] < *gdm*

T. Dan V,2 ὑμῶν *ceteri*] ἐν (< *ld*) ὑμῖν *gld* (*m defic.*).

T. Dan. V,6 τῆς πορνείας (πονηρίας *lfchi*) bleafchi] τῆς πλάνης καὶ (< *d*) τῆς πορνείας *gd* (*m defic.*).

T. Jos. VII,1 εἰς... πρός *ceteri*] ∼ *gdm*.

T. Jos. VII,3 ῥίπτω ἐμαυτήν *ceteri*] ∼ *gdm*.

T. Jos. XI,1 τὸν τοῦ θεοῦ φόβον *ceteri* (*h exc.*)] τὸν φόβον τοῦ θεοῦ *gldm*.

T. Benj. III,4 σκεπαζόμενος *ceteri*] σκεπόμενος *gdm*.

Considering all this, our initial assumption of a common descent of *gldm*, although not capable of definite proof, nevertheless appears to be fully borne out by the facts that have presented themselves so far. We shall discuss below [5] a phenomenon which in this connection must be regarded as a complicating factor : apart from the common errors of *gldm* that were listed above, there are a few characteristic readings of these MSS. which, at first sight, look like other striking examples of the same class, but in fact can claim to be authentic readings which appear to have been lost or corrupted in all other Greek witnesses.

b) In disproof of the theory of a family-relationship between *gldm* one might point to the cases mentioned by H. J. de Jonge,[6] where *bg* seem to have preserved the original text over against *ldmeafchi*. The hypothesis of a common ancestor of *gldm* evidently does not allow for cases where *ldm* join *eaf(chi)* against *g* together with *b*.[7] But we may well wonder whether such agreements between *b* and *g* have indeed been convincingly demonstrated.

If we first consider *T. Zeb.* III,6, an explanation of the absence of βασιλέως in *bg*, different from the one given by H. J. de Jonge, could be attempted either by taking βασιλέως as original and assuming that it has been dropped twice independently,[8] or by regarding it

---

[5] See under 2c.

[6] *Art. cit.* under 6.

[7] One might, of course, argue secondary influence of *b* on *g*, but on the whole, concessions like this do not make a theory more convincing.

[8] Cf. the similar omissions in the case of *Gen.* XL,17 LXX (Sixtine ed.) and of *Gen.* XLV,21 LXX (Grabe's collation of D and certain minuscules).

as an addition that may likewise have originated independently in several MSS. under the influence of LXX-usage.[9] Since, especially in *T. Zeb.*, not only *dm* but possibly also *l* show traces of contamination from α,[10] the latter solution is perhaps slightly preferable. If βασιλέως was still absent from the ancestor of *gldm*, we need not even suppose its having been added more than once within the vertical course of transmission.

It is more difficult to dispense with H. J. de Jonge's second instance from *T. Zeb.* X,4. Yet, I think, one should question his assumption that τέως in *ldmeaf* was added with a view to ἕως γενεῶν in the verse before, since without it the transition between vss. 3 and 4 is particularly harsh, whereas τέως makes perfect sense if it is taken as an independent adverb and translated 'now', 'in the meantime'.[11] Therefore, the omission of τέως in *b* and some ancestor of *g* probably has to be considered a case of haplography, which is not unusual when there is a close sequence of two or more short words. The same explanation goes for the omission of ἐγώ in *eaf*. Whereas in *geafchi* we find independent attempts at correction, the original text seems to have been preserved in *l* and, except for the additional οὖν, in *dm*. The common ancestor of *gldm* must have read like *l*.

Nor do some further instances point to the preservation of the original text in *bg* over against all other witnesses.

T. Sim. III,3 πάντοτε (+ γάρ *k*) *bkg*] ἀλλὰ πάντοτε *ldmeafchi*. The addition of ἀλλά to the harsh, but probably original text of *bkg* very easily suggests itself and may have occurred twice independently.

T. Levi XV,3 θεωροῦντες *bg*] ὁρῶντες *ld* (*m defic.*) μισοῦντες *eafchi*. There is no reason to assume that the reading of *eafchi* goes back to that of *ld*; consequently there is no conjunctive error from which only *bg* would be free.

T. Napht. I,1 τέλους *bg*] τελευτῆς *ceteri*. τέλος with the meaning of "the end of life" is not found elsewhere in the Testaments, τελευτή being the usual word in this connection. Therefore, substitution of τελευτή for τέλος may have taken place more than once independently.

---

[9] The addition of βασιλεὺς Αἰγύπτου to Φαραώ is quite common in the books of *Gen.* and *Exod.* See also *d*'s variant in *T. Jos.* VIII,4. As M. de Jonge pointed out to me, βασιλεύειν in III,3 may also have played a rôle.

[10] See H. J. de Jonge, *art. cit.* under 31.

[11] Cf. *Apc. Esdr.* VI,21 (ed. Tischendorf, p. 31 ll. 30sq.): δὸς τέως τὴν παρακαταθήκην "give now what has been entrusted to thee".

T. Napht. IV,1 ἁγίᾳ *bg*] < *ceteri*. The epithet "holy" may have been omitted by several scribes independently of one another because it must have been considered to be out of place in the case of a writing of Enoch. Besides, "holy" occurs in the Armenian version and if M. de Jonge's conclusions on A's affiliation hold good,[12] this would indicate that *ld(m)* on the one hand and *eafchi* on the other must indeed have omitted it independently. A similar case is

T. Dan VI,2 ἐχθροῦ *bg* (*recte*)] θεοῦ *ceteri*. Here too A supports the reading of *bg* (see Charles, *app. crit. a.l.*). The substitution of θεοῦ can easily be explained in view of the well-known expression βασιλεία τοῦ θεοῦ. Perhaps also the expression στῆναι κατέναντι caused some difficulty of understanding.

Thus far the result of our investigation is clearly in favour of the thesis of a family-relationship between *gldm*. No convincing evidence to the contrary could be adduced since, on closer inspection, none of the supposed conjunctive errors of *ldmeafchi* appeared to be entirely beyond doubt.

c) We have already suggested that in a number of instances *gldm* may have preserved the original text. This possibility was brought home to the present author after noticing the remarkable agreement between some of the readings characteristic of *gldm* and the testimony of the Armenian version as quoted by Charles in his *apparatus criticus*. As one may derive from M. de Jonge's chapter on the Armenian witnesses elsewhere in this volume,[13] Charles' apparatus proved to be generally reliable in this matter, therefore the agreements had to be explained in some way or other. From the outset it was clear that A could not be dependent on *gldm*, while at the same time the text represented by *gldm* could go back either to A or to the Greek original from which this version was made.[14] This means

---

[12] See "The Greek Testaments of the Twelve Patriarchs and the Armenian Version", above ch. VIII, especially p. 130.

[13] *Art. cit.*, p. 127.

[14] A separative error of *gldm* against A, which excludes dependence on the part of A, is e.g. the omission of δι' ἀγγέλου in *T. Jos.* VI,6. Separative errors of A against *gldm*, which exclude the reverse, are amongst others the many omissions that are peculiar to this version. The fact that, moreover, in *T. Zeb.* it presents us, together with *eafchi*, with a much shorter text than the one offered by *b* and *gldm*, also speaks against a dependence of *gldm* on the Greek original behind A. On this subject see the article by M. de Jonge, ch. X of this volume.

that coincidences cannot possibly be accounted for by assuming a direct relationship. Now it is true that a number of them may be classed as entirely fortuitous, but there are cases that cannot be dismissed so easily. There A and *gldm* seem to have preserved traces of a common ancestor which, as a comparison of the readings concerned with those of the other Greek witnesses will presently show, may, for this purpose, be held identical with the archetype itself.[15] That is to say that we are faced with original readings, preserved in *gldm* A, but corrupted in all other extant witnesses. Where this applies, one can, of course, no longer expect to find a conjunctive error either of *gldm* A or of *gldm* themselves. Therefore the variants with which we are concerned have to be classed separately from the ones listed above. A number of them are discussed in M. de Jonge's article. Some further comments are given here.

T. Reub. IV,4 μετανοῶν *gld* (τέκνα μου *m*) "by penitence" A[16]] οὖν *b* ἕως ἐννοιῶν *eafn* ἕως νῦν *chi*. Comparison with I,9 and IV,3 (cf. also *T. Sim.* II,13) shows that this reading fits excellently in the context. The readings of *b* and *eafn*(*chi*) can go back to an original μετανοῶν. It is hardly likely that *b*'s colourless reading gave rise to so different variants.

T. Zeb. II,4 ἐξεχύθησαν *gldm* (for A see Charles, *app. a.l.*)] ἐξελύ-θησαν *ceteri*. Although here the reading of A cannot be relied upon, in support of *gldm* one may point to *Hiob* XXX,16 where ἐκλυθήσεται is substituted for ἐκχυθήσεται by a corrector of א, although the latter translates שפך and is therefore quite idiomatic there. Cf. also *Lam.* II,11.

T. Napht. V,8 ἐν κήποις *gldm* "in the gardens" A (MSS. Z M* W°; the other Armenian MSS. read *sing.*)] ἐκεῖ που *b* παρὼν ἐκεῖ *eaf* παρεκεῖ *chi*. Here too the reading of *gldm* A has much to recommend itself to us. In V,1 we find perhaps a reminiscence of the fact that Naphtali received his visions while tending the flocks (cf. *T. Levi* II,3). In any case Hebr. *T. Napht.* tells this explicitly

---

[15] Of course accepting M. de Jonge's argument in ch. VIII implies that this common ancestor need not ascend further than the hyparchetype of the second branch of the tradition. However, in the text I shall argue that in fact it does because here the readings of II must be preferred to those of I.

[16] The translation of A's variants here and in the following examples is that of M. E. Stone (see M. de Jonge, *art. cit.* [n. 12], n. 31).

(בהיותי רועה בצאן II,1). There Naphtali sees himself and his brothers transported "to the field" (בשדה II,2). Now we find κῆποι mentioned as a place for tending sheep in *Cant.* VI,1 : ποιμαίνειν ἐν κήποις (where κῆποι translates Hebrew גן). It is quite possible that the words ἐν κήποις in *T. Napht.* V,8 preserve a motif stemming from the haggadic tradition behind the Testaments,[17] which became somewhat isolated in the present Greek redaction of Naphtali's visions. The different readings in *beafchi* may well represent independent corruptions of one and the same ἐν κήποις. Particularly the strange ἐκεῖ που of *b* in this way seems to admit of a paleographical explanation : ΕΝΚΗΠΟΙΣ > ΕΝΚΕΙΠΟΙΣ > ΕΚΕΙΠΟΥ.

T. Jos. XIV,5 οὐκ ἔστιν ἔθος (ἔθνος *g* νόμος *l*) *gldm* "there is no law" A] οὐκ ἐστι (+ τοῦτο *c*) *ceteri*. Though one may think of independent additions caused by a misunderstanding of ἐστιν (used in the other Greek MSS. in the sense of ἔξεστιν), the agreement between *gldm* and A is still remarkable. In any case *dm* and *g* have or presuppose exactly the same reading : ἔθος (which in *g* has already been corrupted) so that, if not accepted as original, it should at least count as a common error of *gldm*, though not necessarily of *gldm* A.

T. Benj. VII,4 ἐν τοῖς ἑπτὰ (+ οὖν *d*) κακοῖς *gldm* "with seven evils" A] ἐν τοῖς ἑπτακοσίοις (ἑπτά *a*) ἔτεσιν (< *ea*) *beaf*] ἐν πᾶσι τοῖς κακοῖς *chi*. The situation in the MSS. is most readily explained by assuming that this reading is original. Under the influence of VII,3 ἑπτὰ κακοῖς was probably read as ἑπτακοσίοις (cf. *e*). To this *bf* added ἔτεσιν by way of clarification and *a* changed ἑπτακοσίοις again into ἑπτά under the influence of *Gen.* IV,24. The allusion to this verse of the Bible in what I take to be the original text is so clear and the introduction of the 700 years from vs. 4a so inappropriate, that the latter must be considered secondary.

In two cases it is difficult to reach a definite conclusion. In *T. Zeb.* IV,1 H. J. de Jonge's conjecture ἔλαβον for ἔβαλον still gives the most likely solution to a difficult problem.[18] The corruption

---

[17] On the relationship between the Greek and Hebrew Testament of Naphtali see Th. Korteweg, below, ch. XVI.

[18] For the distribution of variants see under 2a. See also M. de Jonge, *art. cit.*, n. 32.

ἔβαλον may well lie at the basis of the whole textual tradition and, in that case, the variants of *gldm* on the one hand and A on the other could be the results of independent attempts to restore the original sentence. In the same way in *T. Ash.* VI,6 the agreement between *gldm* and A is not apparent. Adaptation of a difficult text like the one preserved in *b* is natural and may have been carried out independently in various witnesses, including A. Nevertheless, as in the case of *T. Jos.* XIV,5, I would tend to regard the *gldm*-reading in itself as very likely a conjunctive error.

3. *The place of* gldm *within the textual tradition*

We have argued that *gldm* probably belong to a separate family as they seem to derive from one common ancestor of which all other witnesses are independent. Does that conclusion indeed call for a radical change in our whole outlook on the textual tradition of the Testaments? In fact the consequences do not seem to be very incisive. Apart from the few readings where we were able to show that only *gldm* A have preserved the original text, no practical result of any importance seems to have suggested itself to us thus far. But if we look again to a place like *T. Zeb.* IV,1,[19] we may well wonder what would happen if we had to reckon with a somewhat higher probability of the true text being preserved there as well in *gldm* A only. The readings of *beaf* are quite identical and not very likely to have originated from independent attempts at correction. The corrupt ἔβαλον for ἔλαβον which they have in common would show them rather to be related to each other in some way. However, we must remember that, given our present textual theory, no direct relationship between the texts of *b* and *eaf(chi)* can be accounted for at all in a case where *gldm* preserve the true text. Common errors that are likely to be conjunctive call for a common ancestor, but according to H. J. de Jonge's hypothesis the only ancestor that *b* and *eaf* have in common is in fact the archetype (ω) of the Greek MSS.-tradition as a whole. And if, as a result of our investigation, the text behind *eaf* need no longer be traced back to a supposed ancestor of *ldmeafchi*, but must be considered an independent witness to the one common hyparchetype of the entire second branch of the

---

[19] One might also find some difficulty in believing that in *T. Napht.* V,8 ἐν κήποις was changed into some expression containing ἐκεῖ in *b* and *eaf* independently.

textual tradition, the main division itself, with its two branches, has not been disturbed thereby and *bk* still belong to the one and *gldmeafchi* to the other of its components.

Can we really be sure? In fact there is only one way that leads to relative certainty and that is by proving that the hyparchetype of *gldmeafchi* is indeed quite independent of that behind *bk* and *vice versa*. Now the first half of this argument has been convincingly stated in H. J. de Jonge's article. It is quite clear that in may cases *gldmeafchi* preserve the original text where *bk*'s witness is faulty or defective. But the reverse is not so easy to demonstrate. In fact I think that we have thus far not yet been presented with really conclusive cases where only *bk* have remained true to the original text, thus showing that they cannot derive from the hyparchetype to which the conjunctive errors in *gldmeafchi* must be traced back. In many places, of course, it is quite possible to defend the superiority of a reading preserved by *bk* only,[20] but then either there is no

---

[20] Some cases where the superiority of the text of *bk* may be seriously considered are the following :

T. Jud. I,5 εὐλόγουν *b*] ἐτίμων *gldeafchi* (*km defic.*). The use of the verb εὐλογεῖν seems to be rather characteristic here. Cp. e.g. *Prov.* XXX,11 : τὴν... μητέρα οὐκ εὐλογεῖ.

T. Jud. V,2 καὶ νότου *bl*] < *gdeafchi* (*km defic.*). The addition of καὶ νότου would have disturbed the symmetry between ἀπὸ ἀνατολῶν on the one hand and ἀπὸ δυσμῶν on the other, whereas omission can easily be accounted for paleographically by the following καὶ νό (μισαντες).

T. Jud. V,4 ἐξ ἑκατέρων *bl*] + τῶν μερῶν *gdeafchi* (*km defic.*). The addition may well be explanatory.

T. Jud. X,2 τῇ τρίτῃ ἡμέρᾳ τῇ νυκτί *b*] τῇ τρίτῃ νυκτί *gldeaf* τῇ τρίτῃ ἡμέρᾳ *m* (*k defic.*). If one takes *b*'s reading to be correct, the variant of *gldeaf* can be readily explained by assuming omission through *homoeoteleuton* of ἡμέρᾳ τῇ.

T. Jud. XXV,2 ἐλαία *b* A] ἡ σελήνη *gldmefchi* (*ka defic.*). Substitution of "the moon" may well have been suggested by the context, whereas ἐλαία seems to derive from *Dtr.* XXXIII,24, the chapter from which also some other elements of this passage are taken.

T. Iss. III,3 πονηρός *bl*] φθονερός *gdmeafchi* (*k defic.*). The use of πονηρός in this context reminds one of Jewish wisdom-literature (*cf. Sir.* XIV,5sqq.), whereas φθονερός seems to be much more the common word in this sense.

T. Iss. IV,5 πορισμόν *b*] περισπασμόν *omn. al.* (*k defic.*). According to J. Amstutz, ΑΠΛΟΤΗΣ, Bonn 1968, pp. 80sqq. the reading of *b* fits best into the context. On the other hand one might regard περισπασμός as belonging to the characteristic vocabulary of wisdom literature.

T. Iss. IV,6 (ἐπιδεχόμενος) ὀφθαλμοῖς πονηρίας *b*] ὀφθαλμὸν πονηρίας *b* *g* ὀφθαλμοὺς

common error in the rest of the MSS., or, if there seems to be one, we may still wonder if its being classed as an error is after all the only way to account for it. Moreover, on closer inspection I could only find two instances of a probable omission because of *homoeoteleuton* that cover the whole second branch of the tradition, the original text still being present in *bk*. They are *T. Jos.* XIX,2 where for διαιρέθησαν καὶ διεσπάρησαν (*bk*) all other witnesses, with the sole exception of *l*,[21] write διεσπάρησαν and *T. Benj.* IX,3, where between ὑβρισθήσεται and καὶ ἐπὶ ξύλου ὑψωθήσεται the words καὶ ἐξουθενωθήσεται are omitted in all witnesses except *bk*. But even if one accepts this evidence as unequivocal, what has been proved is only the independence from *bk*, not the existence of one common hyparchetype behind *gldmeafchi*.

πονηρίας *l* ὀφθαλμοὺς πονηρούς *dmeafchi*. For the peculiar construction of ἐπιδεχ. *c. gen. sing. cf. T. Benj.* VI,4 where it is also found only in *b*.

T. Zeb. III,5 (ὑπόδημα) Ἰωσήφ *b*] ὃ ἐφόρεσαν κατὰ Ἰωσὴφ τοῦ ἀδ. αὐτ. *leafc* (*cf. gA kdmhi defic.*). Is this an explanatory addition to a harsh, but possibly original text like the one given in *b*?

T. Napht. II,9 ἐν τάξει ἐστε *b*] καὶ ὑμεῖς πάντα τὰ ἔργα ὑμῶν ἐν τάξει ποιεῖτε *g* ἔστω πάντα τὰ ἔργα ὑμῶν ἐν τάξει *dmeaf* ἔστωσαν πάντα ὑμῶν ἐν τάξει *c* (*l aliter*). Here the rule *lectio brevior potior* might apply.

T. Gad IV,3 πταίσῃ *b*] πέσῃ *gdleaf* (*kmchi defic.*). Change from πταίσῃ/πταίσητε to πέσῃ/πέσητε is rather common in biblical MSS., especially in minuscules. Cf. the text of *min.* 1 in *II Petr.* I,10 and the readings of several minuscules in *Dtr.* VII,25 and *Sir.* II,8. Responsible are, of course, the spelling of αι as ε and, probably, the use cf. ππ as *ligatura* for π τ. See B. A. van Groningen, *Short Manual of Greek Paleography*, Leiden 1967⁴, p. 44. Cp. also Aesch. *Prom.* 926 παίσας for πταίσας in *Laur. Flor.*

T. Gad IV,4 ἐπιχειρεῖ κατ' αὐτοῦ *bl*] ἐπεχαίρει κατ' αὐτοῦ *g* ἐπιχαίρει αὐτῷ (< *d*) *deafchi* (*km defic.*). Here only *bl* appear to have preserved the original text integrally.

T. Ash. IV,4 στόμα *b*] σῶμα *gdeafchi* (*klm defic.*). Here στόμα seems undoubtedly to be right, whereas σῶμα will have been suggested by the following ψυχήν. Cp. also our argumentation as to *T. Gad* IV,3 above.

T. Jos. XX,1 τὴν ἐπαγγελίαν *bk*] τὰς ἐπαγγελίας *glefc* τὴν γῆν τῆς ἐπαγγελίας *d* (*mahi defic.*). If my conjecture γῆν ἐπαγγελίας is right, the reading of *bk* (together with that of *d*) has preserved the *sing*, whereas the second branch of the tradition substitutes the *plur*.

T. Benj. VI,2 ὁρᾷ ἐμπαθῶς τοῖς φθαρτοῖς *bl*] ἐνορῶ ἐμπαθῶς τοῖς φθαρτοῖς *g* ὁρᾷ ἔμπροσθεν τοῖς φθαρτοῖς *d* ὁρᾷ ἐμπαθῶς τὰ φθαρτά (ἄφθαρτα *f*) *eafc* (*kmhi defic.*). Here only *bl* preserve the original text, although it is also clearly supposed by *gd*.

[21] *l* reads only διαιρέθησαν, possibly through secondary influence of a MS. related to *bk*. A trace of διαιρέθησαν may even be found in *g* when after ἐνέμοντο it adds καὶ δι' ἕνα ἐτηρήτησαν.

Perhaps all this does not sound like a final confirmation of H. J. de Jonge's hypothesis of bifurcate textual development as indeed it is not. To confirm this hypothesis we need a manifest case of conjunctive error of *gldmeafchi* over against *bk* and it must be admitted that such a case is difficult to find.[22] However, on balance, one might be inclined to accept ἡ σελήνη (*T. Jud.* XXV,2), πέσῃ (*T. Gad* IV,3) and σῶμα (*T. Ash.* IV,4) as such, and thereby, in spite of all hesitation, still commit oneself to the theory under examination. For, as long as no more probable solution is suggested, we should look for any evidence, however slight, that is in favour of a hypothesis that thus far has stood its severest tests in a quite satisfactory way.

As it is, this argument by no means implies a preference for the text of one branch of transmission against the other, except for the cases where a common error in one of them is assumed. So the accusations concerning overestimation of the readings of *bk* which some scholars have made against H. J. de Jonge were wide of the mark.[23] In fact during our work on the constitution of the text the defects of the readings offered by *bk* alone were brought home to us quite clearly; only we did not feel thus far the necessity to change our textual theory because of that. Be it as strong or as weak as it may, as a working-hypothesis it did not prove to be false and in fact has rendered valuable service. A decision, however, as to which reading could reasonably claim superiority has in practice never been dictated by this theory alone. After all, textual criticism will always be eclectic throughout, and many questions about what one could call the main roads of textual development are in practice not of primary importance at all and may often turn out to be unsoluble in the end.

---

[22] Of the three instances offered by H. J. de Jonge, *art. cit.*, under 4 the first and second are, in my opinion, not quite cogent, while the third has to be taken as an error of *bk* (omission through *homoeoteleuton*) rather than of *gldmeafchi*.

[23] See H. J. de Jonge's own refutation of the critical remarks of the German scholar J. Becker elsewhere in this volume, pp. 80sqq.

XII

THE NEW EDITIO MAIOR

M. DE JONGE

1. *Introduction; the available evidence*

Most of the studies on the text of the Testaments, the results of which were laid down in the chapters II-XI of this volume, were carried out in the context of the preparation of a new major edition of this pseudepigraph. It is thus necessary to ask what the importance of these investigations has proved to be in terms of the actual preparation of the edition. At the same time it will be useful to sum up briefly the final results of the research and the discussions reported in the preceding chapters.

In chapters II and VIII it became clear that the material at our disposal has increased considerably since R. H. Charles' *The Greek versions of the Testaments of the Twelve Patriarchs*, Oxford 1908. Two new MSS were collated (*l* and *m*), some fragmentary material was discovered (*n*) or studied afresh (*k*, Fm^d). At the last moment Dr M. BeitArié of Jerusalem kindly sent us a microfilm of *h*, but our efforts to procure a new microfilm of *i* failed, so that in this case we had to use the (incomplete) photographs of *i*, made for Charles and preserved in the Bodleian Library, Oxford. All other Greek MSS., however, were collated anew from microfilms or photographs ordered for this edition.

With regard to the versions we can now point to new data about the Serbian translation (see chapters II and IX) and the New Greek version (chapter II). Both are of minor importance: Only very little is preserved in Serbian; it is narrowly related to the equally fragmentary *n*. NGr follows *hi* very closely, and (as Burchard pointed out) it helps us, therefore, to distinguish between α-readings and particular *c*-readings where *h* and *i* are not available. In chapters II and IX it was shown that Charles' information on the Slavic version is very faulty. It became also evident that the value of S is very limited; due to its position between *e* and *af* wa cannot expect it to shed much new light on obscure points. As it mainly supplies us with additional information about a secondary stage in the MS.-tradition, S was not used for the new edition.

A very spectacular increase in the number of MSS. of the Armenian version (see chapter VII) made a new study of this version necessary. Besides the work done by C. Burchard and A. Hultgård particularly M. E. Stone's studies have proved to be of great value for the new edition. Stone's work on a small edition of the Armenian Testaments has run parallel to the last stage of the preparation of the edition of the Greek; in a number of cases the evidence of A proved to be valuable for the reconstruction of the hyparchetype of the *gldm* A *e* etc.—branch of the textual tradition.

2. *Method*

The value of H. J. de Jonge's contribution in chapter II lies in the attempt to give a picture of all the genealogical relationships between the witnesses; to that purpose he applied the usual textcritical argumentation as rigorously and consistently as possible. Between 1970, the original date of the writing of this contribution, and 1975 both its results and the method employed were continually scrutinized while the work on the new edition progressed (see chapter III, particularly the appendix, and chapter XI). In textual criticism there is no escape from subjective evaluation of a great number of individual variants. Even intersubjectively the four people working on the edition could not always reach an unanimous decision, let alone absolute certainty.

In each individual case internal criticism should have the last word. In theory we have to choose the reading which explains all (or nearly all) the others. In practice one will find a great number of instances where no definite judgment is possible and where we cannot trust our own preferences of the moment. Here a consistent search for strict evidence pointing to genealogical relationship is an indispensable help. If in one instance no decision can be made, the combined evidence of a number of carefully selected cases may be conclusive. Even so a number of uncertainties remain, because we possess only part of the MSS. which have existed, and some intermediary stages, consequently, may be missing. Some relationships remain obscure, because even all the combined evidence does not allow a definite conclusion. The graphic representation of genealogical relationships in a stemma will, therefore, never give a complete picture of reality. This is clear when we compare the stemma printed in chapter II to the corrected, and (for the time being) final stemma in chapter III. There are no basic changes, but it is clear that further investigations led to different interpretations of certain phenomena. Next, also the last stemma cannot dispense with dotted lines indicating secondary influence (of *b* on *l*, and of α on *d* and *m*). The distinction of "primary" and "secondary" is to some extent always arbitrary; in any case dotted lines spoil the simplicity of the stemma and are a constant reminder of the fact that reality is more complicated than any theory which tries to give the best possible interpretation of a maximum of phenomena.

Yet we should not overlook that in many instances our investigations led to results that, with due allowance for the limitations inherent in the situation, may be called certain. The survey of our major theories concerning genealogical relationships under 3 will make this clear. At the same time we should state firmly that there is no other method to establish the oldest attainable text of the Testaments. All suggestions to the contrary leading to a plea for an "eclectic" approach as found in the writings of J. Becker and others (see particularly chapter III appendix, chapter X and chapter XVII below) do not offer a real alternative. Nor does it help us if, with Becker, we apply the criteria used in the "traditionsgeschichtliche" approach to a text as a help for the solution of textcritical problems (see chapter X).

3. *Genealogical relationships*

a) R. H. Charles divided the Greek witnesses into two groups, α = *c h i* and β = *a e f b d g*. He gave an eclectic text, often printing the two groups separately, and generally preferred α to β. He even tried to prove that the chief points of divergence of α and β go back to two Hebrew recensions; in this he has not been followed by subsequent writers on the Testaments. But his division between α and β is found very often, mostly because scholars had to rely on Charles' edition with its very complex apparatus and were not in a position to reach their own conclusions independently. Already in 1915, however, J. W. Hunkin tried to show[1] that the α-group,

---

[1] J. W. Hunkin, "The Testaments of the Twelve Patriarchs", *J.Th.St.* XVI, 1915, pp. 80-97.

and more specially *c*, is little more than a late and free recension of the β-text, and that *b* is the best representative of the β-text. His results were fully corroborated by an independent investigation by the present editor in 1953. He added two further sigla : δ = *bgdk* and γ = *aef*.[2]

b) The investigations recorded in this volume have shown clearly that all these sigla, with the exception of α have to be discarded. Neither β nor γ nor δ indicate distinguishable families any longer. The α-group has grown considerably. and it may still be called a (sub-)family. NGr is narrowly related to *h* and *i*. Next, *n* and Serb also belong to this group. There seem to be two branches : *n* Serb and *c*, *h i* NGr.

c) In 1953 I remarked that *e a f* (called γ), though usually following *b d g* (*k*) (called δ) against α, was nearer to α than the other witnesses of the β-group.[3] I also tried to prove that *e* is nearer to δ and *a f* to α. Therefore I assumed a special relationship between *e* and δ and between *a f* and α.[4] H. J. de Jonge proved convincingly that *e* and *a f* should not be taken together as members of one family, but that they are subsequent stages in the development of the text in the more productive of the two branches of transmission, henceforth designated as Family II. The α-witnesses represent the last known stage of the development in Family II, *af* the last but one, *e* the one before *af*. In chapter IX the Slavic version was shown to be situated between *e* and *af*.

d) Within family II a new sub-family has emerged, consisting of *g l d m* (and Fm*d*). It is, however, a very complex family : *d m* and Fm*d* are narrowly connected. Moreover there is clearly secondary influence on *d m* from α (or from the *c h i* NGr-branch of α—we know too little of the *n* Serb-branch to be quite sure). Witness *l* is most interesting. It clearly belongs to *g d m* but it shares many readings with *b*. These can be explained, in many cases, as original readings preserved in *l g* against *d m*; in other instances, however, secondary influence of *b* on *l* is not to be excluded.

[2] M. de Jonge, *The Testaments of the Twelve Patriarchs*. A Study of their Text, Composition and Origin, Assen 1953, pp. 15-23. See also C. Burchard, "Zur armenischen Überlieferung der Testamente der Zwölf Patriarchen", in *Studien zu den Testamenten der Zwölf Patriarchen* (*B.Z.N.W.* 36), Berlin 1969, pp. 1-29, esp. pp. 1-6.

[3] *Op. cit.*, pp. 20-22.

[4] *Op. cit.*, pp. 17-18.

In chapter XI it was shown that *gldm* are an important witness for the *gldmeaf(n)chi*-branch in the textual tradition. This group has, of course its peculiar readings, but particularly if supported by *e*, *eaf* or even *eafchi*, it is an indispensable witness.

e) In chapter VIII the value of the Armenian version was assessed. Its place in the stemma would seem to be between *gldm* and *e*—which means that in cases where *gldm* differ from the other Greek witnesses belonging to the same branch of the tradition, agreement between *gldm* and A indicates that *gldm* in fact have preserved the original text of that branch.

f) The remaining Greek witnesses *bk* are closely related. Often they stand over against all other witnesses to the text, and in each of these cases we have to choose between the reading of *b(k)* and that of the reconstructed hyparchetype of the rest of the tradition. From chapters III and XI it becomes clear that the decision is not always easy. In chapter III H. J. de Jonge attempts to prove that *bk* on the one hand and the rest of the MSS on the other go back to two distinct transliterations from uncial to minuscule writing. This is important for the position of *bk*, because there are not many indisputable conjunctive errors between these two witnesses (see chapter XI), which may now safely be considered as a distinct family (Family I) over against Family II, and it carries the division between the two branches of the tradition, and in fact the archetype, back to a time before the transition from majuscule to minuscule writing in the ninth century. It also has some implication for the date of the Armenian version, belonging to the *gldmeaf(n)chi*-branch in the tradition; here H. J. de Jonge's results link up with those reached independently in chapters VIII and X where a late date of the Armenian version was shown to be likely, because of its sharing the secondary short text in Test. Zebulun found in *eafchi*.

4. *The new edition*

During the preparation of the new edition the evidence in each individual instance was studied on its own merits, against the background of the general picture represented by the stemma and the probabilities suggested by it. Not in all cases, particularly in those where *bk* stand over against the rest of witnesses, could certainty be reached. Where our judgment remains in the balance, we intend to give the *bk*-reading in the text. In an appendix we shall give a list of all places where family I differs from family II. We shall indicate where we regard the reading of family I as superior, where we consider both readings to be of equal value, and where we prefer the text of family II.

In the great majority of cases, however, we have been able to draw a firm line. From the survey given under 3 it is abundantly clear that $b(k)$, g, l, and e are the most important witnesses to the text, and that, in some cases, A gives useful corroborative evidence. *dm* give support for the establishment of the *gldm*-reading in all cases where they are not under the influence of *chi*. *af chi* sometimes help us to distinguish between the individual readings of e and those representative of the *eaf(n)chi*-stage in the tradition. Where they differ from e, however, and e joins *gldm* (A), their evidence is not of importance. The same applies *mutatis mutandis* where *(n)chi* differ from *af*, *eaf*, *gldmeaf* or *b(k)gldmeaf*. In no case have we adopted a reading only attested by $\alpha = (n)chi$ etc. or *eaf(n)chi*.

PART THREE

XIII

THE INTERPRETATION OF THE TESTAMENTS
OF THE TWELVE PATRIARCHS IN RECENT YEARS

M. DE JONGE

A very full and fair survey of recent research is given by J. Becker on pp. 129-158 of his *Untersuchungen zur Entstehungsgeschichte der Testamente der Zwölf Patriarchen.*[1] In the present article I shall limit myself to some main issues, trying at the same time to indicate the development of my own ideas in recent years. Secondly, I shall make some critical remarks on Becker's own contribution to the study of the Testaments, and I shall add a discussion of some points made by J. Jervell and J. Thomas in *Studien zu den Testamenten der Zwölf Patriarchen,*[2] to whose views Becker refers briefly in his "Nachtrag" on p. 419. Finally I shall refer to two dissertations. First D. Haupt's *Das Testament des Levi* (1969),[3] the first book in which Becker's work is used critically, and next A. Hultgård's *Croyances messianiques des Test. XII Patr. Critique textuelle et Commentaire des passages messianiques* (1971), the textcritical aspects of which were discussed earlier in this volume.[4] Two recent annotated translations of the Testaments by J. Becker[5] and B. Otzen[6] will be discussed in a separate article at the end of this volume.[7]

Research before 1953 was dominated by F. Schnapp (who contributed the translation and commentary on the Testaments of the Twelve

---

[1] Leiden 1970.

[2] C. Burchard - J. Jervell - J. Thomas, *Studien zu den Testamenten der Zwölf Patriarchen,* (*B.Z.N.W.* 36), 1969.

[3] The full title is *Das Testament Levi. Untersuchungen zu seiner Entstehung und Überlieferungsgeschichte,* Diss. Halle-Wittenberg 1969 (typescript).

[4] See H. W. Hollander's discussion of the relationship between MS. Athos Laura I 48 and K 116 in chapter VII and M. de Jonge's criticism of H.'s contribution to the study of the Armenian translation in chapter VIII.

[5] In *Jüdische Schriften aus hellenistisch-römischer Zeit* III,1, Gütersloh 1974, pp. 15-163.

[6] In *De Gammeltestamentlige Pseudepigrafer* 7, København 1974, pp. 677-789.

[7] In the composition of this short chapter I used part III "Further research on the Testaments of the Twelve Patriarchs", pp. 85-96 in my article "Recent Studies on the Testaments of the Twelve Patriarchs" in *Svensk Exegetisk Årsbok* XXXVI, 1971.

Patriarchs in Kautzsch's *Die Apokryphen und Pseudepigraphen des Alten Testaments*)[8] and even more by R. H. Charles (who contributed the pages on the Testaments to his *The Apocrypha and Pseudepigrapha of the Old Testament*).[9] Both are works still widely used by non-specialists for quick reference, and the latter has not yet been replaced by a more modern translation. Both regarded the Testaments as a Jewish document, redacted (Schnapp) or interpolated (Charles, following Bousset) by Christian scribes. In the Jewish original, moreover, Jewish interpolations could be detected. But these scholars differed greatly with regard to the composition of the book at the pre-Christian stage and the exact delimitation of the Christian parts. Charles, who minimalized the Christian influence in the Testaments and constructed a textual basis for the removal of the Christian interpolations, won the approval of the great majority of scholars.

The first chapter of my *The Testaments of the Twelve Patriarchs*[10] challenged the Bousset-Charles theory and proved that there is no textual basis for the removal of Christian interpolations. This conclusion has been generally accepted. In the second, most extensive chapter many passages of the Testaments were analysed in order to show that we should speak not of interpolations but of a thorough-going Christian redaction. I maintained, e.g., that T.L. III,5-9 is Christian, that it is an integral part of a very composite picture of seven heavens and that, therefore, the whole must be a Christian composition.[11] On the basis of this conclusion and of similar interpretations of other passages I concluded, somewhat rashly, that the Testaments were the work of a Christian "compilator" or "composer" who used much Jewish material, mainly in a written form. In 1953 I dated this composition in $\pm$ 190-225 A.D. (on the basis of a number of parallel ideas in early Christian literature, mentioned in chapter III of the book); in 1957[12] I went back to the middle or second half of the second century A.D.

---

[8] Tübingen 1900, vol. II, pp. 458-506. Compare his earlier study *Die Testamente der Zwölf Patriarchen untersucht*, 1884.

[9] Oxford 1913, vol. II, pp. 282-367. See also his *The Greek Versions of the Testaments of the Twelve Patriarchs*, Oxford 1908 and his commentary *The Testaments of the Twelve Patriarchs*, London 1908.

[10] Assen 1953.

[11] *Op. cit.*, pp. 46-49.

[12] In "The Testaments of the Twelve Patriarchs and the New Testament", *Studia Evangelica* ed. K. Aland c.s. (*T. U.* 73), Berlin 1959, pp. 546-556 (a paper presented to the "International Congress on the Four Gospels in 1957" in September 1957).

This second part of my thesis was criticized by many subsequent authors. Sometimes this was done with insufficient arguments, as by M. Philonenko (who followed his teacher A. Dupont-Sommer in trying to prove the Essene origin of the Testaments [13] and in a far less extreme way by A. S. van der Woude. [14] To the criticism of these scholars I replied in 1961. [15]

The lively interest around the Qumran Scrolls aroused much interest in the Testaments; they were used as another witness for the double messianism found in the Scrolls. But, on the whole, the results of Qumran research for the analysis of the Testaments have not been very important. Of course Qumran gave us new insight into the background of traditions incorporated in the Testaments, such as the conception of spirits, dualistic elements, the juxtaposition of highpriest and king. It is also significant that we have now 4Q-fragments of the Aramaic Levi-document known from the Cairo Genizah, but Becker rightly denies that the Testaments can have originated in the Qumran community. [16] Benedikt Otzen, one of the first to occupy himself with the possible relationship between the Qumran documents known at that time and the Testaments, [17] was right when he concluded that there are religious and theological similarities, but that no historical connection can be proved.

This negative result did not, of course, vindicate my theory. As I see it now—also after Becker's criticism which is sometimes a little onesided, but always fair—my main shortcomings were the following:

(1) I did not apply "traditionsgeschichtliche" criteria, and occupied myself only very rarely with form-critical analysis. I rightly distinguished the Sin-Exile-Return-passages and the Levi-Judah-passages —Becker considers this an essential step ahead in the study of the Testaments—and also discovered earlier parallels to the S.E.R.-passages, but I did not proceed to a more thorough analysis along

[13] In *Les interpolations chrétiennes des Testaments des Douze Patriarches et les Manuscrits de Qumran*, Paris 1960 (a reprint of two articles in the *Revue d'Histoire et de Philosophie religieuses* of 1958 and 1959).

[14] *Die Messianischen Vorstellungen der Gemeinde von Qumran*, Assen 1957, pp. 190-216.

[15] In "Christian influence in the Testaments of the Twelve Patriarchs", *Novum Testamentum* IV, 1960, pp. 182-235; see now chapter XIV in this volume.

[16] *Op. cit.*, pp. 149-151. B. gives no less than eleven arguments.

[17] In "Die neugefundenen hebräischen Sektenschriften und die Testamente der Zwölf Patriarchen", *Studia Theologica* VII, 1954, pp. 125-157.

"traditio-historical" lines. Here and elsewhere H. Aschermann,[18] K. Baltzer,[19] J. Becker, O. H. Steck[20] and D. Haupt[21] have rightly criticized and supplemented my results.

(2) I should have proceeded more consistently, and, moreover, more critically in my literary analysis. I played down syntactical difficulties, sudden transitions, and similar examples of unevenness, explaining them too easily by means of the theory of a compilator who put together whatever he could find. Having seen the impossible and improbable results of the scissors-and-paste method, I fell into the opposite extreme of assuming coherence and unity where these were not obvious.

(3) I did not investigate the literary genre of "testament". A beginning of such an analysis has since been made by K. Baltzer in 1960 and Becker announces a new study of the subject.[22]

(4) I could have made more of my third chapter dealing with the Christian origins of the Testaments, in which I summed up a number of interesting parallels in early Christian literature. Here I should like to mention Professor J. Jervell's recent contribution to the study of the Testaments.[23] He tries to interpret them as "Interpolationsliteratur" and states rightly that more pseudepigrapha should be studied from this point of view. Since interpolation means interpretation, it is useful to ask how the interpolator worked, which questions he wished to answer and, consequently, in which situation he lived. Concentrating on the passages which speak of Israel and the nations, Jervell comes to the conclusion that the earliest Christian revision[24] took place at a time when not the salvation of the Gentiles, but the salvation of Israel presented a problem. This revision must have taken place at the end of the first century A.D., before the emergence of the so-called "Frühkatholizismus".

---

[18] In *Die paränetischen Formen der Testamente der Zwölf Patriarchen und ihr Nachwirken in der frühchristlichen Mahnung*. Eine formgeschichtliche Untersuchung, Diss. Berlin 1955 (typescript).

[19] In *Das Bundesformular*, Neukirchen 1960, pp. 146-167.

[20] In *Israel und das gewaltsame Geschick der Propheten*, Neukirchen 1967, pp. 149-153.

[21] See note 3.

[22] *Op. cit.*, p. 157; for Baltzer see note 19.

[23] "Ein Interpolator interpretiert. Zu der christlichen Bearbeitung der Testamente der Zwölf Patriarchen", in C. Burchard-J. Jervell-J. Thomas, *Studien zu den Testamenten der Zwölf Patriarchen (B.Z.N.W.* 36), 1969, pp. 30-61.

[24] "Bearbeitung", p. 41, indeed a better term than "interpolation".

Jervell's approach is interesting and basically correct, but it can only supplement other approaches. His conclusions certainly need to be substantiated with a more detailed analysis of the passages involved; the particular views of a redactor or an interpolator become only clear if we know what text he redacted or interpolated. It is here that Jervell wants to prove too much with too few arguments. Moreover, his theory of various stages of Christian redaction, e.g. in the very difficult and varied christological passages,[25] leads too easily to the hypothesis that the first Christian redactor/interpolator had a simple Jewish-Christian christology and that this first Christian revision of the original Testaments occurred at a very early date. In later publications on the Testaments I did not maintain the position I held in my doctoral thesis, without, however, formulating an alternative theory. In 1957, e.g., I contented myself with the general remark : "It is quite conceivable that the Christian author(s) was (were) only the last of a series of collectors and redactors of Testament material, which was transmitted in writing as well as orally, gradually grew in size during the ages and was adapted to various needs".[26] I fought my battle with the protagonists of the Essenes in 1961 and won, I think, but I went off to text-critical work on the Testaments before I had answered H. Aschermann's plea (taken over and supplemented by other German authors) for a "formgeschichtliche" analysis.

Aschermann's dissertation is important because it analyses a number of parenetic and prophetic passages in the Testaments, mainly those which consist of "strings" ("Reihen") of descriptions of vices or virtues, sinful or righteous people, evil or good spirits, of predictions etc. The author also tries to find parallel forms in the Old Testament, in Wisdom literature outside the Old Testament and in the New Testament. He assumes three stages in the original development of the Testaments : a Jewish "Grundschrift" (probably contemporaneous with Ben Sira), a Hellenistic redaction and finally a Christian redaction. He does not, however, indicate clearly which elements he wants to assign to the "Grundschrift" and which to the Hellenistic redaction, nor does he make clear why and how the Testaments were composed. Moreover, he does not express a clear opinion on text-critical matters and does not take into account the Aramaic Levi-material.

---

[25] *Op. cit.*, pp. 47-50, 56-59.
[26] "The Testaments of the Twelve Patriarchs" (see n. 12), p. 550.

Before discussing J. Becker's important study, I mention in passing
two Roman Catholic authors, F. M. Braun and P. Grelot, who have
held an intermediate position in the debates on the Testaments in
recent years. F. M. Braun's article "Les Testaments des XII Patriarches
et le problème de leur origine" (1960)[27] was discussed by the present
author in a short article "Once more : Christian influence in the
Testaments of the Twelve Patriarchs" (1962),[28] to which F. M. Braun
replied in Appendix I "Les Testaments des XII Patriarches et leurs
rapports avec le bas-judaïsme" in his *Jean le Théologien* II (1964).[29]
F. M. Braun regards the Testaments as the work of a Hellenistic Jew
(not of an Essene); they were not interpolated, but underwent a not
very thorough Christian redaction. P. Grelot discussed the Testaments
in a survey-article "Le Messie dans les Apocryphes de l'Ancien
Testament" which appeared in 1962.[30] He comes to the conclusion
that we should speak of a Christian "adaptation", sometimes repro-
ducing the Jewish original with only very small alterations, sometimes
redacting it rather thoroughly. This conclusion enables him to use
the Testaments with some caution as source of material for his
picture of the history of messianic expectation.

J. Becker's book *Untersuchungen zur Entstehungsgeschichte der
Testamente der Zwölf Patriarchen*, very complete and very solid,
is the most important monograph on the Testaments since my own
book of 1953. Becker applies all methods which can reasonably be
applied, and his results are always interesting even when they are
not convincing. Starting from the doubtful presupposition that an
author's ideas should show consistency, he hunts for all inconsistencies
in form and contents; these are very numerous in the Testaments,
as everybody knows who has read them. After Becker has taken
the Testaments to pieces in an extremely thorough manner, he comes
to the conclusion that the "Grundschrift" must have been very small.
In Test. Reuben, e.g., it consists of I,3-10 and VI,9-12, apart from the
opening and closing passages. In Test. Asher only VII,4-7 remains,
apart from the opening and closing formulas. This "Grundschrift"
was Hellenistic-Jewish and dates from the time just before the Macca-

---

[27] *Revue Biblique* LXVII, 1960, pp. 516-549.

[28] *Novum Testamentum* V, 1962, pp. 311-319.

[29] Paris 1964 (the appendix is found on pp. 233-251). This publication is not
mentioned in J. Becker's otherwise admirable bibliography.

[30] See *La Venue du Messie*. Messianisme et Eschatologie (*Recherches Bibliques* VI),
pp. 19-50, esp. pp. 32-41.

bean Revolt. It was variously supplemented many times with homilies, exhortations, apocalyptic visions and midrashic stories about the Patriarchs. This supplementing and redaction must have taken place during the first two centuries before and the first century after the beginning of the common era. Becker speaks of a Hellenistic-Jewish "Sammelbecken". This stage was succeeded by that of Christian redaction. This also was carried out during a large period of time.

One must ask whether Becker, for all his zeal and thoroughness, has really explained the "Entstehungsgeschichte" of the Testaments. His analysis is often useful and illuminating, sometimes overly critical and speculative, but, while he pulls the Testaments to pieces, he does not explain how they ever worked as a whole. Explaining inconsistencies by the theory of gradual growth amounts to giving up the attempt to explain things completely, unless one is able to show how the different redactors at the different stages in the origin of the work arrived at a consistent, or at least integrated, whole.

The solution of two problems is here of utmost importance. First : at what moment are we able to speak of *the* Testaments? Certainly at the moment when an author or a group of authors decided to put together admonitions, exemplary stories about the sons of Jacob and predictions concerning the future within the framework of twelve testaments. I would suggest that this process of composition presupposes the use of a *variety* of material, including variety in ethical or theological emphasis in the material. It is only likely that the author (or group of authors) tried to collect as much as possible and to put it together as neatly as possible even where, strictly speaking, various traditions were not quite congruous. This also has consequences for our use of form-criticism. Forms may have been taken over in order to convey different contents to a different purpose.

Secondly, there is the problem of the Christian elements. We are not allowed to regard everything which is possibly Christian as Christian; we may only say that the Christian redactor(s) regarded it as Christian. On the other hand, we are not allowed to reduce the Christian passages and phrases to an absolute minimum as did Charles and (even more severely) some protagonists for the Essenes. The situation is far more complex. The very fact that Jewish traditions were taken over by Christian groups with or without alterations, and that Jewish documents were used for and adapted to Christian purposes makes it wellnigh impossible to distinguish exactly between Jewish and Christian elements in the Testaments. But it remains important to show how various traditions in the Testaments were used, especially in what form and with what contents and within which groups, in Jewish and Christian circles. We shall return to this problem in the chapters XIV and XVII.

I should like to express my opinion of Becker's book in more or less the same words as his own verdict on my dissertation: There is much to be found in this book which is new and stimulating, and one cannot afford not to use it; but its main thesis is unconvincing. This means that the whole question of the composition and the origin of the Testaments is still very much an open one. The only more or less certain results so far have been reached in the field of textual criticism. There is ample scope for young scholars to try to reach more satisfactory conclusions than Becker's, starting from this author's stimulating and often provocative analysis.[31]

D. Haupt's doctoral dissertation[32] concentrates on the problem of Testament Levi and pays much attention to the problem of the relationship between this Testament and the Aramaic Levi-fragments from the Cairo Genizah and Qumran. Becker tried to show that Greek Test. Levi and the Aramaic material represent only two different developments within traditional Levi-material, that the Levi-fragments are not even the remnants of a Testament, and that, consequently, the comparison with the Aramaic fragments contributes only little to the solution of the problems of literary criticism of the Testaments.[33] Haupt returns to the older theory of literary relationship[34] and proves convincingly that an Aramaic Test. Levi very similar to the text preserved in the fragments served as "Vorlage" for the present Test. Levi. He thinks that this tradition which glorifies Levi as a military and political leader served to legitimate the Hasmonean dynasty and that it originated most likely in the days of John Hyrcanus I. Many Jewish and Christian additions to the original work can be detected, among them redactional elements necessary for the incorporation of the Testament of Levi in the framework of the Twelve Testaments. Haupt does not differ from Becker in the methods

---

[31] See further chapter XVII "Test. Issachar als typisches Testament. Einige Bemerkungen zu zwei neuen Übersetzungen der Testamente der Zwölf Patriarchen".

[32] See note 3.

[33] *Op. cit.*, 69-105.

[34] See e.g. M. de Jonge, *The Testaments of the Twelve Patriarchs*, pp. 38-52 and J. T. Milik, "Le Testament de Lévi en araméen. Fragment de la grotte 4 de Qumran", *Revue Biblique* LXII, 1955, pp. 398-406.

he applies, but he comes to often very different conclusions. This underlines Becker's own concluding remarks at the end of his analysis of Test. Levi. On p. 306 he sums up his results as follows: A comparatively great number of verses can be ascribed to the Christian redaction. In the remaining passages it is very difficult to distinguish between the original testament and the later additions. It may be that the author of Test. Levi had a fairly extensive Levi-tradition at his disposal and redacted this only superficially; more likely, however, extensive additions were made at a later stage in the development of the Testaments. The complexity of Test. Levi and similar results in the analysis of the other testaments are Becker's strongest arguments in favour of the latter alternative. It remains remarkable, however, that exactly in Test. Levi where there is much parallel material no certainty can be reached, whereas in other testaments where such material is lacking clear conclusions are drawn.[35]

J. Thomas' article "Aktuelles im Zeugnis der Zwölf Väter"[36] stands quite apart compared to other recent research on the Testaments by dispensing with serious detailed literary criticism. Always considerations of a more general nature with regard to Jewish ethical instruction force him to assume additions to the supposed original text of the Testaments. The results of his investigation are hardly convincing: He dates the Testaments in pre-Maccabean times; the passages which glorify Levi are regarded as later additions under influence of opinions prevailing in the Qumran sect. The original book is qualified as a "Diasporasendschreiben"; it used Levi as a symbol for the priesthood and Judah as a symbol for the leadership of Palestinian Jewry, whereas Joseph is the symbol of the Jewish diaspora in Egypt. The Testaments invite the Jews in Egypt to join in a movement of penitence together with their brothers in Palestine. God's salvation will be realized on earth only after all main groups in Israel have fulfilled their duty towards God.

Similarly K. H. Rengstorf in a recent article[37] tries to prove that

---

[35] On Test. Levi see also M. de Jonge, "Notes on Testament of Levi II-VII", chapter XV of the present volume.

[36] *Studien zu den Testamenten der Zwölf Patriarchen* (*B.Z.N.W.* 36), Berlin 1969, pp. 62-150.

[37] "Herkunft und Sinn der Patriarchen-Reden in den Testamenten der Zwölf Patriarchen" in W. C. van Unnik ed., *La littérature juive entre Tenach et Mischna. Quelques problèmes* (*Recherches Bibliques* IX), Leiden 1974, pp. 29-47. It gives the text of a lecture held in 1969.

the Testaments of Joseph, Levi and Judah form the nucleus around which the twelve Testaments came into being; the attitude of the brothers towards these three patriarchs is of utmost importance. Joseph is the ideal devout Jew of the diaspora, Levi stands for the priesthood and the temple, Judah for kingship and the Land of Israel. The Testaments, according to Rengstorf, are an appeal to unity, in obedience to the God of the Fathers.

The second part of A. Hultgård's *Croyances messianiques des Test. XII Patr.* gives an analysis of fifteen passages in the Testaments which have significance for the tracing of the development of the messianic beliefs reflected in the Testaments. Each chapter starts with an analysis of the text (never complete and never entirely accurate, as. H. has to work with Charles's material supplemented with direct knowledge of Laura K 116, *l* and the Armenian) which leads up to the construction of an eclectic text. Here very often readings are chosen which are less obviously Christian than others and not always for purely text-critical reasons.[38] The commentary which follows the analysis of the text is mainly restricted to philological remarks and the listing of possible parallels in other Jewish writings. The author does not deal with form-critical matters, nor does he indicate how these passages were incorporated into the Testaments. He concentrates on the individual passages (without indicating why he limited himself to the selected fifteen) and reconstructs three stages in the messianism found in the Testaments—the expectation of an intervention by God Himself, appearing on earth to save Israel and the righteous among the Gentiles; the expectation of the establishment of a new priesthood and a new kingship; and the merging of different expectations into one figure : the Saviour-Priest of T. L. XVIII. Unfortunately H. operates on too limited a scale for his arguments to be convincing. Certainly after Becker's book a limited study of isolated passages has become a wellnigh impossible undertaking.[39]

---

[38] Some examples of this were given above, pp. 130-135.

[39] See also Hultgård's article "L'Universalisme des Test. XII Patr." in *Ex Orbe Religionum. Studia Geo Widengren oblata* I (*Numen Suppl.* XXI), Leiden 1972, pp. 192-207, in which he, among other things, discusses J. Jervell's article "Ein Interpolator interpretiert" mentioned above.

XIV

CHRISTIAN INFLUENCE IN THE TESTAMENTS OF THE TWELVE PATRIARCHS

M. DE JONGE

1. *Introduction*

During the last few years it has become increasingly clear that the problem of the composition and the origin of the Testaments of the Twelve Patriarchs cannot be profitably discussed without taking the Dead Sea Scrolls into account. In his book *The Testaments of the Twelve Patriarchs, a Study of their Text, Composition and Origin* [1]) (the manuscript of which was finished in September 1952) the present author paid only little attention to the parallels between the Testaments and the writings discovered at Qumran, but since then publications like those by A. DUPONT-SOMMER [2]) and B. OTZEN [3]), and especially the discovery of new fragments of an Aramaic Testament of Levi and a Hebrew Testament of Naphtali [4]) have made it abundantly clear that the Testaments have to be studied alongside the Scrolls of Qumran, and that in the course of this study the problem of the relationship between the Jewish and the Christian elements in the Testaments will have to be examined afresh.

In a paper presented to the International Congress on "The Four Gospels in 1957" held at Christ Church, Oxford, 1957 entitled *The Testaments of the Twelve Patriarchs and the New Testament* [5]) the present author tried to sum up the position at that moment with

---

[1]) Assen 1953, quoted below as *The Testaments*.

[2]) E.g. his "Le Testament de Lévi (xvii-xviii) et la secte juive de l'Alliance", *Semitica* IV, 1952, pp. 33-53, compare *Nouveaux Aperçus sur les manuscrits de la Mer Morte*, Paris 1953, pp. 63-84. See also his recent book *Les écrits esséniens découverts près de la Mer Morte*, Paris 1959, pp. 313-319, 364-366.

[3]) "Die neugefundenen hebräischen Sektenschriften und die Testamente der Zwölf Patriarchen", *Studia Theologica* VII, 1954, pp. 124-157.

[4]) See D. BARTHÉLEMY and J. T. MILIK, *Qumran Cave* I, Oxford 1955, pp. 87-91 and J. T. MILIK, *Revue Biblique* LXII, 1955, pp. 398-406; LXIII, 1956, p. 407 n. 1.

[5]) Published in *Studia Evangelica* (*Texte und Untersuchungen zur Geschichte der altchristlichen Literatur, Band* 73). Berlin 1959, pp. 546-556.

regard to the problem of the relationship between the Testaments
and the New Testament. Some two months later A. S. VAN DER
WOUDE published his important book *Die messianischen Vorstel-*
lungen der Gemeinde von Qumran [1]) in which he devotes his second
chapter to "Die messianischen Vorstellungen der Testamente der
Zwölf Patriarchen" (pp. 190-216), discussing the parallels between
the writings of Qumran and the Testaments with regard to the
messianic expectations. M. PHILONENKO's study *Les interpolations*
chrétiennes des Testaments des Douze Patriarches et les Manuscrits
de Qumran [2]) is a monograph devoted entirely to the discussion
of the problems which concern us in this article. This scholar
follows A. DUPONT-SOMMER in assuming a very close link between
the Testaments and the writings of Qumran and in reducing the
Christian influence to an almost negligible minimum.

The aim of the present article is to make a contribution to the
discussion of the problem of the Christian influence in the Testaments by a careful examination of the views put forward by VAN
DER WOUDE and PHILONENKO [3]). The present author is well
aware of the difficulties which the student of this subject meets
on his path. Only part of the Qumran material has so far been
published and for this reason his conclusions can only be provisional.
Moreover scholars tend to differ widely in their treatment of a
number of important problems concerning the origin of the
Qumran documents and in their exegesis of certain passages of
crucial importance. The present author is not a Qumran specialist
and does not regard himself as qualified to express an independent
opinion on the many problems connected with the sect of Qumran
and its writings. In the examination of the views under discussion
all emphasis will be laid upon their treatment of the various
passages of the Testaments individually and upon the opinions
concerning the origin and the background of the Testaments as a
whole.

---

[1]) Assen 1957.

[2]) *Cahiers de la Revue d'Histoire et de Philosophie Religieuses* no 35, Paris
1960, published before in *Revue d'Histoire et de Philosophie Religieuses*,
1958, pp. 309-343; 1959, pp. 14-38. In the present study the 1960-edition
has been used.

[3]) Important also is the IVth part of Max-Alain CHEVALLIER's book
L'esprit et le Messie dans le Bas-Judaïsme et le Nouveau Testament, Paris
1958, entitled "L'Esprit et le Messie dans les Testaments des Douze Patriarches et dans les écrits de Qumran", pp. 111-144.

2. A. S. van der Woude's theory

The views put forward by A. S. VAN DER WOUDE may be sum-marized as follows [1]. The Testaments were originally a Jewish document, but it is impossible to reconstruct the Jewish "Grund-schrift" by removing a number of Christian interpolations, because the Testaments have not only been interpolated but also rewritten and abbreviated. The fragments of an Aramaic Testament of Levi from the Cairo Genizah, which were published in Appendix III of R. H. CHARLES's edition of the Testaments [2] together with a Greek fragment which is incorporated in a tenth century manuscript from Mount Athos, and the fragments published and announced by J. T. MILIK which are in close agreement with these show clearly that the present Greek text of Test. Levi is a very much abbreviated and completely rewritten form of the Aramaic or Hebrew "Vorlage". Still, much original material has been preserved in this way. Unfortunately, he thinks, we are not in a position to to decide whether the original was rewritten before the Christian passages were added or whether the person(s) responsible for the Christian additions were also responsible for the editing of the original material, but VAN DER WOUDE considers the first possibility the more likely one: "Ob der Text schon gekürzt und umgearbeitet wurde, bevor die christlichen Interpolationen in den Text hinein-gerieten, ist nicht zu entscheiden, auf Grund der weniger inter-polierten armenischen Übersetzung jedoch nicht unwahrschein-lich" [3].

VAN DER WOUDE agrees with the present author in that he does not accept the interpolation-theory advocated until recently by nearly all scholars in the field. He does not follow him, however, in assuming that the Testaments are a Christian document written by a Christian author who used much Jewish material in composing it. His arguments against Christian authorship are: 1) The many Hebraisms (or Aramaisms) in the Greek text of the Testaments (see the list in R. H. CHARLES, *The Greek Versions* etc., pp. XXIII ff.) point to an original Jewish document. 2) In the passages in which Levi and Judah are mentioned side by side we should not speak of a "common pattern" (as the present author did) but of a "fest-

---

[1] See especially *op. cit.*, pp. 191-194; pp. 214-216.
[2] *The Greek versions of the Testaments of the Twelve Patriarchs*, Oxford 1908.
[3] *Op. cit.*, p. 193.

geprägter Text". 3) In several places the Armenian version has suffered less from Christian interpolations than the Greek [1]). 4) Several passages which were considered Christian by the present author need not be Christian at all. In his review of VAN DER WOUDE's book in the *Vox Theologica* [2]) J. VAN DER PLOEG remarks that there is not so much difference between VAN DER WOUDE's theory and the present author's conclusions as the former tends to think. Moreover, he says, between these two points of view there is a whole range of possible positions which differ slightly from each other as well as from the two extremes. The present author is inclined to agree with Professor VAN DER PLOEG's views because further study of the Testaments made him change his mind on several points. In 1957 he wrote in his *The Testaments of the Twelve Patriarchs and the New Testament*: "It must be admitted that the picture given in the present writer's book of a Christian author collecting Jewish material and using it for the composition of his book makes too little allowance for the part played by oral tradition in Judaism and Christianity of the first two centuries A.D. It is quite conceivable that the Christian author(s) was (were) only the last of a series of collectors and redactors of Testament material which was transmitted in writing as well as orally, gradually grew in size during the ages and was adapted to various needs" [3]). In this paper I also admitted that in particular the apocalyptical passages of the Testaments (the ones which VAN DER WOUDE discusses) present difficulties to the "composition-theory". The fact that the passages which show a common pattern ("Sin-Exile-Return" and "Levi-Judah") have been used and adapted to Christian needs in a variety of ways, and the fact that some of these passages do not show any trace of Christian alteration at all are strong indications that there was at least one Jewish stage in the composition of these passages and probably also of the whole work. This does not mean, however, that we can return to the earlier interpolation-theory with regard to the apocalyptical passages. The way in which the material found in the fragments of the Aramaic Testament of Levi has been used in the composition of the Testament of Levi incorporated in the Testaments, makes

---

[1]) VAN DER WOUDE thinks he has proved this in at least one case, viz. T. Jud. XXIV (to be discussed below).

[2]) XXIX, 1958, pp. 56-58.

[3]) *Op. cit.*, p. 550.

it abundantly dear that this theory must be dismissed altogether. Also in the apocalyptical passages we cannot expect to find the Messianic ideas of the Jewish author(s) by removing a number of Christian expressions.

So much for VAN DER WOUDE's second point; now we turn to his first one. The problem of the Hebraisms (and / or Aramaisms) in the Testaments was discussed by the present author on p. 163 of *The Testaments*—a passage not referred to by VAN DER WOUDE. It may be pointed out that not all passages which seem to betray a Semitic original have to be translations of such an original [1]; an author who knew the Septuagint can well have composed these passages in a sort of "Septuagint Greek". Secondly the list of Hebraisms drawn up by R. H. CHARLES requires careful sifting; especially fanciful are some of his attempts to find the original meaning of a passage through retranslation into Hebrew or through assuming a confusion between two Hebrew words. Thirdly a number of passages definitely goes back to the LXX (very probably the main theme of T. Issachar was taken from that source! [2]). Fourthly, if there are cases in which we can or must think of a translation from Hebrew or Aramaic (and there are such!) we should bear in mind that this only shows that this particular passage was taken from a Hebrew or Aramaic source—and not even necessarily directly.

As to VAN DER WOUDE's contention that the Armenian translation has fewer Christian interpolations than the Greek text I should like to refer to Chapter I § 3 of *The Testaments* [3]) where, after an analysis of the Armenian version in T. Levi and some other parts of the Testaments I came to the conclusions "that the value of the Armenian version for the reconstruction of the original Greek text has been greatly overrated. Its readings seldom inspire confidence and its omissions disfigure the text in many places" and "that A is of little value for the discovery and removal of Christian additions to the Greek text". VAN DER WOUDE bases his conclusions on the study of only a few passages (which we shall discuss later on) and not on an examination of the whole text or, at least, of a con-

---

[1]) See e.g. the example mentioned in n. 2 on p. 221.
[2]) See *The Testaments* pp. 117 f.; p. 163 n. 5 and p. 206 n. 1 below.
[3]) Pp. 23-34; quotations from p. 30 and p. 34.

siderable portion of it, so that his theory does not seem to be based on sufficient evidence [1]).

VAN DER WOUDE's fourth point makes it necessary for us to discuss the question of method. If we assume (as VAN DER WOUDE and the present author do) that the Testaments in their present form have been used and edited by Christians in one way or another, we must always reckon with the possibility that those passages too which are not evidently Christian do not come from a Jewish hand. VAN DER WOUDE's method of approach resembles to some extent that of CHARLES, BOUSSET and others who removed the more prominent Christian interpolations and presented the remaining, not so obviously Christian parts, as products of a Jewish preformation of Christianity. In the interpretation of a writing with such a complicated history as the Testaments many conclusions will necessarily remain hypothetical, but it seems right to assume that a particular passage is Christian until clear evidence of the contrary is adduced. In other words: The burden of proof does not fall on him who assumes that a certain passage is Christian, but on the scholar who considers a passage Jewish or, more especially, Essene. I should like to repeat here what I wrote in 1957: "The parallels in the Qumran documents are no doubt of great importance for the discovery of pre-Christian elements in the Testaments as well as for the illustration of their general background, but it is far more difficult to use material from the Testaments for the reconstruction of the views of the Qumran sect. At the most the Testaments may, sometimes, give corroborating evidence, viz. in those cases where conceptions found in them agree with those which may definitely be attributed to the members of the Qumran sect. And even then the literary and historical relationship cannot be defined exactly" [2]). This complicated problem cannot, however,

---

[1]) It should be borne in mind that both Sargis JOVSĒPHEANC in his edition of the Armenian version of the Testaments (Venice 1896) and R. H. CHARLES in his apparatus could only use part of the available MSS. Dr. W. C. H. DRIESSEN kindly told me that, according to information received by him, not less than 21 MSS of the Armenian version are kept in the State Library in Erevan in Armenia (CHARLES could only use 1 MS from Armenia, besides 11 from Western Europe). This new material will have to be studied carefully before we can draw definite conclusions with regard to the relationship between the Greek manuscripts and the Armenian version [See now chapter VIII].

[2]) *Op. cit.* p. 555. Originally Essene passages may also have been taken over by a Christian redactor without alteration, because he agreed with

be solved by methodological considerations alone. In each individual case a careful analysis will have to show whether a passage is more likely to be Christian or Jewish. The greater part of this article will be devoted to an examination of a number of disputed passages.

3. M. Philonenko's theory

PHILONENKO goes much further than VAN DER WOUDE. He states that "la parenté entre les *Testaments* et les textes du désert de Juda est, en effet, d'une aveugle évidence" and from this he at once concludes to a "commune origine" [1]). Like VAN DER WOUDE and the present author he assumes that a Hebrew Testament of Levi formed the starting-point for the present collection of Testaments [2]) and that the Aramaic and Greek fragments published by CHARLES and MILIK give us an idea as to the nature and contents of that document. Later on a Testament of Judah and a Testament of Naphtali were composed after this model [3]). These three Testaments were, at a still later stage, abbreviated by a redactor, who omitted many ritual prescriptions and much haggadic material, but added a number of exhortations. This redactor was, according to PHILONENKO, an Essene. The other Testaments were grouped around the three so redacted. "Au terme de cette étape se trouvait constituée une collection de douze Testaments, où de pieuses et pressantes exhortations étaient illustrées par des légendes sur les patriarches". Like F. SCHNAPP [4]) (followed later by CHARLES and BOUSSET) who discovered the hand of a Jewish interpolator in the Testaments, PHILONENKO thinks that a number of important passages were added to the Testaments by yet another Essene, who in the case of T. Benjamin did his job so thoroughly that we should not speak of interpolation but of redaction. This man was responsible for the "Sin-Exile-Return"-passages which, according to PHILONENKO, show a number of interesting parallels with the Psalms of Solomon and must, therefore, like these Psalms, be dated in

---

what he found before him. In such cases the interpreter will have to bear in mind: si duo dicunt idem, non est idem.

[1]) *Op. cit.* p. 3.

[2]) For this and the following see *op. cit.* pp. 4-7.

[3]) With regard to T. Naphtali this hypothesis is a very probable one— see also my *The Testaments*, pp. 52-60. As to T. Judah I should prefer more cautious conclusions (*Ibid.*, pp. 60-71). PHILONENKO does not adduce any proof for these assertions.

[4]) In his *Die Testamente der Zwölf Patriarchen untersucht*, Halle 1884.

the period shortly after 63 B.C.[1]). He also wrote the "Levi-Judah"-passages, passages which deal with the resurrection and a number of universalistic statements. "Il est absolument remarquable que toutes les "interpolations christologiques" appartiennent à la strate que nous venons de situer. C'est là un argument très fort en faveur de l'authenticité de ces textes. Un interpolateur chrétien eût retouché l'ouvrage dans son entier". There are no Christian interpolations at all; the passages which have always been called Christian are in reality the work of the Essene interpolator just mentioned. "Ce n'est point dire cependant, soulignons-le, que la christologie des *Testaments* soit identique aux doctrines messianiques des manuscrits du désert de Juda. Sur bien des points, au contraire, les *Testaments* en majorent et précisent la portée". It should also be borne in mind, PHILONENKO thinks, that any argumentation in these matters is bound to be "caténaire"; in our analysis of the relevant passages we should start with those who present fewest difficulties in order to be able to interpret the more complicated texts with the help of those studied first.

Some critical remarks with regard to PHILONENKO's method would seem to be appropriate. Firstly it seems to be too rash to assume a common origin on the basis of similarity of ideas [2]). Secondly it is to be regretted that PHILONENKO does not examine the relation between the passages which he regards as interpolated and their context in each individual case. His sketch of the history of the origins of the Testaments is too summary to be convincing; moreover he fails to provide clear evidence on many important points. Thirdly: in other passages than those mentioned by PHILONENKO Christian influence also may be recognised—as I hope to demonstrate in a moment. Fourthly: Even PHILONENKO makes the remark that the Christology of the Testaments is not identical with the Messianic ideas of the people of the Dead Sea Scrolls (as

---

[1]) He mentions especially T.Zeb. IX, 5 (discussed below, pp. 240 f.) which, according to him, contains "une claire allusion" to the conflict between Aristobulus II and Hyrcanus II, and T. Jud. XXII, 2 which gives "une allusion non moins claire . . . à l'accession au trône d'Hérode le Grand". These allusions are not clear enough to be convincing. At the most they could give corroborating evidence after it had been proved in another way that these passages of the Testaments were written at that time. The parallels between the S.E.R.-passages and the Psalms of Solomon are of such a general nature that they cannot supply this proof.

[2]) See "The Testaments of the Twelve Patriarchs and the N.T.", pp. 554 f.

far as we know these at present). Of course the possibility of development may not be ruled out; it is even likely that the Messianic ideas of the Qumran sect underwent a gradual change in the course of time, or that there were differences of opinion on this point between various groups within the Essene movement. It is also possible that in the course of this development terms and expressions were used which resemble those which became the usual ones in the Christian Church. The question must be asked, however, how we are to prove that such a development did indeed take place in the sect of Qumran if the only available evidence comes from the Testaments which, if they have not been rewritten by a Christian, were in any case read, copied and commented upon in the Christian Church, which handed them down to us. We cannot regard a number of passages in the Testaments which (to put it mildly) sound Christian as evidence for changed Essene beliefs on the basis of a supposed development within the Essene movement for which we find no proof outside the Testaments. When PHILONENKO tells us: "Si notre démonstration est recevable c'est toute l'histoire des doctrines messianiques au temps de Jésus qui se trouve placée dans une lumière nouvelle" [1]) and when he uses as motto for his study LOHMEYER's word: "Wie dem auch sein mag, der Schluss wird notwendig, dass schon im Judentum das Bild einer göttlichen Gestalt in niedriger Menschlichkeit oder eines Menschen in göttlicher Würde vorhanden war. Und in der Tat scheinen auch die Testamente der Zwölf Patriarchen eine ähnliche Anschauung zu kennen", the question has to be asked whether those far-reaching conclusions are not the result of reasoning in a circle.

The problems under discussion do not only affect the origin and the background of the Testaments and their connection with the Dead Sea Scrolls. If PHILONENKO is right, we shall have to revise our theories concerning the Messianic ideas among the Jews in the period immediately before and after the beginning of our era and, in addition, our views concerning the origins of early Christian Christology. Again, however, it should be said that the problems which concern us here cannot be solved by methodological considerations only. It will be necessary to examine the passages mentioned by PHILONENKO just as carefully as those used by VAN DER WOUDE. To this examination we now proceed.

[1]) *Op. cit.*, p. 60.

4. *Some passages concerning Joseph*

We have just seen that PHILONENKO regards his argumentation as "caténaire". Every scholar who has ever occupied himself with the Testaments will agree with him that it is impossible to argue differently. It seems to me, however, that PHILONENKO gives a wrong interpretation of those links in our chain which are among our strongest, viz. the passages dealing with Joseph, which he mentions last of all, but which should, I think, be discussed first.

In his XIVth chapter [1]) PHILONENKO calls Joseph the central figure in the Testaments—and rightly so. Joseph is the person who possesses all virtues, but who suffers from the hatred and the envy of his brothers. Hippolytus of Rome regards him, like many ecclesiastical authors after him, as a type of Christ [2]). With regard to some passages of the Testaments, e.g. T.B. III, 8 we might be tempted to think that the final redactor of the Testaments takes the same view but from other texts it becomes clear that the Joseph of the Testaments is "le 'type' du Serviteur souffrant, du Juste par excellence, entendons du Maître de Justice" [3]). PHILONENKO criticizes the present author because he assumed the Christian origin of this typology and failed to note that this is already found in Jewish, especially Alexandrian Jewish sources. As an example PHILONENKO mentions Wisd. x, 13-14.

I do not think PHILONENKO has succeeded in proving his case. It need not surprise us that certain Christian notions agree or are closely connected with Jewish ideas, e.g. with those found in Wisdom-literature. In the case of the picture of the ideal Joseph this can be demonstrated at several points. Whether the picture of Joseph which emerges from the Testaments is of Christian origin —and this is not just a matter of stray remarks in individual Testaments but of a picture which is typical of the whole document —can only be decided with the help of a few clear passages. If it can be demonstrated that those are Christian we may assume that

---

[1]) *Op. cit.*, pp. 50-58.

[2]) See *The Testaments*, p. 123, L. MARIÈS, "Le Messie issu de Lévi chez Hippolyte de Rome", *Mélanges J. Lebreton, Recherches de Science Religieuse* XXXIX, 1951, pp. 381-396 and A. W. ARGYLE, "Joseph the Patriarch in Patristic Teaching", *Expository Times* LXVII, 1956, pp. 199-201. Like MARIÈS, PHILONENKO assumes that Hippolytus knew and used the Testaments. I do not think, however, that there is enough evidence to prove— or to disprove—this contention.

[3]) *Op. cit.*, p. 50.

the other passages also have gone through the hands of a Christian redactor and that the Testaments are Christian, at any rate in their present form.

It is indeed possible, I think, to prove that some passages dealing with Joseph can only be Christian in their present form. These passages do not belong to the interpolations mentioned by PHILO-NENKO, but belong to the exhortatory parts of the Testaments. Let us consider PHILONENKO's first passage in his chapter on Joseph, T. Zeb. III, 2-3: ἀλλὰ Συμεὼν καὶ Γὰδ καὶ οἱ ἄλλοι ἐξ ἀδελφοὶ ἡμῶν λαβόντες τὴν τιμὴν τοῦ Ἰωσήφ, ἐπριάσαντο ὑποδήματα ἑαυτοῖς καὶ ταῖς γυναιξὶν αὐτῶν καὶ τοῖς τέκνοις αὐτῶν, εἰπόντες· οὐ φαγόμεθα αὐτήν, ὅτι τιμὴ αἵματος τοῦ ἀδελφοῦ ἡμῶν αὕτη, ἀλλὰ καταπατήσει καταπατήσωμεν αὐτήν,ἀνθ' ὧν εἶπε βασιλεύειν ἐφ' ἡμᾶς . . .

PHILONENKO rightly mentions as parallels Amos ii 6 and Wisd. x 13-14, and he assumes that the author of the Testaments applied the Amos-text to Joseph because he regarded him as one who was perfect and righteous, a type of the Teacher of Righteousness. The brothers in T.Zeb. III, 2-3 speak, however, also of a τιμὴ αἵματος and this expression recalls Matt. xxvii 6, a text which PHILONENKO does not mention [1]). The question has to be answered: Was Matthew influenced by the Testaments or did the author(s) of the Testaments know Matthew? "Price of blood" presupposes violent death, and it is clear that this expression is out of place in a description of what Joseph had to suffer from his brothers. The author of the Testaments must, therefore, have modelled the type after the antitype, and it is quite likely that he had Jesus as antitype in mind. It is, of course, not impossible to suppose that already an Essene writer used the expression "price of blood" for the money which the brothers received when they sold Joseph, because the Teacher of Righteousness had met with a violent death [2]). Such a theory is, however, entirely hypothetical and, in fact, improbable. The Joseph-Christ-

---

[1]) Compare also T.Zeb. II, 2, where Joseph says to his brothers: μὴ ἐπαγάγετε ἐπ' ἐμὲ τὰς χεῖρας ὑμῶν τοῦ ἐκχέαι αἷμα ἀθῷον, ὅτι οὐχ ἥμαρτον εἰς ὑμᾶς with Matt. xxvii 4 where Judas says: ἥμαρτον παραδοὺς αἷμα ἀθῷον. The parallel is striking but we can only use it as corroborative evidence, because the expression "innocent blood" occurs several times in the O.T.

[2]) Assuming that the Teacher was indeed killed by his enemies—a point which many scholars think has not yet been proved convincingly. This problem does not, however, affect our argumentation.

typology is found frequently in the Early Church, and the supposition that the Essenes regarded Joseph as a type of the Teacher
of Righteousness rests only on the evidence supplied by the
Testaments. Moreover we do not know that the Teacher before
his death was betrayed or "sold"—and this is a very prominent
feature ın the N.T.-account of Jesus' death. Until convincing proof
of the contrary can be given, we shall do wise to assume a Christian
origin for T.Zeb. III, 2-3.

Next, PHILONENKO discusses T. Jos. I, 4, 6-7 which does not help
us much further. After this he quotes T. Zeb. IV, 10 according to
the MSS of the α-family: τὸν γὰρ χιτῶνα ἐξέδυσαν τὸν Ιωσῆφ ἐν
τῷ πιπράσκειν αὐτὸν καὶ ἐνέδυσαν αὐτὸν ἱμάτιον δουλικόν.
This passage, like the preceding one, calls Joseph a δοῦλος, because
(according to PHILONENKO) the patriarch wås seen as the type of
the true Servant of the Lord, the Essene Teacher. It is impossible
to disprove this hypothesis. In the most reliable MS, b, ¹) we read
however, that Joseph's brothers stripped off from him τὸν χιτῶνα
τοῦ πατρὸς ἡμῶν and that they put upon him a ἱμάτιον παλαιὸν
δούλου. The reference to the kenosis of Christ (comp. Phil. ii 1-11)
is, I think, obvious, but we cannot prove that this was really in the
author's mind when he wrote this. In T.Zeb. IV, 4 we read that
Joseph ἐποίησε δὲ ἐν τῷ λάκκῳ τρεῖς ἡμέρας καὶ τρεῖς νύκτας—
a detail not mentioned in the Biblical story, where the events
in Dothan all take place during one single day. PHILONENKO says:
"Voilà le trait—étranger au texte biblique—qui donne à notre
récit sa portée symbolique" ²) and we may agree with him here.
He does not, however, connect this with Christ's stay of three days
and three nights in the heart of the earth, mentioned in Matt. xii 40
but with the destiny of the Teacher of Righteousness. "La descente
du fils de Jacob dans la citerne est le "type" de la catabase du
Maître de Justice dans les profondeurs de l'Abîme .... Mais
l'Abîme n'avait pas retenu celui qui y était descendu. Les Testaments nous révèlent, précision intéressante, que Joseph, en qui
nous avons reconnu à nouveau le Maître de Justice, émerge de la
Fosse infernale après trois jours et trois nuits". As parallels from
the Dead Sea Scrolls PHILONENKO mentions 1 QH II, 17; V, 38-39;
VI, 24; VIII, 28-30, passages which speak about the distress of
the Teacher (if we may identify the author of the Hymns with

¹) See The Testaments, pp. 18-22.
²) Op. cit., p. 54.

him). He also points to 1 QH III, 19-20 where the author speaks
of deliverance from the pit and to T. Jos. I, 4 where Joseph says
εἰς λάκκον με ἐχάλασαν καὶ ὁ ὕψιστος ἀνήγαγέ με. I leave aside
the question whether 1 QH really speaks of a descent into the
underworld and ascent from it (it seems to me that the texts just
mentioned have to be interpreted metaphorically like similar
passages in the Old Testament, comp. Is. xxxviii 17; Ps. cvii 17-22;
Ps. xviii 5, 6; Ps. lxxxviii 2-10). The parallel between T.Jos. I, 4
and the passages from the Hodayot is of such a general nature that
no conclusions can be drawn from it. A decisive argument against
PHILONENKO's interpretation of T.Zeb. IV, 4, however, is given
by the fact that the three days and three nights which are well-
known in Christian tradition are nowhere found in the literature
of Qumran. Again we must say: Until convincing proof of the
contrary is given, we shall do wise to regard T.Zeb. IV, 4 as a
Christian passage.

The same is true of T.Gad II, 3-5, a passage about which even
PHILONENKO writes: "Il est évidemment difficile de ne pas penser
à Mt. xxvii 3-9 et CHARLES déclare que la fin du verset 3, omise
par α, est une addition chrétienne [1]). This passage reads in b:
διὸ ἐγὼ καὶ Ἰούδας πεπράκαμεν αὐτὸν τοῖς Ἰσμαηλίταις τριάκοντα
χρυσῶν καὶ τὰ δέκα ἀποκρύψαντες τὰ εἴκοσι ἐδείξαμεν τοῖς
ἀδελφοῖς ἡμῶν. καὶ οὕτως τῇ πλεονεξίᾳ ἐπληροφορήθην τῆς
ἀναιρέσεως αὐτοῦ. καὶ ὁ θεὸς τῶν πατέρων μου ἐρρύσατο αὐτὸν
ἐκ τῶν χειρῶν μου ἵνα ποιήσω ἀνόμημα ἐν Ἰσραήλ. Gen. xxxvii 28
mentions twenty shekels, T.Gad thirty; PHILONENKO thinks that
the latter text was influenced by Zech. xi 12-13 where thirty
pieces of silver are mentioned. "Nos subtils docteurs, lisant le
onzième chapitre du livre de Zacharie, découvraient dans ce berger
que Dieu avait choisi pour paître son peuple, et qui avait été
rejeté, méprisé, estimé à trente sicles d'argent, la figure du Maître".
In CDC XIX, 8 Zech. xi 11 is applied to the Teacher of Righteousness.

It is quite likely that there is a connection between T.Gad II,
3-5 and Zech. xi 12-13; there is, however, also a close link between
Zech. xi and Matthew's description of Judas's treacherous activities (Matt. xxvi 15; xxvii 3 ff.) and it is indeed, as PHILONENKO
says, difficult not to think of Matt. xxvii in connection with

[1]) Op. cit., p. 53.

T.Gad. It is not impossible that a midrash like that found in T.Gad originated in the Qumran sect. But it is a hazardous undertaking to oppose the interpretation of T.Gad. II, 3-5 as a Christian midrash (which is supported by the parallels in Matthew) on the strength of the hypothesis of an example of Essene midrashic thinking for which no parallels can be given.

A few points require a more detailed examination. 1) T.Gad speaks of gold, whereas Gen. xxxvii 28 (Hebr.); Zech. xi 12-13 (Hebr. and LXX); Matt. xxvi 15; xxvii 9 all mention pieces of silver. Only in the LXX-version of Gen. xxxvii 28 pieces of gold are mentioned. The author of T.Gad II, 3-5 must have used the Septuagint, and only because he wished to describe Joseph as a type of Jesus Christ did he connect the *twenty* pieces of *gold* with the *thirty* pieces of *silver* in the peculiar way found in *v.* 3 [1]). 2) PHILONENKO regards the expression τριάκοντα χρυσῶν as a hebraism; one would expect τριάκοντα χρυσία, but the expression in our text is a translation of the Hebr. שלשים זהב. It does not seem necessary, however, to go back to the Hebrew: τριάκοντα (indeclin.) χρυσῶν is an ordinary genitivus pretii. 3) Though it is likely that T.G. II, 3 was written by a Christian the same cannot be said with certainty of the context in which it stands. *V.* 4 tries to connect *v.* 3 with the context by the somewhat illogical statement that because of covetousness Gad was bent on slaying Joseph [2]).

---

[1]) The relationship between the Masoretic text and the LXX presents us with a great number of difficulties. According to F. M. CROSS, *The Ancient Library of Qumran and modern biblical studies*, London 1958, pp. 120-145 the fragments found in Cave IV prove that "the Septuagint reflects accurately a Hebrew textual tradition at home in Egypt in the third-second centuries B.C." and he says that "thanks to the Qumrān manuscripts we have the means to control its evidence (quotations from pp. 134-135). This problem concerns us only in so far as the fact that a Hebrew *Vorlage* of at least some passages of the LXX was known and used in Qumran could explain why various passages of the Testaments (see p. 186 n. 2) go back to a text of the Septuagintal type. It is, however, far more simple to explain these parallels between the Greek Testaments and the Greek text of the Septuagint by assuming direct quotations from the LXX; it would be very remarkable, if the translator of the Testaments and the translator(s) of the LXX had chosen exactly the same wording in a particular passage. In fact we should have to assume that the former, while translating the Testaments had the LXX-translation in mind. Moreover we should not forget that the pre-Septuagintal Hebrew Text was not by any means the only Bible text in use in Qumran. Many MSS found there are, for instance, of a proto-Masoretic type (see further Cross in the book mentioned above).

[2]) See *The Testaments*, p. 101.

In T.B. II, 3 Joseph tells his brother Benjamin that he was flogged by the Ishmaelites. On this verse PHILONENKO remarks: On remarquera que les *Testaments*, comme les évangiles synoptiques, emploient ici le verbe rare et caractéristique de φραγελλόω [1]). If the Teacher of Righteousness was crucified (as he thinks has been demonstrated) he must have been flogged, according to Roman custom; consequently we may read in T.B. II, 3 a reference to the Teacher. This theory does not explain, however, the striking agreement in terminology between T.B. II, 3 and the Gospel-account, so that, again, Christian influence in this verse is quite likely [2]).

At the end of his chapter on Joseph [3]) PHILONENKO discusses the differences between the Hebr. T. Naphtali which we possess in a medieval form [4]) and the Greek Testament found among the Testaments of the Twelve Patriarchs. The Hebr. Testament printed by CHARLES is late and secondary but it may go back to an older text. The present author has tried to prove that both the Hebrew and the Greek Testament go back to an original T. Naphtali, and that the Hebrew which we have is in some places (especially in the visions recorded in Gr. T.N. V and VI) nearer to the original than the Greek [5]). PHILONENKO is of a different

---

[1]) *Op. cit.*, p. 52.

[2]) φραγελλόω is indeed a rare and remarkable word—see W. BAUER, *Wörterbuch zum Neuen Testament*, s.v. who calls it a Christian word, but adds "doch vgl. Text. Benj. 2, 3 u. Aesop aus dem Cod. Paris 1277". The word is a latinism (flagellare). See also A. W. ARGYLE, "The influence of the Testaments of the Twelve Patriarchs upon the New Testament", *Expository Times* LXIII, 1951-'52, pp. 256-258, who thinks that also here the N.T. was influenced by the Testaments.

T.B. II, 3 tells us that after the flogging Joseph was told to run: καὶ φραγελλώσας με εἶπε τρέχειν (so *b; c* plural). PHILONENKO mentions in comparison Ev. Petr. III, 6-7 οἱ δὲ λαβόντες τὸν Κύριον ὤθουν αὐτὸν τρέχοντες καὶ ἔλεγον ... The parallel is not very convincing, and, moreover, a command to run is just what one would expect under the circumstances.

[3]) *Op. cit.*, pp. 55-58.

[4]) Text in CHARLES, *The Greek versions*, Appendix II.

[5]) See *The Testaments*, pp. 52-60. For the fragment of a Hebrew Test. Naphtali found in Qumran our only information is that given by J. T. MILIK in *RB* LXIII, 1956, p. 407 n. 1. According to MILIK it is not possible to establish a connection between this fragment and the Hebrew Testament already known. "La partie conservée relate la généalogie de Bilha dans une rédaction bien plus longue que celle du Test. XII Patr. grec, *Test. Nepht.* I, 6-12". Important is MILIK's remark: "Je crois pourtant maintenir que les Testaments des Douze Patriarches n'existaient pas à l'époque pré-chrétienne, en Palestine du moins".

opinion. According to him the hostile attitude towards Joseph in the Hebrew Testament has to be explained as a reaction from the praise which is bestowed upon Joseph in our Testaments. "Mieux encore, c'est le Maître de justice qu'attaquent les uns et que défendent les autres".

I shall not enter into the details of PHILONENKO's argumentation; the reader may compare the relevant passages in his book and in mine. The principal objection against PHILONENKO's theory is that Joseph who is praised in many passages is not glorified in the Greek Test. Naphtali. In the Greek visions he plays a mysterious rôle which can only be understood if one notices that the picture of Joseph given in the more elaborate account of the visions in Hebr. T.N. II-VI is a very unsympathetic one. The author of the Testaments wanted to remove all things which did not favour his hero and in doing so he even sacrificed the clarity of his account. The same conclusion is reached if one compares the epilogue after the visions in Gr. T.N. VII, 1-3 with Hebr. T.N. III, 13 and VII. In the Hebr. Testament Jacob condemns his favourite son and admonishes his children not to follow him, but to obey Levi and Judah. In the Greek Testament Jacob tells Naphtali that he accepts these two visions as proof for Joseph's being alive—a general statement which is in no way connected with the characteristic features of the visions which even in their Greek form betray an antagonism between Levi and Judah on one side and Joseph on the other. On Gr. T.N. VII PHILONENKO comments: "Le Maître de justice vit mystérieusement parmi les siens" [1], a statement which does not find any support in T.N. V-VII at all.

After the examples given above it does not seem rash to conclude that the Testaments, though perhaps not composed by a Christian author using much Jewish traditional material of all kinds (as I thought in my book), underwent at any rate a thoroughgoing Christian redaction, and that the Christian redactor(s) is (are) responsible for the picture of Joseph as a type of Jesus Christ and as an example for all believers. The contention that already in Qumran Joseph was regarded as a type of the Teacher of Righteousness seems to me to find as yet too little support in the available evidence.

Not only in the passages just mentioned, but also in some

---

[1] *Op. cit.*, p. 58.

further texts which deal with Joseph Christian influence can be discerned—though we shall have to admit that strict proof cannot be given so that they can only supply corroborating evidence. In T.Jos. XVII, 8 (*b*) Joseph says: καὶ οὐχ ὕψωσα ἐμαυτὸν ἐν αὐτοῖς ἐν ἀλαζονείᾳ, διὰ τὴν κοσμικὴν δόξαν μου, ἀλλ' ἤμην ἐν αὐτοῖς ὡς εἷς τῶν ἐλαχίστων. The agreement with Mark x 42-45 and parallel passages is clear, and I think, not accidental. In T.B. III, 8 (*b*) we read: πληρωθήσεται ἐν σοὶ (= Joseph) προφητεία οὐρανοῦ περὶ τοῦ ἀμνοῦ τοῦ θεοῦ καὶ σωτῆρος τοῦ κόσμου, ὅτι ἄμωμος ὑπὲρ ἀνόμων παραδοθήσεται καὶ ἀναμάρτητος ὑπὲρ ἀσεβῶν ἀποθανεῖται, ἐν αἵματι διαθήκης, ἐπὶ σωτηρίᾳ ἐθνῶν καὶ Ἰσραήλ, καὶ καταργήσει Βελίαρ καὶ τοὺς ὑπηρετοῦντας αὐτῷ. PHILONENKO devotes his XIIIth chapter to this single verse [1]). He tries to find Biblical and Jewish parallels for every expression. These cannot be discussed here, but it does not seem superfluous to remark that PHILONENKO admits that the title σωτὴρ τοῦ κόσμου (or a Hebrew equivalent) is not found in the literature of the Qumran sect. About this title he says on p. 17: "Les auteurs des *Testaments*, en élévant le chef de la secte de l'Alliance à cette dignité hors de pair, majorent et précisent sensiblement, reconnaissons-le, la portée des textes de Qumrân". Also with regard to the expression ἐπὶ σωτηρίᾳ ἐθνῶν καὶ Ἰσραήλ Philonenko can only mention parallels from the Testaments themselves. Commenting on T.Jos. XIX, 11 where a similar expression occurs, Philonenko remarks [2]): "Les גוים précèdent ici Israël. Le passage est d'un large universalisme". But he does not answer the question how this universalism tallies with the marked sectarian attitude found in the Qumran Scrolls [3]). Next, it is remarkable that in the two passages from Qumran mentioned by PHILONENKO to illustrate the idea of expiation, viz. 1 QS IX, 3-4 and CDC XIV, 18-20 (where the verb כפר occurs) we do not find that this expiation is brought about by one who gives his life for it, and that is without doubt the central theme in T.B. III, 8. Though certain expressions may be Jewish as well as Christian, the whole passage must have been written by a Christian.

Last of all I should like to mention T.Jos. VIII, 5. W. K. L.

---

[1]) *Op. cit.*, pp. 47-49.
[2]) *Op. cit.*, p. 30.
[3]) See also *The Testaments*, pp. 127 f. and below, p. 218.

CLARKE [1]) and A. W. ARGYLE [2]) have indicated the parallel
between Joseph in his dark prison, who praises the Lord and
Paul and Silas in prison in Philippi (Acts xvi 25). CLARKE pointed
out that the word ἐπακροάομαι is in the LXX and in the N.T. only
found in Acts xvi 25. This parallel too would be better explained,
not by dependence of the N.T. upon the Testaments, but by
dependence of the Testaments upon the N.T.

5. *Levi and Judah*

In a considerable number of apocalyptical passages Levi and
Judah are mentioned together. As has been said before, the present
author assumed in 1952 that these passages were composed by a
Christian author in accordance with a clear common pattern which
glorified Levi's priesthood and Judah's kingship and which was
adapted to Christian needs in a variety of ways. He mentioned
Jub. XXXI, 12-21 and Original Test. Naphtali (comp. Hebr.
T.N. I, 8-10 and VII, 6) as possible sources. After the discovery of
the Dead Sea Scrolls the whole matter had to be reconsidered because
these passages (as many scholars have pointed out) resemble those
in the writings of Qumran where a priestly and a kingly Messiah
are mentioned. We must, therefore, undertake a fresh discussion
of the texts concerned.

VAN DER WOUDE follows G. R. BEASLEY-MURRAY who tried to
demonstrate that "the juxtaposition of the Messiah from Judah
and the Messiah from Levi is too deeply rooted in the fabric of the
book for either element to be discarded" [3]) and he draws the conclusion: "Aus den messianischen Texten der Test. XII ergibt sich
unzweideutig, dass in der Urschrift von zwei messianischen Gestalten die Rede war, d.h. vom Messias aus Levi und vom Messias
aus Juda. Somit entsprechen die messianischen Vorstellungen der

---

[1]) In *Journal of Theological Studies* XV, 1914, p. 599 and *The Beginnings
of Christianity, Part I, The Acts of the Apostles*, ed. Foakes Jackson and
Lake, II, London 1922, pp. 77 f.

[2]) *Expository Times*, LXIII, p. 257 and LXVII, p. 201. ARGYLE also
assumes a parallel between T. Jos. VIII, 3 and Mark xiv 52. This is, however,
not a clear case of parallelism, because Gen. xxxix 11-20 tells us several
times that Joseph had to leave his garment in the hands of Potiphar's wife,
and consequently he had to flee γυμνός (which does not only mean "naked"
but also "lightly clad").

[3]) "The Two Messiahs in the Testaments of the Twelve Patriarchs",
Journal of Theological Studies XLVIII, 1947, pp. 1-12. Quotation from p. 1.

Test. XII denen der Qumrānschriften" [1]). PHILONENKO reaches a similar conclusion along different lines. He too finds a "double messianisme" in several passages of the Testaments which agree with 1 QS and 1 QSa which expect two Messiahs. In other texts, however, belonging to a later stage in the composition of the Testaments these two Messiahs have been joined to form one single Messiah who is son of Levi as well as son of Judah. A similar expectation we find in CDC which also knows only one Messiah. This Messiah is the Teacher of Righteousness [2]).

We cannot discuss here the many and intricate problems connected with the messianic expectations in Qumran and their possible development, but shall content ourselves with a discussion of the passages of the Testaments which are used to shed light upon these problems. We shall start with T. Jud. XXIV which is mentioned first by PHILONENKO[3]) and occupies a prominent place in VAN DER WOUDE's demonstration [4]).

Both authors point out that Num. xxiv 17 plays an important part in the messianic texts of Qumran. CDC VII, 18-21; 1 QM XI, 6 and 4 Q Test. 12, perhaps also 1 QSb V, 27 may be mentioned in this connection. Also T.Jud. XXIV, 1 goes back to this verse, but the author knew it obviously in its LXX-form. We read: καὶ μετὰ ταῦτα ἀνατελεῖ ὑμῖν ἄστρον ἐξ Ἰακὼβ ἐν εἰρήνῃ καὶ ἀναστήσεται ἄνθρωπος ἐκ τοῦ σπέρματός μου, comp. Num. xxiv 17, LXX: ἀνατελεῖ ἄστρον ἐξ Ἰακώβ, ἀναστήσεται ἄνθρωπος ἐξ Ἰσραήλ (and v. 7 ἐξελεύσεται ἄνθρωπος ἐκ τοῦ σπέρματος αὐτοῦ) and Hebr. דָּרַךְ כּוֹכָב מִיַּעֲקֹב וְקָם שֵׁבֶט מִיִּשְׂרָאֵל. How can this important difference between T.Jud. XXIV and the writings of Qumran be explained if T.Jud. XXIV is to come from the same sect as these writings? For PHILONENKO no difficulty seems to exist at all: "Mais l'original hébreu de notre texte était sans doute fidèle à la leçon du texte masorétique", he says. He thinks that the author of T.Jud. XXIV used a florilegium of passages from Scripture dealing with the שֵׁבֶט, because he seems to refer to Is. xi

---

[1]) *Op. cit.*, pp. 215-216.
[2]) *Op. cit.*, p. 10. Compare A. DUPONT-SOMMER, *Nouveaux Aperçus ...*, Paris 1953, p. 83: "Le chapitre XVIII du Testament de Lévi, selon moi, est sans doute le premier témoin de cette messianisation du Maître de justice".
[3]) *Op. cit.*, pp. 8-12.
[4]) *Op. cit.*, pp. 206-209.

and Ps. xlv too. It is quite probable that such a florilegium was used but it cannot be proved that שֵׁבֶט was the key word [1]).

According to VAN DER WOUDE T. Jud. XXIV, 1 is from the hand of a Christian author who read the reference to the Star from Jacob in Num. xxiv 17a and added the following words from the LXX, changing the text before him in such a way that it became a prophecy concerning Jesus Christ. VAN DER WOUDE finds a reference to the remainder of Num. xxiv 17a in T. Jud. XXIV, 5 τότε ἀναλάμψει σκῆπτρον βασιλείας μου and concludes that the original text of this chapter spoke of two Messiahs. As a parallel he mentions CDC VII, 18 ff. where two messianic figures are derived from Num. xxiv 17. In other words: VAN DER WOUDE regards T. Jud. XXIV in its present form as Christian, but he thinks that it is possible to reconstruct the original text which taught the "double messianism" found in the writings of Qumran [2]). If, he asks, in v. 1 and v. 5 the same person is referred to, why do we find the τότε at the beginning of v. 5 ? He points out that the Armenian version which gives a much shorter text, nowhere clearly betrays Christian influence. "Schon daher wäre man genötigt A von vornherein vorzuziehen".

It is clear that T. Jud. XXIV can be divided into two parts and it is quite likely that, originally, this passage dealt with the task attributed to Judah and the rôle played by Levi. But it seems to me an impossible undertaking to reconstruct the original text and to use this original text as new evidence for the messianic expectations of the sect of Qumran. If we examine the beginning of T. Jud. XXIV, 5 which, according to VAN DER WOUDE goes back to the second part of Num. xxiv 17a in the Hebrew, we find that the only word to support this supposition is σκῆπτρον (which in the LXX is used very often as a translation of שֵׁבֶט). Ἀναλάμψει (translated by VAN DER WOUDE with "aufgehen", but "aufleuchten"

---

[1]) In 1 QS V, 24-28 which is quoted as a proof for the existence of such an anthology by PHILONENKO (following J. DANIÉLOU and D. BARTHÉLEMY) the situation is different. There, in line 24 a clear reference to the שֵׁבֶט of Is. xi 4 is found.

[2]) A similar opinion is expressed by R. H. CHARLES in his Commentary on the Testaments, *The Testaments of the Twelve Patriarchs translated from the Editor's Greek text etc.*, London 1908, *in loc.* See also W. H. BROWNLEE, "Messianic motifs of Qumran and the New Testament", *New Testament Studies* III, 1956-'57, p. 197 n. 3 and H. KOSMALA, *Hebräer-Essener-Christen*, Leiden 1959, p. 82. BROWNLEE nor KOSMALA give an analysis of this chapter.

would have been better) is not a probable translation of קָם [1]),
and the combination of σκῆπτρον βασιλείας in *v.* 5 with ῥάβδος
δικαιοσύνης in *v.* 6 points in the direction of Ps. xlv 7 where we
read: שֵׁבֶט מִישֹׁר שֵׁבֶט מַלְכוּתֶךָ (LXX: ῥάβδος εὐθύτητος ἡ ῥάβδος τῆς
βασιλείας σου) [2]). Nor does the Armenian version give any
support to van der Woude's theory. The Armenian equivalent
of τότε is not found in the beginning of *v.* 5, but in *v.* 4 and there
is not much in the Armenian text of *vv.* 1 and 5 to suggest a reference
to Num. xxiv 17. In Charles' retranslation into Greek we read:
καὶ μετὰ ταῦτα ἀνατελεῖ τὸ ἄστρον εἰρήνης τοῦ ἡλίου τῆς
δικαιοσύνης (*v.* 1) .... καὶ ἀναλάμψει σκῆπτρον βασιλείας μου
(var. lect. θαλλήσει ἀπὸ σκήπτρου, *v.* 5) [3]).

We must now discuss the question whether and where Christian
influence is visible in this chapter. As Charles and Philonenko
have pointed out the expressions συμπορευόμενος τοῖς υἱοῖς τῶν
ἀνθρώπων ἐν πραότητι καὶ δικαιοσύνῃ and πᾶσα ἁμαρτία οὐχ εὑρεθήσεται ἐν αὐτῷ (*v.* 1) need not be Christian, because they can
be explained with the help of Ps. xlv 5, Zech. ix 9 and Ps. Sol.
XVII, 36—but, of course, it would not be surprising if they were.
The most important passage with regard to the problem of
Christian influence is, however, T.Jud. XXIV, 2-3: καὶ ἀνοιγήσονται ἐπ' αὐτὸν οἱ οὐρανοὶ ἐκχέαι πνεύματος εὐλογίαν πατρὸς
ἁγίου, καὶ αὐτὸς ἐκχεεῖ πνεῦμα χάριτος ἐφ' ὑμᾶς καὶ ἔσεσθε
αὐτῷ εἰς υἱοὺς ἐν ἀληθείᾳ καὶ πορεύεσθε ἐν προστάγμασι αὐτοῦ
πρώτοις καὶ ἐσχάτοις (text acc. to *b* which wrongly reads προσ-
τάγματι). Van der Woude finds here a reference to Joel iii 1-5
and remarks: "Weiter ist der Gedanke, dass der Geist des Messias
(oder Gottes) in der Endzeit ausgegossen wird, in der spätjüdischen
Literatur genügend belegt". Like Philonenko and Dupont-Sommer
he mentions an interesting parallel from Qumran for the expression
ἐν προστάγμασι αὐτοῦ πρώτοις καὶ ἐσχάτοις. In 1 QS IX, 10
משפטים הרשונים are mentioned, according to which the אנשי היחד

---

[1]) One could mention Job xxv 3 (comp. xi 17), where the LXX, however,
differs completely from the Masoretic Text. See on this verse S. R. Driver-
G. B. Gray, *The Book of Job*, Edinburgh 1921, p. 215.

[2]) See also the following verse: "Thou lovest righteousness and hatest
wickedness, therefore God, thy God, hath anointed thee with oil of gladness
above thy fellows". These two verses are quoted in Hebr. i 8-9 and applied
to Jesus Christ.

[3]) On the value of the Armenian version as a whole, see p. 197 above.

walk until the arrival of a prophet and the Messiahs of Aaron and
Israel (comp. CDC XX, 31). The "last commandments" which are
not mentioned in 1 QS or CDC must be those given in the last days
after the prophet has arrived [1]. This parallel is interesting, but we
should be cautious in accepting it as evidence for a common origin
of (the original text of) T. Jud. XXIV and the writings of Qumran.
As M. A. CHEVALLIER has pointed out [2]), the expression "the first
and the last" is well-known in the O.T. 1 Chron. xxix 29 speaks
of וְדִבְרֵי דָוִיד הַמֶּלֶךְ הָרִאשֹׁנִים וְהָאַחֲרֹנִים. (LXX: οἱ λοιποὶ λόγοι τοῦ
βασιλέως Δαυὶδ οἱ πρότεροι καὶ οἱ ὕστεροι) and 2 Chron. ix
29 of וּשְׁאָר דִּבְרֵי שְׁלֹמֹה הָרִאשֹׁנִים וְהָאַחֲרֹנִים (LXX: καὶ οἱ κατάλοιποι
λόγοι Σαλωμὼν οἱ πρῶτοι καὶ οἱ ἔσχατοι). It is quite possible,
therefore, that the expression in T. Jud. XXIV, 3 means simply
"all commandments, from the first till the last". It is important
to note, that T. Jud. XXIV, 2-3 speaks of the spirit of the *Holy
Father*, tells us that the *M e s s i a h pours down the spirit of
grace* and that the believers *will be his sons in truth* (expressions
spaced in the Greek text given above). Close parallels to these
conceptions are found in T.L. XVIII, 6-8 which reads: (6) οἱ
οὐρανοὶ ἀνοιγήσονται, καὶ ἐκ τοῦ ναοῦ τῆς δόξης ἥξει ἐπ' αὐτὸν
ἁγίασμα μετὰ φωνῆς πατρικῆς ὡς ἀπὸ Ἀβραὰμ πατρὸς
Ἰσαάκ (7) καὶ δόξα ὑψίστου ἐπ' αὐτὸν ῥηθήσεται καὶ πνεῦμα συνέσεως
καὶ ἁγιασμοῦ καταπαύσει ἐπ' αὐτὸν ἐν τῷ ὕδατι (8) αὐτὸς δώσει
τὴν μεγαλωσύνην κυρίου τοῖς υἱοῖς αὐτοῦ ἐν ἀληθείᾳ καὶ οὐκ
ἔσται διαδοχὴ αὐτῷ εἰς γενεὰς καὶ γενεὰς ἕως τοῦ αἰῶνος.

PHILONENKO (who, strangely enough, does not discuss T.L.
XVIII, 6-8 anywhere at length) points to 1 QSb I, 3-5 to explain
T. Jud. XXIV, 2a. In this passage, belonging to the benedictions
for the faithful, we read the prayer: "May the L[ord] bless thee
[from His holy dwelling] and may He open for you from heaven
the eternal source which shall not [fail] .... and may He favour
thee with all blessing[s of heaven and may he ?] thee with the
knowledge of holy ones". No parallel is mentioned for πατρὸς
ἁγίου. As parallel to v 2b he rightly points to Zech. xii 10 where
God says: καὶ ἐκχεῶ ἐπὶ τὸν οἶκον Δαυὶδ καὶ ἐπὶ τοὺς κατοικοῦν-

---

[1]) So VAN DER WOUDE, *op. cit.*, p. 75 n. 3. In CDC XX, 8, 9 ראשונים
and אחרונים are mentioned together, but it is not sure that משפטים is the
accompanying substantive; the translation is uncertain.

[2]) *L'Esprit et le Messie* ...., p. 118 n. 4.

τας Ἱερουσαλὴμ πνεῦμα χάριτος καὶ οἰκτιρμοῦ (LXX, not differing from Hebr.). He does not offer an explanation for the fact that in T.Jud. XXIV the Messiah and not God is the subject, but only states the fact: "C'est le Maître lui-même, et non Yahvé, qui répand l'Esprit de grâce". 1 QH VII, 20 is mentioned as parallel to *v.* 3a: "Thou hast set me as a father to them Thou holdest dear" [1]).

It is to be regretted that PHILONENKO has not dealt with the present author's discussion of T.Jud. XXIV and T.L. XVIII on pp. 89-90 of *The Testaments* and with M. A. CHEVALLIER's careful treatment of these passages on pp. 125-130 of his *L'Esprit et le Messie* [2]), especially as his own demonstration shows at least two serious lacunae: we have seen that he does not explain the expression πατρὸς ἁγίου and that he does not give any parallel from Qumran for the pouring down of the Spirit by the Messiah. The parallels between T.Jud. XXIV, 2-3 and T.L. XVIII, 6-8 and the accounts in the gospels of Jesus' baptism in the river Jordan are obvious (note especially ἐν τῷ ὕδατι in T.L. XVIII, 7 which CHARLES regarded as a Christian interpolation). CHEVALLIER writes: "La parenté du texte de T. Lévi avec les récits du baptême de Jésus est manifeste" [3]). He points out that here as well as in the gospel accounts Is. xi 2 plays an important part and that the "mise en scène" is the same in both cases. The heavens are opened, the Holy Spirit is given to the Messiah, a "fatherly" voice is heard, the Holy Spirit rests upon Him. Only the dove is missing from the account in the Testaments. It can be demonstrated that T. Levi is dependent on the New Testament. In the New Testament the voice declares: "Thou art my son" whereas T. Levi contents itself with an allusion: μετὰ φωνῆς πατρικῆς.

The account in T.Jud. XXIV is shorter than the story in T. Levi but the same elements are found there, and it is clearly Christian too. With regard to T. Jud. XXIV, 2b CHEVALLIER mentions

---

[1]) PHILONENKO mentions also a number of passages where the expression בני אמת occurs; those, however, do not give an exact parallel and need not detain us here.

[2]) The rhetorical question in note 40 on p. 11 can hardly be called a refutation of the views put forward by CHEVALLIER and the present author: "Faut-il préciser que l'auteur du *Testament de Juda* ne fait aucunement allusion, comme le voudraient DE JONGE, *op. cit.*, p. 90 et M.-A. CHEVALLIER, *op. cit.* 130 au baptême du Christ au Jourdain? Ce sont les évangiles qui utiliseront ce motif à nouveau et dans un tout autre cadre".

[3]) *Op. cit.*, p. 129.

Zech. xii 10 and Is. xliv 3 and adds: "Mais jamais dans le Judaïsme l'effusion de l'Esprit n'a été rapportée au Messie; ce point précis est strictement Chrétien" [1].

The fact that the Testaments call the believers sons of the Messiah presents many difficulties to all interpreters. CHEVALLIER remarks: "un tel rapport entre Messie et fidèles n'a aucun précédent connu et n'est en tout cas concevable que dans une perspective chrétiènne". He thinks it possible that a messianic interpretation of Is. xliv 3 (*thy* seed, *thine* offspring) led to this unusual conception. The present author tried to explain it as an example of the vagueness of the Christology of the Testaments which we find in more cases [2]. I QH VII, 20, mentioned by PHILONENKO, does not give an exact parallel because the relationship between the faithful and the author is here compared with various human relationships, viz. that of father and children, nurse and young people, mother and babies. VAN DER WOUDE refers to Ecclus. L, 12 f. where the priests who surround the highpriest are called his sons (so Hebr.; Gr. and Syr.: brothers) [3]. None of these explanations is entirely satisfactory.

Our conclusion with regard to T. Jud. XXIV must be that this is a Christian passage in which possibly material from the Qumran sect (or a related group) has been incorporated. The redaction of T. Jud. XXIV has been so thorough, however, that it is impossible to reconstruct the pre-Christian text of the passage. Consequently there is little in this chapter that can elucidate the messianology of Qumran.

The same can be said of T.L. XVIII. VAN DER WOUDE discusses this chapter on pp. 210-214 of his book. He assumes that this chapter was redacted and interpolated in the same way as T. Jud. XXIV, and he thinks that it is possible to reconstruct the original pre-Christian text though this is far more difficult here than in the case of T. Jud. "Doch scheint es mir möglich, auch in T. Levi XVIII der Urform des Textes, wenigstens im grossen und ganzen auf die Spur zu kommen". VAN DER WOUDE begins with removing a number of interpolations. He regards ἕως ἀναλήψεως αὐτοῦ in *v.* 3, ἐν τῷ ὕδατι in *v.* 7 and ὁ δὲ Ἰσραήλ ἐλαττωθήσεται ἐν ἀγνωσίᾳ

---

[1] We can think e.g. of the Paraclete-passages in John xiv-xvi.
[2] *The Testaments*, p. 90 and pp. 125 f.; comp. John xiv 18.
[3] *Op. cit.*, p. 214; compare, perhaps, I QSb III, 2: "Thy seed".

καὶ σκοτισθήσεται ἐν πένθει in v. 9 as Christian additions and declares: "Übrigens kann man nicht behaupten die Perikope sei christlich". It does not become clear how he can justify his treatment of this chapter in the light of his earlier criticism of the interpolation-theory advocated by CHARLES and BOUSSET. He seems to make the same mistake as these scholars when he removes the obvious Christian expressions and regards the remaining part of the chapter as not necessarily Christian! [1]).

In T.L. XVIII, 1, 2 VAN DER WOUDE finds the contrast between the old wicked priesthood and the new perfect priest from the tribe of Levi, a contrast which is also found or implied in other passages of this Testament. It is remarkable, however, that it is nowhere explicitly stated in T.L. XVIII that the new priest will belong to the tribe of Levi whereas in T. Jud. XXIV, 1 the messianic figure is said to come ἐκ τοῦ σπέρματός μου. The expression τότε ἐγερεῖ κύριος ἱερέα καινόν, ᾧ πάντες οἱ λόγοι κυρίου ἀποκαλυφθήσονται .... in v. 2 agrees excellently with a Christology like that found in the Epistle to the Hebrews. The same can be said of the beginning of v. 3 καὶ ἀνατελεῖ ἄστρον αὐτοῦ ἐν οὐρανῷ, ὡς βασιλεύς: The priest of the last days is at the same time king! [2]).

V. 3b φωτίζων φῶς γνώσεως has been derived from Hos. x 12b LXX. VAN DER WOUDE admits this, but in stead of assuming Christian redaction in this verse which ends with the Christian phrase ἕως ἀναλήψεως αὐτοῦ, he tries to explain the agreement with the LXX with the hypothesis that the author knew the Hebrew original of the LXX-text. "Es ist sicher, dass die Qumrangemeinde einen der Septuaginta ähnlichen Bibeltext gekannt hat". It is, indeed, theoretically possible that the Qumran sect possessed a Hebrew MS which read the Hebrew equivalent of

---

[1]) See also p. 195 above.
[2]) So also M.-A. CHEVALLIER, op. cit., p. 131 n. 1. VAN DER WOUDE, op. cit., pp. 212 f. suggests two possible explanations of T.L. XVIII, 3a: a) It is a Christian addition, see Ignatius, Eph. XIX, 2 and Justin. Dial. CVI, 4, which connects Num. xxiv 17 and Matt. ii 2 (mentioned in The Testaments, p. 154, n. 255); b) a royal star as apocalyptical sign of heaven is referred to. By way of illustration he mentions Matt. xxiv 30, Rev. xii 1-3, Ass. Mos. X, 9, none of which gives an exact parallel. He concludes by saying: "Jedenfalls kann V, 3a nicht beweisen, dass T. Levi XVIII, 1-9 nicht vom levitischen Messias die Rede sei", He forgets to explain why the star which, according to his theory, is always connected with the priestly Messiah, in T. Jud. XXIV as well as in Qumran, is here connected with a King.

φωτίζων φῶς γνώσεως in Hos. x 12b, but this does not seem very likely ¹). Hos. x 12c is used in CDC VI, 11 to give support to the expectation of the eschatological Teacher of Righteousness. We read: עד עמד יורה הצדק באחרית הימים which goes back to the עַד־יָבוֹא וְיֹרֶה צֶדֶק לָכֶם of the Masoretic Text, but does not agree with the ἕως τοῦ ἐλθεῖν γεννήματα δικαιοσύνης ὑμῖν in the LXX. Unless we assume that one Hebrew text was used in T.L. XVIII, 3 and another in CDC VI, 11, or suppose the existence of a mixed text, we cannot explain the peculiar quotation in T.L. XVIII, 3b. It is much easier to assume that the wording of this passage was derived directly from the LXX.

T.L. XVIII, 6-8 has been discussed above; it must be regarded as a Christian passage. It certainly contains more Christian elements than the ἐν τῷ ὕδατι deleted by VAN DER WOUDE as a Christian interpolation.

The only passage from T.L. XVIII which is discussed at some length by PHILONENKO is T.L. XVIII, 9 ²). He pays special attention to the words ἐπὶ τῆς ἱερωσύνης αὐτοῦ τὰ ἔθνη πληθυνθήσονται ἐν γνώσει ἐπὶ τῆς γῆς and he mentions as a parallel I QpHab. XI, 1 ואחר תגלה להם הדעת כמי היים לרב (which comments on Hab. ii 14). This parallel does not seem quite apposite. It is improbable, if not impossible that this refers to the Gentiles; the text is defective, but immediately before and immediately after this passage the conflict between the sect and its Jewish opponents is dealt with ³). With regard to the following passage καὶ φωτισθήσονται διὰ χάριτος κυρίου, ὁ δὲ Ἰσραὴλ ἐλαττωθήσεται ἐν ἀγνωσίᾳ καὶ σκοτισθήσεται ἐν πένθει PHILONENKO points to the

---

¹) See also p. 206 n. 1 above. It should be noted that in the case of the LXX-quotation of Num. xxiv 17 in T. Jud XXIV VAN DER WOUDE does not hesitate to assume Christian redaction.

²) *Op. cit.*, p. 27. About T.L. XVIII in general he writes: "Cet hymne, comme l'a montré A. DUPONT-SOMMER, magnifie le Maître de Justice".

³) See also H. KOSMALA, *op. cit.*, pp. 395-397. PHILONENKO also mentions 1 QMyst. I, 7 and 1 QH VI, 12. The first passage contains a general statement to the effect that knowledge shall fill the earth like justice and that evil shall disappear; it does not speak specifically about the fate of Jews and Gentiles. The passage from the Hodayot is more explicit on this point. According to KOSMALA this passage is mainly concerned with the past; he points to *Qumran Cave I*, 34 bis 3, col. II, 3 ff., where we read that the זרע אדם does not know God and acts wickedly, in contrast to the chosen people, and concludes: "Die Situation ist die gleiche, die Paulus in Rom. i 18-32 beschreibt. See also p. 209 above.

opposition between the Jewish leaders in Jerusalem (which are condemned by the sect) and the chosen few at Qumran (see e.g. CDC III, 13-14, XVI, 3). Again this parallel is not apposite. The contrast is here clearly not between two groups within the Jewish people, but between the Jews and the Gentiles. T.L. XVIII, 9 does not seem to render support to the hypothesis of the Essene origin of T.L. XVIII.

Though T.L. XVIII is Christian in its present form, it may contain elements which come from the Qumran sect or a related group. VAN DER WOUDE points to the fact that the messianic figure in this chapter gives instruction and knowledge (*vv.* 2, 3, 7, 9) like the יורה הצדק in CDC VI, 10 f. and to the reference to Mal. iii 20 in *v.* 4, a verse that stands near to iii 23 which announces the return of Elijah (whom, according to VAN DER WOUDE, the sect identified with the highpriest of the last days). Again, however, the redactor has done his work so thoroughly that it is very difficult to find the pre-Christian and possibly Essene elements.

We must now proceed to an examination of other passages which deal with the position of Levi and Judah. The first is T. Jud. XXI, 1-5, especially the verses 2 and 3, which read in *b*: ἐμοὶ γὰρ ἔδωκε κύριος τὴν βασιλείαν, κἀκείνῳ (Levi) τὴν ἱερατείαν, καὶ ὑπέταξε τὴν βασιλείαν τῇ ἱερωσύνῃ. ἐμοὶ ἔδωκε τὰ ἐπὶ τῆς γῆς, ἐκείνῳ τὰ ἐν οὐρανοῖς. With this we may compare the fragment 1 Q 21, 1 [1]) attributed to a Testament of Levi כהנותא רבא מן מלכות[and 1 QSa II, 11-12 which states clearly that the high priest is higher in rank than the Messiah of Israel. We should note, however, that T. Jud. XXI does not speak of messianic figures from Levi and Judah but of the tribes themselves. The same is true of T. Iss. V, 7. Also in T. Gad. VIII, 1 the two tribes are mentioned: εἴπατε δὲ καὶ ὑμεῖς ταῦτα τοῖς τέκνοις ὑμῶν, ὅπως τιμήσωσιν Ἰούδαν καὶ τὸν Λευί. The rest of this verse, unfortunately, presents us with a text-critical problem. In *b* we read ὅτι ἐξ αὐτῶν ἀνατελεῖ κύριος σωτῆρα τῷ Ἰσραήλ (comp. *a e f, d* σωτήρ), which would point to an expectation of *one* saviour from the *two* tribes; *k, h i, g* and *Arm.* read, however, σωτηρίαν, *c* σωτηρία and this reading may be preferred as lectio difficilior [2]). In that case

---

[1]) *Qumran Cave I*, p. 88.
[2]) So also VAN DER WOUDE, *op. cit.*, p. 197, n. 5.

also in T. Gad. VIII, 1 the two tribes are glorified and not a messianic figure [1]).

In T.N. VIII, 2-3 the patriarch tells his children to command their offspring ἵνα ἑνοῦνται τῷ Λευὶ καὶ τῷ Ἰούδᾳ. After this only Judah is mentioned: διὰ γὰρ τοῦ Ἰούδα ἀνατελεῖ σωτηρία τῷ Ἰσραήλ, καὶ ἐν αὐτῷ εὐλογηθήσεται Ἰακώβ. διὰ γὰρ τοῦ σκήπτρου αὐτοῦ ὀφθήσεται Θεὸς κατοικῶν ἐν ἀνθρώποις ἐπὶ τῆς γῆς σῶσαι τὸ γένος Ἰσραὴλ καὶ ἐπισυνάξει δικαίους ἐκ τῶν ἐθνῶν. VAN DER WOUDE is right in discovering here the hand of a Christian redactor [2]) who made Levi disappear all but completely and glorified Judah as the tribe from which Jesus Christ was born. Originally this passage must have connected salvation with the two tribes; there is no indication that this original passage mentioned two Messiahs. According to PHILONENKO [3]) the present Greek text speaks of the Teacher of Righteousness and he tries to prove his theory by referring to T. Jud. XXIV., 5-6, a passage which belongs to a chapter which was redacted by a Christian, as we have tried to demonstrate above.

T.R. VI, 5-12 and T.S. V, 4-6 present more difficulties. In T.R. VI, 5-12 Judah is only mentioned in passing. Reuben's children will be jealous of the children of Levi but God will protect the latter (v. 7): τῷ γὰρ Λευὶ ἔδωκε κύριος τὴν ἀρχὴν καὶ τῷ Ἰούδᾳ, μετ' αὐτῶν κἀμοὶ καὶ Δὰν καὶ Ἰωσὴφ τοῦ εἶναι ἐπὶ ἄρχοντας. In *The Testaments* p. 88 I thought that the original text only mentioned Levi and Judah. VAN DER WOUDE [4]), however, has pointed out that this combination of names goes back to Num. ii and may very well be original. He also points to 1 QSa II, 14 f. where after the highpriest and the priests the Messiah of Israel and the ראש [.... אלפי ישראל] are mentioned which are told to sit down according to their rank.

The tribe of Levi plays an important rôle in 1 QM; its members are leaders in the Holy War, see e.g. 1 QM XV, 4-8; XVI, 11-14; XVIII, 3-6. Levi dominates so much that the Prince of the congregation of 1 QM V, 1 remains a somewhat shadowy figure. This

---

[1]) W. H. BROWNLEE, N.T.St., III, 1957, p. 197 thinks that also in the Testaments σωτηρία is a messianic title. But the only passage where it is probable that "salvation" is used with this meaning seems to be Isa. li 4-5 in 1 Q Isa.

[2]) *Op. cit.*, pp. 200 f.

[3]) *Op. cit.*, p. 35.

[4]) *Op. cit.*, p. 103 and p. 195, comp. also 1 QM III, 14.

shows a remarkable agreement with the situation presupposed in T.R. VI, 11, 12: αὐτὸς γὰρ εὐλογήσει τὸν Ἰσραὴλ καὶ τὸν Ἰούδαν· ὅτι ἐν αὐτῷ ἐξελέξατο κύριος βασιλεῦσαι πάντων τῶν λαῶν. καὶ προσκυνήσατε τῷ σπέρματι αὐτοῦ ὅτι ὑπὲρ ἡμῶν ἀποθανεῖται ἐν πολέμοις ὁρατοῖς καὶ ἀοράτοις καὶ ἔσται ἐν ὑμῖν βασιλεὺς αἰώνων (text acc. to b). VAN DER WOUDE rightly connects this verse with T.S. V, 4 f.: ἑώρακα γὰρ ἐν χαρακτῆρι γραφῆς Ἐνὼχ ¹) ὅτι υἱοὶ ὑμῶν μεθ' ὑμῶν ἐν πορνείᾳ φθαρήσονται καὶ ἐν Λευὶ ἀδικήσουσιν ἐν ῥομφαίᾳ, ἀλλ' οὐ δυνήσονται πρὸς Λευί, ὅτι πόλεμον κυρίου πολεμήσει, καὶ νικήσει πᾶσαν παρεμβολὴν ὑμῶν (text acc. to b).

In *The Testaments*, p. 89 I assumed that T.R. VI, 11b from ἐν αὐτῷ onwards and T.R. VI, 12 formed an additional note, to be connected with Ἰούδαν. VAN DER WOUDE ²) agrees with this; he thinks that *vv.* 11b-12 refer to Judah and regards T.R. VI, 5-12 as a typical Levi-Judah-passage. Because of T.S. V, 5 and the agreements with 1 QM I am now inclined to assume that also *vv.* 11b-12 originally spoke about Levi and its leadership in days of peace and war. We should note, however, that there are significant differences between the present text of T.R. VI and 1 QM. Levi is said to be king (a title which is nowhere applied to the highpriest or any other priest or priestly figure in the Scrolls and is even avoided to denote the Davidic Messiah ³) and he "will die for us ⁴) in visible, and invisible wars". It does not seem rash to suppose here Christian influence again. The hand of the Christian redactor is also visible, I think, in T.R. VI, 8. There we read: διὰ τοῦτο ἐντέλλομαι ὑμῖν ἀκουεῖν τοῦ Λευὶ ὅτι αὐτὸς γνώσεται νόμον κυρίου καὶ διαστέλλει (so b k; c, β-b g k, S διαστελεῖ; h, g A διατελεῖ) εἰς κρίσιν καὶ θυσίας ὑπὲρ παντὸς Ἰσραὴλ μέχρι τελειώσεως χρόνων ἀρχιερέως χριστοῦ ὃν εἶπεν κύριος.

---

¹) For the "quotations" from Enoch in the Testaments, see *The Testaments*, p. 84.

²) *Op. cit.*, p. 195 f. Like CHARLES he regards ἐν αὐτῷ ἐξελέξατο as a Hebraism (בחר בֹ). It is also possible to translate ἐν as an ἐν instrumentale. The construction ἐκλέγομαι ἐν is quite common in the LXX—see 1 Sam. xvi 9-10; 1 Kings viii 44; xi 32; 1 Chron. xxviii 4, 5; 2 Chron. vi 5, 6; vii 12; Neh. ix 7. Consequently the use of this construction in this passage of the Testaments (if it is used) cannot prove that this was translated from a Semitic original; it may be a "Septuagintism".

³) See VAN DER WOUDE, *op. cit.*, p. 135.

⁴) So c a b g, Aᵇ; h, e, f, part of A, S, ὑμῶν. In V, 12b VAN DER WOUDE translates: "and among you will be a king in eternity". The translation: "and he will be king among you in eternity" should, I think, be preferred.

Translation and interpretation of the last clause (from μέχρι onwards) are difficult. Both the translation "until the consummation of the times of the (an) anointed highpriest, of whom the Lord spoke "and the rendering "until the consummation of the times of Christ the highpriest of whom the Lord spoke" are possible. If we choose the first translation we shall have to explain how the author can restrict Levi's activity to the period which precedes the consummation of the times, when a new highpriest will arise—who will, no doubt, belong to the tribe of Levi Or we may take χρόνων ἀρχιερέως χριστοῦ together and regard this as dependent on τελειώσεως so that the consummation of the times brings the end of the activity of the highpriest and (consequently) of Levi himself —but in that case we must suppose that the author makes a distinction between a "messianic age" and the "coming aeon", a distinction which is found nowhere else in the Testaments. The simplest interpretation is here, again, the Christian one. The Levitical priesthood will be succeeded by Christ as highpriest, as it is taught in the Epistle to the Hebrews; compare, esp. Hebr. vii 11, where we also find the word τελείωσις: εἰ μὲν οὖν τελείωσις διὰ τῆς Λευιτικῆς ἱερωσύνης ἦν, ὁ λαὸς γὰρ ἐπ᾽ αὐτῆς νενομοθέτηται, τίς ἔτι χρεία κατὰ τὴν τάξιν Μελχισέδεκ ἕτερον ἀνίστασθαι ἱερέα καὶ οὐ κατὰ τὴν τάξιν Ἀαρὼν λέγεσθαι. This passage refers to Ps. cx 4, a text which may be alluded to in the ὃν εἶπεν ὁ κύριος of T.R. VI, 8 1).

---

1) We have already pointed out that T.L. XVIII, 1-3 also agrees with the Epistle of the Hebrews. This agreement is striking in T.L. VIII, 11-15, a passage which presents many difficulties. According to VAN DER WOUDE p. 213 this is not an eschatological but a historical passage, dealing with Moses, Aaron and the Zadokite priests, appointed by David. The explanation given in The Testaments, pp. 45-46 should, however, I think, still be preferred. A comparison with Isaac's blessing in Jub. XXXI, 15, 16 renders it probable that Or. Test. Levi spoke of the three offices (v. 11a) which are mentioned in v. 17. In vv. 11b (or 12)—15 we find a later Christian interpretation of the three ἀρχαί which forgets that these offices are to be contemporary and confined to the tribe of Levi. V. 12 deals with Abraham, the believer, v. 13 with the Aaronitic priesthood, and vv. 14-15 with the priestly and kingly office of Jesus Christ.

H. KOSMALA has made some important remarks about the relationship of the Testaments and the Epistle to the Hebrews on pp. 81-91 of his book. He thinks that Hebrews was addressed to people belonging to the circles in which the Testaments originated. He realizes that there are many and intricate problems concerning the relationship between the christian and non-Christian elements in the Testaments, but writes: "Selbst wenn eine kommende kritische Textarbeit einwandfrei feststellen würde, dass die

It is obvious that we are not allowed to speak of a juxtaposition of Levi and Judah in T.R. VI and T.S. V—the latter passage is in marked contrast to T.S. VII, 1-2 (to be discussed presently) which is entirely in keeping with the common pattern found in the other L.J.-passages [1]. Levi is by far the most influential and important person and Judah is hardly mentioned. The same picture emerges from T. Levi. Whereas in T. Jud. XXI Levi and Judah are mentioned side by side (whereby Levi takes precedence of Judah) in T. Levi Judah is very insignificant. He is mentioned in VIII, 14 which we recognized as a Christian passage [2]. Next, in IX, 1 where Judah pays a visit to Isaac together with his father and Levi. In Jub. XXXI we are told how Isaac blessed his two grandchildren on this occasion, but T.L. IX (which goes back to material found in Or. Test. Levi [3]) only mentions Levi and seems to forget about Judah, whose blessing is recorded in his own Testament, viz. in T. Jud. XVII, 5.

The third passage in T. Levi which mentions Judah is II, 11: καὶ διὰ σοῦ καὶ Ἰούδα ὀφθήσεται κύριος ἐν ἀνθρώποις, σώζων ἐν αὐτοῖς (so b k, others ἐν ἑαυτῷ) πᾶν γένος ἀνθρώπων. This verse belongs to a passage in which an angel who appears to Levi in a vision assures him: σύνεγγυς κυρίου στήσῃ καὶ λειτουργὸς αὐτοῦ ἔσῃ, καὶ μυστήρια αὐτοῦ ἐξαγγελεῖς τοῖς ἀνθρώποις καὶ περὶ τοῦ μέλλοντος λυτροῦσθαι τὸν Ἰσραὴλ κηρύξεις (v. 10) and tells him καὶ ἐκ μερίδος κυρίου ἡ ζωή σου καὶ αὐτὸς ἔσται σου ἀγρός, ἀμπελών, καρποί, χρυσίον, ἀργυρίον (v. 12). It is remarkable that vv. 10 and 12 speak about Levi alone, and v. 11 about Levi and Judah; moreover in v. 10 Levi will proclaim concerning him who will save Israel, whilst v. 11 speaks of the salvation of πᾶν γένος ἀνθρώπων. We may suppose that T.L. II, 11 was added later, probably when a later redactor tried to fit Or. Test. Levi into the framework of the twelve Testaments. The passages which glorify

---

eine oder andere der obenerwähnten Wendungen aus den Testamenten Levi und Reuben von einer christlichen Hand nachträglich eingefügt worden sind, so bleibt immer noch die priestlich-messianische Atmosphäre übrig, die von einzelnen Ausdrücken nicht abhängig ist" (p. 88).

[1] It should be noted that in T.S. V, 6 Jacob's prophecy concerning Simeon and Levi in Gen. xlix 7 is altered: The sons of Simeon (not those of Levi) will be few in number and will be divided in Levi and *Judah* (Gen. xlix 7 Jacob, par. Israel).

[2] See p. 222 n. 1.

[3] See *The Testaments*, p. 39.

Levi and Judah seem to belong to a later stage in the composition
of the Testaments; in Or. Test. Levi they did not occur, but at
least one¹ of them was found in Or. Test. Naphtali ¹). We shall
return to this later ²).

VAN DER WOUDE ³) is of the opinion that T.L. II, 10-12 does not
betray any Christian influence; χύριος in *v.* 11 refers to God, as
in *v.* 10. "Er wird mittels Levi und Juda der ganzen Menschheit
erscheinen, mehr besagt *v.* 11 nicht. In Levi und Juda findet Gott
demnach die Organe zur Herbeiführung der endgültigen Erlösung".
In *The Testaments*, p. 50 I called T.L. II, 11 "undoubtedly Christian", because I assumed at that time that the composition of the
Testaments had been the work of one man, who in view of the many
Christian passages could only have been a Christian. At present,
after modifying my theory about the history of the composition
of the Testaments, I take a slightly different view of T.L. II, 11 too.
No doubt the Christian who gave the collection of Testaments its
final form, regarded T.L. II, 11 as a prophecy concerning Jesus
Christ. It is not clear, however, whether he is responsible for the
present redaction of this verse; it is possible that T.L. II, 11 was
given its present form and place by one of the Jewish redactors in
the history of the Testaments, who, of course, interpreted it in his
own way.

Three Levi-Judah-passages still remain to be discussed: T.S.
VII, 1-2; T.D. V, 4, 10 and T. Jos. XIX, 8, 11. As we have seen
T.S. VII, 1-2 differs entirely from T.S. V, 4-6 discussed above. It
reads: καὶ νῦν, τεκνία μου, ὑπακούετε Λευὶ καὶ ἐν Ἰούδα
λυτρωθήσεσθε καὶ μὴ ἐπαίρεσθε ἐπὶ τὰς δύο φυλὰς ταύτας, ὅτι
ἐξ αὐτῶν ἀνατελεῖ ὑμῖν τὸ σωτήριον τοῦ Θεοῦ. ἀναστήσει γὰρ
κύριος ἐκ τοῦ Λευὶ ὡς ἀρχιερέα, καὶ ἐκ τοῦ Ἰούδα ὡς βασιλέα,
θεὸν καὶ ἄνθρωπον. οὕτως (so *b k*, other MSS οὗτος) σώσει πάντα
τὰ ἔθνη καὶ τὸ γένος τοῦ Ἰσραήλ. It is clear that in the present
text the coming of one messianic figure is predicted; it is equally

---

¹) See pp. 207 f. above.
²) H. KOSMALA, *op. cit.*, p. 82 writes: "Viele Anzeichen deuten jedoch
darauf hin, dass die Zweiämterlehre eine spätere Phase in der Entwicklung
des messianischen Denkens darstellt". He mentions the special position of
T. Levi, the only testament, "welches seinen Stamm selbst und seine
besondere Aufgabe für das Wohl Gesamtisraels zum Gegenstand hat ...
Levi Mittlerrolle zwischen Gott und Israel ist über allen Zweifel erhaben
und seine endzeitliche Funktion ist entscheidend".
³) *Op. cit.*, p. 200.

clear that Levi and Judah were mentioned separately in the
original form of the passage. PHILONENKO [1]) regards this as
convincing evidence in support of his theory that in the sect of
Qumran the two Messiahs were gradually united into one, the
Teacher of Righteousness. "Mais quand, plus tard, furent réunis
sur un seul et même personnage — le Maître de justice—les attributs
sacerdotaux et les attributs royaux, le texte fut retouché". Even
the expression θεὸν καὶ ἄνθρωπον must go back to the Hebrew
(Essene) original. "Le Messie attendu est prêtre et roi, Dieu et
homme. Sim. VI, 7 et Benj. X, 7-9 nous ont préparé à comprendre
une telle formule". Neither here nor in his commentary on the two
passages which he mentions PHILONENKO adduces any parallels
from the Qumran writings which can support his supposition. We
shall do well to regard θεὸν καὶ ἄνθρωπον as a Christian expression.
VAN DER WOUDE [2]) removes this as a Christian interpolation
together with the οὕτως .... Ἰσραήλ-clause (because πάντα τὰ
ἔθνη are mentioned before τὸ γένος τοῦ Ἰσραήλ). He thinks that
the original passage predicted the coming of a high-priest from
Levi and of a king from Judah, as instruments in God's hand to
bring about the messianic salvation. In the L.J.-passages discussed
so far, however, we have found that originally only the two tribes
were mentioned, not two Messiahs springing from these tribes, and
it is, indeed, probable that the same expectation was found in the
passage underlying T.S. VII, 1-2. V. 2 tells us that the Lord will
send ὡς ἀρχιερέα and ὡς βασιλέα. The double ὡς is not translated
by VAN DER WOUDE; how we should translate it is not quite
certain, but in view of the Christian context it seems likely that
the Christian redactor wanted to indicate that Jesus Christ was
highpriest and king in a very special way and that, therefore, his
relation to Levi and Judah which were mentioned in the text
before him was a very special one.

T.D. V, 4 speaks, again, about the tribes of Levi and Judah:
οἶδα γὰρ ὅτι ἐν ἐσχάταις ἡμέραις ἀποστήσεσθε τοῦ κυρίου καὶ
προσωχθιεῖτε τὸν Λευὶ καὶ πρὸς Ἰούδαν ἀντιτάξεσθε, ἀλλ᾽ οὐ
δυνήσεσθε πρὸς αὐτούς· ἄγγελος γὰρ κυρίου ὁδηγεῖ ἑκατέρους
ὅτι ἐν αὐτοῖς στήσεται Ἰσραήλ. In this passage there is nothing
specifically Christian. In T.D. V, 10, however, the situation is
more complicated. It reads: καὶ ἀνατελεῖ ὑμῖν ἐκ τῆς φυλῆς

---

[1]) Op. cit., p. 43.
[2]) Op. cit., p. 199.

Ἰούδα καὶ Λευὶ τὸ σωτήριον κυρίου καὶ αὐτὸς ποιήσει πρὸς τὸν Βελίαρ πόλεμον κτλ. Because of the transition from τὸ σωτήριον to αὐτός, v. 11a and v. 13b I assumed Christian redaction and supposed that the αὐτός referred to Jesus Christ. [1]). VAN DER WOUDE [2]) does not agree with this. According to him the αὐτός refers to God, and ἀνατελεῖ must be taken as transitive and not as intransitive. Consequently he does not find any trace of Christian influence in vv. 10-13 (at most ψυχὰς ἁγίων in v. 11 is of Christian origin). Strict proof cannot be given and it is difficult to make a final decision. Possibly this is one of those passages which were written by a Jew, and adopted with few or no alterations by the Christian redactor who interpreted it differently. VAN DER WOUDE remarks about this verse: "Die Stellung der Erlösergestalten aus Juda und Levi wird nicht recht deutlich; eine wichtige Rolle spielen sie jedenfalls nicht; offenbar sind sie nur die Organe Gottes in der Endzeit". In fact, T.D. V does not speak about "Erlösergestalten" at all; in this chapter the tribes themselves are (or were originally, if we adopt the Christian interpretation of v. 10) mentioned as instruments in God's hand.

T. Jos. XIX is an extremely complicated chapter. First there are problems with regard to the text. Vv. 3-7 of this chapter are only found in the Armenian translation and the Armenian of vv. 8-12 differs considerably from the Greek. VAN DER WOUDE prefers the longer Armenian text and his arguments certainly deserve careful consideration [3]). More important, however, are vv. 8-12. In A there is a clear connection between vv. 8-10 and the preceding verses. This passage speaks about a virgin between the horns [4]) and those horns are clearly those of the fourth bull (= Judah) in v. 6. In this verse we are told that the horns of this bull went up to heaven and became as a wall for the flocks. V. 6b also mentions another horn which grows between the two horns just mentioned, but its function is not specified. In v. 8 the virgin gives birth to a lamb that conquers all evil powers (symbolized by beasts and reptiles) to the joy of the bulls, the cow and the harts

---

[1]) See *The Testaments*, pp. 87, 91 ff.

[2]) *Op. cit.*, pp. 196, 205 f.

[3]) *Op. cit.*, pp. 201-204. See also *The Testaments*, pp. 28 f., where I considered it impossible to decide whether the shorter or the longer text is original. [For a new detailed discussion of this chapter, see pp. 133-135 above].

[4]) A number of Armenian MSS reads "harts" instead of "horns". These two words are very similar in Armenian.

(all mentioned in the preceding verses). The picture is confused, but it is clear that in *v.* 6 and *v.* 8 a messianic figure from Judah is referred to in various ways. Therefore it is strange that *v.* 11 suddenly speaks about Levi and Judah, and tells us that "from them shall arise the salvation of Israel". VAN DER WOUDE identifies Levi with the "one cow" mentioned in *v.* 5; it is said that twelve flocks and innumerable flocks drank of the sea of milk, produced by her. For this identification, however, there does not seem to be enough evidence [1]).

"In A ist mit Sicherheit nirgends christlicher Einfluss nach-zuweisen" — so VAN DER WOUDE. It would, however, be very remarkable if a purely Jewish passage spoke of a *lamb*, born from a *virgin* from the tribe of Judah. In Eth. En. LXXX-XC mentioned as a parallel by VAN DER WOUDE and others, we do not find anything of that kind. There are still more difficulties in A: How are we to interpret the mysterious *v.* 7? And why does *v.* 9 mention harts which, according to *v.* 4, had been changed into sheep?

Because of the confusion in A it is difficult to suppose that it represents the original text or is nearer to it than the Greek which has a number of difficulties of its own. The connection between *v.* 2 and *v.* 8 in the Greek is strange. After the dispersion of (first) nine and (later) three lambs a virgin is born from Judah, which, in turn, gives birth to a lamb without blemish. This lamb which has "as it were a lion" on its left hand, destroys all beasts, to the joy of the angels, mankind and the whole earth (*v.* 9, comp. A). In *v.* 11 we read: ὑμεῖς οὖν, τέκνα μου, φυλάξατε τὰς ἐντολὰς κυρίου καὶ τιμᾶτε τὸν Ἰούδαν καὶ τὸν Λευί, ὅτι ἐξ αὐτῶν ἀνατελεῖ ὑμῖν ὁ ἀμνὸς τοῦ Θεοῦ, χάριτι σώζων πάντα τὰ ἔθνη καὶ τὸν Ἰσραήλ (so *b*; *c* adds after Θεοῦ: ὁ αἴρων τὴν ἁμαρτίαν τοῦ κόσμου)—a clearly Christian redaction of the original passage which must have been very similar to the text found in A.

---

[1]) Literally translated this verse reads: "And after this I saw and, behold, twelve young bulls which were sucking one cow, which made a sea of the enormous milk and there drank thereof the twelve flocks and the innumerable flocks". VAN DER WOUDE connects this with 1 Cor. iii 2, Hebr. v 12f. and 1 Petr. ii 2, where milk is used to denote Christian (elementary) teaching. H. SCHLIER, *Th.W.z.N.T.*, I, pp. 644-645 gives a number of parallels from the mystery-religions and the gnosis, where milk is a sacramental element imparting ἀθανασία. I cannot find any connection between these Christian texts or the passages mentioned by SCHLIER and T. Jos. XIX, 5. In our verse we shall have to think of the wealth and fertility of the Holy Land (Exod. iii 8, 17 and often), especially at the end of days (Joel iii 18, Isa. lx 16).

Few things only may be said with reasonable certainty. First, that the present text has undergone Christian redaction, in the Greek as well as in the Armenian. Secondly, that *v.* 11 which speaks about Levi and Judah must belong to a later stage in the transmission of the text—comp. T.L. II, 10-12. Whilst in T.L. originally Levi was the prominent figure, here all emphasis is laid upon Judah. Thirdly, there is no reason to suppose that the original text spoke of messianic figures from Levi and Judah.

PHILONENKO discusses T. Jos. XIX, 8-11 under the suggestive title "L'Agneau de Dieu" [1]. Without discussing the textual problems he follows the Greek text and finds a parallel between T. Jos. XIX, 8 and Rev. xii, 1. The παρθένος of *v.* 8 is, according to him, the holy community from which the Messiah is born. The lamb is the Messiah from Levi, the lion the Messiah from Judah. He does not explain, unfortunately, how the lamb born of a virgin from *Judah* can be the Messiah from *Levi*. Also he does not pay attention to the strange transition from the ἐξ αὐτῆς in *v.* 8 to the ἐξ αὐτῶν (c: ἐκ τοῦ σπέρματος αὐτῶν) in *v.* 11. For his interpretation of the virgin as the holy community he tries to find support in A. DUPONT-SOMMER's interpretation of 1 QH III, 6-18 in his article "La Mère du Messie et la Mère de l'Aspic" [2]. Whatever may be thought of DUPONT-SOMMER's theory [3], it is not at all evident that παρθένος has to be interpreted collectively in our passage.

Looking back upon our investigations in this section we may formulate the following conclusions:

1. In Or. Test. Levi all emphasis must have been laid on Levi, whereas Judah was mentioned only in passing. We might suppose that the author neglected Judah because he knew of a Testament of Judah—or had even written it himself—which glorified that patriarch. In the present Testament of Judah older material has undoubtedly been incorporated [4], but we have reason to suppose that it received its present form, and was turned into a true Testament only at a later stage in the development of the Testaments. Moreover the present Testament also glorifies Levi and assigns the second place to its own patriarch. It is more probable,

---

[1] Chapter VI, pp. 29-30.
[2] *Revue d'Histoire des Religions*, 1955, pp. 174-188.
[3] It is criticized severely by VAN DER WOUDE, *op. cit.*, pp. 144-156.
[4] See *The Testaments*, pp. 60-71.

therefore, that the attitude of Or. Test. Levi has to be explained by the very strong priestly sympathies of its author.

2. The Levi-Judah-passages proper belong to a later stage in the history of the Testaments, at which the Testament of Judah certainly, and probably all other Testaments too, were added to Or. Test. Levi and Or. Test. Naphtali. Quite likely Or. Test. Naphtali had already a Levi-Judah-passage, which may have served as an example when the twelve Testaments were composed.

3. In the original Levi-Judah-passages Levi is honoured more than Judah. It is remarkable that in T.R. VI, 5-12 Judah is kept in the background and that in T.S. V, 4-6 he is not mentioned at all. It is possible that in these two Testaments older material has been used by the author(s) who composed the twelve Testaments. It may not be entirely accidental that these two particular passages belong to the first two Testaments.

4. It is not likely that the original Levi-Judah-passages spoke about two Messiahs; they glorified the two tribes only.

5. In the present Testaments the L.J.-passages have been redacted in several ways in order to serve Christian interests. The Christian redaction belongs to yet a later stage in the composition of the Testaments.

6. The history of the composition of the Testaments is a very complicated one and only parts of it can be traced.

7. As to the problem of the relationship between the various passages of the Testaments and the messianic texts in the Qumran-documents no definite conclusions can be drawn. It seems to me that in the former as well as in the latter a variety of expectations is found. It does not seem possible to define exactly the historical and literary relationship between the material used in the composition of the Testaments and that found in the Dead Sea Scrolls —at least not in the light of our present knowledge. I do not think VAN DER WOUDE's theory (two Messiahs in the "Urschrift" of the Testaments, as well as in the Qumran documents) or PHILONENKO's point of view (two Messiahs in the first period of Qumran and the oldest stratum of the Testaments, one Messiah, the Teacher of Righteousness, later on) do justice to the complexity of the material found in the Testaments (and, we may add perhaps, of that in the Scrolls). PHILONENKO, moreover, has not succeeded in proving his contention that the Messiah spoken of in the Testaments is the Teacher of Righteousness.

6. Further material in T. Levi

With some exceptions VAN DER WOUDE deals in his book only with the passages discussed in § 5. PHILONENKO, however, tries to find support for his theory concerning the origin of the Testaments and to receive more information concerning the history of the Qumran sect and its Teacher in a great number of other passages.

In his second chapter [1]) he discusses T.L. X, XIV en XVI which according to him, belong to the passages that show many points of agreement with the Psalms of Solomon and were written about the beginning of the reign of Herod the Great. In *The Testaments* [2]) the present writer supposed that T.L. XIV-XV served as the model on which the other Sin-Exile-Return-passages in the Testaments were composed, and tried to demonstrate that these two chapters, in a not yet redacted form, belonged to Or. Test. Levi, whereas T.L. X and T.L. XVI, which have the same structure as T.L. XIV-XV and deal with the same subject were added later to fill the gaps caused by the omission of other Or. Test. Levi-material [3]). We cannot enter into this problem here, but will concentrate upon the question whether in these chapters the hand of a Christian redactor may be discovered.

Some of the parallels with passages from Qumran which are quoted by PHILONENKO are of such a general nature that no conclusions can be drawn from them. In connection with T.L. XVI, I καὶ τὰς θυσίας (α: τὰ θυσιαστήρια) μιανεῖτε for instance, he quotes CDC V, 6 (comp. IV, 18-19), I QpHab. XII, 8-9, passages which also speak of pollution of the sanctuary, but this is a very usual reproach to be addressed to wicked priests. With regard to the λόγους προφητῶν ἐξουθενώσητε in T.L. XVI, 2 PHILONENKO quotes CDC VII, 17-18 and in regard to the διώξετε ἄνδρας δικαίους καὶ εὐσεβεῖς μισήσητε I QpHab. X, 13, but, here again, the parallels are too general to give support to any theory whatever.

---

[1]) *Op. cit.*, pp. 13-18.
[2]) See pp. 40-42, and also pp. 83 ff.
[3]) This theory seems to be corroborated to some extent by the new fragments of the Aramaic Test. Levi found in Cave IV. See MILIK, *R.B.*, 1955, p. 399: "Parmi d'autres fragments du même ms, qui ne recoupent pas les textes araméens et grecs connus, il y en a un (ou plutôt deux rapprochés à distance) qui présente un certain intérêt pour la critique littéraire des *Test. XII Patr.*, puisqu'il correspond à T. Lévi XIV, I ss., donc à la partie que l'on considère souvent comme ajoutée postérieurement à l'ouvrage primitif" [See now his publications mentioned in chapter XV, n. 18 (comp. p. 252f.)].

Other parallels quoted by PHILONENKO are Qumran texts, the exact meaning of which is still a matter of debate among scholars; most of these have been interpreted with the help of the Testaments—especially by A. DUPONT-SOMMER [1]). Consequently we find that DUPONT-SOMMER uses the Testaments to support his interpretation of certain texts from Qumran, whereas he and his pupil PHILONENKO use the same Qumran texts to prove that the Testaments are of Qumran origin. This method would not be objectionable if it were certain that extra-Qumran origin in general and that Christian redaction in particular might be excluded, but this, in fact, is not the case.

Important, in this connection, is T.L. XVI, 3-5: καὶ ἄνδρα ἀνακαινοποιοῦντα νόμον ἐν δυνάμει ὑψίστου πλάνον προσαγορεύσετε καὶ τέλος, ὡς νομίζετε, ἀποκτενεῖτε αὐτόν (instead of ὡς . . . αὐτόν α reads ὁρμήσετε τοῦ ἀποκτεῖναι αὐτόν), οὐκ εἰδότες αὐτοῦ τὸ ἀνάστημα, τὸ ἀθῷον αἷμα ἐν κακίᾳ ἐπὶ κεφαλὰς ὑμῶν ἀναδεχόμενοι. δι' αὐτὸν ἔσται τὰ ἅγια ὑμῶν ἔρημα ἕως ἐδάφους μεμιαμμένα. καὶ οὐκ ἔσται τόπος ὑμῶν καθαρός, ἀλλ' ἐν τοῖς ἔθνεσιν ἔσεσθε εἰς κατάραν καὶ εἰς διασκορπισμόν, ἕως αὐτὸς πάλιν ἐπισκέψηται καὶ οἰκτειρήσας προσδέξηται ὑμᾶς ἐν πίστει καὶ ὕδατι (text acc. to b).

PHILONENKO identifies the ἄνδρα ἀνακαινοποιοῦντα νόμον ἐν δυνάμει ὑψίστου with the Teacher of Righteousness. This is not impossible in itself, and we must admit that this was not a usual expression to denote Jesus Christ—except, perhaps, in certain Jewish Christian groups. Still, there is much to be said in favour of a Christian redaction of this passage. In Matt. xxvii 63 Jesus is called ἐκεῖνος ὁ πλάνος (comp. John vii 12). The expression ὡς νομίζετε ἀποκτενεῖτε should be preferred to the α-text followed by PHILONENKO, because it is lectio difficilior and because of the quality of the MSS which support it [2]); this expression gives a good description of what happened to Jesus who conquered death [3]). Next, the phrase τὸ ἀθῷον αἷμα ἐν κακίᾳ ἐπὶ κεφαλὰς ὑμῶν

---

[1]) See A. DUPONT-SOMMER's publicatians mentioned p. 181 n. 2. His theories have been criticized severely by many scholars; see e.g. F. M. CROSS, *op. cit.*, pp. 117-119, pp. 167-173.

[2]) See *The Testaments*, p. 21.

[3]) οὐκ εἰδότες τὸ ἀνάστημα is translated by PHILONENKO and DUPONT-SOMMER as "ne sachant pas qu'il se relèverait". ἀνάστημα is, however, not found with the meaning of "resurrection" which is ascribed to it also in some MSS of the Armenian translation. It means a.o. "height, majesty, prominence" (see LIDDELL-SCOTT, *A Greek-English Lexicon*, s.v.).

ἀναδεχόμενοι in this context reminds us of Matt. xxvii 24, 25 [1]).
In connection with *v.* 4 PHILONENKO refers to 1 QpHab. IX, 9-12
which speaks of the punishment of the wicked priest because of
his sins against the Teacher of Righteousness and his followers,
but does not mention the destruction of the temple, and Ps. Sol.
II, 2 which speaks about the pollution of the sanctuary by the Gentiles, but not of destruction. It is quite likely that this passage was
written by a Christian who regarded the destruction of the temple
in 70 A.D. as a punishment for the crucifixion of Jesus by the
Jews. In *v.* 5 the second advent of the central figure of this chapter
is referred to. "C'est le Maître de justice qui, lors de sa Visite,
accueillera ses fidèles"—so PHILONENKO. As parallel he mentions
CDC VII, 21 where the expression בקץ פקודה הראשון occurs which
is translated as "au temps de la première visite" (comp. the
parallel passage XIX, 11). From the Testaments we may conclude,
PHILONENKO thinks, that this first visitation also was a visitation
by the Teacher and because, in his view, the capture of Jerusalem
by Pompey is here referred to "une conclusion s'impose: aux yeux
des sectaires le Maître de justice passait pour avoir été l'exécuteur
du châtiment sur la ville sainte". The problem of the interpretation
of the very difficult passages from CDC cannot be discussed. Even
so, however, it is clear that PHILONENKO's theory rests upon a
number of suppositions which find little support in the text,
whereas a Christian interpretation does not require any hypothetical
supposition. Likewise there is no reason to assume that the expression ἐν πίστει καὶ ὕδατι does not refer to Christian baptism,
but to Essene lustrations.

Next, PHILONENKO discusses T.L. XIV, 1-2, 5-8 where, amongst
others, the expressions ἀσεβήσητε ἐπὶ κύριον χεῖρας ἐπιβάλλοντες
κτλ. (*v* 1) and οἵτινες ἐπιβαλοῦσι τὰς χεῖρας αὐτῶν ἐπὶ τὸν
σωτῆρα τοῦ κόσμου (*v.* 2) occur. Neither the title κύριος nor the
title σωτὴρ τοῦ κόσμου is used in the writings of Qumran to denote
the Teacher of Righteousness [2]) and we should therefore suppose
that these phrases, in their present form, refer to Jesus Christ.
Not so PHILONENKO who assumes here a "majoration christolo-

---

[1]) See also Matt. xxvii 4; xxiii 35 and T. Zeb. II, 2, mentioned p. 192 n. 1.
PHILONENKO points to 2 Sam. i 16; Ezek. xviii 3, Ps Philo Ant. VI, 11,
but in none of these passages the persons concerned take the blood-guilt
upon themselves—as in Matt. xxvii 25 and T.L. XVI, 13.
[2]) PHILONENKO admits this. In connection with the κύριος-title   he

gique" [1]). We should note, however, that in this chapter and in the following one many expressions are found which are more likely to have originated in a Jewish milieu than in a Christian one, so that we may assume that the Christian redaction of this part of Or. Test. Levi has not been very thorough.

In T.L. X, 2 the expression σωτὴρ τοῦ κόσμου occurs again. In T.L. X, 3 we find the expression ἀλλὰ σχίσαι τὸ ἔνδυμα τοῦ ναοῦ ὥστε μὴ κατακαλύπτειν ἀσχημοσύνην ὑμῶν. According to PHILONENKO this would again refer to the events of 63 B.C., when Roman soldiers intruded into the temple. On this occasion, PHILO-NENKO says, undoubtedly also the temple-veil was rent. None of our sources, however, mentions that this actually happened. PHILONENKO also remarks that this text "nous introduit dans un monde de spéculations assez mystérieux: le Temple est ici considéré comme une personne, et le voile du Temple comme le vêtement du sanctuaire personnifié". He refers to p. 124 of *The Testaments* and p. 197 of J. DANIELOU's *Théologie du Judéo-Christianisme* [2]), but seems to overlook the fact that in both places only Christian parallels are mentioned.

In the third chapter of PHILONENKO's book [3]) T.L. IV is examined. It gives "précisions d'un grand prix sur la fin tragique—et jusqu' ici mystérieuse — du Maître de justice". At a later time the same material was used in the passion-story found in the synoptic gospels.

The methodical objections against PHILONENKO's theory, stated before, could all be repeated in an analysis of his treatment of this chapter; we shall not repeat them here. As to the details we may make the following remarks:

The expression ἐπὶ τῷ πάθει τοῦ ὑψίστου in T.L. IV, 1 cannot be

---

refers to Ps. Sol. XVII, 32 where the messianic king is called χριστὸς κύριος. As this figure is called *His* anointed one in XVIII, 2, it is possible to suppose a deliberate or involuntary alteration from κυρίου to κύριος on the part of a Christian scribe. Comp. also Lam. IV, 20, LXX and Hebr.

[1]) Strangely enough PHILONENKO does not discuss T.L. XIV, 4 where we hear of τὸ φῶς τοῦ νόμου (*b h i*: κόσμου; d κόσμου καὶ νόμου) τὸ δοθὲν ἐν ὑμῖν εἰς φωτισμὸν παντὸς ἀνθρώπου.

[2]) Tournai, 1957. Several interpretations of Matt. xxvii 51 and parallel passages are found in early Christian literature. Part of the material is found on the page from *The Testaments* mentioned in the text and in Campbell BONNER's article "Two Problems in Melito's Homily on the Passion", *Harvard Theological Review*, XXXI, 1938, pp. 175-190.

[3]) *Op. cit.* pp. 19-21

explained with the help of a number of texts from the Hodayot which speak of the sufferings of the author. PHILONENKO rightly characterizes the expression in T.L. IV, 1 as "prémices d'une christologie patripassianiste" but forgets to demonstrate that such a messianology had found adherents in Qumran. Therefore we have to assume Christian influence here; the Christian redactor(s) of the Testaments who lived before the time of the great christological controversies inserted more "patripassianic" passages [1]).

In connection with T.L. IV, 2 .... καὶ γίνεσθαι αὐτῷ υἱὸν καὶ θεράποντα καὶ λειτουργὸν τοῦ προσώπου αὐτοῦ (comp. II, 10a) PHILONENKO rightly points to 1 QSb IV, 25, and in connection with T.L. IV, 3 φῶς γνώσεως φωτιεῖς ἐν Ἰακὼβ καὶ ὡς ὁ ἥλιος ἔσῃ παντὶ σπέρματι Ἰσραήλ to 1 QSb IV, 27, passages which belong to a formula for the blessing of the priests [2]). But here too, Christian redaction is visible in v. 4 where we read: .... ἕως ἐπισκέψηται κύριος πάντα τὰ ἔθνη ἐν σπλάγχνοις υἱοῦ αὐτοῦ ἕως αἰῶνος. πλὴν οἱ υἱοί σου ἐπιβαλοῦσι χεῖρας ἐπ᾽ αὐτόν, τοῦ ἀνασκολοπίσαι αὐτόν. Here the period of Levi's priesthood is limited, as in T.R. VI, 8 [3]); if the author had expected an ideal highpriest from Levi he would have expressed himself differently[4]). Clearly the words υἱοῦ αὐτοῦ refer to Christ though it must be admitted that the title Son of God is by no means exclusively Christian [5]). This Christian interpretation is supported by the fact that the compassion of the Son is bestowed upon all the nations and by the reference to his crucifixion. T.L. IV, 4 reminds us of T.L. XIV, 1 where Christian influence is found. PHILONENKO objects to this Christian interpretation on the ground that this verse does not use the usual word σταυρόω, but ἀνασκολοπίζω. "Comment un chrétien aurait-il pu employer pour la crucifixion de son Seigneur cet ἀνασκολοπίσαι scandaleux?" The answer to this question is, I think, given by Paul who, in Gal. iii 13, quotes Deut. xxi 23 and calls Jesus Christ cursed because he hung on a tree [6]). It is quite

---

[1]) See *The Testaments*, pp. 125 f.

[2]) For the expression φῶς γνώσεως φωτεῖνον φωτιεῖς see, however, T.L. XVIII, 3, discussed on p. 217 f. above, where we found influence of Hos. x 12 LXX.

[3]) See pp. 221 f. above.

[4]) This verse presents PHILONENKO with a difficulty in regard to his exegesis of T.L. XVI, 5. He remarks: ".... l'auteur ne paraît connaître ici qu'une seule et unique Visite marquée par l'apparition du Messie".

[5]) With regard to Qumran PHILONENKO rightly points to 4 Q Flor. line 2, published by J. M. ALLEGRO, *Journal of Biblical Literature*, LXXV,

conceivable that a Christian author (or redactor) deliberately used these words to express the horrible effect of the enmity of the Levitical priesthood.

Interesting is PHILONENKO's comment on v. 6: ὅτι ὁ εὐλογῶν αὐτὸν εὐλογημένος ἔσται, οἱ δὲ καταρώμενοι αὐτὸν ἀπολοῦνται. The αὐτόν is clearly the crucified one of v. 4. PHILONENKO quotes I QpHab. VIII 1-3 (translating the expression ואמנתם במורה הצדק as "leur foi dans le Maître de justice") and remarks: "Ici, comme dans le *Commentaire d'Habacuc* la foi qui sauve, c'est la foi dans le Maître de justice". First it should be pointed out that nothing in v. 6 suggests a "saving" faith in a particular person. Similar expressions occur in Jub. XXV, 22 (in Rebecca's blessing of Jacob), Jub. XXVI, 24 (in Isaac's blessing of Jacob), Jub. XXXI, 17 (in Isaac's blessing of Levi) and Jub. XXXI, 20 (in Isaac's blessing of Judah) and in none of these passages faith in the persons blessed is implied; nor is this the case in Gen. xii 3; xxvii 29 and Tob. xiii 12. Secondly many commentators do not translate the expression in I QpHab. VIII by "faith in" but by "loyalty to" and I think this translation should, indeed, be preferred [1]). Though PHILONENKO's interpretation of either passage cannot be accepted, he rightly discovered parallelism of thought between T.L. IV, 6 and I QpHab. VIII, 1-3. It is clear from the writings of Qumran that loyalty to the Teacher and faith in God were much the same thing in the eyes of the sectarians! It is not at all certain, however, that this parallelism points to common origin; the same passage(s) from Scripture may have influenced both the author of T.L. IV, 6 and the sectarians.

1956, p. 176, where 2 Sam. vi 11 f. is applied to the expected Davidic Messiah. Text and translation of I Q Sa II, 11-12 to which he refers too, are, however, uncertain; see e.g. Morton SMITH, *New Testament Studies*, V, 1959, pp. 218-223.

[6]) In n. 71 on p. 21 PHILONENKO mentions 4 Q pNah. line 8 (J. M. ALLEGRO, *J.B.L.* LXXV, 1956, p. 91) where "one hanged alive on the tree" is mentioned. ALLEGRO refers here to Deut. XXI, 23 (so also VAN DER WOUDE, *Bijbelcommentaren en Bijbelse verhalen*, Amsterdam 1958, p. 58). From the context it is not clear, who is alluded to, and it is even improbable that only one particular figure was meant (see *l.* 7). It should be remarked that also the ἀποσκολοπίσαι which occurs in *b k* gives a good sense. This word means "to remove stumbling-blocks" (see LIDDELL-SCOTT, *A Greek-English Lexicon*, s.v.) and is used in this sense by AQUILA in Ps. lxviii 5; cxix 118; Isa. lvii 14.

[1]) See VAN DER WOUDE, *op. cit.*, p. 159 and H. KOSMALA, *op. cit.*, pp. 390 f.

7. Some passages from T. Benjamin, and T. Zeb. IX, 5-9.

The pericope T.B. IX, 2-5, discussed by PHILONENKO in his chapter IV [1]) which bears the title "Le prophète unique", presents us, like the preceding *v.* 1, with great textual and exegetical problems. Even the generally reliable MS *b* does not seem to give the original Greek text here.

In *v.* 2 we read πλὴν ἐν μερίδι ὑμῶν γενήσεται ὁ ναὸς τοῦ Θεοῦ καὶ ἔνδοξος ἔσται ὑπὲρ τὸν πρῶτον (text acc. to *a e f*) καὶ δώδεκα φυλαὶ ἐκεῖ συναχθήσονται καὶ πάντα τὰ ἔθνη. Which temple is meant is not clear. We could think of an ideal eschatological temple after the manner of Ezek. xl-xlviii, if the text did not go on with the words ἕως οὗ ὁ ὕψιστος ἀποστείλῃ τὸ σωτήριον αὐτοῦ ἐν ἐπισκοπῇ μονογενοῦς προφήτου (*b k* om. προφήτου; *c* reads υἱοῦ αὐτοῦ in stead). Of this figure we hear in *vv.* 3-5: καὶ εἰσελεύσεται εἰς τὸν πρῶτον ναόν (that of Herod? Is the πρῶτος ναός the temple that is now, in contrast to the one yet to come?) καὶ ἐκεῖ κύριος ὑβρισθήσεται καὶ ἐξουθενωθήσεται καὶ ἐπὶ ξύλου ὑψωθήσεται. καὶ ἔσται τὸ ἅπλωμα τοῦ ναοῦ σχιζόμενον καὶ καταβήσεται (var. μεταβήσεται) τὸ πνεῦμα τοῦ Θεοῦ ἐπὶ τὰ ἔθνη ὥσπερ πῦρ ἐκχυνόμενον. καὶ ἀνελθὼν ἐκ τοῦ ᾅδου ἔσται ἀναβαίνων (so *b k*; *c, a e f, g*: μεταβ.: *d*: καταβ.) ἀπὸ τῆς γῆς εἰς οὐρανόν. Ἔγνων δὲ οἷος ἔσται ταπεινὸς ἐπὶ γῆς καὶ οἷος ἔνδοξος ἐν οὐρανῷ.

To whom does the expression ἐν ἐπισκοπῇ μονογενοῦς προφήτου refer? PHILONENKO connects this with T.L. IV, 4 and finds the Teacher of Righteousness here too. He points to the expressions מורה היחיד in CDC XX, 1, יורה היחיד in CDC XX, 14 and אנשי היחיד in CDC XX, 32 where he translates יחיד as "unique" [2]). This translation is not the only one possible. VAN DER WOUDE [3]) rightly draws our attention to the parallel between the אנשי היחיד in CDC XX, 32 and the אנשי היחד in I QS IX, 10 (two passages which show more points of agreement) and supposes that יחד and יחיד are synonyms. But even if PHILONENKO's translation proves

---

The latter remarks that the commentator uses the word אמנה in stead of the אמונה of the Habakuk-text. "Das 'Festhalten am Lehrer der Gerechtig-keit' ist nicht 'Glaube an ihm' im Sinne der christlichen Theologie, d.h. Glaube an die Person des Lehrers selbst, sondern ein getreues Festhalten an ihm inbezug auf seine Verkündigung und Wegweisung".

[1]) *Op. cit.*, pp. 22-24.

[2]) Comp. C. RABIN, "The Teacher of Righteousness in the Testaments of the Twelve Patriarchs?", *Journal of Jewish Studies*, III, pp. 127-128.

[3]) *Op. cit.*, p. 37.

to be the right one, it is still improbable that T.B. IX refers to
the Teacher of Righteousness. This μονογενὴς προφήτης is called
κύριος (a title which is not used in the writings of Qumran to
denote the Teacher of Righteousness[1]). We are told that he
"shall be lifted upon a tree"—a passage which must refer to Jesus
Christ, if we take the parallels in the Testaments into account [2].
Moreover v. 4 which mentions the temple-veil is clearly Christian
(comp. T.L. X, 3) [3]. PHILONENKO's comment on this verse is as
unacceptable as it is ingenious: he thinks that this verse refers to
an outpouring of God's Holy Spirit upon Pompey's soldiers who
rent the veil and supposes that the author was inspired to such a
far-reaching universalism by his hatred of the unworthy priests
which served in the temple. In v. 5, too, we find Christian influence.
As in his discussion of T. Zeb. IV, 1-4 PHILONENKO refers to
passages in the Hodayot which, according to him, mention a
descensus ad inferos of the Teacher. For criticism of this view
see pp. 193 f. above.

Striking is PHILONENKO's interpretation of the phrase καὶ
εἰσελεύσεται εἰς τὸν πρῶτον ναόν. He does not think of a building
(whatever that may have been) but refers to 1 QH VII, 4 where
the author compares his body with a building. This verse he
connects with 1 QH VII, 8-9 where, according to him, the community too is compared with a building. The speculations which
we find here resemble the complex N.T. use of the metaphors
"body" and "building (temple)" and PHILONENKO concludes, "Le
premier Temple, c'est le Temple du corps humilié et outragé du
Maître, son corps de chair. Le second temple, c'est son corps
glorifié, son corps transfiguré, où se rassembleront à la fin des
temps toutes les nations". We shall not enter into a discussion of
1 QH VII, but I should like to point out that nothing in T.B. IX
justifies such an interpretation. In the beginning of v. 2 we read
that the temple where the twelve tribes and all the Gentiles will

---

[1] See p. 232 above.

[2] See p. 234 f. above. Even PHILONENKO writes: "Il est difficile de ne pas
penser aux formules johanniques". His remark that ὑψωθήσεται can be
explained as an aramaism (זְקַף = "to lift up" and "to crucify") does not
render support to his theory concerning the origin of the Testaments. The
Johannine usage can just as well be explained this way (and has, in fact,
been explained this way by a number of scholars, as Philonenko remarks
himself).

[3] Discussed above, on p. 233.

be gathered will be *in the portion of the sons of Benjamin.*

In his fifth chapter [1]) PHILONENKO deals with a passage which, according to most interpreters, deals with the apostle Paul: T.B. XI. Here too we are confronted with a difficult textual problem, because *vv.* 1-2a have come down to us in three different forms, viz. in *c*, βS, and A, and because *vv.* 2b-5 are only found in βS. In *The Testaments* [2]) I defended the view that the βS-text of *vv.* 1-2a is nearest to the original and that *vv.* 2b-5 form a later Christian addition to an already Christian text. PHILONENKO declares, without argumentation, that the Armenian version has preserved the primitive text and assumes that the variants arose in the course of attempts to construct yet another prophecy concerning the Teacher of Righteousness [3]).

The parallels from Qumran which PHILONENKO mentions in connection with the Greek text of *vv.* 1-2 are of such a general nature that they cannot give support to his theory. He rightly refers to the parallels with Gen. xlix 27 (καὶ οὐκέτι κληθήσομαι λύκος ἅρπαξ and διαδιδών τροφήν) but does not consider the possibility that the fact that the quotation is given according to the LXX could point against Qumran origin [4]). The parallel with 1 QH VII, 21 is not convincing, especially as PHILONENKO does not mention any of the numerous passages in early Christian literature which consider Gen. xlix 27 as a prophecy concerning Paul [5]).

As parallel to the anti-jewish and universalistic *v.* 2 PHILONENKO mentions 1 QpHab. VII, 4-5; this passage speaks of the revelation of God's mysteries through the Teacher of Righteousness, but does not mention the nations. Neither T.L. XVIII, 9 [6]) nor T.B. XI, 2 can really be explained by somewhat similar passages from the Dead Sea Scrolls. PHILONENKO also points to Isa. xlix 6,

---

[1]) *Op. cit.*, pp. 25-27.

[2]) P. 34 [See now also chapter VIII, n. 56].

[3]) Comp. VAN DER WOUDE, *op. cit.*, p. 204: "Der armenische Text ist auch hier erheblich kürzer und am zuverlässigsten".

[4]) Hebr. וְלָעֶרֶב יְחַלֵּק שָׁלָל and LXX καὶ εἰς τὸ ἑσπέρας διαδώσει τροφήν. Of the expression ἀγαπητὸς κυρίου in *v.* 2 PHILONENKO remarks that this is nearer to the Masoretic than to the LXX-text of Deut. xxxiii 12. This can, I think, neither be proved non disproved. See on the LXX-quotations also p. 197 and p. 206 n. 1 above.

[5]) See *The Testaments*, p. 122.

[6]) See p. 218f. above.

which tells us that the Servant of the Lord will be a light to the Gentiles, but he forgets to mention where this text is applied to the Teacher in the writings of Qumran.

Finally, in *v.* 5 we find the phrase αὐτὸς ἀναπληρώσει τὰ ὑστερήματα τῆς φυλῆς σου which may be called typically Pauline —comp. 1 Cor. xvi 17; 2 Cor. ix 12; xi 9; Phil. ii 30; Col. i 24 [1]). Again we come to the conclusion that the interpretation which assumes that the Greek text of **T.B. XI** has been redacted by Christians is by far the most likely one.

T.B. X, 7-9 is discussed in PHILONENKO's seventh chapter [2]). This passage deals with the resurrection and the final judgment. The most important passages are ... προσκυνοῦντες τὸν βασιλέα τῶν οὐρανῶν τὸν ἐπὶ γῆς φανέντα ἐν μορφῇ ἀνθρώπου ταπεινώσεως καὶ ὅσοι ἐπίστευσαν αὐτῷ ἐπὶ γῆς συγχαρίσονται αὐτῷ (in *v.* 7), ... ὅτι παραγενόμενον Θεὸν ἐν σαρκὶ ἐλευθερωτὴν οὐκ ἐπίστευσαν (*v.* 8) and .... ὅσα οὐκ ἐπίστευσαν αὐτῷ ἐπὶ γῆς φανέντι (*v.* 9). In order to prove his supposition that in this passage also the Teacher of Righteousness is referred to PHILONENKO mentions the following arguments:

1) Besides τὸν βασιλέα τῶν οὐρανῶν τὸν ἐπὶ γῆς φανέντα he mentions as parallel Or. Sib. III, 47-48 τότ' ἄρ' βασιλεία μεγίστη ἀθανάτου βασιλῆος ἐπ' ἀνθρώποισι φανεῖται. The appearance of a kingdom is, however, not precisely the same as the appearance of the King of heaven Himself on earth. 2) The construction ἐν μορφῇ ἀνθρώπου ταπεινώσεως is typically semitic. But then semitic constructions may have been written by a Christian hand. 3) This "man of humility" is the Ebed Jahwe "dont le Maître de justice, comme nous le revèlent les Hodayot est la saisissante image". Is there, however, in the Hodayot or in any of the other writings found in Qumran a passage where the coming of the Teacher is described as the coming of *the King of heaven* in humble appearance? This seems to be a definitely Christian conception; it can certainly not be derived directly from Deutero-Isaiah. 4) The expression παραγενόμενον Θεὸν ἐν σαρκί betrays a more naïve Christology than that found in the prologue to the Gospel of John. This may be true but does not give us an argument against Christian origin

---

[1]) PHILONENKO mentions Corp. Herm. XIII, 1 in order to prove that this is not exclusively Pauline. Still, we may take this phrase as corroborating evidence for the theory that the present text of T.B. XI, 5 refers to Paul.

[2]) *Op. cit.*, pp. 31-33.

of this expression. 5) In the final judgment the attitude of Jews and Gentiles towards the man whom God sent on earth is the decisive criterion—to this we find a number of parallels in Qumran literature. The repeated use of πιστεύω, however, definitely gives an additional argument in favour of the Christian origin of this passage [1]).

In T.B. X, 8-9 the Israelites are judged first and the Gentiles are judged after them. PHILONENKO remarks that in 1 QpHab. X, 1-5 the order is different but he does not think that this is of any importance. I doubt whether this is true [2]) and should like to point out that the beginning of v. 10 καὶ ἐλέγξει ἐν τοῖς ἐκλεκτοῖς τῶν ἐθνῶν τὸν Ἰσραήλ shows a remarkable parallel with Matt. xii 41 f.

It is clear that the passages from T.B. IX, X, XI discussed here are Christian. The Christian redaction has been far more thorough than in some other parts of the Testaments and it is difficult, if not impossible to reconstruct the pre-Christian text [3]). The Armenian translation of these chapters is much shorter than the Greek text, but we cannot use it in our efforts to find the original [4]).

T. Zeb. IX, 5-7 is a typical Sin-Exile-Return-passage [5]) which warns especially against the sin of dissension: ὅτι ἐν ἐσχάταις ἡμέραις ἀποστήσεσθε ἀπὸ κυρίου καὶ διαιρεθήσεσθε ἐν Ἰσραήλ καὶ δύο βασιλεῦσιν ἐξακολουθήσετε (v. 5, comp. the preceding vv. 1-4). PHILONENKO [6]) and other scholars regard this as a reference to the quarrels between the two brothers Hyrcanus II and Aristobulus II which led to Pompey's interference in Palestinian affairs. We should notice, however, that after the return mentioned in v. 7 (and 8) v. 9 refers to a new exile: the sons of Zebulun are told that they will again provoke the Lord to anger and will be cast away unto the time of consummation. From the author's point of view the events mentioned in v. 5, therefore, belong to the past, and because the exile predicted in the S.E.R.-passages often shows traces of agreement with the Babylonian exile, it is quite possible

---

[1]) See p. 235 above.
[2]) See *The Testaments*, p. 127.
[3]) PHILONENKO also assumes that the (Essene) interpolator of the Testaments did his work so thoroughly in T.B. that we should not speak of interpolation but of redaction; see *op. cit.*, p. 5 and p. 199 above.
[4]) See *The Testaments*, pp. 33 f.
[5]) See *The Testaments*, pp. 83-86.
[6]) *Op. cit.*, pp. 6, 36 f.

that we must think here of the division between Israel and Judah after Solomon. The καίγε πᾶν εἴδωλον προσκυνήσετε in the same verse may then refer to the idol-worship of various kings in Samaria and Jerusalem.

T. Zeb. IX 8 does not belong to the typical S.E.R.-pattern, but agrees in several aspects with other "Messiah"-passages in the Testaments [1]). The *b d g*-text is much longer than that of α, *a e f*, A, S₁. In some other passages, too, the *b d g*-text is longer than that of the other MSS and it is not well possible to decide which of the two recensions is the original one [2]). PHILONENKO thinks that the *b d g*-text was written by a Jew who wanted to supplement the shorter text.

The main problem is, again: To whom does this verse refer? The central figure is called ὁ κύριος and this title is not used in Qumran to denote the Teacher [3]). As parallel to the beginning of the verse we may mention Mal. iii 20 (comp. T.L. XVIII, 4; T. Jud. XXIV, 1); the parallel with 1 QH II, 8-9 mentioned by PHILONENKO is not convincing. No more does 1 QH III, 10 help us to understand the expression αὐτὸς λυτρώσεται πᾶσαν αἰχμαλωσίαν υἱῶν ἀνθρώπων ἐκ τοῦ Βελίαρ. Probably this phrase, like T.D. V, 11 goes back to Ps. lxviii 19 and perhaps also to Eph. iv, 8 f. [4]). The words καὶ ἐπιστρέψετε εἰς τὴν γῆν ὑμῶν in α, *a e f*, A, S₁ belong to the normal S.E.R.-pattern and there is no need to regard it, with PHILONENKO, as reference to the future return of the sect to Palestine. The expression καὶ ὄψεσθε Θεὸν ἐν σχήματι ἀνθρώπου in *b (d) g* is an expanded version of ὄψεσθε αὐτὸν in α, *a e f*, A, S; it is definitely Christian [5]).

It is difficult to say to what extent T.Z. IX has been redacted, but Christian influence is visible in the last two or three verses, certainly in *b d g*, and possibly also in the other MSS (*vv*. 8b, 9).

8. *The eschatological meal*

In the often-quoted passage 1 QSa II, 11-12 rules are given for

---

[1]) See *The Testaments*, p. 91.   [2]) See, however, chapter X, above.
[3]) See pp. 232 and 237 above.
[4]) See, again, *The Testaments*, p. 91.
[5]) PHILONENKO writes: "Rien n'oblige à penser cependant que ces mots soient d'origine chrétienne. Nous avons trouvé en Benj. X, 7 une formule analogue et montré qu'elle n'était pas une interpolation chrétienne". As we could not accept his argumentation in T.B. X (see p. 239 above) we cannot follow him here either.

an assembly and a meal where the highpriest and the Messiah of
Israel will be present. According to some scholars this meal is no
other than the usual common meals of the community, for which
1 QS gives some rules. Others speak of an Essene eucharist, as
prefiguration of the eschatological meal at the end of times.
Also PHILONENKO accepts the existence of a "eucharistie essénienne" and he thinks he has found traces of it in the
Testaments.

I do not think that the writings of Qumran which have been
published so far allow us to speak of an Essene equivalent of the
Christian celebration of Holy Supper [1]). Still, 1 QSa II, 11-22
speaks of a solemn meal at which the highpriest and the Messiah
of Israel will be present and we have to ask whether PHILONENKO
is right when he finds a similar expectation in the Testaments. He
discusses a number of passages from the Testaments in his tenth
chapter [2]) under the title "Le Messie at la Cène". He mentions a
number of paralles, but finds one main difference: Here, again, the
two messianic figures of 1 QSa have been united into one single
Messiah, the Teacher of Righteousness.

The central texts are here T.S. VI, 7 τότε ἀναστήσομαι ἐν εὐφρο-
σύνῃ καὶ εὐλογήσω τὸν ὕψιστον ἐν τοῖς θαυμασίοις αὐτοῦ ὅτι Θεὸς
σῶμα λαβών, καὶ συνεσθίων ἀνθρώποις, ἔσωσεν ἀνθρώπους and T.A.
VII, 3 . . . ἕως οὗ ὁ ὕψιστος ἐπισκέψηται τὴν γῆν, καὶ αὐτὸς ἐλθὼν ὡς
ἄνθρωπος, μετὰ ἀνθρώπων ἐσθίων καὶ πίνων καὶ ἐν ἡσυχίᾳ συντρίβων
τὴν κεφαλὴν τοῦ δράκοντος δι' ὕδατος. οὗτος σώσει τὸν Ἰσραὴλ καὶ
πάντα τὰ ἔθνη, Θεὸς εἰς ἄνδρα ὑποκρινόμενος.

PHILONENKO considers the possibility that the meal is only
mentioned to accentuate the real humanity of the Messiah (comp.
T. Jud. XXIV, 1; T.D. V, 13; T.N. VIII, 3) but rejects this interpretation in favour of the one mentioned above. Is it really possible,
however, that these passages refer to the Teacher of Righteousness?

In T. Sim. VI, 5 we read the phrase κύριος ὁ Θεὸς μέγας τοῦ
Ἰσραήλ, φαινόμενος ἐπὶ γῆς ὡς ἄνθρωπος καὶ σώζων ἐν αὐτῷ
τὸν Ἀδάμ. PHILONENKO finds here a number of semitizing expressions (ὡς ἄνθρωπος, ἐν αὐτῷ, τὸν Ἀδάμ in the meaning of "mankind")—which may, however, just as well be written by a Christian
as by a Jew. The expression φαινόμενος ἐπὶ γῆς ὡς ἄνθρωπος

---

[1]) See e.g. J. v. D. PLOEG, "The Meals of the Essenes", *Journal of Semitic
Studies*, II, 1957, pp. 163-175.
[2]) *Op. cit.*, pp. 38-42.

is clearly Christian—the only parallel mentioned by Philonenko is, again, T.B. X, 7-9 ¹). Also the expression Θεὸς σῶμα λαβών is of Christian origin. Philonenko thinks that this expression points to a hellenistic background—in stead of ἐνσάρκωσις we find ἐνσωμάτωσις which presupposes, he thinks, the pre-existence of the soul—and he remarks: "On a souvent contesté qu'une telle théologie ait pu s'élaborer au sein du judaïsme et aux alentours de l'ère chrétienne: Au sein du pharisaïsme, sans doute, mais à l'intérieur de la secte essénienne de l'Alliance fécondée par l'hellenisme, de telles doctrines eurent la possibilité de s'épanouir". Unfortunately Philonenko does not prove that the possibility which he supposes became reality in the Qumran sect. Until this proof is given we shall do wise to regard Θεὸς σῶμα λαβών as a Christian formula.

In T.A. VII, 3 the expression αὐτὸς (= ὁ ὕψιστος) ἐλθὼν ὡς ἄνθρωπος will have to be regarded as Christian too. The phrase .... ἐν ἡσυχίᾳ συντρίβων τὴν κεφαλὴν τοῦ δράκοντος δι' ὕδατος is a reference to Ps. lxxiv 13: σὺ συνέτριψας τὰς κεφαλὰς τῶν δρακόντων ἐπὶ τοῦ ὕδατος. The change of ἐπὶ τοῦ ὕδατος into δι' ὕδατος ²) and the addition of ἐν ἡσυχίᾳ provide arguments in favour of Christian origin. Moreover there is an interesting parallel in Cyrill of Jerusalem, *Catech.* III, 11 ³) who teaches in connection with baptism that Jesus descended into the water of the river Jordan to kill the dragon: ἐπεὶ οὖν ἔδει συντρίψαι τὰς κεφαλὰς τοῦ δράκοντος (sing. as in our text, comp. Ps. lxxiv 14), καταβὰς ἐν τοῖς ὕδασιν ἔδησε τὸν ἰσχυρὸν .... Finally there is the expression Θεὸς εἰς ἄνδρα ὑποκρινόμενος. Charles translates: "God, speaking in the person of man", and Philonenko: "Dieu parlant par l'intermédiaire d'un homme". One of the meanings of ὑποκρίνομαι is: "to reply, make answer" and "to expound, explain". The person who is answered or to whom the explanation is given is indicated by a dative. The usual meaning is, however: "to speak in dialogue, to play a part, be an actor" (the part played

---

¹) See p. 239 f. and p. 241 n. 5 above.
²) MS *g* (as well as 3 MSS of the Armenian version) reads ἐπὶ τοῦ ὕδατος. Philonenko accepts this as the original text and considers the α, β-*g* text as a Christian alteration. As a rule, however, *g* does not represent the original text when it deviates from the other MSS of the *b d g*-group (see *The Testaments*, p. 18) and therefore it is not likely to be original here too. Its reading must have been influenced by Ps. lxxiv 13.
³) Migne, *P.G.*, XXXIII, col. 441; see also *The Testaments*, p. 152, n. 222.

being put in the accusative), to deliver a speech" [1]). Here, in T.A. VII, 3, the translation "speaking to man" seems possible; the renderings given by CHARLES and PHILONENKO (who do not explain them) are most unlikely. How can the εἰς before ἄνδρα mean "in the person of" or "par l'intermédiaire de"? [2]) Another possible translation is: "God playing the part of man"—though the use of εἰς is not in conformity with classical usage.

Besides these two texts PHILONENKO mentions T. Jud. XXI, 5, T.L. VIII, 16-17 and T.L. VIII, 4-5. T. Jud. XXI is the chapter which speaks about the relationship between Judah's kingship and the much superior Levitical priesthood. Part of it has been discussed already [3]). We now turn to v. 5, where we read: καὶ γὰρ αὐτὸν (i.e. Levi) ὑπέρ σε (i.e. Judah) ἐξελέξατο κύριος ἐγγίζειν αὐτῷ καὶ ἐσθίειν τράπεζαν αὐτοῦ καὶ ἀπαρχάς (α adds: προσφέρειν) ἐντρυφήματα υἱῶν Ἰσραήλ. PHILONENKO points to 1 QSa II, 17f. where the expression שולחן היחד ocurs. This is not a complete parallel, and it seems more likely that T. Judah XXI, 5 goes back to Ezek. xli 22; xliv 16 and Mal. i, 7, 12 where the expressions "my table" and "the table of the Lord" are used to denote the altar in the temple. Levi is allowed to eat of the firstfruits of the choice things brought by the children of Israel like the priests in Ezekiel's temple (see e.g. Ezek. xliv 28-31) [4]). There is no mention here of a common meal.

The same must be said of T.L. VIII, 16 where we read: .... καὶ ἔδεσθε πᾶν ὡραῖον ὁράσει, καὶ τὴν τράπεζαν κυρίου διανεμήσεται τὸ σπέρμα σου. In the following verse ἀρχιερεῖς καὶ κριταὶ καὶ γραμματεῖς are mentioned, as in Jub. XXXI, 15; they will belong to the tribe of Levi. The text continues: ὅτι ἐπὶ στόματος αὐτῶν φυλαχθήσεται τὸ ἅγιον which CHARLES translates as: "For by their mouth shall the holy place be guarded". The reading φυλαχθήσεται is found in e, b d g k and A, but a f, (c), (hi) read ληφθήσεται. The latter reading is preferred by PHILONENKO who writes, in connection with 1 QS: "C'est "sur l'ordre" des fils de Sadoq, des fils d'Aaron, des Nombreux, que l'on est admis à participer aux

---

[1]) See LIDDELL-SCOTT, A Greek-English Lexicon, s.v. Especially in Homer and Herodotus this word is found as an equivalent of the Attic ἀποκρίνομαι (which is found in g).

[2]) This implies that 1 Q p Hab. II, 7-9 used by PHILONENKO to elucidate this passage does not offer a real parallel.

[3]) See p. 219 above.

[4]) See also the reference to this passage in T.L. II, 12.

différents stades de la vie de la Communauté" and he continues:
"Il ne s'agit pas d'autre chose. C'est "sur l'ordre" des prêtres,
des juges et des scribes que l'on prendra part ou non au repas
sacré". As this passage T.L. VIII, 16-17 very likely belonged to
Or. Test. Levi (in some form) [1]) it is possible that something along
the lines suggested by PHILONENKO was originally meant. It
should be borne in mind, however, that it is not certain that
ληφθήσεται is the original reading; that no meal is mentioned
expressis verbis; and that T.L. like Jub. also mentions judges and
scribes.

In T.L. VIII, 4-5 which belongs to a passage where Levi's
installation as (high-)priest is described we find a.o. the phrase:
ἐψώμισεν ἄρτον καὶ οἶνον, ἄγια ἀγίων.. PHILONENKO regards this
as a reference to the wine and the bread of Essene holy meals. The
expression ἄγια ἀγίων "est interessante, car elle souligne le caractère "sacramentaire" du repas". In view of the numerous other
passages of Christian origin I still consider the explanation given
on pp. 45 f. of *The Testaments* the more likely one. T.L. VIII, 1-10
describes a Christian baptismal ceremony, followed by the celebration of the Eucharist [2]).

Our conclusion will then have to be that neither the common meal
of the Essenes nor an eschatological meal like the one they expected
are referred to in the passages discussed in this section. In T. Sim.
VI, 7 and T.A. VII, 3 a meal is mentioned only to accentuate the
real humanity of the Messiah, in casu Jesus Christ. In T.L. VIII,
4-5 we may think of a reference to the Christian Eucharist.

9. *Concluding remarks*

We have reached the end of our critical analysis of the theories
put forward by VAN DER WOUDE and PHILONENKO. In view of
the importance of the problem of the relationship between the
Christian and non-Christian elements in the Testaments for the
study of the New Testament and early Christianity as well as for
the study of the writings and the history of the Qumran sect it
was necessary to discuss their arguments in detail.

The present author has limited himself in the main to the
apocalyptical passages of the Testaments because those were the
ones discussed by the other two authors. For a full discussion of

---

[1]) See *The Testaments* pp. 45 f. and p. 222 n. 1 above.
[2]) See also my discussion of T.L. II-IV on pp. 46-49 of *The Testaments*.

all problems connected with the relationship between the Testaments
and the writings of Qumran we should also investigate and compare
their views on angels and spirits, their ethical teaching and their
attitude towards the worship in the temple. A beginning in this
direction has been made by B. OTZEN and M.-A. CHEVALLIER in their
publications mentioned in the beginning of this article, but much
more will have to be done ¹).

---

¹) See also my article in *Studia Evangelica*, pp. 555 f. In PHILONENKO's
twelfth chapter (pp. 44-46). entitled "L'Archange" we find some remarks
about the angelology of the Testaments and the writings of Qumran. In
T.D. VI, 2 the children of Dan are exhorted: ἐγγίζετε τῷ θεῷ καὶ τῷ ἀγγέλῳ
τῷ παραιτουμένῳ ὑμᾶς and they are warned to take heed of Satan and his
spirits (v. 1). The same angel is mentioned in T.L. V, 5-6. PHILONENKO
recognizes him as the archangel Michael who is mentioned in the Latin
version of Asc. Is. IX, 23 and 1 Q M IX, 15-16; XVII, 6-7. It is remarkable,
however, that this angel is here called μεσίτης θεοῦ καὶ ἀνθρώπων. The same
formula is used for Jesus in 1 Tim. ii 5. Michael is the guardian-angel of
Israel, and also in T. Dan and T. Levi the angel just mentioned protects
Israel—see ἐπὶ τῆς εἰρήνης Ἰσραήλ (T.D. VI, 2), ἐνιυχύσει τὸν Ἰσραήλ
(T.D. VI, 5), ὁ ἄγγελος ὁ παραιτούμενος τὸ γένος Ἰσραήλ (T.L. V, 6).
But in other verses belonging to the same passages more people are included
—see τὸν παραιτούμενον τοῦ γένους τοῦ Ἰσραὴλ καὶ πάντων τῶν δικαίων
(T.L. V, 7), the expression μεσίτης θεοῦ καὶ ἀνθρώπων already mentioned
and perhaps also πάντας τοὺς ἐπικαλουμένους τὸν κύριον (T.D. VI, 3).
The struggle between Israel and its enemies assumes cosmic proportions;
it is a struggle between the servants of God and the powers of Satan.
PHILONENKO rightly points to 1 Q M where we find the same. As parallel
of the expression ἡ βασιλεία τοῦ ἐχθροῦ in T.D. VI, 4 he mentions ממשלת
בליעל in 1 Q M XIV, 9 (comp. XVII, 5, 6 and 1 Q S III, 23; in *The Testa-
ments*, p. 155, n. 271 I wrongly declared that this expression was not Jewish).
There are also points of agreement with the well-known passage of the Two
Spirits in 1 Q S III, 13-IV, 26.
I am not sure whether the more universalistic statements may be called
Essene. It seems quite impossible, however, that T.D. VI, 6-7 was written
by an Essene. Whereas in *v.* 4 we read: οἶδε γὰρ ὅτι ἐν ᾗ ἡμέρᾳ πιστεύσει
Ἰσραήλ, συντελεσθήσεται ἡ βασιλεία τοῦ ἐχθροῦ, *v.* 6 declares ἔσται δὲ
ἐν καιρῷ ἀνομίας τοῦ Ἰσραὴλ ἀφιστάμενος ἀπ' αὐτῶν κύριος, μετελεύσεται
ἐπὶ ἔθνη ποιοῦντα τὸ θέλημα αὐτοῦ (for a discussion of textual problems,
see *The Testaments*, pp. 35 f.; also PHILONENKO regards the text given here
as original). Like other anti-Jewish, universalistic passage this verse will
have been written, or at least thoroughly redacted by a Christian (see
pp. 207, 227 above). See also *v.* 7: τὸ δὲ ὄνομα αὐτοῦ ἔσται ἐν παντὶ τόπῳ
Ἰσραὴλ καὶ ἐν τοῖς ἔθνεσι σωτήρ. It is clear that in T.D. VI important
parallels with views expressed in the writings of Qumran are found—but
again Christian influence is visible.
[F. M. BRAUN O.P.'s article "Les Testaments des XII Patriarches et le
problème de leur origine", *Revue Biblique* LXVII, Oct. 1960, pp. 516-549
appeared after the present study had been sent to the printers. Father
BRAUN's views are discussed in my article "Once more: Christian influence
in the Testaments of the Twelve Patriarchs", *Novum Testamentum* V, 1962,

XV

NOTES ON TESTAMENT OF LEVI II-VII

M. DE JONGE

When, some twenty-five years ago, I was faced with the choice of a subject for my doctoral thesis I also asked the advice of Professor Beek, whose *Inleiding in de Apocalyptiek van het Oud- en Nieuwtestamentisch tijdvak*[1] had then just reached the proof-stage. Like my promotor J. de Zwaan he advised me to go on with the work on the Testaments of the Twelve Patriarchs which I had done for my doctoral examination, and I followed this advice. In the preparation of my *The Testaments of the Twelve Patriarchs. Their Text, Composition and Origin*[2] which was accepted as a thesis for the doctorate by the Leyden Faculty of Theology in 1953 Professor Beek took a lively interest in the conclusions which seemed to present themselves.

It is fitting, therefore, to devote my contribution to this anniversary volume to a subject connected with the Testaments. In the form of a number of notes on some chapters of the Testament of Levi I hope to show how our knowledge of the Testaments has been increased in recent years and to indicate where the real problems are to be found. This contribution should be read together with the present author's survey-article „Recent Studies on the Testaments of the Twelve Patriarchs"[3]. It provides some illustrations to the points raised there and some additional information on literature which has appeared since then. Throughout the author's *editio minima*[4] and the textual material collected

Haarlem 1950.

Assen 1953 (quoted below as *The Testaments etc.*).

Svensk Exegetisk Årsbok XXXVI, 1971, 77-96 [Compare now chapters XII and XIII in this volume].

Testamenta XII Patriarcharum (Ps. V. T. Gr. I), Leiden²1970; for the sigla of the MSS see the introduction to this edition.

for the *editio maior* (which is at present being prepared at Leyden) are used.

1. SOME TEXT-CRITICAL NOTES ON II,3-III,9

The most recent evaluation of the Greek textual evidence can be found in Henk Jan de Jonge's article „Die Textüberlieferung der Testamente der Zwölf Patriarchen" published in 1972[5]. Further studies by the small Leyden team which is preparing a new edition of the Testaments have not led to any important new insights. Family α, now consisting of *n* Serb. *c h i* Ngr. has definitely been shown to be the result of a late recension. The siglum β is to be discarded; the MSS taken together under this siglum do not form a unity, and should simply be indicated as non-α. The most important MSS are *b, l, g* and *e*, and of these *b* is usually the best witness to the original text. This may be substantiated also in an analysis of the textual variants in the descriptions of the two visions of heavens in Testament of Levi.

In T.L. II,3-III,9 we find many variants in (*n*) *c h i* against all others; the most important of these are the following (collation against *b* in editio minima-de J.):

II 5 τουτο ορος Ασπιδος εν Αβελμαουλ	]	om., sed + και ημην εν αυτω
II 7 εκ του πρωτου ουρανου	]	εις τον πρωτον ουρανον
εις τον δευτερον	]	om.
υδωρ	]	+ πολυ
αναμεσον τουτου κακεινου	]	om.
II 8 τριτον	]	δευτερον
παρα τους δυο	]	om.
II 9 αλλους... ασυγκριτους	]	sing. et τεσσαρας om.
οτε ανελθης εκει	]	και εν τω ανελθειν σε εκει
II 10 οτι	]	om.
III 1 επτα	]	δειχθεντων σοι
N.B. Introduction to fragment in *n*	περι των τριων ουρανων ων	
	εδειξεν αυτω ο αγγελος κυριου	
III 2 ο δευτερος	]	και
εις ημεραν προσταγματος κυριου	]	εις ημεραν κρισεως
III 3 τριτω	]	δευτερω

Complex situation at the end of this verse.

b	οι δε εις τον τεταρτον					επανω	τουτων	αγιοι	εισιν.	
eaf	„	„	„	„	„	+ οι	„	„	„	„
g	„	„	„	„	„	−	−	−	„	„
k	−	−	εν δε τω	δ		−	τουτου	„	„	

---

[5] *Z.N.W.* 63, 1972, 27-44 [See chapter 11 in this volume].

d	– – εις	τον	δ δε	ουρανον	–	–	αγιοι εισιν	
l	οι δε „	„	τεταρτον	„	επανω τουτου		„	„
m	– – εν δε	τω δ	ουρανω		–	παντες οι	„	„
n	– – – – –	και επ αυτω εισιν			–	–	„	„
chi	– – – – –	και „	αυτους	„	–	–	„	„

III 4	εν αγιω αγιων	] om.
III 5	αγγελοι	] αρχαγγελοι
	του προσωπου κυριου	] om.
III 9	οι ουρανοι	] ο ουρανος.

That the *n c h i* -text is the outcome of deliberate recensional activity is immediately clear if we look at the description of the various heavens. In the non-α MSS we find twice seven heavens. Both in ch. II and in ch. III the number of seven is reached in a rather complicated manner, but in both cases first three heavens are mentioned which are, later on, connected with another four. II,9 calls these four φαιδροτέρους καὶ ἀσυγκρίτους; in III,3b where (we should follow MS *b*!) we hear „But the (heavens) down to the fourth above these (three just mentioned) are holy"[6]. Both descriptions are obviously the result of intensive redactional activity, but whatever discrepancy there may have been earlier, the final text as we have it is, if not polished, at least consistent.

If we now turn to *c h i* we find that these MSS remove an anomaly in II,7. Levi enters first into the first heaven, whereas in the non-α MSS he goes straight from the first to the second one. It is in this heaven and not between the first and the second that he sees *much* water (not simply: water[7]). In vs 8 the third heaven becomes the second and in the redactional vs 9 only one further heaven is announced. Next at the end of this verse the concluding phrase ὅτε ἀνέλθῃς ἐκεῖ followed by ὅτι in vs 10 is altered into an expression introducing vss 10-12, thereby locating Levi's priestly and prophetic activity in the third heaven and not on earth. This is intelligible as far as σύνεγγυς[8] Κυρίου στήσῃ is concerned – though this expression is regularly used for being priest on earth[9] –

---

[6] I owe these observations to H. J. de Jonge and Th. Korteweg. The essential point is that vs 3b refers to heavens, not to angelic beings.

[7] Another „embellishment" is the doubling of Levi's name in the angels' address in vs 6b where *c h i* read Λευί, Λευί, εἴσελθε. On the use of a double name in address see C. BURCHARD, *Der dreizehnte Zeuge* (F.R.L.A.N.T. 103), Göttingen 1970, 93 n. 136.

[8] *g d e a f* read σύ (<*d*) ἐγγύς, *c h i* ἵστασαι (ἔσωσε *c*) ἐγγὺς τοῦ κυρίου.

[9] See Dt. X, 8, XVIII,5; 2 Chron. XXIX,11 and compare Jub. XXXI,14, also for the following parallel expression λειτουργὸς αὐτοῦ ἔσει (see my *The Testaments*, 50). D. HAUPT, *Das Testament des Levi* (Typewritten diss., Halle-Wittenberg 1969), 34 thinks that Levi's priestly service takes place simultaneously in heaven and on earth (see Jub. XXXI, 14 and 1 QSb IV,25ff.).

but it is clearly less suitable in the case of the prophetic activities mentioned in the rest of vs 10.

Also in ch.III *c h i*, now joined by (the fragmentary) *n*, introduce a
number of variants in order to arrive at the number of three heavens;
c h i implicitly by changing the ἕπτα in III,1 into δειχθέντων σοι, *n* by
introducing the description with the words περὶ τῶν τρίων οὐρανῶν ὦν
ἔδειξεν αὐτῷ ὁ ἄγγελος Κυρίου.[10] Here the α-recension is less succesful than
it was in ch.II. By leaving out ὁ δεύτερος in vs 2, changing 'third' into
'second' in the beginning of vs 3[11] and altering the last part of vs 3, the
heaven mentioned in vs 4 becomes the third one. There ἡ μεγάλη δόξα
dwells, just like in II,10 Levi's meeting with the Lord takes place in the
third heaven. Then, once again, three heavens are mentioned (in vs 5,
vs 7 and vs 8) but the connection between these and the previous three
is not clear. It is obvious in the non-α MSS, in which vss 3b-8 give the
description promised in III,1 of the four heavens only mentioned in II,9.

This comparison between α and non-α in the descriptions of the
heavens makes clear, I think, that the α-text can be explained as the
result of recension of the non-α text. The latter, as we have seen, is very
complicated but consistent. The α-MSS give a much smoother text,
and betray recensional activity in II,10 where earthly activity is transported to heaven, and in the lack of connection between its three heavens
in III,2-4 and the three mentioned in vss 5-7.

In one verse, however, this explanation does not seem to be possible;
in II,5 the non-α MSS identify the mountain which Levi sees in his dream
as 'the mountain of the Shield in Abelmaul'. This constitutes a connection with VI,1 where Levi, after waking up, finds a brass shield on a
mountain which is called Ἄσπις and which is located ἐγγὺς Γεβάλ, ἐκ
δεξιῶν Ἀβιλᾶ. The identification of the mountain in II,5, though intelligible from a redactor's intention to connect the beginning of the vi-
sion(s) with the end, is obviously awkward. It is at least unusual to
identify a visionary mountain with a mountain on earth which is said
to have been visited after the end of the vision. The connection intended

---

[10] J. BECKER, *Untersuchungen zur Entstehungsgeschichte der Testamente der Zwölf
Patriarchen* (A.G.J.U. VIII), Leiden 1970, 37-39 wrongly assumes that α gives a
description of seven heavens in chapter III (however clumsily) and of three heavens
in chapter II. Though he admits that it gives an inferior text in many individual
passages, he prefers the inconsistent composition of α to the consistent picture of
two times seven heavens in β. The scribe of the MS *n* which gives the α-text, understood its meaning better than BECKER.

[11] In III,2 the α-reading εἰς ἡμέραν κρίσεως is obviously secondary compared to
εἰς ἡμέραν προστάγματος κυρίου. It is easier and agrees with the expression used by
all MSS in vs 3.

could better have been inserted in the beginning of II,3. It is quite clear, therefore, why the α-MSS omitted the phrase and substituted a neutral sentence: καὶ ἤμην ἐν αὐτῷ. J. T. Milik considers this the right reading and even fills in a lacuna in the corresponding passages in col. II,1.17 in the parallel 4Q Aramaic Levi-text[12] accordingly. To this text we shall return presently; here, however, we should state that the fact that the α-reading fits better (and seems to conform to another, perhaps earlier version of the same story) does not, in itself, prove its authenticity. The non-α-text clearly gives the lectio durior, but this reading is not impossible. It can be explained as the result of a not quite succesful redactional effort and the α-reading as an attempt to correct it. If the α-reading would be original one asks why the non-α-reading would ever have originated. Also here the non-α MSS give the 'rougher', less polished text.[13]

2. THE COMPOSITION AND REDACTION OF T.L. II-VII

a. Some basic considerations

This leads us to a discussion of some important points in connection with the composition and redaction of T.L.II-VII. In what was just said about II,5 it will have become clear that I am of the opinion that the study of recensional activity and the analysis of redactional activity must be kept apart.[14] There may be parallel phenomena in the time the MSS were copied and in the period the document was composed (and, perhaps, added to), but we should conclude our analysis of the text-

---

[12] See his 'Le Testament de Lévi en araméen. Fragment de la grotte 4 de Qumrân", R.B. 62, 1955, 398-406, esp. 404.

[13] In his *The Greek Versions of the Twelve Patriarchs*, Oxford 1908, R. H. CHARLES prints the text of II,7-10 and III,1-9 in three columns, the middle column giving the text of the α-text of the Armenian version. In his *The Testament of Levi. A first study of the Armenian MSS of the Testaments of the XII Patriarchs in the Convent of St. James, Jerusalem*, Jerusalem 1969, M. E. STONE has shown (on the basis of more MS-material than any scholar before him!) that Aα is clearly the result of recensional activity and that therefore the MSS of this type of text cannot be regarded as of equal value with the other MSS. Nevertheless it represents an Armenian prototype which is not identical with any of the existent MSS or the 'Vorlagen' of existent groups of MSS (*op.cit.*, 30-31). There is no reason to make an exception for Test. Levi II-III (contra CHARLES, and BECKER, *op.cit.*, 46-47, who rashly assumes that Aα, though secondary, goes back to an Armenian 'Vorlage' which is nearer to Greek α!).

[14] See also the present author's 'Textual criticism and the analysis of the composition of the Testament of Zebulun' in *Texte und Textkritik*, ed. J. DUMMER [See chapter X in this volume].

critical data, leading up to the reconstruction of the text which is most likely to be orginal, before we use the results of this study in the analysis of the composition and redaction of the text. In the case of T.L.II-III the earliest text is the 'rougher' non-α-text, best preserved in *b*, and precisely its 'roughness' provides a number of starting points for redactional analysis.

Another remark may be made in advance. The Testaments, in their present form, present a very complicated picture, the different elements of which should be determined with all the methods at our disposal. But after we have analysed the different constituent parts we shall have to explain each testament as a whole, and the Testaments themselves as a deliberate composition. In my doctoral thesis I laid much stress on the activity of the author(s) of the Testaments as 'composer(s)'. Theories of 'interpolation' (R.H. Charles)[15] or 'gradual growth' (J. Becker)[16] do not give a real explanation for the present Testaments. My working-hypothesis is still that the very fact that a man or a group of people wanted to compose testaments of twelve patriarchs made him (or: them) look for all relevant material he (they) could find in order to put this together within a certain framework with a definite, primarily ethical purpose. This material was not only brought together, it was rewritten. The result of this process is obviously still very complex and extremely variegated. Yet we have not completely interpreted the text in front of us before we have explained how the present arrangement and composition makes sense.

In a short article this cannot be proved conclusively for the Testaments, or for the Testament of Levi, or even for T.L. II-VII. I shall try to show, however, that we can receive some insight into the process of redaction and composition if we compare the present chapters with the 4Q Ar.-Levi document published by Milik in 1955 (see 2b) and, next, that the chapters II-VII are complex but not inconsistent (see 2c).

b. *Milik's Aramaic 'Prayer of Levi', its Greek counterpart in MS e and the present Testament of Levi*

Among the many fragments found in the fourth cave at Qumran in some way related to our Test. Levi which J. T. Milik has deciphered and announced,[17] the fragment which he published in 1955[18] is interesting

---

[15] See my *The Testaments etc.*, particularly chapter II.

[16] See also my 'Recent Studies' (note 3), 91-93 [See also chapters XIII and XVII in this volume].

[17] For a full list see J. BECKER, *op.cit.*, 67-72; but add the information given in MILIK's article in the *Harvard Theological Review* 1971 mentioned in n.18.

[18] See note 12 above. In this article he specifies that 4 Q-fragments were the

for several reasons. First, it runs parallel to the Greek text inserted after ἀδικία in T.L.II,3 in MS *e*, just as part of the Genizah fragments published by R. H. Charles find a parallel in a similar addition in the same MS at T.L.XVIII,2. We do not know the provenance of the Greek additions, nor is it easy to establish the exact literary relationship between the Aramaic and the Greek, in the case of the Genizah fragments[19] as well as the new Qumran fragments, but the parallels are sufficiently close to compel us to study them side by side. Consequently, since it proved possible to show that the present Greek Testament of Levi must have known and used tradition(s) preserved in the Aramaic Genizah and corresponding Greek fragments,[20] we can try to use the new material in the same way. Here a second point is of importance: contrary to the majority of the other fragments this text shows agreements with a part of the Greek Testament not yet 'covered' by the Genizah-fragments and the corresponding Greek text in *e*.

In col.II, ll.11-18 of Milik's fragment we read that Levi after ending a prayer goes to his father Jacob, then leaves Abel-main to go to another place. There he sees a vision and/or visions after lying down to sleep. In this vision he sees the gates of heaven and a high mountain reaching to heaven below him. The Greek text inserted in *e* at T.L.II,3 gives only the text of the prayer with a short introduction which does not provide any information about the situation. As we have already seen, the introduction to the vision in Ar.II,14-18 shows points of contact with T.L.II,6. We can also point to II,5 τότε ἐπέπεσεν ἐπ' ἐμὲ ὕπνος and to V,1 where the angel opens τὰς πύλας τοῦ οὐρανοῦ. This raises immediately the problem of the composition of the vision in Test. Levi. Is the use of nearly the same formulae in V,1 and in II,6 an attempt to return to an earlier version of the vision? We should note that Ar.II,18 speaks of תרעי שמיא and that the Aramaic text does not necessarily presuppose more than one heaven. The words τὰς πύλας τοῦ οὐρανοῦ may correspond to this Aramaic expression, and are in any case awkward after the descriptions of several heavens in the previous chapters. In its present context the angel obviously gives Levi access to the highest heaven where the Most

rests of three MSS and he calls the solitary fragment discussed here 4 Q Levi[b]. In *R.B.* 73, 1966, 95 n. 2 he announces that all fragments mentioned in the 1955-article must have belonged to one MS, called 4 Q 213 Test. Levi[a] and that, in the meantime, he has also identified a few pieces of a second MS 4 Q 214 Test. Levi[b]. In his 'Problèmes de la littérature hénochique à la lumière des fragments araméens de Qumran', *H.Th.R.* 64, 1971, 333-378 he publishes a translation of 4 Q Test.Levi[a] 8 III 2-8 (on pp. 344-345).

[19] See my *The Testaments etc.*, 129-131.
[20] So *The Testaments etc.*, 38-52, with conclusion on p. 52.

High dwells, previously described as the highest heaven (III,4). The angel does so after finishing a long speech (II,9-IV,6) in which he describes the heavens which Levi is yet to see, and announces God's judgment on the sinners and God's election of Levi as his priest and servant. This speech is situated between the first three and the following four heavens (II,9, comp. III,3), but in V,1 the latter are no longer in the picture.

Yet, if we would consider II,6-IV,6[21] or alternatively II,7-V,1a[22] as an interpolation in a more original version of the vision we would disregard the fact that IV,2, belonging to this 'interpolation', presupposes the contents of the prayer of Levi preserved in the Ar. and Greek fragments.

In T.L.II,3-5 Levi's prayer follows on a short vision in which he sees the sins of men and 'the fortifications' of Unrighteousness.[23] He prays that he may be saved and immediately after that he receives a vision in his sleep. The order of events is different from that which can be reconstructed from the Aramaic fragment, particularly because the journey to Jacob is only mentioned *after* the vision, in VI,1. Also the words ηὐξάμην Κυρίῳ, ὅπως σωθῶ are a very incomplete and one-sided summary of the prayer of Levi as it is found in the Aramaic and Greek fragments. Levi's desire to be guarded against evil (Greek fragm. vs 7,10) and his appeal to God to destroy evil (id., vs 13) are covered adequately. The latter phrase is also reflected in the announcement of God's judgment on the wicked in III,(1-3), 9-IV,1. But one important point at least is missing: Levi's request to be allowed to serve God. The answer to the prayer given through the angel in IV,2 reflects the contents of the prayer much better and obviously presupposes what Test. Levi in its present form does not mention.[24]

---

[21] Comp. BECKER, op.cit., 261: '5,1 setzt also die Situation aus 2,5 voraus und kennt 2,6ff nicht.'

[22] HAUPT, op.cit., 17f. regards II,6 as the 'original' introduction, because of its parallel with Ar. fragm. Col. II,18. V,1 and Col. II,18 both mention the gates of heaven, but II,6 agrees with the Aramaic fragment in that the angel does not open the gates, but addresses Levi.

[23] With ὅτι τείχη ᾠκοδόμησεν ἑαυτῇ ἡ ἀδικία, καὶ ἐπὶ πύργους ἡ ἀνομία κάθηται one should compare CD IV,12f. and 4 Q Test. 26. In the Greek prayer of Levi in MS e vs 12 Levi asks God τεῖχος εἰρήνης σοι (conj. MILIK: σου) γίνεσθαι κύκλῳ μου, καὶ σκέπη σου τῆς δυναστείας σκεπασάτω ἀπὸ παντὸς κακοῦ. This is a metaphorical expression in the same vein as T.L. II,3b corresponding to the ὅπως σωθῶ of II,4 end. We may compare also καὶ πάντας ἑώρων ἀνθρώπους ἀφανίσαντας τὴν ὁδὸν αὐτῶν in II,3 and Gr. fragm. vs 10 καὶ μὴ κατισχυσάτω με πᾶς σατανᾶς πλανῆσαί με ἀπὸ τῆς ὁδοῦ σου. It is possible that also II,3-4a corresponds to a passage now lost in the Aramaic and not extant in Greek.

[24] So rightly also D. HAUPT, op.cit., 16f. See also II,10; it is interesting to note that in V,2 MS e adds the following words spoken by God himself: (σοι) δοθήσεται ἡ ἱερατεία

T.L.IV,3 reminds one of XIV,3f and the description of the 'new priest' in XVIII,3f. The degree of 'christianization' of these passages can be a matter of dispute; fortunately again a 4Q Levi fragment is preserved with a text which can be compared to XIV,3f. In the translation published by Milik[25] it runs '[...le soleil], la lune et les étoiles [... brillent] au-[dessus de la terre. Ne ressemblez-vous pas au soleil et à] la lune? [Si] vous vous obscuⅰcissez [par l'impiété, que feront tous] les [peuples]? Hénoch n'avait-il pas accusé [les responsables (?) de la perdi]tion. Et sur qui sera la faute, [si] non sur vous, mes fils?' This makes it probable that also in the text behind T.L.IV,3 Levi was compared to a light and to the sun.[26] Also IV,4a may go back to this earlier version, because of its parallel to V,2; T.R. VI,10f. and Jub.XXXI,15. The following verses are obviously Christian[27] including vs 5; apart from the words περὶ αὐτοῦ this verse may reflect Levi's prayer καὶ βουλὴν καὶ σοφίαν καὶ γνῶσιν καὶ ἰσχὺν δός μοι (in Greek fragm. vs 8[28]).

Negatively, it should be noted that in the introduction to the prayer in the Greek and Aramaic fragments much emphasis is laid on cleanliness. We may compare here the emphasis on avoiding ἀκαθαρσία in the non-technical parts of the instructions of Isaac to Levi recorded in the fragments given in the Appendix of Charles, particularly vss 14-18. In the corresponding chapter IX the Greek Testament of Levi pays nearly no attention to this because of his lack of interest in sacrificial matters.[29] The same is true of II,3-4 and IV,2-6 where separation from evil is the issue which receives all the emphasis.

καὶ τῷ σπέρματί σου τοῦ λειτουργεῖν τῷ ὑψίστῳ ἐν μέσῳ τῆς γῆς καὶ ἐξιλάσκεσθαί σε ἐπὶ ταῖς ἀγνοίαις τῆς γῆς (τότε ἔδωκεν). This may, again, be a fragment of the text, of which substantial portions were added at II,3 and XVIII,2.

[25] See n. 18. On pp. 344f. MILIK writes: 'Le contexte de ce passage est celui du ch. 14 du Testament grec de Lévi, mais avec des phrases qu'on rencontre dans les ch. 15 et 16; cette partie du Testament contient des invectives contre le sacerdoce israélite'.

[26] See also I Q Sb IV,27.

[27] See the limitation of the period of Levi's priesthood in the clause ἕως ἐπισκέψηται κτλ., comp. V,2 and T.R. VI,8, and the following sentence. In vs 2 Levi is also designated as God's son, whereas in the Greek fragment he calls himself God's παῖς (vs 17) and ὁ υἱὸς παιδός σου ('Ιακώβ) (vss 15,19). This change need not necessarily be attributed to a Christian author – see The Testaments, 50 and D. HAUPT, op.cit., 14f.

[28] Comp. Is. XI,2 and, perhaps, T.L. II,3a. See also καὶ μέτοχον ποίησον τοῖς λόγοις σου ποιεῖν κρίσιν ἀληθινὴν εἰς πάντα τὸν αἰῶνα, ἐμὲ καί τούς υἱούς μου ... (Gr. fragm. 18). J. BECKER, op.cit., 263f. repeats the theory that the original version of vs 6 read a double σε in stead of the double αὐτόν of the present text. This is possible but cannot be in any way be proved – see also M. DE JONGE, 'Christian influence in the Testaments of the Twelve Patriarchs', Novum Testamentum 4, 1960, 182-235, esp. 224 [Now chapter XIV, 235].

[29] See The Testaments, 39f.

The vision in T.L.II,6-VI,2 leads up to Levi's actual appointment as priest by God himself in V,2. This is preceded by II,10-12 and IV,2-6 where Levi's installation is announced by the angel and where a connection is made between Levi's piety and wisdom and his teaching and preaching to others, even in the present text with his duty to announce the one who is to save Israel. The appointment in V,2 is followed by Levi's investiture in the second vision recorded in chapter VIII. There is a clear connection between VIII,18f and V,7-VI,2, the repetition of the vision underscoring the validity of his calling.[30] Now vs 7 of the Aramaic Genizah-fragments corresponds to T.L.VIII,18f and presupposes that the vision mentioned immediately before is not the first one.[31] It is not too rash to conclude that the Aramaic fragment published by Milik represents essentially the same document as the Cairo Genizah fragments and, in that document, preceded them.

This is corroborated by the following observations: T.L.II,1-2 give a biographical introduction, corresponding to T.L.XI, XII. In XII,5 Levi's exploits in Shechem are connected with his appointment to the priesthood. The *post* is explained as a *propter* in chapters V-VII. The angel gives Levi the command to avenge Dinah and this is recorded in the heavenly tablets (V,2f.).[32] This corresponds to Jub.XXX,17-19,23, and is hinted at in T.L.VI,8a in the complex chapters VI-VII to which we shall return presently. Because of their fragmentary nature we cannot be sure that the Aramaic and Greek fragments mentioned a *propter*, but the *post* is there in vss 78f, the equivalent of T.L. XII,5 and there are left, in vss 1-3, some fragments of a Shechem story which in Charles's edition are rightly put at the head of the fragments at his disposal, before the others which correspond to T.L.VIII end -XIII.

All this should be examined in far greater detail that can be done here; but the examples given may have shown that the Aramaic fragment

---

[30] See also the two visions in the Test. Naphtali and their conclusion in T.N. VII. See also Hebr. T.N. VII,4 ...He said unto me, 'My son, because of the repetition of thy vision my heart has sunk within me'... (transl. R. H. CHARLES, *The Testaments of the Twelve Patriarchs*, London 1908, 225) and the following vs 5; comp. I Sam. III and I Ki. XIX,9-18.

[31] On vss 4-10 = Bodl.fragm.col.a see especially P. GRELOT, 'Notes sur le Testament Araméen de Lévi (fragment de la Bodleian Library, colonne a)', *R.B.* 63, 1956, 391-406. Grelot tries to situate 1 Q 21,1 immediately before this fragment. Comp. J. T. MILIK in *Discoveries in the Judean Desert I*, Oxford 1955, 88f. who also connects fragm. 1 Q 21,7 with it. For criticism see J. BECKER, *op.cit.*, 77-79.

[32] P. GRELOT, *op.cit.* 393-397 connects the peaceful priestly activity mentioned in V,2 with Bodl. fragm a ll 1-2a (to be compared with the מלכות כהנותא of 1 Q 21,1) and the military exploits of V,3 with the מלכות חרבא described in ll 2b-4.

published by Milik belongs to an earlier stage in the transmission of the
document to which also the fragments from the Cairo Genizah must have
belonged. This is evident from the fact that other 4Q-fragments belonging
to the same scroll run partly parallel to Genizah-fragments already
known to us. Further details may perhaps be established after publication
of the full material by Milik and it is to be hoped that then the relationship between the Aramaic and Greek material preserved in the two large
additions (and in the smaller one in V,2?) in e may be determined more
precisely. This much is clear, however, that the publication of Milik's
fragment of 1955 corroborates the conclusion reached by the present
author in 1953. The Testament of Levi presupposes a source which was
much nearer to the stage of tradition reflected in the various fragments
than the Testament itself, and in many cases the fragments can help us
to determine how the author of the Test.XII Patr. used and redacted
his source.[33]

It is difficult to determine the literary genre of 'Original Levi'. In
vs 81 of the Aramaic fragments published by Charles the autobiographical
account with the description of the visions, the punishment of Shechem,
the elaborate instructions to Levi as priest and the biographical summary
(coresponding roughly to T.L.II-XII) ends in the 137th year of Levi's
life, before his death. Then, in vs 82ff, follows an address of Levi to his
sons, roughly corresponding to T.L.XIII, spoken in the year of Joseph's
death equated with the 118th year of Levi's life. The present Testament
of Levi, in XII,6-XIII,1 has concealed this seam somewhat awkwardly,
but effectively. In this way it is able to combine biography, exhortation
and predictions for the future,[34] like the other testaments. Moreover,
as D. Haupt has shown, a number of elements found in vss 82-83 are also
used in the opening passages of the individual Testaments (though only a

---

[33] So also D. HAUPT, op.cit., passim against J. BECKER who assumes a) that there is
only a distant traditio-critical relationship between MILIK's 4 Q-fragment and
T.L. II-V (see op.cit., 72-76, in which he misses the clue provided by T.L. IV,2);
b) that it should be treated apart from the rest of the Aramaic (and parallel Greek)
material. For the latter material BECKER quite unnecessarily presupposes a relatively fixed oral tradition parallel to that behind the present Greek Test. Levi (op.cit.,
77-105, esp. 103-105).

[34] Because of the fragmentary state of 4 Q Test.Levi[a] 8 III,2-8 (see n.18 above)
we are not certain that Or. Levi contained also predictions of the future, but
because of the parallels between this fragment and T.L. XIV this is likely. See also
MILIK's remark on a possible Aramaic text behind T.L. XVI-XVII (to which also
the 'Pesher on the Periods' in 4 Q 180-181 would go back) on p. 123 of his 'Milkî-
ṣedeq et Milkî-reša' dans les anciens écrits juifs et chrétiens', J.J.S. 23, 1972, 95-144.
We should note that in T.L. X (which has no parallel in the fragments) exhortations
are already combined with predictions.

few of them in T.L. I).[35] All this requires further investigation and perhaps we need more material before we can reach definite conclusions.

In any case we may now compare the 4Q 'Amram-fragments which were recently published by Milik.[36] It gives 'the words of visions' recorded by 'Amram, son of Qahat, son of Levi – but on the day of his death. The verbs used are אחוי = 'to show, to tell' and פקד 'to charge'.[37] In 4Q Qahat also published by Milik, father Qahat again 'charges' to hand on what was given to Levi and by Levi to the speaker.[38] It may not be too rash to suppose that the Levi-, Qahat- and 'Amram-material belongs to a series of documents giving priestly final exhortations and visions, preserved in the sectarian priestly circles whose literature was hidden at Qumran. Again, this needs to be investigated more fully after all extant material has published.[39]

c. *The composition of T.L. II-VII*

Space does not permit me to give a detailed analysis of these chapters or to discuss the results of J. Becker and D. Haupt in detail. Perhaps, however, it may be useful to give a survey of the composition of the chapters in the present testament, and to attempt to show that the working-hypothesis mentioned under 2a leads to satisfactory results. It cannot explain all details simply because we still know too little of what the author(s) had in front of him (them). Also we cannot exclude the possibility that the redaction went through different stages before the last one which is definitely Christian; nor is it impossible that glosses

[35] *Op.cit.*, 84-86 and 120-122. HAUPT refers to J. BECKER's treatment of the 'framework' of the Testaments on pp. 158-172 of his book. HAUPT's parallel elements are: mention of Levi's age; synchronization with the years of Joseph's death; the coming together of all sons; introduction to the farewell-address with a verb of saying; the 'Lehreröffnungsformel'. The difference is the use of the first person singular.

[36] '4 Q Visions de 'Amram et une citation d'Origène', *R.B.* 79, 1972, 77-97.

[37] פקד is also used in Ar. fragm. vs 82 and 84 (comp. vs 13 where Isaac teaches Levi).

[38] See '4 Q Visions de 'Amram...', 96f. We should note that Qahat and cAmram are mentioned in T.L. XI-XII and the Aramaic and Greek parallels to these chapters. In the case of Qahat an elaborate explanation of his name is given both in Test. Levi and in the fragments and a vision is recorded (XI,4-6 and fragm. vss 66f.; comp. XI,3 and Greek fragm. vs. 64). His leadership of the nation and his future high priesthood get great emphasis. In the case of cAmram Ar.fragm. vs. 76 explains the name as 'the exalted people' and connects it with the exodus from Egypt. His marriage to Levi's daughter Jochebed receives much attention (XII 4, comp. Ar.fragm. vs 75).

[39] J. T. MILIK regards the Aramaic T. Levi and T. 'Amram as 'preessenian' – see *H.Th.R.* 64, 1971, 345 and *J.J.S.* 23, 1972, 137, 144.

were added later after the actual testament had been composed. I do not think, however, that we can really distinguish stages in the composition of the testament and assign the various verses to these stages.

With these restrictions we can present the following picture: *II,1-2*: biographical details, comp. XI-XII, perhaps 'taken from' Or.Levi. *II,3-5*: Levi's prayer after a vision, introduction to vision of heavenly journey; probably going back to Or.Levi, with the exception of the clearly redactional vs 5b. *II,6-V,6*: highly complex vision of heavenly journey; a number of elements can be traced back to Or.Levi, as was shown above. The final redactor superimposed a system of seven heavens and obviously looked for traditional material to 'fill' this.

II,6 an angel invites Levi to enter.

II,7-8 first three heavens.

II,9-IV,6 speech of accompanying angel.

II,9 announcement of four further heavens; clearly redactional.

II,10-12 announcement of Levi's installation as priest. II,11 a Levi-Judah-addition; in vs 10b Christian influence?[40]

III,1-3 description of first three heavens. Emphasis on the punishment of the wicked. Probably originally connected with:

III,9-IV,1 which gives a description of the final judgment,[41] 'christianized' in IV,1.

III,4-8, after the transitory sentence vs 3b: description of the four highest heavens (in the order 7,6,5,4!) centering around the heavenly cult, of which Levi's priestly activity is to be the counterpart.[42]

IV,2-6 a second announcement and description of Levi's priestly work, in the context of God's hearing Levi's prayer. Clear Christian influence on the present description.

V,1-2 return to the topic of the heavenly journey. Levi sees the Most High and is appointed priest.

V,3-6 Levi's return to earth. Vs 3 the angel commands Levi to punish Shechem and gives him armour and sword.[43] Vs 4 antici-

---

[40] See M. DE JONGE, chapter XIV, 223 f. and comp. J. BECKER, *op. cit.*, 265-267.

[41] See *The Testaments etc.*, 47.

[42] See *The Testaments etc.*, 48f., where a number of (mainly Christian) parallels are mentioned. In its present redaction the passage is undoubtedly Christian, but it incorporates many elements which represent also Jewish (especially Hellenistic-Jewish) thinking on sacrifice – see J. BECKER, *op.cit.*, 267, n.6 and D. HAUPT, *op.cit.*, 42-44.

[43] The belligerent Levi also in T.R. VI, 11-12 and T. Sim. V, 4-5; comp. also P. GRELOT's remarks mentioned in n. 32 and M. DE JONGE, chapter XIV, 220. VI, 3 connects this with his 'zeal for the Lord'—comp. also M. HENGEL, *Die Zeloten* (A.G.J.U. 1), Leiden/Köln 1961, 182-184 and D. HAUPT, *op. cit.*, 27.

pates VI,3ff; Levi tells that he did kill the sons of Hamor. In vss 5-6 Levi asks and receives information about the angel's identity.[44]

V,7-VI,2: conclusion of the vision. Levi goes to his father.[45]

VI,3-VII,4: highly complex description of what happened at Shechem, with various motivations.[46]

VI,3-5 describes what happened (comp. Gen.XXXIV,13-31).

VI,6-7 tries to explain Gen.XLIX,5-7 and (nearly) explains it away – see the ἄλλως ἐποίησεν in vs 6b, and Levi's admission that in his zeal for the Lord (vs 3, comp.V,3-4) he was not sufficiently considerate towards his father.[47]

VI,8-11 various motivations. Vs 8a (perhaps) alludes to V,2-3. Vs 8b-10 mentions expected atrocities in the future and a list of those in the past.[48] Vs 11 agrees with I Thess.II,16b.[49]

VII,1 takes up VI,6f and records Levi's answer to Jacob, presupposing Jacob's remark in Gen.XXXIV,30 (comp. Jub.XXX,25f.) which is not mentioned in T.Levi.

VII,2a alludes to Sir. L,26; it is further explained in vss 2b-3.

VII,4 describes the departure of Jacob's family to Bethel, where the next vision occurs (VIII,1ff).

---

[44] On this angel and his activities see *The Testaments etc.*, 93.

[45] On the geographical names in T. Levi and the Aramaic and Greek fragments see J. T. MILIK, *R.B.* 62, 1955, 403-405. The identification with Γεβάλ, that is the Ebal near Shechem (see also *The Testaments*, 68) may well be an attempt by a scribe to make sense of a text which had become unintelligible to him.

[46] On this section see now especially D. HAUPT, *op.cit.*, 23-27. Columns *a* and *b* of the Cambridge Genizah fragments published by CHARLES are unfortunately too mutilated to be of much use. This account must have given a fuller description of the negotiations on circumcision than T.L. VI,3.

[47] Contrary to what is suggested in the note on VI, 7 in the *editio minima*, ἐμαλακίσθη must be considered as the right reading. The last sentence in vs 7 explains why Jacob did not interfere when his sons attacked Shechem.

[48] Note the καὶ οὕτως in vs 9 and καίγε οὕτως in vs 10!

[49] There must be a literary relationship between these verses (so D. HAUPT, *op.cit.*, 25, n. 68 contra J. BECKER, *op.cit.*, 258, n. 1). The hypothesis that a Christian used this anti-Judaic phrase to crown his description of the complete destruction of Shechem remains more probable than the assumption that T.L. VI, 11 was quoted in Christian anti-Judaic polemic. T.L. VI, 11 may go back to a phrase in Or. Levi – see Jub. XXX, 5 and XXX, 26 (comp. Gen. XXXV, 5) – and may therefore be earlier than the present Testaments; but did this phrase exist in Greek so as to be quoted by a Christian in the first century?

XVI

THE MEANING OF NAPHTALI'S VISIONS

TH. KORTEWEG

I. *Introduction*

As has been rightly observed by a recent author,[1] no more controversial subject in the field of later Jewish literature can be found than that of the origin of the Testaments of the Twelve Patriarchs. Questions that were debated by nineteenth century critics today still give rise to fundamental disagreement among scholars and there are only very few points on which a consensus may be said to exist. It is true that in some respects the discussion has undergone a considerable shift. Theories of interpolation, on the whole, seem to be less popular now than they were a century ago.[2] Consequently there is no longer much confidence in attempts to reconstruct an original Jewish document simply by dropping certain patently Christian passages. On the other hand, those scholars also who consider the Testaments in their present form as a Christian composition, thereby following a view first advocated by K. J. Nitzsch and afterwards modified by M. de Jonge, must concede that the materials from which the book draws are mainly of Jewish origin and were probably circulating in some form or other in Jewish circles about the beginning of our era. Moreover, new methods of literary criticism have been applied to the study of the Testaments too, especially that of form-criticism. Accordingly, a number of scholars have hoped to gain new insight into the structure of the book as a whole by trying to isolate as far as possible the more or less independent units of which

---

[1] "Er is nauwelijks een onderwerp te bedenken, waarover zoveel verschil van mening bestaat als over de ontstaansgeschiedenis van de Test. der twaalf patriarchen".—A. S. van der Woude in Th. C. Vriezen and A. S. van der Woude, *De Literatuur van Oud-Israël*, 1973[4], p. 361.

[2] Attention may be drawn, however, to the attempts of J. C. O'Neill to reintroduce this typical nineteenth century approach in New Testament criticism in his recent commentary on the *Epistle to the Romans*. No doubt a lot of injustice has been done to many eminent critics of the last century by simply by-passing their theories as 'out of date', in stead of judging them on their own merits.

it is believed to consist. Notable among them is J. Becker whose
*Untersuchungen zur Entstehungsgeschichte der Testamente der zwölf
Patriarchen* appeared in 1970. His general view and several of his
particular opinions have already been dealt with elsewhere in this
volume.[3] In this connection we may illustrate his critical method
by pointing briefly to his analysis of the passages from *T. Napht.*
with which this paper is concerned. They are chapters V-VII of
the Greek Testament, which are paralleled by chapters II-VII of
the Hebrew document called צוואת נפתלי בן יעקב to which attention
was first drawn by M. Gaster in 1893.[4]

According to Becker it is of crucial importance that in the course
of the narrative of Naphtali's first vision, as it is contained in ch. V
of the Greek Testament, we find a threefold repetition of the intro-
ductory formula καὶ ἰδού (vss 2.6.8). This means that we are confronted
by "not one or two, but three dreams put into a sequence without
a material connection, but nevertheless in 5, 1; 6, 1; 7, 1 presented
as a single dream".[5] That the dreams are in fact unrelated is apparent
as soon as we observe that their meaning can only be understood
if each is explained individually. In the parallel account of Naphtali's
visions in Hebrew the situation is quite different. There it is clearly
impossible to separate three dreams from one another. This leads
Becker to assume that the Greek Testament, where the dividing
lines are still visible, must, on the whole, represent the earlier stage
of composition, whereas the Hebrew Testament shows unmistakable
signs of later adaptation and harmonization. This impression is
confirmed moreover by the fact that the author of the Hebrew
seems to be strongly opposed to the figure of Joseph who, in the
Greek Testaments, is always presented as a model of virtue and
wisdom. In fact this deprecatory tendency may well have started
from the rather sudden introduction of Joseph in an unfavourable
sense in VI,6.8 of the Greek Testament, but those verses clearly
interrupt the context and have to be omitted from a reconstruction
of the original.

As far as the dissimilarity in the evaluation of Joseph is concerned,
Becker more or less repeats one of the objections already made by

---

[3] See especially ch. X and ch. XIII.

[4] M. Gaster, The Hebrew Text of one of the Testaments of the XII Patriarchs,
Proc. of the Soc. of Bibl. Archaeology XVI (1893-94), pp. 33sqq.

[5] *O.c.*, p. 107.

Charles, in the Introduction to his edition of 1908, against Gaster's assumption that in the Hebrew document we have recovered the original form of *T. Napht.*[6] After Charles had concluded his discussion of the newly published text by dismissing it as a "Hebrew *réchauffé* of a late and conflate character", the case was not reopened until as late as 1953, when M. de Jonge tried to show that both the Greek and the Hebrew narrative probably derive from one source which he called *Or. Napht.* Becker, however, thinks that form-criticism still leads to the position held by Charles and that there is not much to be said in favour of De Jonge's assumption of an original document underlying both the Greek and the Hebrew *Testament of Naphtali.* It seems to me, on the contrary, that there is a great deal to say in support of it and that form-criticism will never lead very far if it is applied too mechanically. In order to show this, a new attempt will be made to compare the Greek and Hebrew accounts of Naphtali's visions, each within its different setting. In this way some fresh light may be thrown on their mutual relationship. At the same time, I hope to offer a small contribution to the further clarification of the vexing problem of the origin of the Testaments as such. My general impression is that the composition of that title, which has come down to us in a number of Greek MSS. and several translations, shows many secondary developments of Jewish materials of probably diverse origin. In some cases these developments suggest that the author responsible for them may well have been a Christian.

II. *Naphtali's visions in the Greek Testament*

Together with ch. IX, ch. I,1-4 provides the biographical framework of the Greek Testament. In I,5 the patriarch's last words to his sons begin with the twofold introduction-formula that is common in wisdom literature. Next, from I,6-12, Naphtali presents us with full details of his genealogy, adding some special information about his mother (vss 9-12).[7] In II,1 the life story of the patriarch first continues,

---

[6] R. H. Charles, *The Greek Versions of the Testaments of the Twelve Patriarchs*, Oxford 1908, pp. LIIsq.

[7] I only mention in passing that J. T. Milik, Prière de Nabonide et autres récits d'un cycle de Daniel ..., *R.B.* 63 (1956), p. 407 n. 1 has announced a yet unpublished fragment of a Hebrew Testament of Naphtali, containing Bilhah's genealogy "dans une rédaction bien plus longue que celle du Test. XII Patr. grec, *Test. Nepht.* I,6-12". According to Milik "l'identification est hors de doute, puisque le héros du récit appelle Bilha 'ma mère', Jacob 'mon père' et Dan '(mon) frère'".

but then is suddenly interrupted from vs 2 onwards with a long piece of exhortation which does not come to a close until the end of ch. III. In ch. IV we have what has been termed by De Jonge a S.E.R.-passage.[8] A remarkable feature in it is the repetition of the sin-exile-return pattern in vss 4sq.: having been brought back into the land of their fathers, Naphtali's sons will sin again and be scattered over the face of the earth "until the Lord's compassion (τὸ σπλάγχνον Κυρίου) shall come, a man working righteousness and showing mercy to all those who are far off and all those who are near" (vs 5). The last words remind us strongly of *Eph.* II,17 (cf. II,13), where we find a description of the coming of Christ Jesus (vs 13; cf. ἐλθών vs 17)[9] with his mission of peace ὑμῖν τοῖς μακρὰν καὶ... τοῖς ἐγγύς. Probably however, we must here reckon with an allusion to *Is.* LVII,19 LXX: εἰρήνην τοῖς μακρὰν καὶ τοῖς ἐγγὺς οὖσιν, a passage that may also have had an immediate influence on *T. Napht.* IV,5. In any case it is important to notice that ch. IV ends with a prophecy announcing the coming of an eschatological saviour.

In ch. V there follows the account of the first vision. The particle γάρ (vs 1) can be taken to suggest a link with the preceding section,[10] but before we can decide if such a connection makes sense, we must proceed to an interpretation of the vision itself. The scene is set "on the Mount of Olives, east of Jerusalem, when the sun and the moon were standing still" (vs 1). Isaac commands his grandsons to run as fast as they can and catch the heavenly bodies in front of them. As a result Levi gets hold of the sun while Judah catches the moon. The use of the verbs προσδραμεῖν/ἐπιδραμεῖν and κρατεῖν should be noted. Next Levi "being as the sun" (vs 4) is given twelve βαία φοινίκων by a certain young man. At the same time Judah

---

[8] On these passages in general see M. de Jonge, *The Testaments of the Twelve Patriarchs...*, Assen 1953, pp. 83-86. Neither the pattern itself nor its repetition are, of course, limited to the *Test. XII Patr.* Cf. e.g. *Ass. Mos.* V-VI and on the whole matter O. H. Steck's fundamental study quoted below in n. 31.

[9] On the "coming" of a saviour cf. G. D. Kilpatrick, Acts 7, 52, ἔλευσις, *J.T.S.* 46(1945), pp. 136-145. In the Testaments the motif is connected with an eschatological figure from Levi and Judah. I think it originally belonged to the deuteronomic concept of a "prophet like Moses". Afterwards also a royal or a priestly figure could be expected to "come". I hope to set out my views on this matter on another occasion.

[10] The particle γάρ does not necessarily provide a link with the immediately preceding passage, it can also refer further back. Cf. J. D. Denniston, *The Greek Particles*, Oxford 1970², pp. 63sqq. Or it can simply mark a transition.

is shining as the moon and beneath his feet appear twelve rays (ἀκτῖνες). This description of Levi and Judah is a clear reminiscence of the passages in the Testaments where a similar portrait of an eschatological saviour is given. In e.g. *T. Levi* XVIII,4 the coming of a "new priest" is announced, who will "shine as the sun" (οὗτος ἀναλάμψει ὡς ὁ ἥλιος). We may also compare *T. Jud.* XXIV,2 where we hear that from Judah's seed a man will arise who is like "the sun of righteousness" and especially *T. Levi* IV,3 where there is a promise to Levi that he shall be "like the sun" to all Israel (ὡς ὁ ἥλιος ἔσῃ παντὶ τῷ σπέρματι Ἰσραήλ). It would seem evident that the description of Levi's and Judah's glory in *T. Napht.* V,4 has been consciously modelled on the same pattern. Besides, against this background we can also explain why in vss 3sqq. the remaining brothers, including Naphtali himself, stay so utterly unsuccessful, although Isaac had clearly addressed them all. The author of the Greek Testament understands the race to be for the messianic dignity of resembling the sun or the moon [11] and therefore limits his attention to the two tribes to whose province this dignity belongs. Vs 5 goes on stressing their unity and it is interesting to note that in this connection the verbs that were used in vs 2 recur although in a quite different sense. This confirms the impression, already awakened by the incongruities of vs 4 relative to the beginning of the story, that in these two verses we are confronted by at least some amount of redactional activity.

The pictures change without transition. In vs 6 an enormous bull appears and to judge from the use of the verb πιάσαι (cf. vss 2sq.) and the participle φθάσας in vs 7 (cf. vs 3: ὁ Ἰούδας φθάσας ἐπίασε τὴν σελήνην) another race begins between the brothers to get hold of it, won this time by Joseph who is lifted up with the bull into the height. Thereupon this scene too breaks off and by way of the stereotype καὶ ἰδού something new is announced. To Naphtali there appears a γραφὴ ἁγία prophesying the exile of the "twelve sceptres of Israel". This concludes the first vision.

In ch. VI,1 we hear that after seven months Naphtali receives a second vision. Jacob and his sons are standing on the shore of the sea of Jamnia. In front of them a ship comes sailing by, bearing the name "Jacob", and they all embark. A terrible storm blows

---

[11] Compare the use of the sun and the moon as symbols for royal dignity in passages like *Ps* LXXXIX,36sq.

Jacob away while standing at the helm. In vss 5-7 there is a lively account of a shipwreck. With vs 5 we may compare *Jonah* I,4 LXX : καὶ τὸ πλοῖον ἐκινδύνευσε συντριβῆναι and *Mc.* IV,37 : ὥστε ἤδη γεμίζεσθαι τὸ πλοῖον. Vs 6 recalls two passages from *Acts* XXVII : first the attempt of the sailors to abandon ship during the storm by escaping on a boat (vss 30-32), then the rescue of part of Paul's company who cling to planks that were floating around after the ship had been wrecked (vs 44). These features seem to form part of a standing description. Here again the unity of Levi and Judah is stressed (vs 6). Moreover, it is to Levi's prayer (vs 8) that the final salvation is due. The storm calms down and the ship reaches land safely (τὸ σκάφος ἔφθασε ἐπὶ τὴν γῆν cf. *John* VI,21 : καὶ εὐθέως ἐγένετο τὸ πλοῖον ἐπὶ τῆς γῆς ...). In vs 10 we read how Jacob also returns and a general rejoicing follows. Here the second vision closes. As we have seen, it shows clear traces of a composition according to the more or less fixed pattern which is often detected in stories about a rescue from distress at sea. The rescue itself is the main point of the narrative. Naphtali's vision describes how the ship named "Jacob" has to endure a terrible storm in which it is nearly wrecked. From vs 9, however, we have to conclude that after all nothing serious has come to pass, in spite of the suggestion to the contrary to which the "planks" (σανίδες) of vs 6 at first seem to give rise. At the end peace and general rejoicing prevail. The words εἰρήνη and ἀγαλλίασις remind us of passages in the Testaments like *T. Levi* XVIII,5.(13).14, where the same terms are used to express eschatological bliss. Since they often have this function in the Septuagint as well as in the rest of later Jewish literature, we may wonder whether the joy of *T. Napht.* V,4 does not convey the same idea.

This suggestion seems indeed to accord well with the explanation of Naphtali's dreams given by Jacob in VII,1 : δεῖ ταῦτα πληρωθῆναι κατὰ καιρὸν αὐτῶν πολλὰ τοῦ Ἰσραὴλ ὑπομείναντος.[12] Everything will be accomplished after Israel withstands a great deal of suffering. The implication is that the fulfilment alluded to, can only be that eschatological restoration, to which the chapter immediately preceding the visions refers as do certain particulars within the visions themselves. Throughout them a kind of gradual development is visible. At the end of the first dream the exile is spoken of (V,8), in ch. VI a storm

---

[12] Cf. the similar remark after Joseph's vision in *T. Jos.* XIX,10.

indicates new sufferings for the house of Jacob,[13] but after the intercession of Levi the whole matter concludes on a note of peace and joy. That this conclusion had already been in view from the beginning is suggested by the way in which the eschatological functions of Levi and Judah are stressed even in the first vision. So Jacob's interpretation seems to be perfectly natural and there is no need with M. de Jonge to stigmatize his words as "not quite fitting here".[14] In fact they show us what sense the author of the Greek Testament would like us to make of Naphtali's record about his visions. In their present form the dreams are meant to provide a parallel to the eschatological pattern set out in ch. IV. Together they illustrate the line along which the history of Israel is to develop, first towards the exile and then towards the final restoration hinted at in VI,9.10. Since according to the eschatology of the Greek Testaments it is from Levi and Judah that the final salvation issues, their part in the visions also receives full attention. Apart from them only Joseph is mentioned by name. The reason for this we do not yet perceive. In any case it is not suggested by the story as we find it in the Greek Testament. We shall be able to say more about it, if we now turn to our next subject which is an analysis of the parallel account of Naphtali's visions in the Hebrew document.

III. *Naphtali's visions in Hebrew*

The Hebrew Testament opens with a short dialogue between the patriarch and his sons. In I,5 he exhorts them to fear the Lord. Next follows a prophecy of future apostasy introduced in vs 8 by יראתי 'I fear' (cf. *T. Benj.* IX,1 ὑπονοῶ) and in vs 10 a second time by ידעתי which recalls the frequent οἶδα of the Greek Testaments. Naphtali announces that his sons will forsake the Lord[15] and follow after the customs of "the peoples of the lands".[16] This will happen because they will join the sons of Joseph and separate from Levi and Judah. This is further elaborated in vs 10. We hear that the

---

[13] Cf. the repetition of the S.E.R. scheme in ch. IV.

[14] *O.c.*, p. 56.

[15] The verb תעה "apostatize" occurs several times in the book *Ez.* in rather stereotype passages: XIV,11; XLIV,10 (2×); XLIV,15; XLVIII,11 (2×). Cf. especially XLIV,10: תעו אחרי גלוליהם.

[16] This resembles the idiom of *Chron.* In *Neh.* X,29 those who decide for the law of God are characteristically called כל־הנבדל מעמי הארצות אל־תורת האלהים.

בני יוסף will depart from YHWH, the God of their fathers, and afterwards seduce "the sons of Israel" to do the same. So they will be the cause of the exile that is to follow as a punishment. Linked up with this prophecy is the account of the first vision (ch. II-III).

Naphtali receives it while he is tending his sheep (בהיותי רועה בצאן II,1). Although the Greek Testament tells us nothing about this circumstance, we may see a comparison in *T. Levi* II,3 where Levi begins the account of his first vision by pointing to a similar situation: ὡς δὲ ἐποιμαίνομεν ἐν 'Αβελμαούλ... Naphtali watches himself and his brothers while they are in the field with their flocks. This time not Isaac, but Jacob himself summons his sons to a race. When they ask what will be the goal, Jacob points to the sun, the moon and the stars. Levi and Judah each grasp a staff (מרדע), whereupon Levi jumps upon the sun, while Judah sits down on the moon. The rest of the brothers content themselves with the stars, with the exception of Joseph who refuses to listen to his father's command and is determined to stay on earth, while this is appropriate for the son of a woman.[17] While Joseph is still speaking to his father, a bull appears (III,1). Jacob tells him to get hold of the bull and ride upon him. This time Joseph obeys and Jacob thereupon disappears (III,2sq.). For four hours Joseph proudly rides his bull (III,4), but then a conflict with Judah breaks out because Judah has twelve rods (מרדעות) in his hands and Joseph only one (III,6). Joseph succeeds in depriving Judah of ten out of the twelve rods that were in his possession (III,7) and then persuades ten of his brothers to depart from Levi and Judah (III,8sq.). The result is that only Benjamin is left to them (III,11sq.). A mighty tempest (רוח גדולה) now separates Joseph from his brothers (III,12) and all are scattered. This brings the vision to a close. When Naphtali tells his father about it, Jacob declares the whole thing to be an idle dream, because it has not been repeated (כי לא משנה הוא III,13).

Nevertheless after a short time a repetition takes place. Naphtali watches Jacob and his sons while they are standing on the shore of the Great Sea (ים הגדול IV,2). In front of them a ship comes sailing by without a sailor and without a pilot בלא מלח ובלא איש cf. Gr. *T. Napht.* VI,2: ἐκτὸς ναυτῶν καὶ κυβερνήτου). Jacob throws himself into the sea, his sons, Levi and Judah first (IV,4), follow

---

[17] Joseph's words are here of a proverbial character and fit in with his general reputation for wisdom.

after him. The ship's cargo consists of "all the goodness of the world"
(כל טוב שבעולם IV,6). In IV,7-9 we hear about the name of the ship.
According to an inscription written on the mast it belongs with
its cargo to the son of him who is blessed by God (בן ברכואל IV,8).
From this Jacob concludes that God has blessed him not only on
land, but also on the sea (IV,9). In order that each of his sons may
get his share he commands them to seize anything they can get.
Here the wording strikingly resembles that of II,2 :

II,2	IV,10
בניי רוצו ותיפסו	בני עתע תתגברו
לפניי כל אחד אשר	וכל אחד בה שיתפוס
יעלה בחלקו	הוא חלקו

The twelve sons each must try to get their חלק.[18] The use of the
verb תפס recalls κρατεῖν in the Greek Testament V,2sqq. But the
remarkable thing, which has no parallel in Greek, is surely this
close similarity of the framework in which both visions are set.

This time the result of the competition among the brothers is
that Levi climbs the main mast of the ship, Judah the smaller mast,
while the rest of the brothers, again with the exception of Joseph,
each take an oar (IV, 11-13). Jacob acts as steersman (IV,13).
In spite of his father's summons Joseph refuses to take his oar.
Instead Jacob entrusts him with one of the rudders (IV,15) and,
before disappearing (V,1), instructs each of his sons (IV,16). Soon
a quarrel arises between Joseph, now acting as the only helmsman,
and Judah who, from his mast, determines the course the ship has
to take. As a result the ship goes wrong and is dashed on a rock
(V,5). Levi and Judah come down from their masts and with their
brothers safely reach the shore (VI,1). On his return Jacob finds
his sons scattered around, one here, the other there (מטורפין אחד הנה
ואחד הנה VI,2). After a short dialogue with his sons in which they
blame Joseph (VI,4), he puts everything in order again (VI,5-7) and
ends by upbraiding Joseph severely.

When Naphtali also reports the second vision to his father, Jacob
bursts into tears (VII,1). The reason for this appears to be that
the second dream is obviously a repetition of the first one (על הישנות ⋯
החזון VII,4). And since the purport of both dreams is the same,
they have to be taken as one (חזון אחד הוא VII,5). This means that

---

[18] Cf. Gr. *T. Iss.* V,5 : μερίς and our discussion under IV,2 below.

the prophecy contained in them will be fulfilled : because of Joseph Israel shall be led captive (VII,4). Naphtali now finishes his report with an exhortation to his sons which clearly resumes I,8-10 : "Therefore (על כן), my sons, I command you (מצוה cf. the frequent ἐντέλλομαι in the Greek Testaments) not to unite with the sons of Joseph, but only with Levi and Judah".

If from the framework of Naphtali's visions in the Greek Testament it appears that both of them must be related to the promise of an eschatological saviour in IV,5, the setting in the Hebrew document is different. Here the visions are meant to illustrate Naphtali's prophecy concerning the rebellion against Levi and Judah of which his sons will be guilty. The main point of this warning as well as of the visions is clearly the contrast drawn between Levi and Judah on the one hand and Joseph on the other. As we have seen, the על כן of VII,6 reconnects the content of the visions with the predictions already given in ch. I. The catch-word now is not restoration, but apostasy. Of course in VI,5-7 we read how Jacob saves his sons from the trouble in which they have involved themselves. But what follows is not general rejoicing, as in the Greek Testament, but a severe reproach addressed to Joseph (VI,8sq.). And on hearing his son's report about his second dream, Jacob breaks into tears. It is curious that in the Greek Testament also we hear of tears shed by Jacob on being informed by Naphtali about his dreams, but, as we shall see presently, there the motive behind them is entirely different. In Greek the visions end on a note of joy pointing, according to Jacob's interpretation, to the final salvation which shall dawn when Israel's sufferings have come to an end. This obviously leaves no more room for either tears or warning. In Hebrew the last word is apostasy and the gloomy prospect of exile that is to follow in its wake.

IV. *Original elements*

A comparison of the Greek and Hebrew account of Naphtali's visions shows them to be related on many points. Thus the question arises about what kind of relationship we have to assume. As we have seen, the problem has been the subject of a lively debate among scholars ever since Gaster first tried to solve it by arguing for the priority of the Hebrew document. His conclusions were discarded by Charles who himself took what nearly amounted to the reverse position, and that position is, even in a more radical form, the one still maintained by J. Becker in his *Untersuchungen*. The form-critical arguments advanced by the latter, however, cannot conceal the fact that they rest on a strong bias against whichever of two alternative accounts appears to be the more elaborate and the more consistent with itself. To me it seems that, although we cannot neglect formal aspects, the matter at stake is above all one of content and general purport. If, as Becker rightly observes, the Hebrew text of Naphtali's visions is fuller and more coherent than the Greek, then this does not by itself and on mere formal grounds imply that it is also secondary, let alone that because of this it should be taken for granted that the Hebrew account depends directly on the Greek Testament. Now as regards the more substantial aspects of both narratives neither Charles nor Becker have done very much to destroy a decisive argument first put forward by Gaster and afterwards worked out in detail by De Jonge, which I may here quote in Gaster's original words: "The Greek counterpart of the Hebrew makes no sense and has no meaning at all; whilst the Hebrew is rounded off, and complete and perfectly clear".[19] Since, moreover, De Jonge has convincingly demonstrated that most particulars of the Greek account can only be understood if we compare their setting in the Hebrew narrative, whereas the reverse cannot anywhere be applied, general priority in my opinion has still to be assigned to the form in which Naphtali's visions appear in the Hebrew document, however late its present redaction may be. Of course one could object that my own analysis has been an attempt to show that in fact the Greek account does make sense in itself. This objection, however, would overlook a difference which we have already noted in passing, but which, in this conection, becomes a matter of primary importance: namely that whereas in the Hebrew document the content of the visions is intimately related to their framework, in the Greek Testament this relationship is largely of an artificial character and betrays a considerable amount of redactional activity. This will now be pointed out in some detail.

(1) In the analysis of the Hebrew account of Naphtali's visions occasional attention was paid to the close correspondences between them. Instead of presenting a full survey here, I might add just one

---

[19] M. Gaster, *o.c.*, p. 42.

important item to the list : in both visions the central motif is a
quarrel about leadership between Levi and Judah on the one hand
and Joseph on the other, leading to a division among Jacob's sons.
Now it is of crucial importance to realize that these correspondences
have a very special meaning. According to the theory advanced by
Jacob in III,13; VII,4sq. the visions must resemble one another so
closely in order to count as one. This in turn is to safeguard the
outcome of the prophecy contained in them. A single dream is taken
by Jacob to be no more than an idle delusion. If we now look to
the Greek Testament, the first thing we note is that there also
Naphtali's visions are referred to as constituting a pair (VII,1 :
τὰ δύο ἐνύπνια). Nevertheless the reason for it is nowhere apparent.
In fact, precisely those correspondences which are so striking in the
Hebrew account, are entirely lacking in the Greek. In the first vision
there is a race but no conflict between Levi-Judah and Joseph, in
the second (ch. VI) the conflict seems to have left some traces in
vs 6, but we do not find anything like a race. On the other hand,
in the first vision apart from the race nothing else happens at all,
while in the second full stress is laid on the tempest and the raging
of the sea which Jacob's sons have to endure on their journey.
So an expression like that of VII,1, which seems still to attach some
significance to the fact that there are two visions, is not borne
out by the actual account as found in the Greek Testament, whereas
in the Hebrew the importance given to the fact that the second
dream is only a repetition of the first is fully motivated by the
numerous internal correspondences between them.

Now it is beyond doubt that the theory which makes fulfilment
of a dream depend on its being repeated is of ancient oriental origin.[20]

---

[20] For this theory, of which *Gen.* XLI,25 gives a particularly striking example,
cf. Artemid. *Oneirocr.* IV,27 : τοὺς πολλάκις ὁρωμένους ὀνείρους, εἰ μὲν ἐκ μικρῶν
διαστημάτων βλέποιντο, ἀεὶ τὸ αὐτὸ σημαίνειν νόμιζε, τούτου δὲ ἕνεκα ὁρᾶσθαι
πολλάκις, τοῦ μᾶλλον αὐτοὺς προσέχειν καὶ πιστεύειν. The motif already occurs
in the Epic of Gilgamesh; cf. F. M. Th. de Liagre Böhl, *Het Gilgamesj Epos vertaald
en toegelicht*, Amsterdam 1958[3], pp. 129sq. In Herodotus there is one example in
I,107sq. Cf. H. R. Immerwahr, *Form and Thought in Herodotus*, Cleveland, Ohio 1966,
p. 163 n. 39, who supposes oriental tradition : "the duplication of the dream seems
to be unique in Herodotus...; it may have been in the Eastern tradition about
Cyrus, for duplicate dreams are common there...". In like manner How and Wells,
A Commentary on Herodotus, Oxford 1950[4], on 107,1 : the τῶν μάγων οἱ ὀνειροπόλοι
are "a genuine Oriental feature". Other possibilities are referred to by D. Fehling,
Die Quellenangaben bei Herodot (Unters. z. ant. Lit. u. Gesch. 9), Berlin-New York
1971, p. 143.

Thus in our case, there is no reason why we should in any event attribute it to the fancy of a late Hebrew author. However, the decisive point to be made in this connection concerns the observation that the same concept in all probability already formed part of the primitive substance from which the present Greek Testaments have been composed. This is shown by the parallel in *T. Levi* VIII,1.18. In this chapter Levi opens his report on the second vision dealing with his installation as a priest with the following words: "There again I saw something like the former" (πρᾶγμα ὥσπερ τὸ πρότερον vs 1). In vs 18 we hear about the conclusion at which he arrived: "And when I awoke, I understood this vision to be like the other one" (ὅτι τοῦτο ὅμοιον ἐκείνου ἐστιν). For this we have a counterpart in the Aramaic fragment from the Bodleian Library col. a l. 11: חזון הוא דן וכדן.[21] This implies that the idea of a pair of visions both having the same purport is not peculiar to the Greek *T. Levi*, but belongs to an older stratum of the material as it is found in the Aramaic fragments.[22] Hence we may conclude that this concept probably also dominated the account of Naphtali's visions in its original form. That its prominence in the present Hebrew document is not due to a late redactor is at least strongly suggested by the fact that it is not entirely absent from the Greek either, although here it is only preserved in a rudimentary form without further consequences either for the content of Naphtali's dreams or for their interpretation as given by Jacob. Now if the close correspondence between Naphtali's visions together with the theory underlying it are indeed primitive features, it is immediately clear that in the Greek Testament redactional activity must have gone to great lengths to disturb the original coherence and meaning of the whole.

(2) As we have seen, the perspective in which Naphtali's visions in the Greek Testament are placed is mainly that of the eschatological salvation spoken of beforehand in IV,5 and, within the visions themselves, referred to in VI,10; VII,1. This could explain the use made in the description of Levi and Judah in V,4sq. of standing features borrowed from eschatological passages elsewhere in the Testaments. Whereas in the Hebrew Testament Levi and Judah end up

---

[21] P. Grelot, *R.B.* 63(1956), pp. 399sq. proposes כדו ו as an emendation of וכדן.

[22] On the different opinions concerning the relationship between the Greek *T. Levi* and the Aramaic fragments see M. de Jonge's remarks near the end of his survey in ch. XIII.

by sitting on the sun and the moon and Judah is holding twelve rods signifying his leadership over his brothers, in the Greek the main accent is on the radiance resulting from Levi being *like* the sun and Judah *like* the moon. Accordingly the rods have become twelve rays appearing under Judah's feet, while to Levi an equal number of palm branches is given. The parallelism which thus exists between them is even extended to a unity in vs 5: both come near to one another and embrace. In the meantime the other brothers have withdrawn from the stage. The interest of the author is entirely centered on the relationship between the principal actors themselves. Therefore De Jonge may well have hit the mark with his reference to the combination of priesthood and kingship which, according to an early Christian view, existed in Christ.[23] This, of course, would imply that the author of the Greek *Testament of Naphtali* was a Christian.

As to this possibility a few remarks seem to be called for at this point. First of all, as to the eschatological colouring of the description of V,4sq., we should remind ourselves that precisely the eschatological passages found throughout the Testaments often bear a manifestly Christian stamp. We may even surmise that the Greek author was sometimes at odds with the dominant position which the material he used assigned, even with regard to Judah himself, to the person of Levi. So in *T. Napht.* VIII,2b.3 a traditional exhortation to obey Levi and Judah is followed by a promise, which might be taken as a correction inspired by the redactor's point of view, namely that from Judah salvation shall come not only for Israel, but also for the righteous amongst the gentiles. Also in *T. Napht.* V,5 the stress laid on the unity between Levi and Judah may well display a Christian interest. Secondly, the chapters from *T. Napht.* with which we are concerned here contain some phrases which almost look like an echo of the N.T. In the case of IV,5 I have already pointed to *Eph.* II,17. Moreover, the only exact parallel to the βάϊα φοινίκων which has been discovered in the whole of Greek literature until now occurs in *John* XIII,13.[24] Of course, in cases like these the possibility of

---

[23] *O.c.* (n. 8), p. 54.

[24] A parallel expression is given by Porph. *De abst.* IV,7 (ed. Nauck, p. 239 l. 25) to explain the originally Egyptian βάϊς: σπάδικες τοῦ φοίνικος. This expression is also pleonastic, for σπάδιξ is in its turn explained by Plut. *Quaest. conv.* VIII,4,3 (724A) as κλάδον τοῦ ἱεροῦ φοίνικος.

another explanation can never be excluded. Still the very presence of a tendency towards the enhancement of Levi and Judah in their combined eschatological functions makes De Jonge's suggestion at least worthy of consideration. In any case, if Christian influence is to be assumed at all in the passages under consideration here, it is certainly impossible to account for it by a theory of interpolation. The changes to which this influence would have given rise are far too subtle and too intricately interwoven with the fabric of the whole to allow an explanation like that. So it is e.g. quite evident, that the glorification of Levi and Judah in V,4.5 not only refers back to the prediction of IV,5, but also anticipates the role which according to VI,8 is assumed especially by Levi in the rescue of his brothers from the shipwreck which had dispersed them. It is to the saving activity of Levi and Judah that the final restoration of Israel shall be due.

Now whatever Jewish or Christian purpose the framework of Naphtali's visions in the Greek Testament should be supposed to serve, it is clear that because of it many motifs contained in the materials used by the redactor had to be severely strained and distorted. So the verbs used in the context of the race in V,2.3, προσδραμεῖν and κρατεῖν occur again in V,5 with quite a different meaning. Moreover, it remains strange that in both Naphtali's dreams compared with Levi, Judah and Joseph, the other brothers so completely disappear into the background. This seems the more striking since in other passages of the Greek Testaments it is clear that, although Levi and Judah occupy a position of preeminence, the part played by their brothers is not merely that of bystanders. On the contrary, a text like T. Jud. XXV,1sq., which certainly contains some primitive material, clearly suggests that each of the brothers gets his special share. It is this μερίς which in T. Iss. V,5 is described as a blessing bestowed on Jacob's sons by the Lord through the mouth of their father. It implies all kinds of worldly riches. Exactly the same concept we meet with in the Hebrew T. Napht. II,2 and again in IV,10, where Jacob tells his sons to run (רוץ = Gr. προσδραμεῖν) for their share (חלק). If, in the first vision, only sun, moon and stars, and a bull are mentioned in this connection, the ship which appears in the second vision is loaded with "all the goodness of the world". With all this Jacob has been blessed by the Lord and he now wants to hand it over to his sons in turn: each of them receives what is due to him, while at the same time the preeminence of Levi and

Judah is safeguarded in that they take possession of the sun and
the moon in the first vision and of the two big masts in the second.
Both times Joseph alone presents a problem and in each case his
refusal to take part then sets the stage for further action. Thus
we find that in the Greek account the motif of a race, apart from
being confined to the first vision only, is entirely subservient to
the glorification of Levi, Judah and Joseph, to the exclusion of
the other brothers, whereas in the Hebrew it has preserved its full
meaning in both visions, a meaning moreover that is linked up with
a primitive concept which has left its stamp even on some of the
materials by now only attested in the Greek Testaments.

(3) This brings us to that which in my opinion is the central issue.
It was noted above that among the many corresponding features
which bind together Naphtali's visions in their Hebrew redaction,
belongs also what has to be considered the central motif of each,
viz. the quarrel about leadership between Levi and Judah on one
side and Joseph on the other. In the Greek account this whole
symmetry proved to be conspicuously absent. Even the fact that
in VI,6 as in V,5 the unity of Levi and Judah is stressed—a unity
which according to VI,6 exists over against Joseph—acquires within
the present context no intellegible meaning for the story as such.
In fact, it never appears why Joseph is mentioned at all. Now it
is true that J. Becker regards his role in the second vision as being
due to an early interpolation. As a general rule, however, the deletion
of a passage should not become too easy a substitute for explaining it.
In this case a satisfactory explanation of what, at first sight, looks
like senseless incoherence, seems quite possible as soon as it is granted
that by imposing his design on the materials at his disposal the author
of the Greek Testament could hardly avoid creating a certain amount
of obscurity. On the basis of this assumption we may now venture
the following reconstruction of what, in all probability, came about.

First, the motif of a storm scattering Jacob's sons was transferred
from the first to the second vision, the reason for this being partly
that it was so completely suited for a shipwreck story, partly that
in a course of events reaching its climax in the glorification of Levi,
Judah and Joseph, there was no longer much use for it. Once all
reference to a quarrel between these protagonists (which in the Hebrew
Testament provides the clue to the whole) had been dropped, the idea
of a storm following as a punishment obviously had to go the same
way. Moreover, why should a storm continue to separate a company

part of which had already disappeared into the air, leaving the others standing as they did on the earth? On the other hand, if in the second vision every notion of a dispute between Judah and Joseph about whom should direct the ship's course had to be cleared away, then another reason for the disaster, which inevitably was to precede the soteriological climax of the narrative, had to be invented. For this purpose the author could now avail himself of the storm motif dropped in the first dream, while at the same time using the opportunity to introduce some other set features of shipwreck stories such as an escape by way of a boat in the midst of the storm,[25] the floating around in the water on planks (σανίδες)[26] and the prayer of a righteous man which saves the whole crew.[27] In this way also the disappearance of Jacob, which, although a necessary ingredient of the story, in the Hebrew Testament has something enigmatic about it, could now be explained as being caused by the wind that had blown him away. As will be obvious, by bringing into play all these expediences the author of the Greek Testament eventually had to change the pattern of the story as a whole, directing it towards an entirely new climax. We have seen, that this is now provided by vv 8-10: as a result of Levi's prayer the sons of Jacob are saved from their dispersion. But why were they dispersed at all? To this question the only answer left by now is to refer to the tempest so vividly described in vss 4 sq. The tempest itself, however, appears wholly unmotivated. It is just the disaster needed in a story which according to the design of its author should result in a rescue operation.

Now all this seems to leave the explicit mention of Levi, Judah and Joseph in VI,6 quite pointless. Even if from the interest shown in the unity of the first two in V,5 we could understand why the same feature should have been preserved where it occurred in the original form of the second vision, this does not explain why also Joseph should still have a part to play. In the Hebrew account, of course, the importance attached to his person is quite obvious. There Joseph is made responsible for Israel's rebellion against the leadership of Levi and Judah which leads to the exile. Must the

---

[25] Cf. *Acts* XXVII 30.

[26] Cf. *Acts* XXVII,44.

[27] Cf. *Acts* XXVII,24. Moreover it is instructive to compare with *T. Napht* VI,5 the parallels listed above on p. 266 from *Mc.* IV,37 and *Jonah* I,4LXX.

reference to Joseph in the Greek Testament VI,6 still be taken in the same unfavourable sense? We have seen that Becker clearly answered this question in the affirmative while at the same time suggesting that we are faced with an interpolation. To me this seems rather improbable. In the Greek Testament Joseph doesn't act at all before the disaster has already reached its climax and even then only to save his life. There is nothing dishonourable about that. Moreover, as to the actual meaning of Joseph's flight within the present context, more attention should be paid in my opinion to Jacob's reaction in VII,2: "I believe that Joseph is alive, because I see always that God shall include him within your number". If this is to be connected with the preceding visions at all (and to my mind the τότε with which vs 2 opens undeniably points in that direction), the most likely reference seems to be to the escape by boat spoken of in VI,6. So in the Greek Testament there is no shred of evidence that this flight should even in the least lead to Joseph's discredit. On the other hand, it is easy to point out that far from owing to an interpolation all this represents a deliberate device by the Greek author. For Jacob's words in VII,2.3 must have belonged originally to a haggadic tradition to which there is also a reference in the Greek *T. Napht.* II,1. Because of his speed Naphtali is compared to a hind and is therefore appointed by Jacob to act as a messenger. Now two of the targumim on *Gen.* XLIX,21 after a similar characterization of Naphtali add a remark which in this context strikingly reminds us of Jacob's words in reaction to the report of Naphtali's dreams. As one of Naphtali's feats as a messenger we hear of the fact that "he brought the news to our father Jacob first of all, that Joseph was still living".[28] To me it seems clear that this provides the necessary background for a scene as depicted in Gr. *T. Napht.* VII,2. In the source on which the Greek author was drawing Jacob must have been expressing his belief in a message to some such effect, delivered a moment before by his son Naphtali. Instead of hearing about this message, however, we must now content ourselves with the short hint contained in the second vision. Even so it is still Naphtali's function to convince his father that Joseph is alive. With this the author now connects a theme that is highly characteristic

---

[28] So the *Fragmentary Targum* and the *Targum Ps.-Jonathan* in J. Bowker's translation (*The Targums and rabbinic Literature*, Cambridge 1969, pp. 286 and 280; cf. also the materials collected in the note on p. 291).

of his personal treatment of the Joseph story throughout the Testaments. The tears of Jacob in vs 3 (which in the supposed original may have been meant as tears of joy) obviously remind him of the many tears over Joseph's misfortune shed elsewhere in the Testaments, e.g. in *T. Zeb.* I,5sq. where Zebulon tells how he was weeping about Joseph in secret for fear of his brothers. It is just in the same fashion that Naphtali here apologizes about his reluctance to tell Jacob of the sale of Joseph by confessing that he was afraid of his brothers (ἀλλ᾽ ἐφοβούμην τοὺς ἀδελφούς μου). So the common κλαυθμός, as we find it in VII,4 of the Greek Testament, although not quite in keeping either with the visions or with the first part of ch. VII itself, fits in nicely with the general tendency displayed in the fragments of the Joseph story, distributed over the various Testaments in order to serve as a kind of agglutinating substance keeping the present Greek collection together.

This suggests that the entire seventh chapter offers a prime example of the rather clumsy effort by which the author of the Greek Testaments reworks a motif which originally belonged to genuine haggadic tradition. By doing this he seems to have had at least a double purpose. First, taking up the motif of Naphtali's role as a messenger to inform his father about the fact that Joseph was still alive obviously enabled him to give an entirely new appearance to Joseph's presence in Naphtali's dreams now his role could no longer be that of the main actor around whom the whole drama evolved. Secondly, by connecting this motif with other elements of the Joseph story, Naphtali's biography, which with ch. VII assumes what to some extent looks like a completed form,[29] is now also connected with those of the other patriarchs, in which the motif of Joseph's selling is usually one of the more prominent features.

By now there can no longer be any doubt that the interpretation of Naphtali's visions as we find them in the Greek Testament depends

---

[29] If my view on VII,2sq. is correct, these verses resume II,1 and with it provide a biographical framework in which materials from various origins have been inserted. On the whole the link between biography and paraenesis is more strongly accentuated in the Greek Testaments than in the preserved Hebrew and Aramaic fragments. Possibly the wisdom-teaching of *T. Napht.* II,2sqq. had originally no connection with the biographical motif of II,1 at all, whereas the biographical 'unit' itself served as an introduction to the testament proper, mainly consisting of moral and religious instructions.

to a far greater extent on the framework supplied by the redactor, than on the materials to which this had to give shape. Within this framework and consequently also within the Greek redaction of the visions themselves Joseph is always spoken of favourably. There is no mention of his attempts to stir up his brothers against the authority of Levi and Judah and a warning against his dangerous influence is found neither here nor anywhere else in the Greek Testaments. Instead in ch. VII the Greek redactor reminds us of the significance which he usually attributes to the Joseph story, namely that of bringing to the forefront either the honest dealing or the sin and subsequent repentance of each of the patriarchs. To this redactor moreover Joseph himself always represents the very embodiment of virtue and piety. As we have seen, the reverse holds true for the narrative of the Hebrew document. This therefore must stand much nearer to the original from which also the Greek redactor drew his materials. In an appendix I shall show that the hostility towards Joseph as well as the idea of a contrast between him and Levi and Judah are indeed not to be taken as a tendency introduced by a medieval Jewish author, but as primitive features in keeping with a whole set of concepts which, as far as I can see, must have prevailed in the religious milieu from which the tradition underlying the Testaments probably drew its origin.

In the meantime I may conclude my discussion of how we should disengage the original elements contained in the different redactions of Naphtali's visions by pointing out with appropriate emphasis that neither the Greek Testament nor its Hebrew counterpart can on its own account be taken as an adequate representative of the haggadic tradition which underlies both, and which may or may not already have taken the form of a 'testament' itself. As to the Greek account, the previous discussion will have made this abundantly clear. As to the Hebrew, however, some further comments may yet seem desirable. First then, let us remember that the motif of Naphtali acting as a messenger and informing his father that Joseph is still alive, which certainly derives from primitive haggadic tradition, nowhere occurs in the Hebrew document at all, whereas in the Greek Testament it has only been partly misplaced. The same might apply to a somewhat obscure passage in the course of Naphtali's report on his first dream found in Gr. *T. Napht.* V,8. Personally I think a case can be made for considering this verse as indeed containing some primitive substance, especially if the reading ἐν κήποις of *gldm* A is accepted as original.

Then also the Greek Testament could be interpreted to represent Naphtali in one detail at least engaged as a shepherd while he receives his visions.[30] However, a prediction of the exile at the end of the first vision neatly conforms to the general design of the Greek redactor and is probably intended to contrast with the idea of a final rescue, which, by virtue of its place at the end of the second dream also functions as a conclusion to the whole. Therefore here also we must reckon with the possibility of misplacement. In any event, in the Hebrew document no trace of it can be found at all and this may be due to a deliberate omission. On the other hand this text, apart from the general priority that according to my previous discussion has to be assigned to its narrative content as such, contains some features which, though being unparalleled in the present Greek *T. Napht.*, yet show a somehow primitive origin by the striking resemblance which they bear to similar passages elsewhere in the Greek Testaments. A situation like this was already indicated above in the description of the cargo with which the ship appearing in Naphtali's second dream is loaded according to Hebr. *T. Napht.* IV,6sqq. To this I may now add such instances as the remark on Naphtali's "good old age" in Hebr. *T. Napht.* I,1 : בא בשבה טובה, with which one should compare e.g. Gr. *T. Iss.* VII,9 : καὶ ἀπέθανε... ἐν γήρει καλῷ. If, moreover, we ought to translate the subsequent ובא שלם בגברתו not with Charles as "and had completed his years of strength", but as "and had remained in good health, in his strength", the comparison might even include that which follows the words quoted from *T. Iss.* VII,9 : πᾶν μέλος ἔχων ὑγιὲς καὶ ἰσχύων (cf. *T. Napht.* I,2 : ὑγιαίνοντος αὐτοῦ). To mention only one more point, the dialogue between Naphtali and his sons as recorded in the Hebrew *T. Napht.* I,2-8a finds an interesting counterpart in the Greek *T. Levi* XIX,1-3. One should especially compare the patriarch's solemn invocation of God as a witness to the promise of obedience made by his sons in Hebr. *T. Napht.* I,8a and *T. Levi* XIX,3. Of course the whole scenery represents a development of biblical passages such as *Josh.* XXIV 14-27.

From all this it is clear that original elements deriving from a haggadic tradition pertaining to Naphtali's visions are sometimes present in both, sometimes only in one of the accounts which have come down to us. This means that, since in this situation neither

---

[30] See further in ch. XI.

of them is likely to represent the immediate source of the other, we must assume an original document on which both have drawn independently. In this document, however, the meaning of Naphtali's visions must have come nearest to that which is still attached to them by the late Hebrew redactor. In the Hebrew Testament Naphtali's account is straightforward and coherent in respect of almost every detail, whereas in the Greek we discovered a considerable amount of tension between the materials used by the redactor and the framework to which they were adapted. In their original form Naphtali's visions had no properly eschatological implication at all. They were simply a prediction of future apostasy brought about by the sons of Joseph and of the coming exile. At the same time they implied a warning for the patriarch's sons to stay with Levi and Judah and not to rebel against the divinely appointed rulers which, in a lengthy succession, were to proceed from these tribes. Since for the Greek author these rulers all contracted into one eschatological saviour issuing from Levi and Judah, who brings about the final restoration of Israel as well as the salvation of the Gentiles, the contrast with Joseph had to lose almost all of its meaning. That is why the prospect of gloom and apostasy that must have been prominent in the original document, and remains characteristic of the present Hebrew redaction, was changed into a really "happy ending". Whether the manner of this change is in all details conceivable within a Jewish milieu is a question on which I do not here venture to make a final decision.

APPENDIX

JOSEPH'S ROLE IN THE HEBREW TESTAMENT OF NAPHTALI
AND ITS BACKGROUND IN POST-EXILIC JUDAISM

By the first chapter of Hebr. *T. Napht.* Joseph is already made responsible for the coming exile. The בני יוסף will cause the בני ישראל to desert the Lord and to separate from Levi and Judah. In the first vision ten tribes yield to Joseph's attempts at seduction, whereas only Benjamin remains with Levi and Judah. The second vision inculcates this contrast between Levi-Judah and Joseph even further. In ch. VII Jacob concludes from Naphtali's report about his dreams that his sons shall go into exile because of the corruption on the part of the sons of Joseph (על משחת בני יוסף אתם גולים vs 4). Naphtali ends with a final exhortation to his sons not to join the company of the בני יוסף, but to cling to Levi and Judah.

All this clearly represents a late development of the scheme which has stamped the outline of the history of Israel given in II *Kings* XVII,7sqq., the so-called deuteronomic view of history.[31] The main characteristic of this construction is that the whole history of the twelve tribes from their first arrival into the land onwards (and sometimes even from the exodus) is viewed in the perspective of the exile seen as a judgement executed first on the northern kingdom, afterwards on the southern also.[32] The result of this whole history is merely a progressive alienation from YHWH followed by a final punishment that brings everything to its close.

The origin and early development of this view can provide us in many respects only with matter for speculation. As for e.g. II *Kings* XVII,7-23 an attempt has been made to reconstruct an earlier stage of the text, in which only the northern kingdom played a part and which, therefore, could derive from pre-exilic deuteronomic circles.[33] However, an essential feature of the deuteronomic view of history, as it is known to us, is precisely that the downfall of the northern and the southern kingdoms follow one another in a close sequence. If one wants to go further back, one should appeal, not to an earlier stage of II *Kings* XVII,7-23, but rather to *Ps.* LXXVIII which should probably be dated considerably earlier than is usual today.[34] In this psalm, which so obviously bears the stamp of

---

[31] Cf. above all O.H. Steck, *Israël und das gewaltsame Geschick der Propheten* (WMANT 23), Neukirchen 1967, pp. 66sqq.

[32] Apostasy from the exodus onwards is assumed in *Pss* LXXVIII; CVI; also in II *Kings* XVII,14; XXI,15; *Jer.* VII,25. For the pattern as such, cf. M. Noth, *Überlieferungsgeschichtliche Studien*, Tübingen 1967[3], pp. 100-110.

[33] Cf. O.H. Steck, *o.c.*, p. 66sq. n. 4.

[34] Cf. O.H. Steck, *o.c.*, p. 110sq. n. 6. *Ps.* LXXVIII has been assigned to a deuteronomic milieu by H. Schmidt, Die Psalmen, *H.A.T.* 1934, a.l. Unlike authors like Kraus and Steck I consider this a very plausible conjecture. The features derived from sapiental instruction are quite consonant with it, for, as has become more and more widely recognized, there always existed intimate relations between deuteronomic theologians and wise men. See W. McKane, *Prophets and Wise Men* (Studies in Biblical Theology 44), London 1966[2], pp. 107sq.; J. Maffroy, Sagesse et loi dans le Deutéronome, *V.T.* 15(1965), pp. 49-65; C.M. Carmichael, Deuteronomic laws, wisdom and historical tradition, *J.S.S.* 12(1967), pp. 198-206, J. Marböck, *Weisheit im Wandel. Untersuchungen zur Weisheitstheologie bei Ben Sira*, Bonn 1971, pp. 82sqq.; M. Weinfeld, Deuteronomy —the present state of inquiry, *J.B.L.* 86(1967), pp. 256sq.; 262; id., *Deuteronomy*

deuteronomic theology, Israel's disobedience eventually leads to the
rejection of the sanctuary at Shiloh (vss 60sq.) by YHWH, and
according to vs 67 also to that of "the tent of Joseph" and of
"the tribe of Ephraim". In contrast with this stands the glorification
of the tribe of Judah and the cult on Mount Zion at the conclusion
(vss 68sq.). David is the divinely appointed king (vss 70-72). The
deuteronomic circle behind *Ps.* LXXVIII evidently saw the destruction
of the sanctuary at Shiloh as a historical precedent for the judgement
executed on the northern kingdom as a whole. In *Jer.* VII,12-15 we
can still see it function as an example used to reinforce the announcement of coming doom : here also the rejection of Shiloh goes
hand in hand with that of Ephraim.[35] The difference between
Ps. LXXVIII and Jeremiah's temple speech is only that the latter
now uses the example of Shiloh's destruction against the temple
of Jerusalem itself, which according to him is also moving towards
its doom. On the other hand the ideology Jeremiah attacks here
seems to be nearly identical with that glorification of Mount Zion
and the sacral kingship which, as we have seen, forms the central
message of *Ps.* LXXVIII. Thus it almost seems, as if the deuteronomic
'sages' responsible for *Ps.* LXXVIII are opposed by Jeremiah with
the assistance of their own weapons.[36] In his preaching, the rejection
of Ephraim and the tent of Joseph no longer functions as a dark
foil against which the legitimate cult on Mount Zion and the kingship
bestowed by God on the house of David more gloriously shine forth,
but as a foreboding of the judgement which the southern kingdom
also cannot escape.

It is this whole set of presuppositions which forms the background
of the writing of history as it was practised in deuteronomic circles.
The history of the twelve tribes, of the northern as well as of the

---

and the Deuteronomic School, Oxford 1972; C. J. Labuschagne, Redactie en Theologie
van het boek Deuteronomium, *Vox Theol.* 43(1973), pp. 171-184.

On the other hand, the anti-Samaritan tendency which Kraus and other scholars
attribute to *Ps.* LXXVIII is, as far as I can see, not in the least apparent. The
rejection of the sanctuary at Shiloh can hardly be taken as directed against a community
like that of the Samaritans, which itself rejected this sanctuary as false! Cf. J. Macdonald,
The Theology of the Samaritans, London 1964, pp. 17sqq.

[35] On the destruction of the sanctuary at Shiloh, cf. Th. C. Vriezen, *De Godsdienst
van Israël*, Zeist 1963, p. 70.

[36] By way of a different argument McKane (*o.c.*, pp. 102-112) is led to the same
conclusion, viz. that Jeremiah opposes an early "'nationalization' of international
wisdom" represented by deuteronomic חכמים.

southern, is viewed by them as nothing but a continuous movement towards apostasy from the "Law" and from the "Covenant", finally leading to the ultimate catastrophe. The process of reflection, however, which went on in these circles did not end with this. At the close of II *Kings* XVII 7-23 we already find a passage which points in a new direction and which therefore must be regarded in its present context as secondary, I mean vss 21-23a.[37] There we find a hint of the division of David's kingdom. As is shown by I *Kings* XI,11-13, the original author of the Books of Kings had taken this division to be the work of God, as a punishment for Solomon's idolatry. The usual translation of II *Kings* XVII 21 however, which following Luther finds the same view here also, is in my opinion untenable. The subject of קרע according to the following ימליכו cannot be YHWH.[38] In this passage the division of the kingdom is rather seen as the work of Israel itself,[39] which rejects the divinely established house of David and chooses Jeroboam to be king instead. The movement of idolatry which sets in after his election can now be seen as no more than a prolongation of the initial apostasy represented by the very separation of Israel from Judah itself.

As has clearly been recognized by such scholars as G. von Rad[40] and M. Noth,[41] it is this picture which has been worked out fully in the Books of Chronicles. Although the author of these books still shows knowledge about Ahijah's prophecy (cf. II *Chron.* IX,29; X,15) and traces Jeroboam's kingship back to a divine appointment (cf. II *Chron.* X,15; XI,4), neither Solomon's idolatry nor the content of Ahijah's prophecy are touched upon further. Instead we read in II *Chron.* X,19 that Israel separated (יפשעו) from the house of David

---

[37] See the survey of opinions in O. H. Steck, *o.c.*, p. 66 n. 4. I think that the addition includes הנביאים and tries to explain vs 20 fin. : עד אשר השליכם (cf. vs 23a : עד אשר הסיר). Vs 23b is an excellent sequel to vs 20 and is closely linked with vs 24 (Asshur!).

[38] Taking YHWH as subject would imply reading ימליך in stead of ימליכו. The early corruption could be explained by assuming that a scribe had taken offense at the idea of YHWH appointing Jeroboam to be king, now the latter's idolatry was mentioned in the same context.

[39] Probably one must read *ni.* with *Vulg.* Cf. the picture drawn in *Ass. Mos.* II. In vs 3 the verb *abrumpere* is used for the secession of the ten tribes. R. H. Charles, *The Assumption of Moses...*, London 1897, p. 9 translates "will be apostates", E.-M. Laperrousaz, *Le Testament de Moïse*, Paris 1970, p. 115: "feront sécession".

[40] G. von Rad, *Das Geschichtsbild des chronistischen Werkes* (BWANT IV,3), 1930.

[41] M. Noth, *o.c.*, especially pp. 171-180.

until the present day. To the author "all Israel" is from this time onwards only represented by Judah and Benjamin.[42] In addition, in II *Chron.* XI,13-15 we read that priests and levites come to Jerusalem, because Jeroboam's idolatry makes it impossible for them to remain true to the cult prescribed by the law of YHWH. In their wake follow all those מכל שבטי ישראל who want to seek YHWH, the God of Israel (vss 16sq.). As a result we find "all Israel", that means all those who still cling to YHWH, together in Jerusalem around the throne of David and the legitimate cult on Mount Zion administered by priests from the tribe of Levi. In the period following the exile old ideals, like those we have met in *Ps.* LXXVIII, apparently came to life again. At least the way of writing history that we find in the Books of Chronicles shows clear traces of their influence.

G. von Rad especially has emphasized the degree of unreality that appears as soon as this view is compared with the actual situation in which the author of *Chronicles* himself must have lived. Since the time of Nehemiah the people who had returned from the exile were named יהודים, a designation that frequently occurs e.g. in the Book of Esther.[43] This group considered itself as the "holy remnant" [44] to which YHWH had been merciful again in spite of the sins that had been committed.[45] The atmosphere, however, which is so characteristic of the prayers of confession which we find in *Neh.* IX,6sqq. and *Ps.* CVI and which also pervades much of later Jewish piety,[46] seems to be entirely strange to the author of the Books of Chronicles. To him Judah and Benjamin without reservation represent "all Israel" in as much as they "are the properly loyal tribes which have stuck to the divinely established monarchy and to the true cult... In this way according to the special design of the author of Chronicles, post-exilic history is connected with the period before the exile and even with the patriarchs as the holders of the promise"

---

[42] Cf. Von Rad, *o.c.*, pp. 19sqq.; 25sqq.; 34sqq.

[43] To be exact : 40x. Cf. Von Rad, *o.c.*, pp. 24sq.

[44] Use and background of this concept cannot be discussed here. In my view it originally belonged to the atmosphere of the sacral kingship, protected by YHWH against total annihilation.

[45] Cf. *Neh.* IX,31 (also vss 27sqq.): the pattern which we find here is borrowed from *Jud.* II,10sqq. and also occurs in *Ps.* CVI,43-47; on this last passage see O. H. Steck, *o.c.*, p. 112 n. 14.

[46] On prayers of confession in later literature, see Chr. Burchard, *Untersuchungen zu Joseph und Aseneth* (WUNT 8), Tübingen 1965, pp. 104-107.

(G. von Rad).[47] Since the split of the monarchy apostasy and sin are found only among the northern tribes. Those from the north who do not want to participate come to Jerusalem. Thus in II *Chron.* XV,9 we read that members of the tribes of Ephraim, Manasseh and Simeon join the reform movement started by Asa. According to II *Chron.* XXX,10 couriers are sent by Hezekiah to invite all Israel to the celebration of a legitimate Passover in Jerusalem. Although they encountered scorn and contempt everywhere in the land of Ephraim and Manasseh, nevertheless a few accepted their invitation and came to Jerusalem.

In II *Chron.* XV,3 sqq. moreover, a curious view is developed concerning the period preceding the division of the kingdom. We hear of a time during which Israel lived "without the true God, without a priest who gave instruction and without law". As far as we can gather from the context, the period of the judges is meant.[48] In the opinion of the Chronicler the turning point arrives no earlier than the reign of David.[49] David first gives to the Levites the position that is due to them, not only as regards the cult, but also with respect to the instruction in the law, which virtually falls entirely to their lot. The author of Chronicles apparently takes such a lively interest in their claims, that it has not unreasonably been conjectured by some scholars that the attempt to enforce them was one of the major aims which guided him in writing.[50] In any case the identification

---

[47] *O.c.*, p. 24.

[48] Accordingly the idea of a godless generation following on Joshua found in *Jud.* II,10sqq. has disappeared. Cf. Von Rad, *o.c.*, p. 78.

[49] Saul is, of course, passed over. Cf. Von Rad, *o.c.*, p. 79. Von Rad's suggestion that *Ps.* LXXVIII has to be dated after *Chronicles* because Saul plays no part in it, does not carry conviction: first, the glorification of David at the expense of Saul does not originate with the author of *Chron.* and, secondly, the arrangement of *Ps.* LXXVIII is not primarily chronological. Vs 67 resumes vs 9 and in vss 68-72 the rejection of the northern tribes (= Ephraim), which is the main theme of vss 9-67, is contrasted with YHWH's election of the sanctuary on Mount Zion and the davidic kingship. I cannot agree with B. D. Eerdmans, *The Hebrew Book of Psalms*, O.T.S. IV, Leiden 1947, pp. 379sqq., who thinks that the spalm simply breaks off when the author has arrived at his own time. To get an exact chronological sequence Eerdmans has to suppose that vs 9 has been misplaced.

[50] This has been cogently argued by G. von Rad, *o.c.*, p. 61; 81sqq. On p. 130 he compares *Chron.* with P: "Dort war das zentrale Anliegen der von Moses geordnete Kult der Aaroniden an der Stiftshütte. Hier ist es der von David geordnete Dienst der Leviten an der Lade". Von Rad's opinion is severly criticized by M. Noth, *o.c.*, pp. 173sq., but it has found the support of W. Rudolph and M. Weinfeld.

of the Levites with teachers of the law seems to be more or less to his credit,[51] a fact which deeply influenced the later development of the Jewish religion. In this way also the divinely established royalty of David is laid as the foundation of the legitimate cult of the true God in which the Levites play such a prominent part. In Qumran we even meet the idea that the law had been hidden ever since the days of Eleazar, the first high priest, until it was again openly proclaimed by Zadok under the rule of David.[52] Although the role which in this connection is attributed to Zadok may reflect the special concerns of the Qumran community, this view on the pre-Davidic period is basically no other than that of II *Chron.* XV,3sqq. Serving YHWH according to the law and the covenant is strictly connected with loyalty towards the house of David. On its side are the tribes of Judah and Benjamin, which have remained free from apostasy, and to them, as we have seen, priests and Levites assemble as well as those from among "all Israel", including Ephraim and Manasseh, who remain faithful to YHWH.

In my opinion mainly the same concept is found in several writings belonging to a later period. The community of Qumran is especially

---

[51] Cf. M. Weinfeld, *Deuteronomy and the Deuteronomic School*, Oxford 1972, p. 54: the author of *Chron.* "invested the Levites with the robes of the teacher-priests in keeping with his purpose of glorifying the Levites at the expense of the priests". According to Weinfeld, *ibidem* "the Levites became the interpreters and teachers of the written law only in the post-exilic period". The same functions are attributed to the Levites in the *Test. XII Patr.* and related literature. A few points may be mentioned. First there is the genealogical list of Levi's sons found both in the Greek Testament and in the Aramaic fragments. It is also found in I *Chron.* XXIII,6 and besides only in priestly tradition (*Gen.* XLVI,11; *Exod.* VI,16; *Josh.* XXI,27). Further, according to I *Chron.* XXIII,4 the Levites have to act as "officers and judges" (שפטים ושטרים). The same combination of words occurs in *Deut.* XVI,18, but there the Levites are not yet mentioned! (Cf. G. von Rad, *o.c.*, p. 61). In *Deut.* XVI,18 the Septuagint translates: κριταὶ καὶ γραμματοεισαγωγεῖς, in *I Chron.* XXIII,4: γραμματεῖς καὶ κριταί. Thus it is quite in the Chronicler's line when in *T. Levi* VIII,17 κριταὶ καὶ γραμματεῖς are predicted to arise from the tribe of Levi. P. Grelot, Notes sur le Testament araméen de Lévi, *R.B.* 63 (1956), pp. 395sq. points to the parallel not only of *Jub.* XXXI,15, but also of I Q *Sa.* I 24, where we read that the sons of Levi will present themselves לשרים ולשופטים ולשוטרים. The Chronicler's identification of the שפטים ושטרים mentioned in *Deut.* XVI,18 with the Levites has apparently exerted a strong influence. Of course, the identification may already have been current before in the circles from which the author of *Chron.* originated.

[52] *C.D.* VII,2sq.

worthy of our attention in this respect. It is a well-known fact that in this circle more than anywhere else a high value was set on the concept of a covenant with YHWH. In the so-called Damascus Document there is a kind of review of the past starting with II,14sqq., which intends to show that since the time of the so-called Watchers of heaven [53] history has been a continuous movement of apostasy from YHWH and his commandments. Over against the mass of apostates, however, there is always a small minority which holds true to the covenant. In IV,2 the sons of Zadok are identified with the שבי ישראל, that part of Israel which turns to YHWH and departs from Judah to the land of Damascus.[54] The Levites join them. In I Q *p.Hab.* XII,4 the same group is called the פתאי יהודים, "the simpleminded Jews". The community's link with Judah is even closer in IV Q *p. Nah.* III,4sq. where we read that when Judah's glory will be revealed in the end of days, the simpleminded of Ephraim (פתאי אפרים) will leave their seducers alone and join Israel. According to IV,5sq. the רשעי אפרים will have to empty the cup of God's anger, after Manasseh has first had its turn. Even earlier the "city of blood" from *Nah.* III,1 had been identified with Ephraim in II,1sq., and in II,8 we hear of people who have led this tribe astray. The idea underlying all this is apparently that Ephraim and Manasseh represent the corrupted part of the nation, whereas those among them who want to keep faithful to YHWH must depart from their native tribes and join "Israel". That this concept never comes quite clearly to the front will have to be accounted for by the fact that after all the real interest of the Qumran community may not have gone far beyond the very contrast between apostates and members of the true community of the Covenant, which they believed themselves to embody. Compared with this the old division of tribes was a scheme that for the main part continued its existence on paper only, turning up e.g. in the illusory visions and images of the War Scroll. There we find in I,2 the sons of Levi joining the sons of Judah and Benjamin [55] for the battle against the sons of Darkness, while these are supported in their turn by the מרשיעי ברית,

---

[53] These are the same as the ἐγρήγοροι mentioned several times in the Testaments.

[54] Cf. G. Vermes, *Scripture and Tradition in Judaism* (Studia Post-Biblica 4), Leiden 1973², pp. 43-49.

[55] They are explicitly called the גולת המדבר. E. Lohse, *Die Texte aus Qumran*, Darmstadt 1971², p. 294 n. 2 correctly observes that afterwards the "sons of light" are said to consist of the twelve tribes. Thus we have here the same discrepancy to which Von Rad pointed in the case of *Chron.*

the defilers of the covenant. It is true that Ephraim and Manasseh are not mentioned in this connection. But when the Damascus Document in VII,12sq., commenting on *Is.* VII,17, speaks of the separation between the two houses of Israel which had happened when Ephraim departed from Judah [56] (שר אפרים מעל יהודה), the name "Ephraim" has clearly been used to denote the apostate part of the nation and must not, with some scholars,[57] be taken as a veiled designation of the community itself. The vagueness that persists even here seems again to result from the fact that, after all, the issue at stake is not the tribal division, but only the contrast between the apostates (נסוגים) on one side and the faithful (מחזיקים) on the other. This does not alter the fact that on the background the set of ideas, dominating the representation of Israel's history which we found in the Books of Chronicles is still present: law and covenant are closely related to the faithful tribes Levi, Judah and Benjamin, which for this reason are considered to embody "all Israel", together, of course, with those members of the other tribes who have remained faithful to YHWH.

To me it seems evident that the warnings which Naphtali addresses to his sons in the Hebr. *T. Napht.* must be seen against this background. They have to join Levi and Judah and to beware of the בני יוסף. Now exhortations to obey Levi and Judah are to be found in the Greek Testaments as well, even in a rather overwhelming number. But there this contrast with Joseph, which becomes so meaningful when we see it in the perspective of later Jewish literature appears nowhere. Only in his redaction of Naphtali's visions the Greek author has not been able to clear it away completely: in both dreams, but especially in the second (VI,5), the motif of an opposition between Levi-Judah and Joseph still shines through. From this it seems justifiable to conclude that its connection with the so-called Levi-Judah passages is indeed primitive. It explains their original meaning: apostasy from Levi and Judah amounts to abandonment of law and covenant, both of which in the eyes of post-exilic religious thinkers guaranteed the existence of the Elect People.

---

[56] Following Rabin, Van der Woude en F. F. Bruce (*Biblical Exegesis in the Qumran Texts*, Den Haag 1959, pp. 32sq.) translate שר with "became ruler over".

[57] See e.g. A. S. van der Woude, *Die messianischen Vorstellungen der Gemeinde von Qumran*, Assen 1957, pp. 44sqq. Cf. also J. Maier, *Die Texte vom Toten Meer II*, Basel 1960, p. 52 (note on *C.D.* VII,12sq.). I agree with Maier that Van der Woude's interpretation is not convincing.

XVII

TESTAMENT ISSACHAR ALS „TYPISCHES" TESTAMENT

*Einige Bemerkungen zu zwei neuen Übersetzungen
der Testamente der Zwölf Patriarchen*

M. DE JONGE

1. *Einleitung*

1974 sind kurz nacheinander zwei Übersetzungen der Testamente
der XII Patriarchen, versehen mit Einleitungen und kurzen Anmerkungen, erschienen: die von Benedikt Otzen in der Reihe *De Gammeltestamentlige Pseudepigrafer* Band 7 [1] und die von Jürgen Becker
in der neuen Herausgabe *Jüdische Schriften aus hellenistisch-römischer
Zeit*, III,1.[2] Weil beide Beiträge Versuche darstellen, den heutigen
Stand der Forschung auf dem Gebiet der Testamente in einer für
Nicht-Spezialisten zugänglichen Weise wiederzugeben und weil sie in
der Praxis — ebenso wie das bei den Beiträgen von F. Schnapp
in *Die Apokryphen und Pseudepigraphen des Alten Testaments* und
von R. H. Charles in *The Apocrypha and Pseudepigrapha of the
Old Testament* der Fall war [3] — als „Gebrauchsbücher" großen
Einfluß auf die Verwendung der Testamente haben werden und
vielleicht auch auf die weitere Forschung, scheint uns eine kritische
Besprechung angebracht.

Im Folgenden wird, nach einer kurzen Darstellung beider Bücher,
zunächst auf die Auffassungen eingegangen werden, die beide Autoren
hinsichtlich des *Textes* der Testamente haben — einiges im Anschluß
an das, was darüber in Kap. II-XI dieses Bandes bemerkt ist —,
sodann sollen beider Ansichten über *Entstehung und Datierung* der
Testamente besprochen und schließlich beide Übersetzungen (mit
Anmerkungen) des Testaments Issachar näher betrachtet werden.
Damit soll auch im Einzelnen deutlich werden, um was es in der

---

[1] København 1974, S. 677-789.

[2] Gütersloh 1974, S. 17-163.

[3] Vgl. meinen Aufsatz „The interpretation of the Testaments of the Twelve Patriarchs
in recent years", Kap. XIII dieses Bandes.

heutigen Forschung der Testamente geht. Der Leser wird bemerken, daß der Autor dieses Artikels diesen beiden Publikationen sehr kritisch gegenüber steht und der Ansicht ist, daß die Zeit für ihr Erscheinen noch nicht reif war.

2. *Anlage*

Beide Veröffentlichungen haben, wie zu erwarten, ungefähr die gleiche Anlage. Das Hauptgewicht liegt auf der Übersetzung mit den Anmerkungen; Becker faßt textkritische Noten und inhaltliche Anmerkungen in einem Apparat zusammen, Otzen hält sie mit Recht getrennt. Vorausgeht eine Einleitung, die bei Otzen 20 Seiten, bei Becker 15 Seiten umfaßt. Otzen behandelt der Reihe nach : den Namen der Schrift; die literarische Gattung; die Struktur und den Inhalt; Quellen und Parallelstellen; Intention, Zeit und Ort der Abfassung und die Textüberlieferungen (jetzt erst!), und schließt mit einer ausführlichen Literaturliste, sowie einer kurzen Erörterung über die Anlage der Übersetzung.

Becker informiert nach einer kurzen Einführung zunächst über die handschriftliche Überlieferung und die Editionsarbeit; danach über verwandtes Material und Abhängigkeiten; die Entstehungsverhältnisse; die Theologie der Test. XII und den Aufbau der Schrift. Schließlich gibt er eine kurze Auswahl aus der Literatur. Von vorneherein ist ein Unterschied festzustellen : J. Becker hat aufgrund seiner früheren ausführlichen Arbeit *Untersuchungen zur Entstehungsgeschichte der Testamente der Zwölf Patriarchen* (1970) viel deutlicher eine eigene Meinung über die komplizierten Probleme, vor die die Testamente uns stellen, als Otzen, der vorsichtiger und zurückhaltender ist und sich bewußt ist, wie beschränkt seine (und überhaupt unsere) Kenntnisse sind.

3. *Der Text*

Beiden Autoren ist die Existenz des griechischen Materials bekannt, das M. de Jonge in der zweiten Auflage seiner *Testamenta XII Patriarcharum* erwähnt [4] und das von H. J. de Jonge [5] analysiert ist;

---

[4] Leiden 1964, [2]1970. Otzen zitiert allerdings nur die erste Auflage.

[5] „Die Textüberlieferung der Testamente der zwölf Patriarchen" (1972), vgl. „Les fragments marginaux dans le MS. *d* des Testaments des XII Patriarches" (1971), jetzt Kap. II und Kap. IV dieses Bandes.

ebenso die des neuen armenischen Materials, das in den Veröffentlichungen von C. Burchard, M. E. Stone und A. Hultgård [6] erwähnt ist. Sie verwenden es aber nicht für ihre Ausgaben (Otzen) oder nur sporadisch (Becker, der manchmal Bezug nimmt auf Hultgårds *Croyances Messianiques*). Das ist sehr zu bedauern, weil auf diese Weise kein wirklichkeitsgetreues Bild der Textüberlieferung geboten wird. Zugegeben sei, daß das armenische Material noch schwer zugänglich ist, und daß eine Zahl kleinerer Fragmente wie Fm^d und *n* wenig Wert haben. Aber auch schon vor ihrer Veröffentlichung in der kommenden neuen Leidener Edition hätten die Handschriften *l* und *m* leicht für diese zwei Übersetzungen kollationiert werden und so zu einer mehr ausgeglichenen Bewertung der Gruppe *g l d m* in ihren Relationen mit *b* (*k*) und mit *e a f* (*chi*) beitragen können.

Ein wesentliches Manko ist auch, daß beide Autoren einer tiefgehenden Auseinandersetzung mit H. J. de Jonges „Die Textüberlieferung der Testamente der zwölf Patriarchen" aus 1972 [7] aus dem Wege gehen. Otzen steht dessen Ergebnissen positiv gegenüber, wenn er sich auch fragt, ob de Jonge *b* und *k* nicht zu direkt mit dem Archetyp verbindet. Er hat aber die Ergebnisse dieses Artikels nicht mehr benützen können, weil die Übersetzung und die Anmerkungen bereits fertig waren, als er ihn in die Hand bekam. [8] Glücklicherweise hat das keine großen Folgen für seine Übersetzung, weil er im Prinzip *b* gefolgt ist (in M. de Jonges Ausgabe von 1964) und weil er auf alle Stellen, an denen er von *b* abweicht, hinweist. Das bedeutet aber, daß im Apparat viele Varianten, namentlich aus *chi* oder aus einzelnen Handschriften vorkommen, die aufgrund der bisherigen Forschung in Leiden besser hätten weggelassen und/oder durch andere ersetzt werden können. So hält Otzen unabsichtlich den durch die Ausgabe von Charles geweckten Eindruck weiter aufrecht, daß die entscheidende Wahl die ist zwischen einer α-Lesart und einer β-Lesart!

Schwieriger ist der Sachverhalt in der Übersetzung von Becker. Genauso wie 1970 hält er 1974 an der Existenz von zwei „Familien" α und β fest, die er als „Kristallisationszentren mit je bestimmten Eigentümlichkeiten bei fließenden Grenzen" [9] kennzeichnet. Diese vage Formulierung macht es ihm möglich, einen eklektischen Text zu

---

[6] Siehe M. de Jonge, „The Greek Testaments of the Twelve Patriarchs and the Armenian Version", oben Kap. VIII.

[7] Jetzt Kap. II dieses Bandes.

[8] A.a.O. S. 690 und 696.

[9] A.a.O. S. 21.

übersetzen. Die dabei unumgängliche Subjektivität verteidigt er durch
den Hinweis auf die Vorrangigkeit der inneren Textkritik.[10] In dieser
Hinsicht zeigt er eine größere Affinität zu A. Hultgård als zu
H. J. de Jonge, dessen Artikel er zwar nennt, aber nicht einer wirklich
kritischen Besprechung unterwirft. An anderer Stelle in diesem Band
hat H. J. de Jonge ihn seinerseits deswegen kritisiert.[11] Das Ergebnis
ist eine Übersetzung, die auf einer sehr subjektiven Textkonstitution
beruht. Bei der Analyse seiner Übersetzung des Testaments Issachars
soll gezeigt werden, daß dabei zwei Prinzipien zu dominieren scheinen:
die Anwendung der Regel *lectio brevior potior* und eine Anpassung
von Beckers Textkritik an seine Einsichten über die Komposition
der Testamente.

Becker gibt ziemlich ausführliche textkritischen Anmerkungen in
seinem Apparat; doch sind viele im Grunde überflüssig, und zudem
sind sie — wie oben bemerkt wurde — unvollständig trotz seiner
scheinbaren Präzision.

4. *Die Entstehungsgeschichte*

Bei der Charakterisierung der Standpunkte der beiden Autoren
hinsichtlich der Entstehungsweise der Testamente können wir am
besten von Beckers Erörterungen ausgehen, die verständlicherweise
auf die in seinem Buche von 1970 verteidigten Theorien zurückgreifen.
Otzen bespricht diese Theorien bei der Bestimmung seines Stand-
punktes.

Was „verwandtes Material und Abhängigkeiten" betrifft (S. 21-23),
ist B. sehr vorsichtig. Literarische Abhängigkeit ist nirgendwo nach-

---

[10] So z.B. a.a.O. S. 22.

[11] Siehe „The earliest stage of the textual tradition of the Testaments of the
Twelve Patriarchs", Kap. III dieses Bandes, insbesondere S. 80-86. Auf S. 20 nennt
Becker nur ein konkretes Beispiel: „Wenn aber diese 'reinen' Hyparchetypen Kon-
struktion sind und Stellen wie z.B. TL 2-3 oder TSeb 6-8 zeigen wie β gemeinsam
gegen α stehen, bzw etwa b und dg zusammengehen, wird man β nicht einfach
auflösen sollen, sondern trotz interner Differenzen von einer (Groß-) Familie sprechen
müssen". Die tatsächlich wichtigen Abschnitte T.L. II-III und T.Z. VI-VIII sind oben
besprochen. Auf S. 248-251 wurde gezeigt, daß die *chi(n)* Varianten in T.L. II-III
sekundär sind; das impliziert eine Familienverwandtschaft in α, besagt aber nichts
über die anderen MSS. Auf S. 149-152 wurde versucht, plausibel zu machen, daß
in T.Z. der längere Text in *bgldm* (nicht nur *b* und *dg* wie Becker meint) der ursprüngliche
ist; wenn das so ist, steht die Gruppe *eaf* mit einer deutlich sekundären Lesart
neben *chi* gegenüber *bgldm* — ein deutlicher Grund, das siglum β aufzugeben.

weisbar. Selbstverständlich kannte der Autor die Erzählungen über die Söhne Jakobs in der zweiten Hälfte von Genesis und er ließ sich inspirieren durch den Segen Jakobs und den des Mose in Genesis XLIX (und die darauf folgende Abschiedsszene) bzw. in Deuteronomium XXXIII, aber was das parallele jüdische Material anbelangt, dürfen wir nur von „relativ fester mündlicher Tradition" sprechen, die durch verschiedene Schriften aufgenommen und weitergegeben ist. Das gilt für Test. Juda III-VII und namentlich für Test. Levi, von dem wir viele Cairo-Genizah-Fragmente und Qumranfragmente besitzen. Was die letztgenannten betrifft, hat B. sich nicht durch die Kritik von D. Haupt[12] überzeugen lassen. Es bleibt bei ihm bei „entfernter traditionsgeschichtlicher Verwandtschaft". In dem Artikel „Notes on Testament of Levi II-VII' habe ich zu zeigen versucht, daß man wohl entschieden weiter gehen muß und von einer schriftlichen Quelle reden kann, die durch den Autor von Test. Levi tiefgreifend umgearbeitet ist.[13] Im Hinblick auf die Visionen in Test. Naphtali ist B. der Meinung, daß der Grundstock des mittelalterlichen hebräischen Testaments Naphtali zurückgreift auf unser heutiges Testament Naphtali und später erweitert wurde. Auch dagegen ist viel einzuwenden; an anderer Stelle dieses Bandes hat Th. Korteweg, unter Rückgriff auf meine Darlegung von 1953[14] m.E. überzeugend nachgewiesen, daß das hebräische Test. Naphtali Elemente bewahrt hat, die auch in der Vorlage unseres Testamentes Naphtali vorhanden gewesen sein müssen und bewußt in dem heutigen Testament ausgelassen oder verändert worden sind.[15]

Aus S. 679-682 seines Buches kann man entnehmen daß Otzen zum größten Teil mit Becker übereinstimmt. Nur im Hinblick auf Test. Naphtali zieht er die Theorie vor, daß hebr. Test. Naphtali und unser griechisches Test. Naphtali auf eine gemeinsame Quelle zurückgehen oder wenigstens auf eine gemeinsame Tradition (siehe seine Bemerkung zu V,1-8). Außerdem weist er, ebenso wie B. an anderer Stelle, auf die Parallelen hin die mit synagogaler Paränesetradition und den dualistischen Varianten in Qumran bestehen, und auf Schemata wie das „Sin-Exile-Return-pattern" und die eschatologische Rolle von Levi und Juda. Nirgendwo (noch nicht einmal

---

[12] D. Haupt, *Das Testament des Levi*, Diss. Halle 1969.
[13] Siehe Kap. XV dieses Bandes, insbesondere S. 257.
[14] *The Testaments of the Twelve Patriarchs*, Assen 1953, S. 52-57.
[15] Kap. XVI dieses Bandes.

im Test. Naphtali!) kann man nach ihm von literarischer Abhängigkeit
sprechen, und niemals können wir auf eine Herkunft aus demselben
Kreis oder demselben Milieu schließen.

Becker nimmt an, daß die Entstehungsgeschichte der Testamente
lange und kompliziert gewesen ist (S. 23-27). Die Ergebnisse der
christlichen Bearbeitung sind einfach zu unterscheiden und zu entfernen; die Bearbeitung muß im zweiten Jahrhundert stattgefunden
haben. Otzen ist in diesem Punkt mit ihm einverstanden (S. 690-691),
weist aber in diesem Zusammenhang nachdrücklich auf die Bedeutung
des Beitrags von Jervell[16] hin. Was übrigbleibt bildet keine Einheit.
Becker unterscheidet eine deutlich einheitliche „Grundschrift" und
einen darauf folgenden „anonymen Wachstumprozeß im Bereich des
Judentums". Er sieht sich zu dieser Hypothese gezwungen, weil das
in den Testamenten angesammelte Material nach Form und Inhalt
sehr verschiedenartig ist und viele Dubletten und sogar Widersprüchlichkeiten aufweist. In seinem Buch sagt er darüber : „So lassen sich
von der Gattung und vom Inhalt her diese einzelnen Zusätze der
zweiten Schicht gut voneinander abheben. Doch will es nicht gelingen,
darüberhinaus in der zweiten Schicht auch zeitlich, geschweige denn
geographisch, verschiedene Stufen voneinander abzugrenzen. Die zweite
Stufe innerhalb der Geschichte der TP ist demnach als ein Sammelbecken zu bezeichnen, in dem sehr verschiedene Bearbeitungsvorgänge
vereint sind, die im einzelnen im geschichtlichen Dunkel liegen".[17]

Wie schon oben bemerkt wurde,[18] muß das Gespräch mit Becker
hier einsetzen. Indem er eine Grundschrift rekonstruiert, „deren
geschlossene kompositorische und theologische Formung den Schluß
erzwingt, daß hier ein Verfasser unter Verwendung manchen traditionellen Stoffes ein einheitliches Werk schuf" (S. 24), macht er es
sich zu leicht : er verzichtet einfach auf eine Erklärung, warum
50 Prozent des Textes später angeschwemmt sein sollen. Wir werden
weiter nach einer Theorie suchen müssen, die die Testamente als
eine „Einheit-in-Verschiedenheit" erklären kann. Die Entstehung der
„Einheit-in-Verschiedenheit" wird man in erster Linie auf dem Niveau
der Komposition und Redaktion der zwölf verbundenen Testamente
vermuten, und man muß die Frage stellen, ob Beckers Grundschrift
mehr ist als ein mit Hilfe literarkritischer Operationen rekonstruiertes
Idealbild. Auf dieses Problem soll in § 5 eingegangen werden.

---

[16] Jervell wird übrigens auch von Becker genannt (S. 23).
[17] *Untersuchungen zur Entstehungsgeschichte ...*, S. 373f.
[18] Siehe Kap. XIII, S. 188-190, Kap. X, S. 153-160; vgl. auch Kap. XV, S. 251f.

Otzen ist viel vorsichtiger; auf S. 682-685 gibt er zunächst die
Auffassungen von R. H. Charles und J. Becker wieder, ohne sich
selbst an eine Aufteilung in Grundschrift und Redaktion zu wagen.
Die Hypothese M. de Jonges, es handele sich um eine christliche
Schrift, die von jüdischem Material Gebrauch macht, weist er entschieden zurück, spricht also von der christlichen Bearbeitung einer
jüdischen Schrift, macht aber weiter keine Aussage.

Becker meint, daß die Grundschrift und die späteren Hinzufügungen
in der Diaspora entstanden sind, vielleicht (vgl. die dem Joseph
zugeschriebene zentrale Position) in Ägypten. Was die Datierung
anbelangt, nimmt T.N. V,8 eine Schlüsselposition ein, weil die Syrer
die Letzten sind in einer Reihe von Völkern, die Israel unterdrücken.[19]
Das ergibt 198 v.Chr. als terminus a quo. Aufgrund der Kritik an
dem jerusalemer Priestertum in T.L. XIV etc., die nach Becker
Kritik an der Hellenisierung enthält, könnte man an die Periode
von 200-174 v.Chr. denken; es sei klar, daß weder der makkabäische
Aufstand noch die Entweihung des Tempels vorausgesetzt werden.[20]
Trotz der vielen Parallelen zur Qumranliteratur kann nicht auf einen
essenischen Ursprung der Testamente geschlossen werden; es gibt
zu viele fundamentale Unterschiede.

Mit Letzterem ist Otzen einverstanden, aber in allen anderen
Punkten weicht er von Becker ab. Aus T.N. V,8 schließt er nur
auf einen terminus ad quem von ± 60 v.Chr. (Ankunft der Römer
in Palästina). Fürs übrige sieht er keine Möglichkeit, die Testamente
genauer zu datieren als zwischen ± 150-50 v.Chr., in der Zeit, in
der nach ihm das Problem des Verhältnisses von „Levi" und „Juda"
akut war. Die Argumente für eine Entstehung in der Diaspora hält
er nicht für überzeugend — wir können genauso gut an hellenisierende
synagogale Kreise in Palästina denken — schließlich gibt es viele
Parallelen zu den in Qumran gefundenen Schriften.

Wir wenden uns nun einer Analyse der Übersetzung und Anmerkungen beider Autoren zum Testament Issachars zu, um von da
aus einige Bemerkungen über die Komposition dieses Testamentes
und der Testamente im allgemeinen zu machen. Die Wahl fiel auf

---

[19] Zur Unbrauchbarkeit dieses Verses für die Datierung der heutigen Testamente
siehe M. de Jonge, *The Testaments*..., S. 55 und Th. Korteweg, Kap. XVI, S. 280f.

[20] In seiner Anmerkung zu T.L. XIV,8 sagt er aber: „Angesichts der Typik der
Aussagen wird man zu TL 14 eine konkrete Historisierung kaum vertreten können.
Sicher ist nur, daß allgemein Hellenisierungstendenzen angegriffen werden".

dieses Testament, weil es die für die Testamente zentrale Tugend
der ἁπλότης beschreibt [21] und also für die Paränese der Schrift
bezeichnend ist. Zudem zeichnet sich in der Bibel Issachar in keiner
Weise vor den anderen Jakobssöhnen aus, und es gab offenbar wenig
außerbiblisches haggadisches Material über ihn, sodaß die Behandlung
dieses Patriarchen als exemplarisch für den Aufbau des Ganzen der
zwölf Testamente angesehen werden kann.

5. *Test. Issachar bei Otzen und Becker*

a) *Kapitel I-II*

Der biographische Anfang von Test. Issachar I,3-II,5 (gleich nach
dem Einsatz I,1-2) ist ohne Zweifel kompliziert. I,3-15 läuft auf die
Erklärung des Namens Issachars hinaus, und dabei wird von den
Angaben von Gen. XXX,14-18 Gebrauch gemacht. Der dort im
Gespräch zwischen Lea und Rahel gegebene Hinweis auf die Art
und Weise, wie die Ehen von Jakob mit Lea und Rahel zustande
kamen, wird (plastisch!) ausgearbeitet (vgl. Gen. XXIX,15-30). In
Kap. II wird dieses Thema weiter ausgesponnen. In I,7a wird schon
gesagt daß es um zwei Liebesäpfel ging. In I,8 überläßt Rahel Jakob
der Lea eine Nacht lang für Rubens Liebesäpfel; aber in I,14 wird
genauer gesagt, daß Jakob ihr für einen Liebesapfel eine Nacht lang
überlassen wurde. Daran schließt II,4 mit der Mitteilung an, daß
Rahel den Jakob für den zweiten Apfel noch eine weitere Nacht
abtrat. Dazwischen wird von einem Engel aus dem Himmel erklärt,
daß Rahel zwei Kinder gebären wird, weil sie Enthaltsamkeit dem
Zusammensein mit ihrem Mann vorzieht. Die Verteilung der Kinder
auf Lea und Rahel ergibt damit sechs-zwei statt acht-null. „Denn
aufgrund der Liebesäpfel sah der Herr sie an" (II,2 Ende, par II,4
Ende). „Denn er sah, [22] daß sie um der Kinder willen mit Jakob
zusammen sein wollte, aber nicht aus Lüsternheit".

Die Zahl zwei wird also in Verbindung gebracht mit zwei Nächten
und zwei Kindern. Der Hinweis auf Enthaltsamkeit und die Betonung
des Kindergebärens als des einzigen Zwecks der sexuellen Beziehung
kommen unerwartet, ebenso wie die Mitteilung am Schluß, daß

---

[21] Siehe J. Amstutz, ΑΠΛΟΤΗΣ. *Eine begriffsgeschichtliche Studie zum jüdisch-christlichen Griechisch*, Bonn 1968, S. 64-85.

[22] Becker übersetzt frei: „denn er wußte"; oder liest er ᾔδει statt εἶδε? *d* liest οἶδε.
Vgl. Beckers Bevorzugung von οἶδεν mit *de* vor εἶδεν in IV,4.

Rahel die Liebesäpfel nicht aufaß, sondern im Haus des Herrn aufstellte und dem Priester des Höchsten brachte, der in jener Zeit amtierte (II,5).

Otzen gibt sich zufrieden mit der Feststellung der Widersprüchlichkeiten, Becker aber greift zurück auf die Hypothese, die er auf S. 335f. seines Buches entwickelt hat und die er in seiner Anmerkung zu II,1 kurz wie folgt zusammenfaßt: „T Is 2 ist zweischichtiger Nachtrag, der wohl zugleich 1, 7a verursachte. Die ursprüngliche Darstellung in T Is 1 war an der Zahl der Äpfel desinteressiert. Über diese wird in 2, 1-3 und 2, 4f. in verschiedener Weise spekuliert".

Bevor wir diese Hypothese besprechen, ist es nötig einige textkritische Bemerkungen einzufügen.

In Kap. II folgen sowohl Otzen als auch Becker dem b-Text,[23] aber in Kap. I gibt es verschiedene Stellen, wo sie, sei es einzeln sei es gemeinsam, von b abweichen.

I,1. ἠγαπημένοι b] -μένα dl, h; -μένου m eaf, ci (g. def.) Otzen und Becker lesen den genitivus singularis der einen sehr guten Sinn ergibt. Es ist aber auch möglich, anzunehmen, daß ἠγαπημένοι als lectio durior ursprünglich ist. Das neutrum pluralis ist dann eine Anpassung an τέκνα, der genitivus singularis eine (andere) Anpassung an πατρός.

I,3. Mit Recht wählen Otzen und Becker „Ruben" statt der falschen Lesart von b „Jakob".

I,5. Es ist nicht einzusehen, warum Otzen der c-Lesart ἅπερ γίνονται ἐν τῇ γῇ Χαράν κτλ. folgt statt der schwierigen, und deshalb vorzuziehenden Lesart ἃ ἐποίει ἡ γῆ 'Αρὰμ ἐν ὕψει κτλ. in b und vielen anderen MSS.

I,6. Hier nimmt Otzen die offensichtlich erklärende Hinzufügung in chi „denn der Herr überging mich und ich habe Jakob keine Kinder geboren" in seinen Text auf — zu Unrecht!

I,7. Otzen läßt mit eaf, chi das παρθενίας nach τὸν ἄνδρα weg.

I,8. Otzen nimmt das verdeutlichende „Rahel" mit chi, dm auf.

I,9-10. Hier finden wir in chi den kleinen Satz μὴ καυχῶ, καὶ μὴ δοξάζου nicht am Anfang von V. 9, sondern anstelle von τί οὖν am Anfang von V. 10. Becker folgt hier chi, weil er den Text dieser MSS. für sinnvoller hält. Das ist nicht evident; aufgrund der Tatsache, daß chi in diesem Kapitel viele sekundäre, erklärende oder „glättende" Lesarten hat, gebe ich auch hier dem Nicht-chi-Text den Vorzug.

---

[23] In II,5 liest Becker „Priester" statt „Priester des Höchsten" mit chi.

I,11. Der nicht-*chi* Text ist hier syntaktisch und inhaltlich (Wiederholung von ὁ δόλος) unglücklich; *chi* geben hier den Inhalt wieder in einem kürzeren flüssigen Satz. Becker hält den Nicht-*chi*-Text für sekundär. Zu Unrecht m.E., weil der *chi*-Text sich einfach als Verbesserung des Nicht-*chi*-Textes erklären läßt, und nicht einzusehen ist, warum der flüssige *chi*-Satz von späteren Abschreibern so kompliziert gemacht sein soll.

I,13. Hier liest *chi* zusätzlich „Jakob", offenbar zur Verdeutlichung. Otzen übernimmt das.

I,14. Hier liest der *chi*-Text: „Doch für die Liebesäpfel gebe ich dir für eine Nacht den Jakob". Das überflüssige καὶ εἶπε Ῥαχήλ (auch im Vorhergehenden hat Rahel das Wort) wird weggelassen; und weiter wird direkt zurückgegriffen auf V. 8, das (wie wir sahen) mit Gen. XXX,15f. übereinstimmt. Es ist nicht einzusehen, weshalb die Varianten entstanden wären, wenn der *chi*-Text ursprünglich wäre. *l* und *d* gehen völlig eigene Wege (*d* auch in II,2-4); die anderen Nicht-*chi*-MSS. stimmen im großen und ganzen mit *b* überein: „Und Rahel sagte: 'Nimm einen Liebesapfel, und für einen will ich dir ihn geben für eine Nacht'". Der Zusammenhang „ein Apfel - eine Nacht" liegt implizit auch in II,4 vor. Aber die Tatsache, daß Lea ermuntert wird, den übriggebliebenen Apfel zu nehmen, suggeriert, daß es bei diesem einen Tausch von einer Nacht für einen Apfel bleibt — das ergibt in diesem Zusammenhang selbstverständlich Schwierigkeiten und erfordert eine Korrektur.

Otzen und Becker folgen hier dem *chi*-Text, wobei bei Becker deutlich wird, wie er Text- und Literarkritik verbindet. In seiner Anmerkung zu diesem Vers sagt er: „... das Interesse an der Zahl der Äpfel steht unter Einfluß aus V. 7a. α steht im Einklang mit V. 8". V. 7a ist nach ihm später in Kap. I zusammen mit den zwei Teilen von Kap. II hinzugefügt. Der α-Text hätte, obwohl auch dort 7a zu finden ist, in V. 14 die ursprüngliche Fassung besser bewahrt.

Wer aber Textkritik und Untersuchung von Komposition und Entstehung sorgfältig trennt, weil nicht einzusehen ist, warum die Erwägungen von mittelalterlichen Schreibern von MSS. zu denen der Autoren/Redaktoren aus viel früherer Zeit [24] immer parallel laufen sollen, wird hier einige kritische Bemerkungen machen. Erstens: in einem kompliziert konstruierten Ganzen wie Test. Issachar I-II sind

---

[24] Siehe oben Kap. X, S. 153-160. Man vergleiche für das Folgende auch meine Darstellung in *The Testament of the Twelve Patriarchs*, S. 77-81.

erklärende Lesarten und glättende Konstruktionen sekundär im Verhältnis zu den lectiones difficiliores, die sie voraussetzen. Otzen und
Becker wählen zu oft den einfacheren Text und der Leser, der ihre
Textentscheidungen vergleicht, muß wohl folgern, daß sie wenig konsequent vorgehen. Zweitens muß man fragen, ob die Komplexität
des biographischen Teils des Test. Issachar wie Becker will, durch
die Annahme zweier Stadien erklärt und dann das erste Stadium
der Grundschrift der Testamente zugeschrieben werden muß. Hiergegen
ist einzuwenden :

a) Wenn jemals ein gesondertes Dokument, das von der Geburt
und Namensgebung Issachars handelte, bestanden haben sollte, dann
wäre damit noch nicht gesagt, daß es zum Grundstock des Testaments
gehört haben muß; es könnte in bearbeiteter und angepaßter Form
vom Autor der Testamente in Kap. I aufgenommen sein.

b) Weiter ist auffällig, daß die verschiedenen Variationen des Themas
„zwei", die in II,1-3 und II,4-5 folgen, doch in einen Zusammenhang
gestellt sind mit dem, was in Kap. I behandelt wird. Ein Vergleich
mit Gen. XXX,14-24 zeigt, daß T. Iss. I,3-15 zurückgreift auf
Gen. XXX,14-18. Daran versucht anschließend T. Iss. II zu erklären,
warum Lea nach Gen. XXX,19-21 noch einen Sohn gebar und warum
das der sechste war; danach wird auch Gen. XXX,22-24 in die
Betrachtung einbezogen, ein Stück, das von der Aufhebung der Un-
fruchtbarkeit Rahels spricht. Der Schluß von II,2 und der letzte
Satz von II,4 geben eine Erklärung von Gen. XXX,22 und stellen
damit eine explizite Verbindung mit den zuvor genannten Liebesäpfeln
her.

c) Die in Kap. II angesprochenen Themen passen gut zum Ganzen
des Test. Issachar. Die Einstellung gegenüber der Sexualität in II,1-3
steht in Übereinstimmung mit der in III,5 (ein Vers, den Becker
zum Grundstock rechnet), und Rahels Gabe an Gott durch den
Priester hat sein Pendant in Issachars Opfern in III,6 und V,3
(Verse, die ebenso zu Beckers Grundstock gehören).

Aufgrund dieser Überlegungen gibt es keinen Grund, die Entstehung
der Testamente durch die Annahme einer allmählichen Hinzufügung
von verschiedenartigen Teilen zum Grundstock zu erklären. Selbstverständlich ist die Komposition dieser Kapitel ungeschickt, es bleiben
Unausgeglichenheiten und Widersprüche (Vgl. z.B. was oben zu I,14
bemerkt wurde), aber es gibt doch mehr Einheit in der endgültigen
Form als mit einem Wachstumsprozeß à la Becker erklärt werden
kann. Man muß wohl voraussetzen, daß diese Kapitel eine sehr

komplizierte Vorgeschichte gehabt haben und daß der Autor keine
strenge Form und keine vollständige Einheit von Gedanken angestrebt
hat.

b) *Kapitel III-V*

Der paränetische Teil Test. Iss. III-V hat die Tugend. ἁπλότης,
zum Thema. In einer sorgfältigen Arbeit hat J. Amstutz[25] gezeigt,
welch einen zentralen Platz dieser Begriff nicht nur im Test. Issachar,
sondern auch an anderen Stellen der Testamente einnimmt. Seine
Folgerung „... daß ἁπλότης für die Überlieferung die in den Test. XII
Patr. greifbar wird, ein „Inbegriff" für das Idealbild des Frommen
ist"[26] beruht in erster Linie auf einer Exegese von T.L. XIII,1;
T.R. IV,1; T.S. IV,5 und vor allem von T.B. VI (wo „der gute Mann"
gezeichnet wird). Seine Argumentation braucht hier nicht wiederholt
zu werden. Dann bespricht Amstutz ausführlich unser Testament.
Er zeigt, wie das Bild Issachars als γεωργός aus Gen. XLIX,14f.
LXX entnommen und sofort in III,1-2 mit εὐθύτης τῆς καρδίας
und ἁπλότης (zusammen auch in IV,6 genannt) verbunden wird.
Diese ist die allumfassende Tugend, die im folgenden in eine Menge
Tugenden zerlegt und mit einer Menge Untugenden kontrastiert wird.
Amstutz bemerkt, daß auch in T.R. IV,1 das harte Bauernleben
mit der ἁπλότης verbunden wird (vgl. auch die Parallele zwischen
diesem Vers und T.Iss. III,5) und aus dem Vergleich mit Juda und
Levi (und Gad) in Kap. V folgert er, daß der Autor die Bauernarbeit
als einen dem Issachar von Gott gegebenen Lebensauftrag sieht.
V,8 faßt das Vorhergehende zusammen in dem Satz: „Ihnen (d.h. Levi
und Juda) nun gehorcht und wandelt in der Lauterkeit eures Vaters".[27]
Amstutz betrachtet die paränetischen Kapitel III-V als Einheit.
Becker gebraucht wieder sein Seziermesser und kommt zum folgenden
Ergebnis:[28] T.Iss. IV handelt von ἁπλότης, und T.Iss. V parallel
dazu vom Bauernleben. V,1 ist eine redaktionelle Klammer, V,8b
ebenso. Bei genauerem Zusehen wird deutlich, daß wir in Kap. III,
wo diese zwei Themen zusammenkommen, das Motiv der ἁπλότης
leicht entfernen können. Wir müssen also folgern: In dem Grundstock
war nur die Rede von Issachar dem Landmann und dessen Nächsten-

---

[25] S. Anm. 21.

[26] A.a.O. S. 72.

[27] A.a.O. S. 72-75.

[28] Vgl. seine Anm. a zu IV,1 und *Untersuchungen zur Entstehungsgeschichte...*,
S. 336-342.

liebe; das Thema der ἁπλότης wurde damit erst später verbunden. Zum ersten Stadium des Test. Issachar gehörte allein Kap. III außer den Hinzufügungen über ἁπλότης und V,1(Rest),2-6. In seinen Anmerkungen zu Kap. III und IV schließt sich Otzen Beckers Theorien an.

Das, worum es im *jetzigen* Testament geht, ist also bei Becker und Otzen zum größten Teil sekundär. Die Frage ist aber, ob Becker seine Analyse wirklich beweisen kann, und ob die ganze literarkritische Operation nicht völlig überflüssig ist.

Daß in Kap. III die Hinweise auf ἁπλότης enfernt werden können, ist, in Anbetracht der Zusammensetzung dieses Kapitels aus vielen kleinen Sätzen, nicht erstaunlich. In III,1-2 wird das Thema der ἁπλότης mit dem Bauernleben in Zusammenhang gebracht, und zwar nicht nur als Einleitung dieses Kapitels, sondern auch des ganzen Teils III-V. In III,3-4 finden wir ein aus vier Teilen bestehendes Unschuldsbekenntnis, das auf einen fünften positiven Satz πορευόμενος ἐν ἁπλότητι ὀφθαλμῶν hinausläuft. Dann folgt ein weniger deutlich strukturiertes Stück, in der zweimal (V. 6a, V. 7b) gesagt wird, wie Jakob sich klarmachte, daß Issachars ἁπλότης von Gott gewollt war und gesegnet wurde. Das mag uns nach III,2 überflüssig vorkommen, für den Autor war es offenbar sehr wichtig. Er kommt denn auch in V, 3-6 unter nachdrücklichem Hinweis auf den Jakobssegen in Gen. XLIX,14f. darauf zurück. Ein weiterer Punkt der Überein-stimmung ist die Tatsache, daß Gottes Segen mit Issachars Fröm-migkeit verbunden wird. Er zeigt in III,6f., V,3-6 seine Gottesfurcht im Darbringen von Dankopfern und Erstlingsgaben an Gott. In III,8 wird neben der Liebe zu Gott auch die Liebe zum Nächsten genannt, und das ist das Thema von V,1-2.

Nach einer allgemeinen einleitenden Ermahnung πορεύεσθε ἐν ἁπλότητι καρδίας in IV,1 folgt eine negativ beschreibende Reihe mit fünf Teilen, die hinauslaufen auf das positive: der ἁπλοῦς... μόνον ἐκδέχεται τὸ θέλημα τοῦ θεοῦ (IV,2-3). Nach der Feststellung, daß die Geister des Irrtums keine Macht über ihn haben (V. 4a), beginnt in V. 4b-6 eine neue negative Reihe mit vier Teilen, die in V. 6a hinausläuft auf πορεύεται γὰρ ἐν εὐθύτητι ζωῆς, καὶ πάντα ὁρᾷ ἐν ἁπλότητι, chiastisch gefolgt von zwei näheren Bestimmungen, die mit V. 4a und V. 3b korrespondieren.

Wieder beginnt V, 1 mit einer Ermahnung φυλάξατε νόμον θεοῦ, τέκνα μου, καὶ τὴν ἁπλότητα κτήσασθε. Auch hier sind also ἁπλότης und strenge Einhaltung des Gesetzes miteinander verbunden; und die Einhaltung des Gesetzes, so 1b-2, äußert sich als Einhaltung der zwei großen Gebote, der Liebe zu Gott und der Liebe zum Nächsten, besonders zum armen, schwachen und unterdrückten Nächsten, wie das schon in III,6-8 deutlich wurde. Auf den bereits erwähnten Teil V,3-6 folgt dann ein lose eingefügter Levi-Juda-Abschnitt, auf die wiederum eine abschließende Ermahnung, ἁπλότης einzuhalten, folgt.[29]

Es ist denn auch nicht verwunderlich, daß das am Ende des Testaments (Kap. VII) etwas unerwartet vorkommende Unschulds-bekenntnis, eingeleitet von dem Satz „Ich bin mir keiner Sünde zum Tode bewußt" (V. 1b), in dem negative und positive Aussagen ver-bunden sind, hinausläuft auf eine Unterstreichung der zwei großen Gebote in V. 6. Hierauf folgt übrigens in V. 7 wiederum die Mitteilung, daß jeder Geist Beliars von denen, die so leben, fliehen wird.

Amstutz hat überzeugend dargelegt,[30] wie ἁπλότης, Furcht des Herrn und Einhaltung des Gesetzes hier und an anderer Stelle in den Testamenten zusammengehen, und wie die Einhaltung des Gesetzes in der Liebe Gottes und des Nächsten zusammengefaßt wird.[31] Er zeigt auch, daß die Verbindung von Bauernleben und ἁπλότης auch außerhalb der Testamente oft gefunden wird.[32]

Es ist also sehr gesucht, wenn Becker zwischen ἁπλότης und dem Bauernleben und zwischen ἁπλότης und dem Doppelgebot eine Tren-nung vornimmt. Für die Trennung von Beruf und „tugendhaftem Vorbild" beruft er sich auf T.Zeb. VI-VIII, selbstverständlich auf den von ihm (zu Unrecht)[33] für ursprünglich gehaltenen kurzen Text.

---

[29] Der Zusammenhang besteht (s. oben) in der Tatsache, daß der dem Issachar gegebene Auftrag mit dem des Levi und Juda verbunden wird. Issachar wird Levi und Juda untergeordnet (so sogar auch Joseph in T.Jos. XIX,11 f.). Daß Gad an dieser Stelle erwähnt wird ist noch von keinem befriedigend erklärt worden. Becker in seiner Anm. zu V,7 (S. 83) nennt das L.-J.-Stück einen „Nachtrag", erklärt aber in Wirklichkeit damit nichts.

[30] A.a.O. S. 64-72. Im Vorhergehendem wurde von seiner Analyse der Paränese im Test. Issachar ein dankbarer Gebrauch gemacht.

[31] Über die Liebe zu Gott und die Liebe zum Nächsten im Judentum und im frühen Christentum vgl. jetzt K. Berger, *Die Gesetzesauslegung Jesu. Ihr historischer Hintergrund im Judentum und im alten Testament*, Teil I (*W.M.A.N.T.* 40), Neukirchen-Vluym 1972, insbes. S. 56-257; und auch A. Nissen, *Gott und der Nächste im Antiken Judentum. Untersuchungen zum Doppelgebot der Liebe* (*W.U.N.T.* 15), Tübingen 1974, insbes. S. 224-244.

[32] Siehe a.a.O. S. 73 (und S. 75), und auch J. Becker, *Untersuchungen zur Ent-stehungsgeschichte...*, S. 336, Anm. 2 und 4.

[33] Siehe Kap. X, insbes. S. 149-152.

Was das zweite betrifft : Im Hinblick auf das Unschuldsbekenntnis in III,3-4 bemerkt Becker, daß es ein traditionelles Stück ist, das ursprünglich nichts mit ἁπλότης zu tun hat, wie die Dublette VII,1-6 beweist. Wenn aber ἁπλότης, Einhaltung des Gesetzes und das Doppelgebot für den Autor der Testamente direkt zusammenhängen, dann wird in III,3-4 und 6-8, IV,2-3 und 4-6, V,1-2 und VII,1-6 in vielen Variationen das eine Hauptthema dieses Testaments (und aller Testamente) beleuchtet. Zudem zeigt die detaillierte Analyse von Amstutz eindrücklich dass nicht nur die positiven Beschreibungen in diesem Testament, sondern auch gerade die negativen mit der Beschreibung und Bestreitung von Sünden in anderen Testamenten viele Anknüpfungspunkte haben.

Bei der Analyse dieser Kapitel kann die von Becker im Gefolge H. Aschermanns [34] und G. von Rads [35] angewandte Formanalyse gute Dienste leisten (vgl. übrigens auch Amstutz!). Die Unschulds-bekenntnisse und „negativ beschreibenden Reihen" sind bekannte literarische Formen, in die der Autor seine Ermahnung kleidet und mit deren Hilfe er sein Hauptanliegen deutlicher macht. Daß sie zum Teil traditionelles Material enthalten, ist wahrscheinlich, obwohl auffällt, daß viele Verbindungslinien zu anderen Teilen der Testamente gezogen werden können. Daß aber z.B. aufgrund der Form von T.Iss. VII,1-6 und aufgrund der Tatsache, daß es eine Dublette zu III,3-5 bildet, gefolgert werden kann „Es war sicher ursprünglich selbständig, hat es doch weder mit dem Beruf Issachars, noch mit der Tugend der Lauterkeit etwas zu tun",[36] verstehe ich nicht. Ebensowenig verstehe ich, weshalb denn III,3-5 als Teil des Kapitels III (ohne die Hinweise auf ἁπλότης) wohl, VII,1-6 jedoch nicht zum Grundstock der Testamente gerechnet werden sollte. Auch hier stellt sich heraus, daß die Hypothese der Existenz eines Grundstockes überflüssig ist.

An diesem Punkt angelangt, ist es ratsam noch kurz nachzugehen,

---

[34] *Die paränetischen Formen der „Testamente der Zwölf Patriarchen" und ihr Nachwirken in der frühchristlichen Mahnung.* Eine formgeschichtliche Untersuchung. Diss. masch. Berlin 1955. Über die negativ beschreibende Reihe s. S. 30-44, und über Unschuldsbekenntnisse S. 63-77 (insbes. 65-67).

[35] G. von Rad, „Die Vorgeschichte der Gattung von 1 Kor 13, 4-7", in *Gesammelte Studien zum A.T.* I (*Theol. Bücherei* 8), München 1958, S. 281-296 (Erstmals in 1953 veröffentlicht).

[36] A.a.O. S. 343 und Anm. c zu VII,1 auf S. 83 seiner Übersetzung. Vgl. auch Anm. a zu IV,2ff. auf S. 81 seiner Übersetzung : „... Das kleine Gedicht war ursprünglich selbständig".

welche textkritischen Entscheidungen Otzen und Becker in Kap. III-V gefällt haben.

III,3a. Becker liest das Präsens εἰμι mit *a*, *chi* statt ἤμην in den anderen MSS., weil das die lectio durior ist. Wir müssen hinzufügen : Auch weil hier eine negativ beschreibende Reihe anfängt, die qua Form vom Kontext abweicht. Becker folgt hier Aschermann, der sagt : „Zwischen diesen Aussagen ist eine Reihe, ein typisches Unschuldsbekenntnis eingeschaltet. Sie beginnt mit V. 3; Ihr Anfang ist durch den Tempuswechsel markiert".[37] Es ist aber wirklich die Frage, ob das textkritische Argument hier die Kompositionskritik stützen kann. Das Präsens in V. 3a kann eine unwillkürliche Anpassung an das direkt (in allen MSS.) vorhergehende πορεύομαι sein. In V. 4 wird zweimal der Aorist gebraucht.

III,3b. Otzen und Becker ziehen das φθονερός der anderen MSS. dem πονηρός von *bl* vor. Dieses mehr allgemeine Wort könnte aber den Vorzug verdienen vor dem mehr spezifischen φθονερός; man achte z.B. auf den Zusammenhang zwischen πονηρός, φθονερός und βασκαίνω in Sir. XIV,3-10!

III,4. Der letzte Satzteil πορευόμενος ἐν ἁπλότητι ὀφθαλμῶν (ein positiver Abschluß der negativen Reihe, vergleichbar mit ähnlichen kleinen Sätzen am Ende anderer Reihen, s. oben) wird mit dem in V.5 folgenden διὰ τοῦτο von Becker mit *g*, *chi* ausgelassen.[38] Nach B. wird also ein in der Kompositionsgeschichte festgestelltes Phänomen, die Verbindung mit ἁπλότης, von dem, was in den MSS. geschieht, bestätigt : auch dort wird. ἁπλότης hinzugefügt.[39]

III,6. Becker wählt den eindeutig glättenden Text von *chi*, Otzen folgt mit Recht dem Text der Nicht-*chi*-MSS. Zu Unrecht läßt Becker auch τότε ἐγώ am Ende des Verses mit *chi* aus.

III,8. Becker folgt dem c-Text (nicht α, wie er sagt); es handelt sich um eine Variante von sekundärer Bedeutung.

IV,4-6a. Wenn wir eine Zahl von weniger wichtigen Varianten übergehen, begegnen wir in IV,4-6a bei Becker einem typischen Beispiel einer Bevorzügung der lectio brevior. Während er in seiner Anmer-

---

[37] A.a.O. S. 66. S. auch Anm. 11 dort.

[38] Otzen läßt, unerwartet, nur διὰ τοῦτο aus.

[39] Aschermann erwähnt die Existenz dieses kleinen Satzes überhaupt nicht. Dadurch wird es ihm einfacher, auch das καὶ οὐκ ἐνενόουν ἡδονὴν γυναικός in V. 5 zur Reihe zu rechnen und den Satz durch spätere Hinzufügungen mit dem Leben des (verheirateten) Issachar verbunden sein zu lassen. Auch Becker betrachtet den einschlägigen Text in V. 5 als ursprünglich zur Reihe gehörig.

kung b zu III,2b eine Zahl von Auslassungen in der armenischen
Übersetzung als sekundäre Kürzungen bezeichnet (vgl. auch V,6-7),
folgt er in den soeben genannten Versen A in der Auslassung von
ἵνα μὴ ἐν διαστροφῇ μιάνῃ τὸν νοῦν αὐτοῦ in V. 4 Ende, und
οὐ βασκανία ἐκτήκει ψυχὴν αὐτοῦ in V. 5 mit dem Argument,
daß so der (ursprüngliche) zweigliedrige Parallelismus besser zu seinem
Recht komme. Weil die Handschriften in V. 6a nach εὐθύτητι und
ἁπλότητι mehrere Substantive im Genitiv hinzufügen,[40] müsse auch
hier der kurze armenische Text ohne Genitive ursprünglich sein. Wieder
jedoch empfiehlt es sich, die weniger geglättete Lesart als ursprünglich
zu betrachten, und das ist in keinem dieser Fälle die lectio brevior.
Auch im Rest von V. 6 folgt Becker (gegen Otzen) zu Unrecht
dem einfacheren Text, und nicht dem, den wir in b (gl) finden.

V,1. Wieder folgt Becker der kurzen Lesart; mit chi wird ἐντολὰς
κυρίου καί ausgelassen. Dieser Satzteil sei eine Hinzufügung unter
dem Einfluß von IV,6 und V,2a.

V,4. Nach εὐλόγησε muß in b σε durch Haplographie ausgelassen
sein, und Otzen fügt es mit Recht ein. Becker liest εὐλογήσει σε
mit l, eaf. Doch ist mit Rücksicht auf V. 5 ein futurum in V. 4 nicht
wahrscheinlich. Die Komposition ist schwierig, und wird durch ein
futurum nicht einfacher; Nur die Substitution von σε durch ὑμᾶς
in V. 4 (siehe gd(m), hi) und von σοι durch ὑμῖν in V. 5 (siehe g(a))
bringt wirklich Erleichterung. Wie dem auch sei, wir werden in
V. 4-5 ein Zitat in direkter Rede sehen müssen — vgl. den Hinweis
auf den Segen Jakobs in V. 6!

V,8. Am Schluß dieses Kapitels weicht Otzen plötzlich unnötiger-
weise vom b-Text ab. In V,8 liest er τῇ ἁπλότητι τῆς καρδίας ὑμῶν τοῦ
πατρὸς ὑμῶν (mit c), einen Text, der wahrscheinlich durch eine
Verschreibung mit späterer Korrektur zustande gekommen ist; dann
zieht er das glättere τῷ δὲ Γάδ in c dem ὅτι καὶ τῷ Γάδ in den
anderen MSS. vor, trotz der Tatsache, daß er in einer Anmerkung
bemerkt, daß die zweite Form noch deutlich zeigt, daß diese Wendung
in diesem Zusammenhang sekundär ist.

c) *Kapitel VI und VII*

Textkritisch ist über Kap. VI wenig zu bemerken.[41] In VII,1-6
folgt Otzen ganz dem b-Text, obwohl man darüber streiten kann,

---

[40] Das Variantenmuster ist noch komplizierter als B. vorgibt. l liest ἐν ἁπλότητι ζωῆς.
[41] In V. 1 gibt B. πανουργίᾳ in ch(i) den Vorzug vor κακουργίᾳ in den anderen MSS.
(geringe Abweichungen in d und m).

ob die lectio durior καὶ ἀλήθειαν am Schluß von V. 5 nicht durch
Auslassung eines Verbs entstanden ist (ἐποίησα *dm, af;* ἠγάπησα
e; ἐφύλαξα *chi* + εὐσέβειαν ἠγάπησα *c; lg* om wegen *hmt*). Becker
folgt *hi.* In V. 6 entscheidet Becker sich wieder für die glatte *chi*-
Lesart, ohne deutlich zu machen, wie daraus jemals der komplizierte
Nicht-*chi*-Text [42] entstanden sein könnte. Aus seinen *Untersuchungen
zur Entstehungsgeschichte* [43] geht deutlich hervor, daß er in *chi* den
ursprünglichen Text des später eingefügten und dann biographisch
aufgefüllten Teils V. 1-7 gefunden zu haben meint. In V. 7 wählt
Otzen unerwartet den *chi*-Zusatz καὶ τῆς γῆς nach τὸν θεὸν τοῦ
οὐρανοῦ. In V. 8-9 folgt Becker konsequent *chi*, die hier die lectio
brevior haben. Otzen übersetzt den *b*-Text, einschließlich der Hinzufügung „der fünfte", der nur in diesem MS. gefunden wird.

Die Komposition von Kap. VI-VII stellt uns vor drei Probleme:
Den Zusammenhang zwischen dem sog. „Sin-Exile-Return"-Abschnitt
in Kap. VI und dem Rest des Testaments, die Position von VII,1-6(7?)
und die Funktion von VII,7b. Zu jeder dieser Fragen eine kurze
Bemerkung.

In Kap. VI,1-2 ist das Element Sünde aus dem S.E.R.-Schema
konkret mit einem Verlassen der ἁπλότης und des Bauernbetriebes
verbunden. Weil kein S.E.R.-Stück „von Haus aus" eine ähnliche
Aussage über eine Tugend oder ein Laster kenne,[44] hält Becker diese
Verbindung für sekundär. Vollkommen willkürlich, aber im Anschluß
an seine früheren Hypothesen, hält er dann den Hinweis auf die
ἁπλότης und alles, was weiter in V. 1 erwähnt wird, für sekundär,
während der Verfasser des Grundstocks wohl gegen das Aufgeben
des Handwerks gewarnt hätte. Mit Recht ist für Becker die Reinheit
des S.E.R.-Schemas hier kein stichhaltiges Argument;[45] es ist in den
Testamenten verschiedenartig bearbeitet. Gerade deswegen gibt es
keinen Grund, anzunehmen, daß die eine Verbindung wohl, die andere
dagegen nicht ursprünglich ist.

Das Unschuldsbekenntnis in VII,1-6(7?) kommt unerwartet, aber

---

[42] Hier ist mit Otzen die Lesart von *b* ὡς τέκνα μου vor der Lesart ὑπὲρ τὰ τ.μ.
in *gldm eaf* zu bevorzugen.

[43] Siehe S. 343, Anm. 4.

[44] *Untersuchungen zur Entstehungsgeschichte* ..., S. 342.

[45] Siehe *The Testaments of the Twelve Patriarchs*, S. 83-86. In T.Z. IX,5 wird z.B.
die Beschreibung der Sünde unmittelbar mit der in IX,1-4 bestrittenen Zwiespalt in
Zusammenhang gebracht.

nur der, der eine „reine" Form konstruieren möchte, wird durch das Vorhandensein dieses Teils gestört werden. Vielleicht war der Autor der Testamente hier so sehr auf das konzentriert, was für ihn der Kern der Sache war (siehe den Zusammenhang zwischen diesem Teil und Kap. III-V, der oben aufgezeigt wurde!), daß er es für wünschenswert hielt, dieses Wesentliche nochmals auszusprechen. Jedenfalls wird mit der Hypothese einer späteren Hinzufügung die Schwierigkeit nur von einem Autor auf einen Redaktor verschoben, der dann das getan haben müßte, was einem Autor nicht zugeschrieben werden kann.

Das Problem von VII,7b betrifft den Text und die Interpretation. Es geht um den Satz ἔχοντες μεθ᾽ ἑαυτῶν τὸν θεὸν τοῦ οὐρανοῦ, συμπορευόμενος τοῖς ἀνθρώποις ἐν ἁπλότητι καρδίας, Die MSS. *m eaf hi* lesen hier συμπορευόμενοι. In seiner Übersetzung folgt Becker diesem Text mit großer Zurückhaltung, während er in seinem Buch beide Möglichkeiten offenläßt.[46] Otzen liest den accusativus singularis, verbindet jedoch ἐν ἁπλότητι καρδίας mit τοῖς ἀνθρώποις, aber das hält Becker wegen der Parallele mit T.Jud. XXIV,1 (vgl. T.D. V,13; T.N. VIII,3)[47] mit Recht für unwahrscheinlich. Es ist deutlich, daß VII,7 in seiner heutigen Fassung nicht beschreibt, was jeweils geschehen wird, wenn sich die Söhne Issachars die Ermahnungen ihres Vaters zu Herzen nehmen, sondern daß gehorsamen Söhnen die Aussicht auf eine neue Zeit geboten wird. Dann wird Gott mit den Menschen wie ein Mensch verkehren, der durch ἁπλότης gekennzeichnet sein wird. „Die Stelle kann nicht anders verstanden werden als als Schilderung der wiederkehrenden Urzeit in den Tagen des Messias... Der Messias, der dann erscheint, wird verwirklichen das höchste Ideal : ἡ ἁπλότης", so Amstutz,[48] der mit de Jonge darin übereinstimmt, daß dieser Abschnitt christlich ist. Auch Becker stimmt dem zu, aber er denkt dabei selbstverständlich an eine spätere christliche Bearbeitung — wie diese vorgenommen wurde und wie eingreifend sie war, wird aber nicht deutlich.

---

[46] Vgl. die nuancierte, jedoch nicht ganz durchsichtige Argumentation auf S. 344-346 seines Buches.

[47] S. auch *The Testaments of the Twelve Patriarchs*, S. 35, wo zudem darauf hingewiesen wird, daß *hi* ebenso wie *c* nach ἐν ἁπλότητι καρδίας ein αὐτοῦ einfügen, und also überhaupt keinen Zusammenhang mit τοῖς ἀνθρώποις herstellen.

[48] A.a.O. S. 84.

6. *Zusammenfassung und Ausblick*

Die ausführliche Besprechung der Art und Weise, in der Otzen und Becker mit Test. Issachar verfahren, hat, wie ich hoffe, gezeigt, daß man ihre Übersetzung und ihre Anmerkungen nur sehr kritisch benützen kann. Das von ihnen gebotene textkritische Material ist unvollständig und ihre Rekonstruktion des ursprünglichen Textes beruht sehr oft auf subjektiven Überlegungen. Subjektivität ist in der Textkritik nie ganz auszuschließen, aber sowohl beim Feststellen der großen Linien wie auch in den Einzelentscheidungen ist ein konsistenteres Vorgehen möglich als diese beiden Autoren, jeder auf seine Art, gezeigt haben. Die neue *editio maior* wird das, wie ich meine, beweisen.

Hinsichtlich der Komposition und der Entstehungsgeschichte dieses Testaments (das, wie oben dargelegt wurde, als Beispiel gewählt wurde, weil die Situation hier als repräsentativ für die Testamente im ganzen betrachtet werden kann) ist deutlich geworden, daß Beckers Betrachtungsweise in ihren Ausgangspunkten und ihren Ergebnissen abzulehnen ist. Otzen ist viel weniger konsequent und viel weniger dezidiert als Becker, aber es stellte sich heraus, daß er doch an einigen wichtigen Punkten Becker folgt. Oben wurde versucht, das behandelte Testament als eine Einheit zu erklären, also als eine Komposition eines Autors oder einer Gruppe von Autoren, in der verschiedenartiges Material verarbeitet wurde. Es ist unnötig, in der Entstehungsgeschichte des Test. Issachar zwei nachdrücklich unterschiedene jüdische Phasen anzunehmen; auf jeden Fall ist es unmöglich, zu beweisen, daß jemals ein reiner, der Form und dem Inhalt nach konsistenter „Grundstock" bestanden hat.

In § 5 ist viel, was zum Thema gehört, unbehandelt geblieben. Die Paränese dieses Testaments kann nur im Zusammenhang mit der Paränese des ganzen Werks behandelt werden; eine systematische Analyse dieser Paränese ist nötig. Viele Parallelen in anderen jüdischen und frühchristlichen Schriften wurden nicht in die Betrachtung einbezogen — es sei hier bemerkt, daß die Anmerkungen von Otzen und Becker, teilweise natürlich in Wiederaufnahme älterer Forschungsergebnisse wie z.B. des immer noch wertvollen Kommentars von R. H. Charles,[49] viel brauchbares Material bieten. Auch wurde das Verhältnis zwischen den jüdischen und den christlichen Elementen

---

[49] *The Testaments of the Twelve Patriarchs*, London 1908.

in den Testamenten — ein grundsätzliches Problem für die endgültige Interpretation dieses Buches — außer Betracht gelassen.

Gerade weil es hier um eine so wichtige Sache geht, möchte ich zur Frage der christlichen Elemente im Rahmen der Analyse des Test. Issachar noch einige Bemerkungen machen. Zunächst ist klar, daß wir das Problem in Test. Issachar nicht einfach durch die Annahme einer Interpolation lösen können. VII,7b — wie auch immer es abzugrenzen ist — fällt bestimmt nicht aus dem Rahmen; im Gegenteil, es paßt auf natürliche Weise in das Ganze des Testaments. Andererseits kann man nicht ohne weiteres sagen, daß das Testament eine christliche Komposition ist, bei der von jüdischem Material Gebrauch gemacht wurde. Diese Lösung, die von mir 1953 verteidigt wurde, später aber modifiziert wurde, ist wahrscheinlich ebenso vereinfachend wie die Interpolationstheorie.[50]

Wie kompliziert die Sache ist, wird deutlich, wenn wir uns fragen, worauf im jetzigen Test. Issachar der Ton liegt.

In I-II liegt der Ton auf der ἐγκράτεια — näher erläutert in II,3 —, und auf dem Geben von Gaben an die Priester und den Tempel. Wir haben gesehen, daß in III-V, namentlich in III,5 und III,6, IV,3 daran angeschlossen wird. Weiter liegt in der Paränese von III-V und VII der Ton auf ἁπλότης als vollkommener Ausrichtung auf das Gesetz Gottes, die in der Liebe zu Gott und der tätigen Anteilnahme am Nächsten besteht.

Es stellte sich als selbstverständlich heraus, daß ein Levi-Juda-Abschnitt und ein Sin-Exile-Return Abschnitt eingebaut und mit der Paränese verbunden wurde. Schließlich wird in Aussicht gestellt, daß der Gott des Himmels ἐν ἁπλότητι καρδίας mit den Menschen auf der Erde verkehren wird.

Können diese Ideen unter der Überschrift „typisch jüdisch" oder „typisch christlich" zusammengefaßt werden? Wohl kaum. Die der philosophischen Asketik des Späthellenismus eigene Tugend der ἐγκράτεια spielt z.B. eine wichtige Rolle bei Philon.[51] Wenn er über Henoch als Symbol der μετάνοια und der βελτίωσις redet, bemerkt er an einer Stelle „Er wird also versetzt aus Unwissenheit in Bildung, aus Unvernunft in Einsicht, aus Feigheit in Mannhaftigkeit, aus Gottlosigkeit in Frömmigkeit und weiter aus Genußsucht in Enthaltsamkeit (καὶ πάλιν ἐκ μὲν φιληδονίας εἰς ἐγκράτειαν), aus Ruhm-

---

[50] Vgl. auch oben Kap. XIII, S. 186 und S. 189.

[51] Siehe W. Grundmann s.v. ἐγκράτεια in Th.W. II, S. 338-340.

liebe in Bescheidenheit".[52] An anderer Stelle sagt Philon : „φιλοσοφία δὲ ἐγκράτειαν μὲν γαστρός, ἐγκράτειαν δὲ τῶν μετὰ γαστέρα, ἐγκράτειαν δὲ καὶ γλώττης ἀναδιδάσκει" (Congr. 80) und in Vit. Mos I,28, wo er eine vergleichbare Unterscheidung macht, bemerkt er, daß Mose γαστρί τε γὰρ ἔξω τῶν ἀναγκαίων δασμῶν, ὡς ἡ φύσις ἔταξεν, οὐδὲν πλέον ἐχορήγει, τῶν τε ὑπογαστρίων ἡδονῶν εἰ μὴ μέχρι σπορᾶς παίδων γνησίων οὐδὲ ἐμέμνητο. Die Zähmung der Lust bringt eine Anschauung mit sich, die den Zweck der Ehe in der Kinderzeugung sieht. Auch das ist ein auch außerhalb von Judentum und Christentum vorkommender Grundsatz.[53]

Auch bei Josephus finden wir ihn : In seinem großen Bericht über die Essener in B.J. II §119-161 sagt er gleich am Anfang : „Sie verwerfen die sinnlichen Freuden als Frevel, erachten aber die Enthaltsamkeit (ἐγκράτεια) und das sich nicht von der Leidenschaft beherrschen lassen als Tugend".[54] Darum stehen sie auch der Ehe ablehnend gegenüber. In §160f. spricht Josephus jedoch von einer zweiten Gruppe (τάγμα) der Essener, der nur hinsichtlich der Ehe andere Auffassungen hat. Diese Essener heiraten wohl, wenn auch nach längerer und genauer Vorbereitung; charakteristisch für sie ist auch : „Während der Schwangerschaft ihrer Frau ... enthalten sie sich des ehelichen Verkehrs, ein Beweis dafür, daß sie nicht um der Lust, sondern um der Kinder willen heiraten". Dem entspricht Josephus' eigene Auffassung. In c. Apionem II §199 bemerkt er μῖξιν μόνην οἶδεν ὁ νόμος τὴν κατὰ φύσιν τὴν πρὸς γυναῖκα, καὶ τοῦτο εἰ μέλλοι τέκνων ἕνεκα γίνεσθαι.

Wer nun aufgrund dieser Parallelen auf einen hellenistisch-judischen Ursprung des Test. Iss. schließen würde, irrte sich; ἐγκράτεια ist auch im frühen Christentum eine hochgeschätzte Tugend (I Kor. VII,9; I Clem. XXXVIII,2; Ign. Polyc. V,2; Polyc. Phil. V,3 etc.). Ebenso

---

[52] Abr. (17), 24. Deutsche Übersetzung von J. Cohn in *Die Werke Philos von Alexandria*, ed. L. Cohn, I, Breslau 1909.

[53] S. auch Ios. 43, Deter. 102, Quaest. Gen. IV,86. Über Philos Stellung zur Frau und der Ehe s. I. Heinemann, *Philons griechische und jüdische Bildung*, Darmstadt 1962, S. 231-292, der auch auf hellenistische Parallellen hinweist. Allgemein : H. Preisker, *Christentum und Ehe in den ersten drei Jahrhunderten*, Eine Studie zur Kulturgeschichte der Alten Welt, Berlin 1927, insbesondere I „Die Umwelt des Christentums in ihrer Stellung zur Ehe", (S. 13-99), und W. A. Meeks, „The Image of the Androgyne : Some uses of a symbol in earliest Christianity", *History of Religion* 13,3 (February 1974), S. 165-208, insbesondere I „Woman's Place" (S. 167-180).

[54] Deutsche Übersetzung von O. Michel-O. Bauernfeind, *De Bello Judaico/Der Jüdische Krieg* I, Darmstadt 1959.

ist es ein allgemein akzeptierter Gedanke, daß der Zweck der Ehe im Kindergebären besteht (Justinus, Apol. I, 29,1; Athenagoras, Legatio XXXIII,1; Minucius Felix, Octavius XXXI,5 etc.). Clemens Alex., der mit weitem Blick das Leben seiner Zeit überschaut, viele Auffassungen von Nichtchristen und Christen Revue passieren läßt und dabei die gnostische Askese zurückweist, faßt in Strom. III,57 die christliche Auffassung wie folgt zusammen: „Die menschliche Enthaltsamkeit nun, ich meine die von den Philosophen der Griechen gelehrte, verlangt, daß man mit der Begierde kämpft und ihr nicht zu ihren Taten zu willen ist; die von uns dagegen gelehrte, daß man überhaupt nicht begehrt; sie hat also nicht das Ziel, daß man sich trotz der vorhandenen Begierde beherrscht, sondern daß man sich der Begierde selbst enthält. Diese Enthaltsamkeit ist aber auf keine andere Weise zu gewinnen als durch die Gnade Gottes".[55] Und in III,58 folgert er daraus für die Ehe: „Auch wer zum Zweck der Kindererzeugung geheiratet hat, muß Enthaltsamkeit üben, damit er nicht einmal sein eigenes Weib begehre, das er lieben sollte, indem er mit keuschen und sittsamen Willen Kinder zeugt". Als negatives Beispiel führt er dann in III,59 Engel (vgl. Gen. VI), die ἀκρατεῖς γενόμενοι ἐπιθυμίᾳ ἁλόντες aus den Himmel gefallen sind (vgl. T.R. V,5-7, T.N. III,5) an.

Clemens hätte der Haltung Rahels und dem Beispiel Issachars, wie sie im T.Iss. beschrieben sind, beistimmen können! J. Amstutz widmet einen großen Teil seiner Arbeit über ἁπλότης dem Material aus dem Hirten des Hermas.[56] Dabei fällt auf, wie eng Enthaltsamkeit und Einfalt hier — ebenso wie im Test. Issachar — verbunden sind. Amstutz weist zu Recht hin auf Hermas' eigene Charakterisierung als ὁ ἐγκρατής, ὁ ἀπεχόμενος πάσης ἐπιθυμίας πονηρᾶς καὶ πλήρης πάσης ἁπλότητος καὶ ἀκακίας μεγάλης in Vis. I,2,4. Die vielen Beispiele, die Amstutz weiter nennt, brauchen hier nicht wiederholt zu werden. Wohl aber müssen wir noch zwei Abschnitten in denen ἁπλότης zentrale Bedeutung hat, unsere Aufmerksamkeit schenken: ersten dem dieser Tugend gewidmeten Mandatum II, in dem zunächst in V. 2-3 καταλαλία zurückgewiesen wird (aktiv und passiv, man darf

---

[55] Deutsche Übersetzung von O. Stählin in *Bibliothek der Kirchenväter* II,17, München 1936.

[56] A.a.O. S. 132-155. Amstutz weist, im Gefolge E. Petersons, *Frühkirche, Judentum und Gnosis*, Rom-Freiburg-Wien 1959 (insbes. S. 209-220 „Einige Beobachtungen zu den Anfängen der christlichen Askese") auch auf andere asketische und enkratitische Äußerungen in der frühen Christenheit hin.

noch nicht einmal einem Verleumder zuhören). Danach in V. 4 wird gesagt : ἐργάζου τὸ ἀγαθὸν καὶ ἐκ τῶν κόπων σου ὁ θεὸς δίδωσίν σοι πᾶσιν ὑστερουμένοις δίδου ἁπλῶς, μὴ διστάζων, τίνι δῷς. Πᾶσιν δίδου, πᾶσιν γὰρ ὁ θεὸς δίδοσθαι θέλει ἐκ τῶν ἰδίων δωρημάτων. Die Parallelität, einerseits zu T.Iss. III,3-4 und andererseits zu III,6-8 (vgl. T.Z. VI,4, VII,2) ist schlagend. Zweitens der Schilderung der. ἁπλοῖ in Sim. IX,24,1-4, in der der Ton auf das μηδὲν κατ᾽ ἀλλήλων ἔχοντες und das πάντοτε σπλάγχνον ἔχοντες ἐπὶ πάντα ἄνθρωπον, καὶ ἐκ τῶν κόπων αὐτῶν παντὶ ἀνθρώπῳ ἐχορήγησαν ἀνανειδίστως καὶ ἀδιστάκτως. Darum segnet Gott auch in Anbetracht ihrer ἁπλότης alles was sie unternehmen (vgl. T.Iss. III,7; V,4-6).

Es gibt noch mehr übereinstimmende Züge zwischen dem Hirten des Hermas und den Testamenten der XII Patriarchen,[57] aber es ist schwierig, daraus auf eine literarische Abhängigkeit oder einen historischen Zusammenhang zu schließen. Wohl aber müssen wir die Frage stellen, ob nicht für die Testamente gelten kann, was für den Hirten des Hermas gilt, daß nämlich die Versuche, die jüdischen Quellen bzw. eine jüdische Grundschrift zu rekonstruieren, zum Scheitern verurteilt sind. In vielen Schriften des frühen Christentums sind jüdische, hellenistische und namentlich auch jüdisch-hellenistische Traditionen verwendet und verarbeitet, und zwar in der Weise, daß sie ein integrierender Bestandteil dieser Schriften geworden sind. Solche Traditionen wurden im frühen Christentum anscheinend häufig aufgenommen. Auch wenn bei der weiteren Erforschung der Testamente tatsächlich bewiesen werden sollte, daß die Idee, zwölf Testamente nach einem bestimmten Muster zu schreiben und zu einer Sammlung zusammenzufügen — unter Verwendung allen verfügbaren Traditionsmaterials — vorchristlich ist, und daß also die heutigen Testamente eine christliche Schrift sind die jüdisches Material verarbeitet, müßten wir uns vergegenwärtigen, daß eine geistesgeschichtliche Scheidung zwischen „jüdisch" und „christlich" oft unmöglich und daher literarkritisch wenig sinnvol ist. Sowohl bei der Bearbeitung einer bestehenden jüdischen Sammlung als auch bei einer Komposition, bei der viel jüdisches Traditionsmaterial in mancherlei Form verwendet wurde, werden christliche Autoren ohne weiteres vieles haben übernehmen können, weil es völlig zu dem paßte, was sie weitergeben wollten. In beiden Fällen werden sie auch jüdische Vorstellungen nicht ver-

---

[57] S. mein Buch *The Testaments of the Twelve Patriarchs*, S. 119f. (ganz vorsichtig und gar nicht erschöpfend).

ändert haben, weil es ja die Söhne Jakobs waren, die zu ihren
Söhnen sprachen!

Wie vorsichtig wir sein sollten, wird auch deutlich, wenn wir im
Test. Issachar auf einige Punkte, die auf den ersten Blick typisch
jüdisch zu sein scheinen, achten. Rahel und Issachar bringen Gott
ihre Gaben durch einen Priester dar (II,5; III,6, vgl. V,3). In 1953
bemerkte ich schon dazu, daß das hier Gesagte zu dem, was in
der frühen Kirche über das Opfern von Gaben bekannt ist, paßt;[58]
insbesondere wies ich auf die Traditio Apostolica von Hippolyt hin,
in der der Bischof der rechtmäßige Nachfolger des Priesters ist.
Jedoch schon in I Clem. XLI-XLIV sieht der Autor eine deutliche
Parallele zwischen den Priestern und Leviten des alten Bundes und
den Amtsträgern des neuen.[59] A. Jaubert hat in einem lehrreichen
Aufsatz „Thèmes lévitiques dans la Prima Clementis"[60] auf die
Bedeutung der levitisch-priesterlichen Gedanken für die Auffassung
von τάξις in ersten Clemensbrief hingewiesen. Im gleichen Aufsatz
weist sie auch auf den merkwürdigen Abschnitt XXXI-XXXII hin,
wo über den Segen, den Abraham, Isaak und Jakob empfangen,
gesprochen wird. Jakob wird τὸ δωδεκάσκηπτρον τοῦ Ἰσραήλ gegeben
(XXXI,4), das auch viele Gaben Gottes empfängt. „Von ihm (d.h.
Jakob) stammen nämlich alle Priester und Leviten ab, die dem Altar
Gottes dienen; von ihm stammt der Herr Jesus dem Fleische nach;
von ihm stammen die Könige, Herrscher und Fürster durch Juda ab;
seine übrigen Stämme stehen nicht in geringem Ansehen, da Gott
die Verheißung gab : Dein Same wird sein wie die Sterne des Himmels"
(XXXII,2).[61]

Mlle Jaubert weist mit Recht hin auf die merkwürdige Stellung
des „der Herr Jesus dem Fleische nach" (vgl. Röm. IX,4) zwischen
(zunächst) Levi und den von ihm abstammenden Priestern und (sodann)
Juda mit den von ihm abstammenden Königen. Der Autor drückt
sich hier nicht deutlich aus, er suggeriert mehr als er expliziert;
doch muß im Hintergrund eine Tradition stehen, die Levi und Juda
verherrlicht, und schon vor Clemens wird Jesus nicht nur mit Juda,

---

[58] S. *The Testaments of the Twelve Patriarchs*, S. 80f.

[59] So I Clem. XLIV,4 ἁμαρτία γὰρ οὐ μικρὰ ἡμῖν ἔσται, ἐὰν τοὺς ἀμέμπτως καὶ
ὁσίως προσενεγκόντας τὰ δῶρα τῆς ἐπισκοκῆς ἀποβαλῶμεν.

[60] *Vig. Christ.* 18, 1964, S. 193-203. S. auch ihre Ausgabe mit Kommentar, *Sources
Chrétiennes* no 167, Paris 1971.

[61] Übersetzung von J. A. Fischer, *Die Apostolischen Väter*, Darmstadt ⁴1964. Das
letzte Zitat ist im A.T. keine Zusage an Jakob sondern an Abraham (Gen. XV,5 etc.).

sondern auch mit Levi in Zusammenhang gebracht worden sein.[62]
Auch an diesem Punkt wird bei Clemens schon angedeutet, was bei
Hippolyt expliziert wird. Man kann selbstverständlich nicht behaupten,
daß Clemens die Testamente kannte, aber die deutliche Erwähnung
des δωδεκάσκηπτρον in XXXI,4, dem vorhin besprochenen Abschnitt,
und die Betonung der großen Herrlichkeit der zwölf Stämme am
Ende von XXXII,2 weisen auf eine Betrachtungsweise der Söhne
Jakobs hin, die mit dem, was in den Testamenten gefunden wird,
verwandt ist. Daraus wird auf jeden Fall verständlich, warum die
L. J.-Abschnitte in den Testamenten eine ähnlich wichtige Rolle spielen,
und warum z.B. in Test. Issachar V,7-8 jedenfalls doch ein Hinweis
auf die Herrlichkeit und den Auftrag von Levi und Juda hinzugefügt
wird.

Man hüte sich in der Erforschung der Testamente der zwölf Patriarchen vor vereinfachenden Lösungen. Jüdische Parallelen weisen
nicht auf jüdischen Ursprung hin, christliche Parallelen weisen nicht
auf eine christliche Komposition hin. Eine genauere Untersuchung
der spezifisch christlichen Elemente in ihrem Zusammenhang mit den
nicht spezifisch christlichen wird erweisen müssen, ob die Theorie
einer christlichen Bearbeitung oder die einer christlichen Komposition
zu bevorzugen ist.

---

[62] Siehe *The Testaments of the Twelve Patriarchs*, S. 124f.

INDEX LOCORUM

A. OLD TESTAMENT

B. APOCRYPHA AND PSEUDEPIGRAPHA
(except Testaments of the Twelve Patriarchs)

C TESTAMENTS OF THE TWELVE PATRIARCHS

D. DOCUMENTS DIRECTLY RELATED TO THE TESTAMENTS OF THE TWELVE PATRIARCHS

E. QUMRAN DOCUMENTS

F. NEW TESTAMENT

This index was compiled with the help of J. Nauta